D0215092

Psychological Concepts

Among the scientific advances over the last one hundred years, those in psychological science rank among the most prolific and revealing. The analyses of human intelligence and cognition, of human consciousness and self-awareness, of human memory and learning, and of human personality structure have opened up new avenues towards a deeper understanding of the human nature, the human mind, and its evolution. These new insights, whilst meeting high standards of research methodology, have also given rise to a conceptual grid that connects hitherto divergent lines of research in the human and behavioural sciences, leading up to present-day neuroscience.

The Editors, both past presidents of the International Union of Psychological Science (IUPsyS), bring together a distinguished panel of international experts in the attempt to unravel, in a comparative cross-cultural and historical approach, changing contents and functions of psychological key concepts (such as intelligence, cognition, mind and the self). Their findings help to guide psychological theorizing, psychological experimentation and field research, and in so doing they apply behavioural science insights to the improvement of human affairs. Prepared under the aegis of the International Union of Psychological Science, the book exemplifies a concept-driven international history of psychological science.

With its team of distinguished researchers from four continents, *Psychological Concepts: An International Historical Perspective* outlines the history of psychology in a truly innovative way.

Kurt Pawlik is Professor of Psychology at the University of Hamburg, Germany (1966–). He received his PhD in psychology from the University of Vienna (Austria). His research specializations include: psychology of individual differences, neuropsychology, psychological assessment and psychometrics, environmental, and international psychology. He is past president (*inter alia*) of the German Society of Psychology, the International Union of Psychological Science, and the International Social Science Council.

Géry d'Ydewalle is Professor of Psychology at the University of Leuven, Belgium (1980–), where he also received his PhD. His research specializations include: perception and memory, neuropsychology, applied research on genetic risk perception and decision making, film perception, and psychology of the internet. He is past president (*inter alia*) of the Belgian Psychological Society, the International Union of Psychological Science, and a member of the Belgian Royal Academy of Science.

Psychological Concepts

An International Historical
Perspective

**Edited by Kurt Pawlik and
Géry d'Ydewalle**

*Under the auspices of the International Union of
Psychological Science*

Psychology Press
Taylor & Francis Group
HOVE AND NEW YORK

First published 2006 by Psychology Press
27 Church Road, Hove, East Sussex BN3 2FA

Simultaneously published in the USA and Canada
by Psychology Press
270 Madison Avenue, New York, NY 10016

*Psychology Press is an imprint of the Taylor & Francis Group, an
informa business*

© 2006 the International Union of Psychological Science

Typeset in Times by Garfield Morgan, Swansea, West Glamorgan
Printed and bound in Great Britain by TJ International Ltd, Padstow,
Cornwall
Cover design by Lisa Dynan

All rights reserved. No part of this book may be reprinted or
reproduced or utilised in any form or by any electronic, mechanical,
or other means, now known or hereafter invented, including
photocopying and recording, or in any information storage or
retrieval system, without permission in writing from the publishers.

The publisher makes no representation, express or implied, with
regard to the accuracy of the information contained in this book and
cannot accept any legal responsibility or liability for any errors or
omissions that may be made.

This publication has been produced with paper manufactured to strict
environmental standards and with pulp derived from sustainable
forests.

British Library Cataloguing in Publication Data
A catalogue record for this book is available from the British Library

Library of Congress Cataloging in Publication Data
Psychological concepts : an international historical perspective /
[edited by] Kurt Pawlik and Géry d'Ydewalle.
      p. cm.
   "Under the auspices of the International Union of Psychological
Science."
   Includes bibliographical references and index.
   ISBN 1-84169-533-5
   1. Psychology–History. 2. Psychology–Philosophy–History.
I. Pawlik, Kurt. II. d'Ydewalle, Géry. III. International Union of
Psychological Science.
   BF81.P59 2006
   150.9–dc22

                                                     2006003611

ISBN13: 978-1-84169-533-4
ISBN10: 1-84169-533-5

Contents

List of tables and figures

List of contributors

James R. Averill, Department of Psychology, University of Massachusetts, Amherst, MA 01002, USA

Rossana De Beni, Dipartimento di Psicologia Generale, Università di Padova, Via Venezia 8, I-35131 Padova, Italy

John W. Berry, Psychology Department, Queen's University, Kingston, ON, Canada, K7L 3N6

Maria A. Brandimonte, Università Suor Orsola Benincasa, Via Suor Orsola 10, I-80135 Naples, Italy

Nicola Bruno, Università Suor Orsola Benincasa, Via Suor Orsola 10, I-80135 Naples, Italy

Nandita Chaudhary, Department of Human Development, Lady Irwin College, University of Delhi, New Delhi, India

Simona Collina, Università Suor Orsola Benincasa, Via Suor Orsola 10, I-80135 Naples, Italy

Michael C. Corballis, Department of Psychology, University of Auckland, Auckland, New Zealand

Cesare Cornoldi, Dipartimento di Psicologia Generale, Università di Padova, Via Venezia 8, I-35131 Padova, Italy

Géry d'Ydewalle, University of Leuven, Psychology Department, B-3000 Leuven, Belgium

Volker Gadenne, Institut für Philosophie und Wissenschaftstheorie, Johannes-Kepler-Universität Linz, A-4040 Linz, Austria

Simona Gardini, Dipartimento di Psicologia Generale, Universita di Padova, Via Venezia 8, I-35131 Padova, Italy

Willy Lens, University of Leuven, Psychology Department, B-3000 Leuven, Belgium

George Mandler, University of California, San Diego, CA, USA (& University College London, UK). Psychology/UCSD 0109, 9500 Gilman Drive, La Jolla, CA 92093-0109, USA

Lars-Göran Nilsson, Department of Psychology, Stockholm University, S-10691 Stockholm, Sweden

Kurt Pawlik, University of Hamburg, Psychology Institute, Von-Melle Park 11, D-20146, Hamburg, Germany

Martin Pinquart, Department of Developmental Psychology, University of Jena, D-07749 Jena, Germany

Boele de Raad, University of Groningen, Department of Psychology, Grote Kruisstraat 2/1, 9712 TS Groningen, The Netherlands

Jerker Rönnberg, Department of Behavioural Sciences, Swedish Institute for Disability Research, Linköpings University, S-581 83 Linköping, Sweden

Rainer K. Silbereisen, Department of Developmental Psychology, University of Jena, D-07749 Jena, Germany

Robert J. Sternberg, School of Arts and Sciences, Tufts University, Ballou Hall, 3rd Floor, Medford, MA 02155, USA

Louise Sundararajan, Rochester Psychiatric Center, 691 French Rd., Rochester, NY 14613, USA

Harry C. Triandis, University of Illinois, 1 Lake Park Road, Champaign, IL 61822, USA

Maarten Vansteenkiste, University of Leuven, Psychology Department, B-3000 Leuven, Belgium

Nicholas J. Wade, Department of Psychology, University of Dundee, Dundee DD1 4HN, UK

Qi Wang, Department of Human Development, Cornell University, Martha Van Rensselaer Hall, Ithaca, NY 14853-4401, USA

Foreword

The International Union of Psychological Science has fostered the publication of some 60 book volumes. Although the majority of these were collections of state-of-the-art essays on facets of psychology arising from International Congresses of Psychology, handbooks, or specialized directories (see *Psychology: IUPsyS Global Resource* for a full listing of all Union works), this volume is the Union's first to deal with the history of psychological concepts, constructs, and ideas. It was a daunting undertaking managed intelligently by the editors, Kurt Pawlik and Géry d'Ydewalle, with outstanding continuing support from Psychology Press. Like all Union products, this volume deals with the selected topics by situating them in the international context; the selection of authors, too, was determinedly diverse internationally so as to insure the broadest perspectives and sensitive treatments. The editors' vision, as presented in their Chapter 1, has been achieved. Readers will find fundamental concepts illuminated in new ways that will make this volume a stimulating one for scholars, teachers, and students—perhaps even prompting new research paths. The Union is deeply appreciative of the editors' efforts and the generous contributions of our expert international authors.

J. Bruce Overmier
President, International Union of Psychological Science
December, 2005

Preface

Among the advances in the evolution of science over the last one hundred years, those in psychological science seem to rank among the very prolific and revealing. The analyses of human intelligence and cognition, of human consciousness and self-awareness, of human personality structure, or of human memory and learning have opened up unexpected new avenues towards a deeper understanding of the human nature, the human mind, and its phylogenetic and cultural evolution. At the same time, the history of these discoveries and insights into the *condition humaine*, while meeting high standards of research methodology, also constitutes a focus, in the literal sense, of converging lines of research in the human and behavioral sciences at large, including recent comparative anthropological or cross-cultural study and exciting discoveries from research in neuroscience. In this sense, the study of the history of psychological science both reflects and re-orients transdisciplinary theorizing about human behavior, its nature and basic coordinates.

In this volume a distinguished panel of international experts sets forth to comply with the editors' invitation to unravel, in a comparative cross-cultural and historical approach, the changing content and function of psychological key concepts: in guiding psychological theorizing, psychological experimentation and field research, and in applying behavioral science insights to the improvement of human affairs. In this way, the book also constitutes an attempt towards a concept-driven history of psychological science. And by comparing styles of approach between chapters, the reader may also sense a salient, often-quoted characteristic of psychology as a discipline: its unity in diversity. Appreciating such multidisciplinarity-within-the-discipline as a potential rather than a problem of psychology, we did not wish to exercise any editorial policy that would infringe on it.

Prepared and published under the aegis of the International Union of Psychological Science, the book may help bringing together psychological thinking hitherto rooted in different theoretical and cultural traditions and promote their comparative study in the behavioral sciences. Given the history of this publication as outlined in the introductory Chapter 1, the editors are deeply grateful to all contributors for their readiness to take part in this challenging task, to Psychology Press, notably Mr Michael Foster and Ms Rohays Perry, for their continuous encouragement and professional patience, and to the numerous colleagues in the global psychological community whose comments, ideas and criticisms proved most helpful in the planning of this volume. May it serve as a stimulating text furthering the study of the history of psychology and its research paradigms.

Kurt Pawlik   Géry d'Ydewalle
Hamburg, Germany   Leuven, Belgium
                              December, 2005

1 A historical and comparative study of concepts and constructs in psychology

Kurt Pawlik and Géry d'Ydewalle

The approach to the history of psychology taken by this volume differs from familiar history texts. In this chapter the rationale of this approach is explained and followed up into the design and aim of the book. As a point of start, we will first look at alternative modes of collating facts of history in psychology, their merits and their shortcomings—all the while keeping in mind Hermann Ebbinghaus's (1885) often-quoted dictum of psychology's "long past albeit short history still". The latter has been borne out ever so often in the recent "boom" of history texts in psychology, several of them spurred by the celebration of centennial anniversaries of research laboratories (Hearst, 1979), of national societies of psychology (like that of the American Psychological Association in 1992, of the British Psychological Society in 2001, or of the German Society of Psychology in 2004) or simply by the ubiquitous attention to the recent "turn of the millennium" (Fuller, Walsh, & McGinley, 1997). Already, the accumulated literature on the history of psychology is far too numerous to be referenced here in detail. Instead, we will take a comparative look at alternative approaches, with reference to illustrative literature.

Styles of uncovering the history of psychology

It seems that there is more agreement among scientists on the goals in studying the history of science than among historians on those of the science of history itself:

- Is history an objective rational science, yielding results that can claim to stand, irrespective of a historian's frame of reference? Or is history to be understood as a portrayal (a reconstruction) of selected moments in, and documents on, the past, chosen according to a historian's strategy of search or way of interpretation?
- If so, by what criteria will such search be guided, and how is what will be worth the exercise of historical reconstruction or fact collection to be decided?

- Can we yet give a new sense, if not answer, to the Hegelian question of whether one can learn anything from history, and derive from its study transferable insights (in the sense of explanations or predictions)?
- Or can history at best furnish case studies of essentially unique circumstances, actors and events, "stories" told by the past with no lesson to be learned from them for the future?
- Is the notion of (some) empirical lawfulness in the course of history tenable at all? Is the apparent covariation (and interaction) between antecedent, concomitant, or just "collateral" events in the evolution of psychology and their consequences a distracting illusion or heuristically fruitful to guide the professional historian of psychology?
- And still more general: can psychology itself, as a science and as a profession, learn lessons from its own past and history (Pawlik, 2004)?

However tempting, for the purpose of this volume we cannot dwell on these and other fundamental questions of historical reflections in psychology; yet we should keep them in mind as proper caveat against drawing all too quick generalizations from the comparative historical essays that make up this volume. Instead, we would like to join with Edwin G. Boring, who expressed this so well in the Preface to the first edition of his classic text *A history of experimental psychology*:

> The experimental psychologist . . . needs historical sophistication within his own sphere of expertness. Without such knowledge he sees the present in distorted perspective, he mistakes old facts and old views for new, and he remains unable to evaluate the significance of new movements and methods. . . . A psychological sophistication that contains no component of historical orientation seems to me to be no sophistication at all.
>
> (Boring, 1929, p. ix)

As any student of the history of psychology will soon detect, there is more than one way or one style of uncovering the discipline's past. In fact, one can distinguish at least five approaches to the study of history of psychology, depending on whether it takes off from leading personalities (authors/researchers) and institutions, proceeds by temporal (periods in time) or regional (countries, language zones) traditions of study, or goes by schools of thought or paradigms of methodology. And, of course, there can by any number of combined approaches, Boring's aforementioned book serving as a first and fine example (see also Boring, 1942, or the recent *Illustrated history of psychology* by Lück & Miller, 1999). More often, though, texts on the history of psychology seem to concentrate on one preferred mode of study as a road map guiding the search for facts and their presentation.

Organizing a history of psychology around *leading personalities* unfolds a scenario of authors considered influential, like Wundt, Thorndike, or Skinner in psychology proper or Sherrington and Wiener from physiology and cybernetics, respectively. The three volumes by Kimble, Wertheimer, and White (1991), Kimble, Bonneau, and Wertheimer (1996), and Kimble and Wertheimer (1998) can serve as an excellent recent example. A companion approach looks at the history of psychology through the eyes of the actors themselves, that is, through autobiographies of eminent authors. The series on the history of psychology by invited autobiographies as initiated by Murchison (1961) is the classic example, which has been taken as a model also in other language communities (e.g. Pongratz, Traxel, & Wehner, 1972). And there is a rich resource of literature of self-initiated autobiographies by leading names in psychology, beginning with Wundt's late *Erlebtes und Erkanntes* (Wundt, 1920) or, more recently, with Skinner's highly readable three-volume autobiography (Skinner, 1976, 1979, 1984). Still another variant of this type of history of psychology takes off from representative personal documents or statements reflecting the development of the discipline, like the annual addresses of successive presidents of the American Psychological Association (Hilgard, 1978) or their equivalent, for example, in the German Society of Psychology (Schneider, 2005).

Histories of psychology *by institutions* look into the role that a university department, a clinic or research institution has played in the history of psychology, like the precursors of present-day psychology at Harvard University, the impact (or missing or unsuccessful impact) originating from psychology in academies of science around the world or the history of international organizations in psychology (Rosenzweig, Holzman, Sabourin, & Bélanger, 2000). This approach provides valuable information on infrastructures that gave rise to the development of psychology as a discipline.

A third type of history studies the course of psychology during selected *periods of time*, as during political oppression in Germany by the Nazi regime (Geuter, 1985; Pawlik, 1994) or in the years of the Cultural Revolution in China (Jing, 1994), or in a certain *region or language community* (see for example Pawlik & Rosenzweig, 1994, or the survey by Clark, 1957, of the development of psychology in the first half of the twentieth century in the USA).

In a fourth approach, *schools of thought*, like associationism, behaviorism or psychoanalysis up to modern cognitivism or constructivism, are chosen as rationale for categorizing and integrating dates and dynamics in the history of psychology. The resourceful volume by Woodworth and Sheehan (1964) can serve as an early example for this approach, which has since become an organizing scheme for numerous excellent accounts of theoretical psychology and its historical roots (see, for example, Hall & Lindzey, 1970; Koch, 1959–1963; or Marx & Hillix, 1963).

In historical accounts of *specific fields* of psychology, like research on memory, on individual differences or psychological therapy, the preference seems to go for a fifth type of history writing in psychology: one by *paradigms of theory or methodology*. Thus in clinical psychology, for example, a history of psychotherapy will often be organized by reference to major therapeutic methodologies like psychoanalysis, behaviour therapy, cognitive behaviour therapy, and their later derivatives. Conversely, means and limitations of early research on head and brain injury, electro-encephalographic techniques of research, advances in the chronometric analysis of cognitive performance, or functional magnetic resonance tomography may be paradigms of methodology highlighted in designing a history of neuropsychology.

It should go without saying, but should be stressed nonetheless, that each of these modes of studying the history of psychology is a valid one in itself, can yield salient insights into the evolution of the discipline and may provide the kind of orientation called for in the quote from Boring as to enhance "psychological sophistication". Yet, unless special attention is paid, all five approaches can lack in one challenging aspect: theoretical and conceptual coherence. Clearly, there is significant connectivity in theory construction and concept formation across different research contexts, forming a "red thread" between laboratories and schools of thought apparently unconnected at the surface or even unnoticed by the actors in question.

Furthermore, one and the same concept term may be employed in different research traditions, thereby varying in meaning, operationalization, and theoretical context. The concept of "self" (see Chapter 15) can serve as an instructive example. And international psychology abounds with examples of supposedly equivalent concepts that differ significantly between languages and cultures in connotation and concept-building roots. Pawlik and d'Ydewalle (1996) gave the example of the Freudian German-language concept of *Trieb* (*instinct* vs. *drive*), and Chapter 6 unfolds the multitude of meanings of *emotion*. With concepts serving as building blocks in theory construction, such historical or cross-cultural divergence must be taken into account in the design and in assessing the validity of research on derivations from them.

Considerations like these gave rise to the idea of exploring the salience of an approach to the *history of psychology by key concepts*, taking concepts like intelligence, consciousness or mind as starting points for historical and cross-cultural comparison, thereby cutting across more familiar paths of history writing.

Concepts and constructs in psychology

According to one recent distinction in social science, the term *concept* would refer to "*specific* ideas covering crucial aspects of a *narrow* variety of behavior", whereas *construct* would be used for "*general* ideas covering crucial aspects of a *wide* variety of behavior" (Zeller, 2005, p. 665, emphasis by the present authors). In this terminology (and without disputing for the moment its obvious vagueness), "intelligence" would constitute a construct, whereas a hypothesized ability like "perceptual speed" could qualify as a concept.

For the purpose of this volume, we used (and proposed to the contributing authors) a wider notion of *concept* in the sense of a core or source element of a psychological theory, like *personality*, *motivation*, or *self*. As salient nuclei in theory construction, such concepts will differ in meaning between rival theories and may also carry different connotations in different contexts of language and culture. Following from this delineation, conceptual units at the operational level, like *behaviour* or *reaction* or *stimulus*, should not fall under the purview of this project.

It is in this sense that the expression *conceptual history* is used for the approach followed in this volume. It entails diachronic (historical) and synchronic (cross-sectional, cross-cultural) explanation and comparison of core concepts. In this understanding, *construct* then refers to a conceptual variant or component of a psychological concept, typically conceived ("constructed") out of research grounded in an articulated theory. For example, "secondary motivation" would constitute a construct in behavioral learning theory.

Clusters of ideas thereby identified as *psychological concepts* share a charm and risk: One makes reference to them by common-language words (see the examples given two paragraphs earlier), which can have a long-standing tradition in pre-empirical (philosophical or other) thinking about human nature. This may contribute to the appeal of psychology within the humanities and also highlight psychology's social relevance—yet, for the price and risk of ambiguity in conceptual content and implications. Think of a concept like *intelligence* and its multitude of meaning at different times in history, in belletristic literature, or its cultural and philosophical roots (cf. Chapter 8). At the same time, variations in connotative (and still more so in denotative) meaning of a concept can also prove suggestive in theory development and keep psychological thinking embedded in the cultural matrix of a society and open to requests for indigenization of psychology (Sinha, 1981).

Although this can lend special weight on a comparative conceptual history of psychology, one is also reminded of points of critique expressed in recent years, notably by scholars from the developing world, that in psychology concepts and theories covertly import (and afterwards take for granted) Western traditions of thinking about human nature. Such traditions can reach far back in time and can be rooted in classical European philosophy; they form a *Weltanschauung* (way of conceiving, or thinking about, the world), not necessarily shared by other cultures. An example is the distinction between linear versus circular notions of time in European as compared to African thinking (Boon, 1998) or the Western notion of communication as being explication-bound as compared to the Confucian

Chinese notion of communication as context-bound (Lin-Huber, 2001). This being said, a comparative analysis of psychological key concepts also contributes to theoretical psychology at large and to the epistemology of research on human behaviour and the human mind (see also O'Donahue & Kitchener, 1996).

In preparing this volume, the editors had ample opportunity to experience the aforementioned twist of "charm and risk" when choosing psychological concepts as templates for studying lines of history in psychology. In the next section, the steps and procedures followed in pursuing this aim are presented: In selecting key concepts for their theoretical saliency and in bringing together a international body of experts that could be persuaded to undertake this task with the editors.

Design and aim

This book has a history of its own which goes back to steps taken by the Standing Committee on Research of the International Union of Psychological Science (IUPsyS) in the late 1980s. Lars-Göran Nilsson, then chairing this committee, submitted a research project on a taxonomy and classification of key concepts in psychology. The Executive Committee of IUPsyS approved the project in 1991. A first full report on the project progress was provided by Nilsson at the meeting of the IUPsyS Executive Committee in Montreal in 1993. As stated explicitly by him in a personal communication, he considered as a dream the production of a textbook on concepts. Unfortunately, such an outgrowth of the project remained a dream for a more than a decade.

A milestone occurred in 1997, with an informal lunch meeting in Stockholm between several members of the IUPsyS Executive Committee (involving particularly Kurt Pawlik, Past President of the IUPsyS and then Chair of the IUPsyS Standing Committee on Publications and Communication) and Michael Forster, managing director of Psychology Press. New ideas for the IUPsyS publication programme were explored, and among them there was also a suggestion for a comprehensive book on the history of psychology from an *international* perspective (possibly to be conducted as a collaborative research project with the International Union of the History and Philosophy of Science, which then did not materialize, however). And there was the other driving idea, ever since the first exchange between by Kurt Pawlik and Michael Forster, that the approach of such a new history text should proceed by key concepts of psychology, rather than by key authors, institutions or schools of thought. Further discussion of the scope agreed on a need to include indigenous psychology and so go beyond a history of European and US psychology. Other items to be covered were cross-disciplinary trends and a history of how concepts changed as they were introduced and modified internationally; for example, Freudian concepts with different breadth and idiomatic meanings when translated into different cultures. And there was the suggestion to focus on a more concentrated, integrated volume directed to a wider audience that might not be as rich in detail but that might have more impact. Still in 1997, the IUPsyS Executive Committee formally endorsed the launch of a project, under the direction of the editors, on the conceptual history of psychology from an international perspective.

Further brainstorming on the task took place at subsequent IUPsyS Executive Committee meetings, particularly at a meeting in Stockholm in 2000. The idea gradually consolidated for a history book of concepts in psychology as a history of concepts and ideas within and across historical/cultural contexts and as derived from layman's concepts. Discussions also included the question whether this is a possible and doable book at all.

In April 2001, letters and e-mails were sent by the editors to all Presidents and Secretaries-General of the National Members of IUPsyS. First, the project idea was introduced. In the book, the historical–theoretical trend lines of construct development were expected to be described, and analyzed in a comparative manner, for a small number of well-chosen key concepts of psychological theory.

The preparation of such a volume was expected to be demanding in more than one respect. Its success was to depend on the good choice of concepts, of a proper analytical approach and, last but not least, of competent and devoted authors. As authors will often be more familiar with the theoretical evolution of constructs within their own area of specialization and/or regional/linguistic competence than with a construct's historical evolution across theories and/or regional/linguistic contexts, the editors of the book also invited the Presidents and Secretaries-General of the National Members of IUPsyS to initiate, as broadly as possible, an e-mail-based discussion network to share with the editors thoughts and proposals as to: (1) the principal doability and usefulness of such a book; (2) ideas on the analytical approach to be followed in a comparative–historical study of construct evolution in psychology; (3) thoughts and proposals as to a wise choice of key concepts to be considered; and (4) proposals as to authors/contributors to be contacted.

A large number and rich variety of responses were received, all of which enthusiastically endorsed the project idea. At the same time, many suggestions were made as to the criteria for choosing the key concepts as well as to nominate particular authors. Therefore, the editors decided to convene an informal discussion meeting (on 4–5 July 2001) in conjunction with the Sixth European Congress of Psychology in London. All IUPsyS Executive Committee members were invited, as were those Presidents and Secretaries-General of the National Members of IUPsyS who had provided comments to the mailing of April 2001. At that meeting, proposals for criteria to choose key concepts, for criteria for choice of authors and (regional, sub-topical) companion-authors as well as for a possible International Editorial Advisory Board were discussed at length. Two tentative lists of approximately 20 concepts were compared, in order to explore the criteria for selection. Although the two lists were drafted independently by two participants, the overlap of the concepts in the two lists was striking.

Thereafter started a lengthy exercise by the editors to choose a limited number of key concepts. We explored the subject index of major introductory textbooks of psychology as well as the subject index of the *Annual Review of Psychology* over the last ten years. This yielded a list of 184 concepts. By clustering concepts as a function of largely overlapping content (e.g. "affect", "mood", and "emotion") and selecting within each cluster the most representative concept name (e.g. "emotion"), we were able to restrict this list considerably. A further selection was made as a function of a distinguished history of a concept, its central position in psychology, and its potentially different meanings in different cultures. New concepts from emerging subdisciplines in psychology (e.g. "modularity") were not retained. Finally, the resulting list was compared with the two tentative lists of the London meeting, and a very limited number of discrepancies were solved by further discussion among the editors. The final list, which thereafter remained unchanged despite some difficulties encountered in finding respective chapter authors willing to cover a particular concept was as follows:

- cognition
- consciousness
- culture
- (individual) development
- emotion
- imagery
- intelligence
- language
- learning/memory
- mind
- motive/motivation
- perception
- personality/individuality
- social/self.

Whereas selecting the key concepts was a difficult exercise, choosing the authors was, as a first step, much easier. They had to be leading authorities in the research field of the concept, its historical and international perspectives, come from as many different regions/countries in the world as possible, and be willing to meet our deadline. They were invited to be a key contributor to this book publication project of IUPsyS and introduced to the concept-centered comparative–historical approach to be followed in the book. As a lead author, their task was to write a synoptic portrait of what they would see to be the significant status of the concept (or conceptual field) in psychological science at large, its historical development and possible cultural variability, and evolving designs of research the concept gave rise to.

All 14 authors, in the first row of invitations, enthusiastically endorsed the idea of the book; unfortunately, only a handful were willing to meet the deadline. We continued sending new invitations, but for a few concepts finding a chapter author proved very problematic. This unfortunately jeopardized the original publication schedule, challenging the patience of colleagues and of the publisher. It also challenged our intention to bring together authors from all around the world, and to represent psychology beyond our own (Western) hemisphere. Nevertheless, we were finally able to assemble for the 15 chapters an illustrious tableau of leading authors from 11 countries and 4 continents (America, Asia, Europe and Oceania), who were prepared to work on their chapters as historical analyses from a comparative international perspective.

References

Boon, M. (1998). *The African way*. Sandton, South Africa: Zebra Press.

Boring, E. G. (1929). *A history of experimental psychology*. New York: Century.

Boring, E. G. (1942). *Sensation and perception in the history of experimental psychology*. New York: Appleton-Century-Crofts.

Clark, K. E. (1957). *America's psychologists: A survey of a growing profession*. Washington, DC: American Psychological Association.

Ebbinghaus, H. (1885). *Üeber das Gedächtniß: Untersuchungen zur experimentellen Psychologie*. [On memory: Investigations into experimental psychology.] Leipzig: Duncker & Humblot.

Fuller, R., Walsh, P. N., & McGinley, P. (1997). *A century of psychology: Progress, paradigms and prospects for the new millennium*. London: Routledge.

Geuter, U. (1985). Nationalsozialistische Ideologie und Psychologie. [National-socialistic ideology and psychology.] In M. G. Ash & U. Geuter (Eds.), *Geschichte der deutschen Psychologie im 20. Jahrhundert* [History of German psychology in the 20th century] (pp. 172–200). Opladen, Germany: Westdeutscher Verlag.

Hall, C. S., & Lindzey, G. (1970). *Theories of personality*. New York: Wiley.

Hearst, E. (Ed.). (1979). *The first century of experimental psychology*. Hillsdale, NJ: Lawrence Erlbaum Associates Inc.

Hilgard, E. R. (Ed.). (1978). *American psychology in historical perspective*. Washington, DC: American Psychological Association.

Jing, Q. (1994). Development of psychology in China. *International Journal of Psychology, 29*, 667–675.

Kimble, G. A., Bonneau, C. A., & Wertheimer, M. (Eds.). (1996). *Portraits of pioneers in psychology* (Vol. 2). Washington, DC: American Psychological Association.

Kimble, G. A., & Wertheimer, M. (Eds.). (1998). *Portraits of pioneers in psychology* (Vol. 3). Washington, DC: American Psychological Association.

Kimble, G. A., Wertheimer, M., & White, C. L. (Eds.). (1991). *Portraits of pioneers in psychology* (Vol. 1). Washington, DC: American Psychological Association.

Koch, S. (Ed.). (1959–1963). *Psychology: A study of a science*. New York: McGraw-Hill.

Lin-Huber, M. A. (2001). *Chinesen verstehen lernen*. [Learning to understand Chinese.] Berne, Switzerland: Huber.

Lück, H. E., & Miller, R. (Ed.). (1999). *Illustrierte Geschichte der Psychologie*. [Illustrated history of psychology.] Weinheim, Germany: Psychologie Verlags Union.

Marx, M. H., & Hillix, W. A. (1963). *Systems and theories in psychology*. New York: McGraw-Hill.

Murchison, C. (Ed.). (1961). *A history of psychology in autobiography* (Vol. I). New York: Russell & Russell.

O'Donahue, W., & Kitchener, R. F. (Eds.). (1996). *The philosophy of psychology*. London: Sage.

Pawlik, K. (1994). Psychology in Europe: Origins and development of psychology in German-speaking countries. *International Journal of Psychology, 9*, 677–694.

Pawlik, K. (2004). Was die Psychologie aus ihrer Geschichte lernen kann. [What psychology can learn from its history.] In G. Mehta (Ed.), *Die Praxis der Psychology* [The practice of psychology] (pp. 51–68), Vienna, Austria: Springer.

Pawlik, K., & d'Ydewalle, G. (1996). Psychology and the global commons: Perspectives of international psychology. *American Psychologist, 51*, 488–495.

Pawlik, K., & Rosenzweig, M. R. (Eds.). (1994). The origins and development of psychology: Some national and regional perspectives. (Special Issue). *International Journal of Psychology, 9*, 665–756.

Pongratz, L. J., Traxel, W., & Wehner, E. G. (Eds.). (1972). *Psychologie in Selbstdarstellungen*. [Psychology in autobiographies.] Bern, Switzerland: Huber.

Rosenzweig, M. R., Holtzman, W. H., Sabourin, M., & Bélanger, D. (2000). *History of the International Union of Psychological Science (IUPsyS)*. Hove, UK: Psychology Press.

Schneider, W. (2005). Zur Lage der Psychologie in Zeiten hinreichender, knapper und immer knapperer Ressourcen: Entwicklungstrends der letzten 35 Jahre. [On the state of psychology in times of sufficient, tight and still tighter resources: Trends of development over the last 35 years.] *Psychologische Rundschau, 56*, 2–19.

Sinha, D. (1981). Non-Western perspectives in psychology: Why, what and whither? *Journal of Indian Psychology, 3*, 1–9.

Skinner, B. F. (1976). *Particulars of my life*. New York: McGraw-Hill.

Skinner, B. F. (1979). *The shaping of a behaviorist*. New York: Alfred A. Knopf.

Skinner, B. F. (1984). *A matter of consequences*. New York: New York University Press.

Woodworth, R. S., & Shehan, M. R. (1964). *Contemporary schools of psychology*. New York: Ronald Press.

Wundt, W. (1920). *Erlebtes und Erkanntes*. [The experienced and the cognized.] Stuttgart, Germany: Alfred Kröner Verlag.

Zeller, R. A. (2005). Measurement error, issues and solutions. In K. Kempf-Leonard (Ed.), *Encyclopedia of social measurement, Vol. 2* (pp. 665–676). Amsterdam: Elsevier–Academic Press.

2 Cognition

Maria A. Brandimonte, Nicola Bruno, and Simona Collina

Introduction

William James (1890/1983) argued that a degree of vagueness can be beneficial to science when attempting new research directions. A strikingly
similar opinion was vented by Marvin Minsky a century later:

> It often does more harm than good to force definitions on things we
> don't understand. Besides, only in logic and mathematics do definitions
> ever capture concepts perfectly. The things we deal with in practical life
> are usually too complicated to be represented by neat, compact expres-
> sions. Especially when it comes to understand minds, we still know so
> little that we can't be sure our ideas about psychology are even aimed
> in the right directions. In any case, one must not mistake defining
> things for knowing what they are.
>
> (Minsky, 1988, p. 20)

The fact that both opinions were set forth by students of cognition is
perhaps no coincidence. As we shall see, different conceptual aspects have
come to be crystallized within the current definition of cognition through a
convoluted and blurry path, in common usage, in philosophy, as well as in
psychological theorizing.

A glimpse of common sense usages can be obtained from dictionary
definitions. Consider Webster's (1913 edition):

> Cog*ni"tion\, n. [L. cognitio, fr. cognoscere, cognitum, to become
> acquainted with, to know; co- + noscere, gnoscere, to get a knowledge
> of. See {Know}, v. t.] 1. The act of knowing; knowledge; perception. 2.
> That which is known.

This underscores a crucial difference between two usages of the same term.
The first is a process: cognition as something that humans do (along with
several other animals). The second is a product: cognitions as mental representations that surface to consciousness when we perceive, reason, or

form mental images. At the very beginning of his *Principles*, William James (1890/1983, p. 1) used the term in the second sense: "Psychology is the science of mental life, both of its phenomena and their conditions. The phenomena are such things as we call feelings, desires, cognitions, reasonings, decisions, and the like . . .". Conversely, at the beginning of *Cognition and reality*, Ulrich Neisser (1976, p. 1) relied on the first: "cognition is the activity of knowing: the acquisition, organization, and use of knowledge". The difference is not, as one might suspect, merely a matter of conceptual change after the so-called "cognitive" revolution (Neisser, 1967). Consider the American Heritage Dictionary of the English Language (4th edition, published in 2000):

> Cognition\, n. 1. The mental process of knowing, including aspects such as awareness, perception, reasoning, and judgment. 2. That which comes to be known, as through perception, reasoning, or intuition; knowledge.

This reiterates the earlier distinction between process and product, but also adds one (crucial) adjective. Cognition is not merely a process, but a "mental" process. In what is perhaps the most influential definition (Neisser, 1967), cognition indeed refers to the mental process by which external or internal input is transformed, reduced, elaborated, stored, recovered, and used. As such, it involves a variety of functions such as perception, attention, memory coding, retention, and recall, decision-making, reasoning, problem-solving, imaging, planning and executing actions. Such mental processes involve the generation and use of internal representations to varying degrees, and may operate independently (or not) at different stages of processing. Furthermore, these processes can to some extent be observed or at least empirically probed, leading to scientific investigation by means of methods akin to those of the natural sciences.

The duality of the concept of "cognition" and its origins

As a word, *cognition* originates from Latin. Latin philosophers used the word *cognitio* as a translation of the Greek *gnosis*, which the Western philosophical tradition translates as *knowledge* (French: *connaissance*, Italian: *conoscenza*, German: *Erkenntniss*). Technically, knowledge is verifiable description, as distinguished by mere belief, that is, description that is assumed to be true but not verified. Thus, to have knowledge of X is to have a procedure to ascertain that X is true. For the present purposes, we suggest that relevant philosophical doctrines may be broadly classified in two general categories. In the first, the procedure is one that establishes an identity between X and our knowledge of X, or at least between their corresponding structures. We will refer to this as the *mappings* doctrine. In the second, the procedure is simply one of presentation: Knowing X is simply an "encounter", an event whereby X becomes present. Borrowing a term from a different context (Quine, 1960), we will refer to this as the *qualia* doctrine.

Forms of the mappings doctrine were typical of the Pre-Socratic philosophers, of Plato, of philosophers from Aristotle, to Thomas Aquinas, and of the Renaissance natural philosophers such as Giordano Bruno. The purest form was perhaps the doctrine of *eidola* set forth by Epicurus, who hypothesized minuscule images detaching from objects to reach the knower's soul, thus preserving the identity with the originating object (Pastore, 1971). Epicurus's idea closely resembles the empiricist notion that objects exert impressions on the sense organs (Locke, 1694/1979). Romantic idealism added, somewhat obscurely, the notion that the mapping is created by a subjective act (Fichte, 1794/1982; Hegel, 1807/1931). The mappings doctrine is explictly present in many modern approaches, such as logical positivism. Wittgenstein, for instance, wrote: ". . . a proposition is true or false only as an image of reality . . ." and ". . . there must be an identity between the image and the object . . ." such that ". . . mutual relations between parts of the object correspond to mutual relations between elements of the image . . ." (Wittgenstein, 1927/1961, prop. 2.15). Note that mappings imply a dualism of object and representation. The problem posed by such dualism was made explicit by Descartes (1637/1994), who argued that awareness of an object is no warranty of true knowledge. Kant's "Copernican" revolution (1781/1999) attempted to solve the problem by stressing the subjective, rather than objective, character of the mapping. In his view, the mapping is no longer a relation of identity, objectively describable, but one of production ("synthesis") based on internal constraints ("*a priori* categories").

Quine (1960) coined the term *qualia* to define the qualitative content of experience. An early form of the qualia doctrine was proposed by the Stoics, who distinguished between knowledge of objects that manifest themselves directly, and knowledge of signs that refer to objects in an indirect fashion. Developments of the Stoic doctrine can be traced in, among others, Berkeley (1710/1988) and in what later came to be known as *phenomenology* (Husserl, 1931/1977). In the *qualia* approach, direct knowledge is in essence self-validating. The experience of X is our encounter with X, and as such must be taken at face value. In the encounter, the object manifests itself to consciousness, which in turn consists of a "transcending" operation towards the object (Husserl's term).

On the other hand, the conceptual precursor of cognition as a mental process is not *gnosis* but *nus*, "that whereby the soul reasons and understands" (Aristotle, writing *ca.* 350 BC), which the philosophical tradition translates as *understanding* (French: *entendement*, German: *Verstand*). The Latin translation, *intellectus*, has the same root as intelligence, and is preserved in Italian (*intelletto*). The notion is often reported as corresponding to that of a generic thinking faculty. A quick perusal of some representative definitions, however, clarifies that the notion was in fact limited to cognitive processes that we would today identify with thinking, reasoning, and problem solving, and was therefore more restricted than the modern notion of cognition. Thomas Aquinas (1225/1947), for instance, stressed the internal character of *intellectus*, arguing that the word derived from *intus legere*, to read within, and pertained to cognitive acts aimed at the essence of things, as distinguished by their mere sensible qualities. Kant defined understanding as "the power to know in general". Aristotle proposed a notion of "intuitive" understanding, defined as the faculty to grasp abstract principles involved in formal reasoning, and Kant argued for a "judging" faculty, operating according to *a priori* principles. Bergson (1907/1998) proposed a notion of "operative" understanding, which stressed creativity: the faculty of creating varieties of utensils and manufacts. However, Locke's *Essay on human understanding* (1694/1979) aimed to show "how we come by any knowledge", and to reject any role of innate ideas in such process. The notion implies a larger role for perception, or at least sensation, in cognition.

Evolution, artificial intelligence, and the naturalization of cognition

As shown briefly in the preceding section, philosophical precursors of the cognition concept reveal an intricate conceptual history, with both senses of the modern concept surfacing and resurfacing either alone or in combination. In general, when considering doctrines of knowledge, the duality of process and product is apparent in the idea of mapping between known objects and the corresponding representations. Interestingly, the nature of the mapping oscillated between a more or less "objective" notion of the relationship between object and knowledge, and a notion stressing a subjective contribution. Debates between stimulus-based and constructivist theories of perception and cognition are strongly reminiscent of these two ways of considering mappings. Stimulus-based theories, such as that championed by Gibson (1979), emphasize similarities between structural properties of the environment and structural properties of perceived or conceived cognitive products, and propose that a sort of objective link is naturally given between them, by the properties that are represented in the spatial–temporal structure of incoming stimuli. Constructivist theories, such as the Gestalt and the neo-Helmholtzian approach, rejected the existence of such objective link and suggested that human cognition requires internal constraints and active reconstruction from incomplete or ambiguous stimulation.

The distinction between what we have here called the *qualia* and the *mappings* approaches was voiced explicitly by Gestalt theorist Kurt Koffka (1935, p. 75), who argued that the starting point in the study of the human mind is the question: "Why do things look as they do?" Koffka noted that the question has two aspects: a qualitative aspect and a "cognitive" aspect.

From the standpoint of the qualitative aspect, he argued, the question applies simply to the appearance of things, as we experience them. As such, it would apply even to a world of pure illusion. From the standpoint of the cognitive aspect, instead, the question is concerned with the problem of how the appearance of things relates to how things actually are. As a student of Husserl, Koffka (and many other Gestaltists) exposed the idea of a methodological primacy of the first aspect over the second. The choice had the merit of reminding psychology, in a period of rampant behaviorism, of the existence of inner conscious contents that remained unexplained by stimulus–response laws, and remained genuine problems. At the same time, however, it eschewed the idea that conscious contents are also always directed toward external objects. Brentano (1874) strongly argued that such "aboutness" is specific of mental phenomena, and modern debates on what is today often called the "symbol grounding" problem (Harnad, 1987) are wary of the difficulty of accounting for the aboutness of mental content.

Current approaches stressing the notion of cognition as perception–action cycle controlled by internal schematas, priors, and decisions (Neisser, 1976) may be construed as one attempt to overcome the opposition between stimulus-based and constructivist theories (see also recent attempts to develop an "embodied" approach to cognitive processes, for instance, as in Clark, 1997). However, links between current theories of cognition and concepts that were used within the philosophical debate should be established with great caution, because current concepts unavoidably include notions that came from two later developments. The first of these, the theory of evolution (Darwin, 1859) provided a radically new criterion for evaluating how organisms learn about their environment. Before evolution, epistemologists struggled with concepts such as Kant's *Ding an sich* (the "thing in itself", as opposed to its phenomenal appearance) and debated whether knowledge was acquired or innate. By providing a conceptual framework for considering cognition as an adaptive faculty, evolution provided a radically new means for evaluating truth, or at least the degree of efficacy associated with the process of acquiring knowledge— not as access to "reality" (however defined) but as a means to warrant survival by gaining adequate knowledge of one's environment. In addition, evolution provided a powerful framework for understanding how organisms may possess knowledge at birth, and how such knowledge may nonetheless be acquired—not at the time-scale of the individual, but during the evolutionary history of the species.

The second development, the distinction between hardware and software within artificial intelligence, played a crucial role in defining what cognition may be and how it should be studied. Before the advent of artificial intelligence, attempts to approach the study of cognition through the methods of the natural sciences (as opposed to philosophical speculation) had to rely on biology, that is, on the idea that cognition can ultimately be explained by understanding the workings of the nervous system. The notion that cognitive processes could be taken as computational algorithms provided a radically new option. If cognitive processes are the software of the mind, then cognition can be studied using the tools of computer science, and quite independently of their actual implementation in a human nervous system, a non-human animal's, or even in a machine. This notion was critical to the cognitive revolution in psychology, and has now found wide acceptance in philosophical circles (see Block, 1995).

Mind, body, and cognitive explanation

The problem of understanding how cognitive processes relate to neural processes may be considered a manifestation of an older, and broader, conceptual issue stemming from the mind/body dichotomy. The issue originates with Cartesian dualism, and permeates approaches to cognition. Are mental and cerebral states two separate entities? Can the mental states be reduced to brain states? And, if so, what is the nature of the interaction between the two? During the centuries, questions such as these have been the object of heated debate. Fechner (1860/1966) reported that the fundamental idea behind psychophysics came to him when striving to solve the problem of the connection between the body and the mind. By formulating quantitative laws of relations between mental contents ("sensations") and bodily stimuli, he believed that one could prove how mind and body are one aspect of the same unity. Descartes' dualistic position posited an epistemological primacy of mental contents, although he admitted that mind and body had to interact somehow. For this reason, according to Sternberg (1999), Descartes' theory should be considered both mentalistic and interactionistic. In Locke's theory, on the contrary, the body had the major influence on the mind. Humans are born without knowledge, and through the senses (body) they process information that only later will be used by the mind for storage and retrieval. In general, materialist philosophers (for instance, De La Mettrie,1748/1990; Ryle, 1949) denied that the mind was ontologically different from the body, and suggested that it be studied by same methods borrowed from the natural sciences. Other researchers took the opposite position and denied the body a role in influencing human behavior, while others supported the existence of both entities, suggesting an interaction.

Many students of cognition agree that cognitive competence should be explained by coordinating three levels of analysis (Marr, 1982): implementation, algorithm, and computational problem. Explanations at the level of implementation refer to the brain substrate that underlies each cognitive function. For example, it refers to the neurological circuits involved every time we want to retrieve a word from the mental lexicon. Thus, on the one hand, implementation refers to the body. Explanations at the level of the algorithm, on the other hand, correspond to the processes required to perform a cognitive activity considered purely as procedures, independently of the substrate carrying them out. For example, to correctly produce a word (e.g. to destroy), we need to retrieve information about its meaning (e.g. the act of breaking into pieces), its syntactic properties (the grammatical category and the syntactic complements it selects), its phonological characteristics. In this sense, explanations at the level of the algorithm refer to the mental operations involved in cognitive function. Explanations at the level of the computational problem, finally, refer to the constraints that apply on both the implementation of cognition and on the implemented algorithms. At this level, crucial to understanding cognition are the biological and environmental contexts of cognition taken as an adaptive process that subserves specific functions within defined ecological niches. Thus, the computational problem refers to the mind but also to the body, as well as to the interaction of both with the environment. Recent speculations about the gene *FOXP2* and its relationship with language in the evolutionary history of our species are an excellent example of this level of explanation (see Chapter 9).

Not all theorists, however, concur with Marr's three-pronged line of attack. Many researchers, for example, believe that we still know so little about neural circuits that it makes sense to study cognition independently (Simon, 1981). The most important argument for studying the mind independently of the body derives from the computer analogy (Phelps, 1999). In this view, although the relevance of the brain functions as the hardware that actually performs the computation is acknowledged, the nature of cognitive performance is captured by the instructions given in the software (Johnson-Laird, 1983). In this sense, the actual hardware carrying out the instructions is irrelevant: It could be neuronal circuits, chips, or anything else (Putnam, 1967). Other researchers argue for reductionist explanations, suggesting that in order to understand cognition we first need to discover the neural correlates of it (Crick, 1994). These researchers reject the idea that we can draw a distinction between software and hardware, a position that finds strong support in connectionist models of cognitive processes. According to many authors (Gazzaniga, 2001; Posner, 1989), recent brain imaging techniques now make it possible to study brain activity *in vivo*, revealing the actual structure of connections between brain processes (Hunt, 1999).

Nevertheless, one position is to assume that brain research helps to study human behavior, another is to assume that brain data are sufficient to explain cognition (Phelps, 1999). The way we name colors is an example of this impasse (Tabossi, 1994). According to Tabossi (1994), a simple example as how we put a chromatic continuum (color) into discrete entities (names) is a good example of the risk we may incur when we underestimate the importance of a multidisciplinary approach to the cognition problem. Indo-European languages have complex systems to name colors. However, some populations of New Guinea have just two different terms: One refers to the red and the yellow and is named "bright"; the other refers to blue, green, black and is named "dark" (discussed in Tabossi, 1994). According to linguistic relativism (Whorf, 1956), names are given to colors on the basis of cultural factors, and therefore culture (language, values, and so on) deeply influences cognition. For instance, according to this hypothesis, it is easier to recognize a color when a name is available for it. Data collected using a multidisciplinary approach have shown that this is false. In fact, perceptual studies demonstrate that color perception is quite independent from culture. Red, green and blue, for instance, are also more discriminable than other colors when there is no specific name for them. Quite independently of culture, the primate visual system codes color along three opponent dimensions: red/green; yellow/blue; black/white. In addition, some researches revealed that red and yellow are better instances for "bright" than pink or ochre (Rosch, 1978). These results reveal the complexity of the processes, and strongly remind us of the risks involved in underestimating the utility of a multidimensional approach to cognition (Tabossi, 1994).

Cognition and representation

Most theories of cognition assume that the mind forms internal representations (minority exceptions are ecological and embodied theories). For this reason, an overview of the conceptual history of cognition would not be complete without a survey of different approaches to mental representation. As we have seen, representation was implicit in several "mapping" attempts to account for knowledge formation by philosophers. In modern cognitive research, the notion takes more or less this form: If we want to understand the mental algorithms involved in cognitive processes, we must understand the nature of the data that these algorithms input, process, and output. Therefore, we need to understand how minds represent features of the world (McNamara, 1999). Nonetheless, the nature and role of representation have been one of the most controversial issues in cognitive research. Research in this area has generated an abundance of theory, together with contrasting positions and heated discussions. The controversial question has mainly concerned the definition of format and organization of knowledge stored in the mind and, as a consequence, the description of how mental representations are formed.

Many theorists have proposed that language represents the central scaffolding for cognition. In this vein, Wittgenstein (1927/1961, p. 115) observed: "The limits of my language mean the limits of my world" and Sapir (1921, p. 162) proclaimed: "We see and hear and otherwise experience very largely as we do because the language habits of our community predispose certain choices of interpretation." An equally acclaimed tradition, however, has argued that there are many thoughts that transcend words. So, for example, James (1890/1983, p. 255) noted: "Great thinkers have vast premonitory glimpses of schemes of relations between terms, which hardly even as verbal images enter the mind, so rapid is the whole process." Einstein (cited in Schlipp, 1949, p. 228), in a striking fulfillment of James's characterization, reported: "These thoughts did not come in any verbal formulation. I very rarely think in words at all. A thought comes, and I may try to express it in words afterwards." Thus, according to many other theorists, words and phrases appear to cut the world up more coarsely than does thought (Pylyshyn, 1981, 2003). According to Pylyshyn, for example, there are many concepts for which there is no corresponding word. More seriously, one can have thoughts while perceiving contents that *cannot* be expressed in words, thereby implying that the grain of thoughts is finer than that of a person's *potential* linguistic vocabulary (Fodor, 2001; Pinker, 1994; Pylyshyn, 1984). In *The language instinct* (1994), Stephen Pinker offered several arguments to support his view that natural language is inadequate as a medium for thought and that the primary medium of thought is an innate propositional representation system.

According to the propositional theories of knowledge representations, any well-specified set of data can be represented in a single format, i.e. propositions. A propositional representation is a general formalism for representing human knowledge; it is defined as the smallest unit of knowledge that can stand as an assertion and can be true or false (McNamara, 1999). Propositions are not words. They are thoughts or ideas that *can be* expressed in words, but which are mostly expressed through special notations (see e.g. Kintsch, 1974) that specify the *relation* among words and the *argument* of the proposition (McNamara, 1999, p. 117). Within the knowledge system, a statement is not a sentence in any natural language; rather, it is a "language of thought", commonly referred to as *mentalese* or *lingua mentis* (Fodor, 1975). More recently, the idea that natural language cannot be the medium of thought because of inherent ambiguity and instability has been proposed by many cognitive scientists (Block, 1995; Fodor, 2001) who argue that there must be many more concepts than there are words and that, unlike concepts, the meaning of a particular word may depend on many pragmatic factors.

Most of our memory for persons, objects, and events from the past is based on non-verbal thinking. The functional role of mental images and of visual–spatial representations in memory has been documented since the time of the ancient Greeks (Yates, 1966). However, the properties of visual–spatial representations and the mechanisms by which they mediate human behavior have been clarified only recently by cognitive research (Cooper & Lang, 1996). The fundamental tenet of analogical theories of knowledge representation is that the properties of human behavior are too rich to be explained by a single form of representation (Kosslyn, 1980, 1994). According to this view, mental states must include sensory contents as well as verbal contents. This is the basic premise of Paivio's dual code view of mental representations, as well as the "perceptual symbol system" concept introduced by Barsalou (1999, 2003). Paivio's (1971) dual coding theory has been one of the most useful theoretical distinction in the field of memory. Given its explanatory value, Paivio's dual coding theory has remained substantially unchanged up to the present time (Paivio, 1975, 1986, 1991). The theory assumes that cognitive behavior is mediated by two independent but interconnected systems, which are specialized for encoding, organizing, storing, transforming, and retrieving information. The verbal system is regarded as a more abstract, logical mode of representation, whereas the imagery system is assumed to be a more concrete, analogical mode. The most important assumptions of the theory concern the independence and interconnectedness of the two systems. "Independence" means that either system may work or be influenced in isolation of the other; "interconnectedness" means that information can be transferred from one system to the other. An important corollary of the independence assumption is that the two codes may be additive in their effects (Paivio, 1975, 1986, 1991).

Analogical representations differ markedly from propositional representations (Kosslyn, 1980; Paivio, 1971, 1986, 1991). What distinguishes the analogical aspects of our memories from other aspects and, more generally, from propositional representations, is that analogical representations correspond in non-arbitrary ways to the external objects or events that they represent (Cooper & Lang, 1996; Kosslyn, 1980; Palmer, 1978; Shepard & Cooper, 1982). More specifically, there is some degree of "isomorphism" between an object in the world and its analogical representation in the person's mind. This kind of *complementarity* may be schematic, including only salient features of an object or global information about the object's structure, or it may be more concrete, including metric (spatial) information about shape and size (Cooper & Lang, 1996; Kosslyn, 1980, 1994). The evidence consistent with analogical representations and processes is too extensive to be discussed here. To give the reader the flavor of this long and heated debate, we will mention some well-known results, which are commonly considered a milestone in the research on visual imagery, namely, Shepard and Metzler's (1971) experiments on mental rotation. These authors found that the time to judge whether two line drawings represented the same three-dimensional object was a linear function of the angular disparity between the two figures. This result, which generated ample discussion within the field, was taken as the first and more striking evidence that the mental events and transformations during mental rotation are similar to those occurring during perception of the same real event. The mind, according to this view, passes through intermediate states that correspond to the intermediate states it passes through while perceiving.

During the past 20 years, research in cognition has turned from mere demonstrations of the functional role of visual–spatial representations in memory to investigations of the properties and format of such representations, of their relationship with working memory and verbal/semantic long-term memory, as well as with abstract non-visual information. Attention has been devoted to the general question of what processes (and related representations) subserve the use of visual–spatial memory. Indeed, there is ample agreement that visual–spatial memory can neither be investigated in isolation, nor be considered a monolithic structure (Cooper & Lang, 1996; Farah, Hammond, Levine, & Calvanio, 1988). To the contrary, the literature offers strong evidence that visual–spatial memory can both exceed and yet still be influenced by abstract/verbal processes. Although these two depictions of the relationship between language and thought might seem at odds, research in a number of domains of perceptual memory suggests that they may both be accurate. For example, individuals' ability to successfully recognize difficult-to-verbalize colors (Heider, 1972), faces (Polanyi, 1966), and non-verbal forms (Attneave, 1957) reveals the substantial degree to which knowledge can often transcend linguistic skill. Yet these domains are not immune to the influence of language, as revealed by the recognition advantage of easily named colors (Lucy & Shweder, 1979), the impact of post-event verbal information on memory for faces (Greene, Flynn, & Loftus, 1982), and the influence of verbal labels on memory for form (Carmichael, Hogan, & Walter, 1932). In short, cognitive representations can both exceed and yet still be influenced by language (Schooler, Fiore, & Brandimonte, 1997).

The discussion on mental representations is strictly related to modern cognitive theory, but it may be open to critical considerations that are present in the history of thinking (see Barsalou, 1992; Cornoldi & Logie, 1996; Kaufmann, 1996). Recently, researchers have argued that the value of representations in cognitive science has been exaggerated (e.g. Brooks, 1991; Thelen & Smith, 1994; van Gelder & Port, 1995). Many of these researchers have suggested that we should eliminate representations from cognitive models and focus instead on the relationship between the cognitive system and the environment or on the sub-representational dynamics of cognitive systems. However, in defense of the concept of "representation", other authors (Markman & Dietrich, 1998, 2000) have proposed a different interpretation by introducing the notion of a "mediating state" as a common ground in the study of cognition.

In analyzing the use of mental representations in psychological theories and computer models, Markman and Dietrich (1998) suggested two central issues that in their view a defense of representation should deal with. First, a defense of representation should clarify the core notion of representation that seems to be common to most approaches to cognitive processing, in order to provide the philosophical foundation for the use of representation in cognitive models. Second, a defense of representation should analyze how the concept is used in cognitive models in practice, that is, the pragmatic aspects of representation.

As defined by Markman and Dietrich (1998), "mediating states are internal states of a cognitive system that carry information about the environment external to the system and are used by the system in cognitive processing". Mediating states form a common ground in the study of cognition in that all cognitive theories posit the existence of mediating states. Markman and Dietrich (1998, 2000) specify the characteristics of a mediating state in terms of the following four necessary and jointly sufficient conditions: (1) There is some entity with internal states that undergo changes; (2) there is an environment external to the system which also changes states; (3) there is a set of informational relations between states in the environment and the states internal to the system (the information must flow both ways, from the environment into the system, and from the system out to the environment); and (4) the system must have internal processes that act on and are influenced by the internal states and their changes. In this perspective, the label "representation" can be restricted to a particular subset of mediating states. For example, one may refer to representations as only those mediating states with a particular *type of content* (e.g. propositional). Markman and Dietrich (1998, 2000) argue that this way of restricting mediating states to particular subsets may not be critical for most cognitive explanations but rather has a role in a *theory of content*. Given that all cognitive scientists (even anti-representationalists) agree that cognitive systems include some kind of internal states that carry content (i.e. they accept the existence of mediating states), this definition, according to these authors, provides a good *ouverture* to the discussion on representations and processes in cognition.

From the point of view of mediating states, one may reconcile the apparent disagreement between representationalists and anti-representationalists. Markman and Dietrich (1998) argue that disagreements over whether there are representations are better understood in terms of mediating states, as different researchers focusing on different aspects of cognition and using different kinds of mediating states will be able to explain what they are observing. According to the authors, this definition of a mediating state is quite general. It is intended to capture the general notion that there is *internal* information used by organisms or systems that mediates between environmental information coming in and behavior going out. As a consequence, this notion might be one with which all cognitive scientists can agree. However, the current debate reveals that not all cognitive scientists agree on the concept of mediating states as proposed by Markman and Dietrich (1998). For example, Clapin (1998) argues that not all internal representational states carry information about their contents and that being a mediating state is not essential to being a representation. In fact, they argue, although many people think that information is the basis for a theory of representational content they do not suggest that *every* representational state is information carrying. Therefore, Markman and Dietrich's notion of a mediating state is not one that can form the basis of all accounts of representation (Clapin, 1998). As an alternative approach, Clapin (1998) suggests a careful taxonomy of which representational properties are required for which cognitive processes, without assuming that all representations share all the same properties.

In sum, the current state of the art indeed reveals that the debate about the nature of cognition is still lively and productive, and it will probably push forward our knowledge of the human mind for a long time to come.

References

Aquinas, T. (1225/1947). *The summa theologica*. Translated by Fathers of the English Dominican Province, Benziger Bros. On-line. Available: http://www.ccel. org/a/aquinas/summa/home.html

Attneave, F. (1957). Transfer of experience with a class-schema to identification-learning of patterns and shapes. *Journal of Experimental Psychology*, *54*, 81–88.

Barsalou, L. W. (1992). *Cognitive psychology: An overview for cognitive scientists*. Hillsdale, NJ: Lawrence Erlbaum Associates Inc.

Barsalou, L. W. (1999). Perceptual symbol systems. *Behavioral and Brain Sciences*, *22*, 577–609.

Barsalou, L. W. (2003). Abstraction in perceptual symbol system. The Royal Society. Published on-line, 22 May 2003.

Bergson, H. (1907/1998). *Creative evolution*. New York: Dover.

Berkeley, G. (1710/1988). *A treatise concerning the principles of human knowledge*. La Salle, IL: Open Court (Original work published in 1710).

Block, N. (1995). The mind as the software of the brain. In E. E. Smith & D. Osherson (Eds.), An *Invitation to cognitive science, Vol. 3, Thinking* (pp. 377–425). Cambridge, MA: MIT Press.

Brentano, F. (1874). *Psychology from an empirical standpoint*. London: Routledge.

Brooks, R. A. (1991). Intelligence without reason. *Proceedings of the 12th International Conference on Artificial Intelligence*. Sydney, Australia.

Carmichael, L., Hogan, H. P., & Walter, A. A. (1932). An experimental study of language on the reproduction of visually perceived form. *Journal of Experimental Psychology*, *15*, 73–86.

Clapin, H. (1998). Information is not representation. *Psycoloquy*, *9*, 64.

Clark, A. (1997). *Being there: Putting brain, body and world together again*. Cambridge, MA: MIT Press.

Cooper, L. A., & Lang, J. M. (1996). Imagery and visual–spatial representations. In E. L. Bjork & R. A. Bjork (Eds.), *Memory* (pp. 129–164). San Diego, CA: Academic Press.

Cornoldi, C., & Logie, R. H. (1996). Counterpoints in perception and mental imagery: Introduction. In C. Cornoldi, R. H. Logie, M. A. Brandimonte, G. Kaufman, & D. Reisberg (Eds.), *Stretching the imagination: Representation and transformation in mental imagery* (pp. 3–30). New York: Oxford University Press.

Crick, F. (1994). *The astonishing hypothesis*. New York: Scribner.

Darwin, C. (1859). *On the origin of species by means of natural selection*. London: Murray.

De La Mettrie, J. O. (1748/1990). *L'homme machine: A study in the origins of an idea* (A. Vartanian, Trans.). Princeton, NJ: Princeton University Press.

Descartes, R. (1637/1994). *Discourse on method*. In E. S. Haldane & G. R. T. Brown (Eds.), *The philosophical works of Descartes*. Cambridge, UK: Cambridge University Press (Original work published 1637).

Farah, M. J., Hammond, K. M., Levine, D. N., & Calvanio, R. (1988). Visual and spatial mental imagery: Dissociable systems and representations. *Cognitive Psychology, 20*, 439–462.

Fechner, G. T. (1860/1966). *Elements of psychophysics* (Vol. I). New York: Holt, Rinehart and Winston.

Fichte, J. G. (1794/1982). *Science of knowledge (Wissenschaftslehre)*. Cambridge, UK: Cambridge University Press.

Fodor, J. (1975). *The language of thought*. Cambridge, MA: Harvard University Press.

Fodor, J. (2001). *The mind doesn't work that way: The scope and limits of computational psychology*. Cambridge, MA: MIT Press.

Gazzaniga, M. (2001). *The new cognitive neuroscience*. Cambridge, MA: MIT Press.

Gibson, J. J. (1979). *The ecological approach to visual perception*. Boston, MA: Houghton Mifflin.

Greene, E., Flynn, M. S., & Loftus, E. F. (1982). Inducing resistance to misleading information. *Journal of Verbal Learning and Verbal Behavior, 21*, 207–219.

Harnad, S. (1987). *Categorical perception: The groundwork of cognition*. Cambridge, MA: Cambridge University Press.

Hegel, G. W. F. (1807/1931). *The phenomenology of mind* (2nd ed., J. B. Baillie, Trans.). London: Allen & Unwin (Original work published 1807).

Heider, E. (1972). Universals in color naming and memory. *Journal of Experimental Psychology, 93*, 10–20.

Hunt, E. (1999). What is a theory of thought? In R. J. Sternberg (Ed.), *The nature of cognition* (pp. 3–51). Cambridge MA: MIT Press.

Husserl, E. (1931/1977). *Cartesian meditations* (Dorian Cairns, Trans.). The Hague: Martinus Nijhoff.

James, W. (1890/1983). *Principles of psychology*. Cambridge, MA: Harvard University Press (Original work published 1890).

Johnson-Laird, P. (1983). *Mental models: Towards a cognitive science of language, inference and consciousness*. Cambridge, MA: Harvard University Press.

Kant, I. (1781/1999). *Critique of pure reason*. Cambridge, MA: Cambridge University Press

Kaufman, G. (1996). The many faces of mental images. In C. Cornoldi, R. H. Logie, M. A. Brandimonte, G. Kaufman, & D. Reisberg (Eds.), *Stretching the imagination: Representation and transformation in mental imagery* (pp. 77–118). New York: Oxford University Press.

Kintsch, W. (1974). *The representation of meaning in memory*. New York: Wiley.

Koffka, K. (1935). *Principles of Gestalt psychology*. London: Lund Humphries.

Kosslyn, S. M. (1980). *Image and the mind*. Cambridge, MA: Harvard University Press.

Kosslyn, S. M. (1994). *Image and the brain: The resolution of the imagery debate*. Cambridge, MA: MIT Press.

Locke, J. (1694/1979). *An essay concerning human understanding*. Oxford: Clarendon Press (Original work published 1694).

Lucy J. A., & Shweder, R. A. (1979). Whorf and his critics: Linguistic and nonlinguistic influences on color memory. *American Anthropologist, 90*, 923–931.

Markman, A. B., & Dietrich, E. (1998). In defense of representation as mediation. *Psycoloquy, 9*, 48.

Markman, A. B., & Dietrich, E. (2000). In defense of representation. *Cognitive Psychology, 40*, 138–171.

Marr, D. (1982). *Vision.* San Francisco, CA: Freeman.

McNamara, T. (1999). Single-code versus multiple-code theories in cognition. In R. J. Sternberg (Ed.), *The nature of cognition* (pp. 113–135). Cambridge, MA: MIT Press.

Minsky, M. (1988). *The society of mind.* New York: Simon & Shuster.

Neisser, U. (1967). *Cognitive psychology.* Englewood Cliffs, NJ: Prentice-Hall.

Neisser, U. (1976). *Cognition and reality.* San Francisco, CA: Freeman.

Paivio, A. (1971). *Imagery and verbal processes.* New York: Holt, Rinehart and Winston.

Paivio, A. (1975). Perceptual comparisons through mind's eye. *Memory & Cognition, 3,* 635–647.

Paivio, A. (1986). *Mental representations: A dual coding approach.* New York: Oxford University Press.

Paivio, A. (1991). *Images in mind: The evolution of a theory.* New York: Harvester Wheatsheaf.

Palmer, S. E. (1978). Fundamental aspects of cognitive representation. In E. Rosch & B. Lloyd (Eds.), *Cognition and categorization* (pp. 259–303). Hillsdale, NJ: Erlbaum.

Pastore, N. (1971). *Selective history of theories of visual perception, 1650–1950.* London: Oxford University Press.

Phelps, E. A. (1999). Brain vs. behavioral studies of cognition. In R. J. Sternberg (Ed.), *The nature of cognition* (pp. 295–323). Cambridge, MA: MIT Press.

Pinker, S. (1994). *The language instinct: How the mind creates language.* New York: William Morrow.

Polanyi, M. (1966). *The tacit dimension.* New York: Peter Smith publishers.

Posner, M. (1989). *Foundations of cognitive science.* Cambridge, MA: MIT Press.

Putnam, H. (1967). The nature of mental states. In W. H. Capitan & D. D. Merrill (Eds.), *Art, mind, and religion* (pp. 37–48). Pittsburgh, PA: University of Pittsburgh Press. (Original title "Psychological predicates") (Reprinted in D. M. Rosenthal, ed., 1971).

Pylyshyn, Z. W. (1981). The imagery debate: Analogue media vs. tacit knowledge. *Psychological Review, 88,* 16–45.

Pylyshyn, Z. W. (1984). *Computation and cognition.* Cambridge, MA: MIT Press.

Pylyshyn, Z. W. (2003). Return of the mental image: Are there really pictures in the brain? *Trends in Cognitive Science, 7*(3), 113–118.

Quine, W. V. O. (1960). *Word and object.* Cambridge, MA: MIT Press.

Rosch, E. (1978). Principles of categorisation. In E. Rosch & B. Lloyd (Eds.), *Cognition and categorization* (pp. 27–48). Hillsdale, NJ: Lawrence Erlbaum Associates Inc.

Ryle, G. (1949). *The concept of mind.* Chicago: University of Chicago Press.

Sapir, E. (1921). *Language: An introduction to the study of speech.* New York: Harcourt, Brace and Company.

Schlipp, P. A. (1949). *Albert Einstein: Philosopher-scientist.* Cambridge, UK, Cambridge University Press.

Schooler, J. W., Fiore, S. M., & Brandimonte, M. A. (1997). At a loss from words: Verbal overshadowing of perceptual memories. *The psychology of learning and motivation: Advances in research and theory* (Vol. 37, pp. 291–340). San Diego, CA: Academic Press.

Shepard, R. N., & Cooper, L. A. (1982). *Mental images and their transformations.* Cambridge, MA: MIT Press.

Shepard, R. N., & Metzler, J. (1971). Mental rotation of three dimensional objects. *Science, 171,* 701–703.

Simon, H. A. (1981). *The science of the artificial.* Cambridge, MA: MIT Press.

Sperber, D., & Wilson, D. (1986). *Relevance: Communication and cognition.* Cambridge, MA: Harvard University Press.

Sternberg, R. J. (Ed.). (1999). *The nature of cognition.* Cambridge, MA: MIT Press.

Tabossi, P. (1994). *Intelligenza naturale e intelligenza artificiale.* Bologna: Il Mulino.

Thelen, E., & Smith, L. B. (1994). *A dynamic system approach to the development of cognition and action.* Cambridge, MA: MIT Press.

van Gelder, T., & Port, R. (1995). It is about time: An overview of the dynamical approach to cognition. In R. Port & T. van Gelder (Eds.), *Mind as motion: Explorations in the dynamics of cognition* (pp 1–43). Cambridge, MA: MIT Press.

Wittgenstein, L. (1927/1961). *Tractatus Logicus-philosophicus.* New York. Humanities Press (Original work published 1927).

Whorf, B. L. (1956). The relation of habitual thought and behavior to language. In B. L. Whorf & J. B. Carroll (Eds.), *Language, thought, and reality: Essays by B. L. Whorf* (pp. 35–270). Cambridge, MA: MIT Press.

Yates, F. A. (1966). *The art of memory.* Chicago: University of Chicago Press.

3   Consciousness: Psychological, neuroscientific, and cultural perspectives

Volker Gadenne

From a historical viewpoint, consciousness is one of the most remarkable phenomena. Some time ago, it was regarded as the genuine subject of psychology. Then, in the first half of the twentieth century, mainstream psychology rejected consciousness as an object of science. Although not many behaviorists held the radical view that there were no mental states, most of them accepted the methodological position that the mental could not be studied scientifically and was useless for the explanation of behavior. In the course of the cognitive revolution, consciousness was reintroduced, and became a major subject of several disciplines. Now thousands of psychologists, neurobiologists, cognitive scientists, linguists, and philosophers address to that subject (cf. Baars, 2003). New journals were founded and many interdisciplinary conferences were organized. Yet some psychologists have remained suspicious of this development and still hold that consciousness should be left to philosophy, theology, and art. But they seem to be in the minority.

Concepts of consciousness

The word "consciousness" has its origin in the Greek *syneidesis* (as used, e.g. by Heraclitus) and the Latin *conscientia* (cf. Jung, 1933). Suppose that a person A knows something, perhaps some fact not accessible to everybody. However, a second person, B, knows that fact, too. In this case, B has *syneidesis* (used, for example, by Sophocles in his *Antigone*), or *conscientia*. Now, assume that B is not another person, but an instance in A's mind that knows about A's actions, and judges them as moral or unmoral. Here *conscientia* means what we now call "conscience". There is still another meaning of *syneidesis/conscientia*: Leave out the moral aspect and conceive of B as an inner state or instance that perceives, or reflects on, what happens in A's mind. This is the idea which became central to many systems of philosophy: consciousness as a sort of *reflection*, or intimate knowledge of own mental states. For example, I see an apple and I am, simultaneously, *aware of* the fact that I see an apple. Or I am in a state of fear, and I *experience* that state.

The idea of consciousness as a kind of reflection can be found through-out the whole history of philosophy and psychology (e.g. Descartes, Locke, Leibniz). John Locke defined consciousness as the perception of what passes in a person's own mind. Such an *inner perception* seems to presuppose mental states of a *metalevel*, which are directed towards the mental states on the basic level. The latest version of this view has been brought forward by Rosenthal (1993). He claims that a mental state M's being conscious is M's being accompanied by a simultaneous *higher-order thought* about M.

But the concept of consciousness has also been used in a different way. Franz Brentano (1874/1973) proposed to call any mental state "a consciousness" (he did not believe in unconscious mental states). For example, a perception is "a (state of) consciousness" of an external object. The perception's being conscious Brentano called "inner consciousness", because it is consciousness of a mental, that is, an "internal" object.

There are still some more uses of the word. We say that a person is conscious of certain facts, that someone is conscious of doing something, that a person can lose or regain consciousness, etc. It has been argued that the concept is rather unclear, and probably useless as a scientific term. It seems, however, that the main uses can be reduced to three, which are related and fairly clear.

We have, first, *conscious states* or events, such as a perception, thought, or emotion. The term "consciousness" is sometimes used to denote such a conscious state, or the total of a person's conscious states. There is, second, a mental state's *property of being conscious* (of being experienced, perhaps because of some higher-order state). This property is also called "consciousness". Third, we ascribe the property "conscious" to a person to say that he or she is, at that moment, capable of having conscious states at all, which means that they are *awake*, and not in dreamless sleep or coma.

The view of consciousness one has is necessarily shaped by what one thinks about the *unconscious*. The question whether unconscious mental states exist has been controversially discussed for many centuries. Freud was not the first to assume an unconscious mental life. Unconscious states were postulated by Leibniz, Kant, and Herbart (see Brentano, 1874/1973). Helmholtz postulated "unconscious inferences". However, the dominant view at that time was that the idea of an unconscious mental is absurd, or even contradictory. It was mainly psychoanalysis that changed this view after its influence on psychology began to grow in the 1920s. During the second half of the twentieth century, psychologists got used to the idea that only a part of human information processing corresponds to conscious events.

What has psychology found out about consciousness? It has investigated this phenomenon from different perspectives. The oldest approach is the *phenomenological* one. In the course of the cognitive revolution, the per-spective of *information processing* became dominant. The most current approach is the *neuropsychological*. We will discuss these approaches or perspectives in succession. Finally, we will ask whether the concept of consciousness, as well as consciousness itself, is culture dependent.

The phenomenological perspective

The phenomenological approach to consciousness is the oldest one. By "phenomenological" I here mean not only the movement founded on the works of Edmund Husserl (cf. Herzog, 1992; Spiegelberg, 1994), but any attempt to describe the mental as it is *given in experience*. William James's (1890) famous description of the *stream of consciousness* is phenomenology in this wide sense. Gestalt psychology, the Würzburg School, and the school of Wundt and Titchener also contributed to this kind of research (cf. Boring, 1950). Any mental phenomenon, say, anger or happiness, can be investigated phenomenologically. But what can be said from this perspective about consciousness in general? What is the structure of a conscious state, and its typical properties? Here are some results (for an overview, see Gadenne, 1996):

- As James demonstrated, conscious states or events are always *personal*. The elementary mental fact is not *this sensation* or *that thought* but *my sensation* or *my thought*. Conscious states are necessarily *subjective*, they exist only as experienced by a subject.
- Consciousness is *unified*. We experience our sensations, feelings, and thoughts as part of one single consciousness. This *unity* encompasses the different experiences a person has at a given moment as well as her experiences across time.
- We do not experience unextended moments, but short, *structured intervals*. For example, we do not hear "thunder pure", but "thunder-breaking-upon-silence". We do not hear isolated sounds, but "this sound-following-the-sound-that-just-faded-away". A conscious state encompasses what was given a moment before, and what is just coming.
- Conscious states are always *structured*. As Gestalt psychology objected to sensationalism, the basic data of consciousness are not "sensory elements", but *wholes*. The mind organizes stimuli into coherent figures. We see, for example, not isolated points on a paper, but a person, or a face. A fundamental feature of this organization is the structuring of the perceptual field into *figure* and *background*.
- Many conscious states are *about* something or *directed* toward something. Brentano called this directedness the *intentionality* of a conscious state. There is no perception, belief, hope, or fear that is not *of* or *about* an object (which need not really exist). Brentano thought that intentionality is the characteristic feature that demarcates the mental

from the physical. However, whereas many mental states seem to be intentional, especially those with a *propositional content*, sensations and some feelings seem to lack that special property. For example, a pain or a feeling of tiredness is not, like a belief, *of* or *about* an object.

- There are, in addition to sensations and images, conscious states that do not refer to an object (e.g. an experience of astonishment, confusion, or hesitation). The psychologists of the Würzburg School (Külpe, Ach, Bühler, Marbe) systematically investigated such *imageless states*, which they called "Bewusstseinslagen" (translated as "conscious attitudes").
- Consciousness comes in different *degrees of attention*. This holds for whole conscious states as well as for their parts. In any conscious state, we can distinguish the *center* of our attention from the *periphery* within the field of consciousness. Things on the periphery are not unconscious though they receive little attention.

What is the epistemological status of such statements about consciousness? Their empirical basis is the researcher's own experiences, or the experiences reported by other persons. Note, however, that a claim such as "People structure the perceptual field into figure and background" not only refers to one person, or to several, but is a *general* assumption. It is a general hypothesis, which anybody can test, and eventually criticize, on the basis of his or her own experiences. As long as no deviating results are reported, such a hypothesis can be accepted as empirically confirmed.

Note also that phenomenological research is not necessarily the same as *introspection*. Brentano already argued that it is not possible to *observe* own mental states in the same way we observe external objects. There are some simple mental phenomena we can inspect without destroying them, for example, a persisting toothache, a sensation of warmth, or an afterimage. But if we shifted our whole attention to our process of thinking, that thinking would immediately stop. And if we managed to concentrate on an emotion of fear or anger, that emotion would have probably subsided at that moment. Nevertheless we *experience* such mental states, and this is a source of knowledge, too.

The access to own mental states is of course limited in scope. Contemporary psychology is concerned with many processes that are completely inaccessible to conscious experience but can be studied with experimental methods. People *can* experience and describe facts of consciousness like those reported by Gestalt psychology. They are *not* able to detect and describe the "elements" of the mental, and the laws governing their connections. If researchers require subjects to scrutinize their mind introspectively, as the Wündt/Titchener school did, these subjects will not report experiences but speculations.

The aforementioned properties of consciousness refer to *normal* conscious states. In addition, psychology is interested in *altered* states of consciousness, which include dreaming, hypnotic states, hallucination (induced by drugs or sensory deprivation), consciousness in meditation, mystical experiences, pathological conscious states (e.g. paranoid beliefs). In some of these cases, properties characteristic of normal states are lacking. In schizophrenia, for example, the *unity* of consciousness seems to be missing: Cognitive and affective processes seem to be disorganized, and the patients often experience a kind of dissociation between them. In mystical experiences, and in meditation, some people claim to have been in a state of *pure consciousness*, that is, consciousness without any sensory content or intentional object (Rao, 2002).

The phenomenological approach has been most positively received in areas of clinical psychology, and by the *humanist school* of psychology (Bühler & Allen, 1982; Spiegelberg, 1972). It never became a main paradigm of general psychology. In basic psychological research, the role and the scientific value of subjective data are still controversial. Some researchers reject it altogether, others grant the heuristic value of subjective data. It seems that at least some theoretical models of cognitive psychology have their sources in the experience of mental processes. Consider processes such as *rehearsal* in memory or the *rotation of mental images*. They would probably never have been studied with experimental methods, if the researchers had not consulted their own experiences. Recently, some neuro-scientists and cognitive scientists have argued that is was time to reintroduce the phenomenological approach into the study of consciousness (see Varela, 1996, 1998).

The perspective of information processing

In the second half of the last century, cognitive psychology was well estab-lished as the dominant paradigm. Psychologists were no longer concerned with reinforcement schedules or drive theories. They were mainly interested in subjects like perception, attention, memory, knowledge, problem solving, and language, which they interpreted as *human information processing*. By and by, they also began to take up the old subject of *consciousness*. But in contrast to the schools in the first half of the century, they were much more interested in the *function of consciousness in information processing*, than in phenomenological questions.

When cognitive psychologists speak of consciousness, they sometimes use this concept simply as a collective for all higher mental activity. In this case, the concept is unproblematic, but rather superfluous. Much more interesting is the attempt to introduce "consciousness" as a theoretical term. For example, consciousness was associated with the "limited-capacity system" in Broadbent's "filter theory" of attention, or with the *short-term store* or *working memory* in the multistore models of memory (e.g. Atkinson & Shiffrin, 1968). According to that view, the function of consciousness is to briefly hold small amounts of carefully selected information from the sensory registers or the long-term store, in order to execute cognitive operations.

Somewhat later, Mandler (1975, 1985) proposed to interpret consciousness as *focal attention*, a theoretical construct previously introduced by Neisser (1967). According to Neisser's theory, sensory information is first processed by (parallel) *preattentive processes*, which monitor unattended sensory inputs for important information. Only a small part of the environmental information is selected as relevant and processed in more detail. Selected and fully processed stimuli become the contents of *focal attention*.

Mandler's suggestion has two interesting implications. First, a large part of cognition seems to go on *unconsciously*. Second, the contents of consciousness, which we experience as the basic data of the mental, are actually more or less complicated (unconscious) *constructions*. Lashley and Miller had emphasized before that it is the result of cognition, not the underlying process, that appears spontaneously in consciousness (Miller, 1962). For example, we are conscious of an item, say, a number, in a recognition task, but we do not experience the mechanism of high-speed scanning while we try to remember that item. We form grammatically correct sentences, and are conscious of the words and phrases, but we do not experience the rules and corresponding processes that guide the construction of those sentences. While psychoanalysis was mainly interested in unconscious wishes and attitudes, cognitive psychology postulates rather "cold" unconscious processes. But both share the view that the mental includes much more than the conscious.

The discovery of parallel processing suggested that an adequate model of the mind should contain a hierarchy of processors, which work, to a certain degree, independently of each other. Processors at the bottom level of such a system should be concerned, for example, with the detection of optic or acoustic stimuli, or with the control of elementary movements. Such a system needs a *central processor* (or *executive*), which controls and organizes the whole activity from the top down. Bobrow and Norman (1975) assumed that the central processor of the human cognitive system is the seat of consciousness: Consciousness controls the process that schedules resources, and decides among alternatives, in cognition as well as in action. Shallice (1972) also emphasized the function of consciousness to select between alternative conceptualizations or conflicting tendencies on the sublevels of the system. A similar idea was put forward by Frith (1981, 1992).

Baars (1983, 1988) developed a theory of consciousness that integrates elements from the above views. He also regards human information processing as distributed, i.e. complex processing is performed by specialized processors. Such a system has to integrate information from different sense modalities. It needs a *global database* that serves this integration and provides information to the system as a whole. Consciousness is assumed to reflect a special operating mode of that global data base: Conscious contents reflect coherent global representations.

All these hypotheses are closely connected. They all regard consciousness as an instance or process at the top (or at the center) of the human information processing system. Many cognitive psychologists now agree that consciousness is characterized by certain formal, or functional properties. Conscious processes are contrasted with automatic ones: The *conscious* ones are said to be *serial, flexible, domain specific, relatively slow, resource limited, and not perfectly reliable. Automatic* processes are *parallel, rigid, domain unspecific, fast, resource unlimited, and highly reliable.* Concentrated thinking and problem solving is a typical kind of conscious processing, while, for example, feature analysis in perception is automatic.

This view fits well into an evolutionary perspective according to which consciousness emerged as an efficient system for problem solving. Systems for automatic processing are the earlier ones in evolution. They are efficient in specific environments but do not help individuals when environments change and pose new problems. Conscious processing, characteristic of higher organisms, enables an individual to create modified strategies of action that help to adapt to new situations.

However, not all cognitive scientists agree that consciousness corresponds to the top (or central) level of processing. According to Jackendoff (1987), conscious contents are only to be found on the *intermediate level*, i.e. on the level of (not concepts and propositions, but) sensations and images of the various modalities (visual, auditory, etc.). Is Jackendoff right? Interestingly, this leads back to *phenomenological* questions: Are there, in addition to sensations and images (i.e. the states characterized by *qualia*) *imageless* conscious states, as the Würzburg School claimed? If the Würzburg School was right, Jackendoff must have overlooked the imageless part of consciousness. Gadenne and Oswald (1991) and Gadenne (1996) discuss how phenomenological knowledge and the results of cognitive psychology can be jointly used to answer questions concerning consciousness.

The neuroscientific perspective

The hypothesis that the brain is the seat of consciousness was already held by some ancient Greek philosophers and physicians, who had observed the consequences of brain damage. Aristotle, however, regarded the heart as the seat of the mind, an influence we can still find in literature and in ordinary language. In contemporary (Western) academic psychology, this is no longer controversial. Most psychologists consider the brain as the physical basis of the mind. This does not necessarily imply that they hold a form of reductive physicalism. Not many scientists commit to the view that conscious states are literally identical with certain brain states, or that the subjective aspect of experience could be reduced to some physical property. The major view can best be described by what has been called the *principle of supervenience* (Kim, 1996, p. 10): A difference in mental states implies a difference in physical states. Put otherwise, mental events cannot happen independently of the brain. This leaves open whether the mental is identical, or can be reduced to, physical processes.

Knowledge about mind and brain comes from different sources. The earliest discoveries were based on brain lesions or brain disease: Changes in consciousness or behavior after brain damage must be due to the function of the area destroyed. Selective destruction of brain tissue has been performed in animal experiments, and in some cases did involve people, too, for example, in *frontal lobotomy*, as used in the treatment of schizophrenia (for a criticism of neurosurgery, see Valenstein, 1980).

Another method is electrical stimulation (with thin metal or glass electrodes) of single neurons, or groups of neurons, and the observation of the effect on these neurons, on global behavior, or on reported conscious states. Penfield discovered that the somatosensory cortex is related to the body surface, i.e. there is a point-to-point connection between the cortical surface and the body surface (Penfield & Rasmussen, 1950). In a similar way, the skeletal muscles are represented on the surface of the motor cortex.

In 1929 Berger introduced the electroencephalogram (EEG), the first of the non-invasive procedures. The EEG is used for recording electrical activity from the cerebral cortex. A person's EEG may be synchronized (wave-like shape) or desynchronized (no repeating waves). Alpha waves (8–12 hertz) are characteristic of a drowsy subject. A fast desynchronized EEG is typical of a waking, aroused state, and of dreaming sleep. Thus, the EEG reflects the general state of consciousness. But it is also used as an indication of single sensory or motor events (event-related potentials).

In the last three decades, the methods of *neuroimaging* (e.g. magnetic resonance imaging or positron emission tomography) have been developed to record the activity in all parts of the brain and use a computer to build up a three-dimensional picture. Such a picture shows in which brain structures there is enhanced activity while a subject is, for example, hearing, reading, or thinking.

In general, the results achieved with these different methods have converged. Here are some further results, which were of major importance in the physiological study of consciousness (cf. Kolb & Wishaw, 1996):

- The *primary auditory cortex* in the temporal lobe receives inputs from the sound receptors of the ears, and the *primary visual cortex* in the occipital lobe is the destination for the pathways from the visual receptors of the eyes. The primary cortical areas are necessary (although not sufficient) for *conscious sensations* of the different modalities.
- The function of the *primary visual cortex* for consciousness is dramatically demonstrated by *blindsight* (Pöppel, Held, & Frost, 1973; Weiskrantz, 1986). Patients with lesions to primary visual cortex report have no visual experiences, i.e. they are blind. In certain experiments, however, such patients can successfully perform visual tasks (discriminate colors, or guess the direction of a moving stimulus). Blindsight demonstrates the difference between *conscious* and *unconscious cognition*.

- Higher cognitive functions, such as short-term memory and attention, cannot be assigned to single areas. For example, structures relevant for *short-term memory* were found in the frontal, parietal, and temporal lobes. The function of *attention* seems to be located in the prefrontal, but also in the parietal lobe.

- Damage in the large area of the *frontal lobes* often causes a change of personality traits, mainly loss of social inhibitions, decrease in conscientiousness, failure to plan ahead or to carry-out plans (but no loss in general intelligence), indecision and perseveration, apathy, and decrease in general anxiety.

- The two hemispheres of the cerebrum are not totally symmetrical in higher cognitive functions. In particular, there is a link between *one hemisphere* (in most people the left one) and *language*. In addition, the left hemisphere (in most persons) is better in analytical thinking (processing words and digits). The right hemisphere is superior at visuospatial processing, recognizing faces, and at perceiving and interpreting emotions (Gazzaniga, 1985; Sperry, 1971). This was first found in *split-brain* patients, i.e. patients whose two hemispheres were separated by cutting the connecting pathways between them. These results have later been confirmed in studies with non-invasive methods on normal persons. It has been controversially discussed whether a split brain produces *split consciousness*, at least during the time intervals when the two hemispheres act independent of each other (Nagel, 1971).

- A *conscious decision* is correlated with a cortical event that occurs shortly before the decision. Kornhuber and Deecke (1965) asked subjects to perform simple bodily movements, such as flexing a finger, choosing for themselves when to perform the action. They recorded the electrical activity in the cortex and found a slow negative potential in the supplementary areas of the motor cortex as a correlate of the subject's decision. In later experiments, Libet demonstrated that such a *readiness potential* begins about 350 milliseconds before the subject becomes aware of his or her decision. It has been controversially discussed whether this result proves that conscious decisions are causally determined by unconscious brain events (Libet, 1985).

- Consciousness also depends on *subcortical* structures. In experiments with cats, it was demonstrated that the core of the brainstem contains structures which control *arousal* (Moruzzi & Magoun, 1949). It turned out, however, that there is no single structure or physiological mechanism corresponding to the psychological concept of arousal. The brainstem *reticular formation* contains distinct centers controlling cortical arousal and sleep.

- The foregoing results deal with macrostructures of the brain and their relevance for consciousness. It has also been asked what *microprocesses* are necessary to produce conscious states and activity. In some studies, the researchers found, as a correlate of wakefulness and dreaming, a

40-hertz oscillation in special groups of neurons connecting thalamus and cortex (Llinás & Ribary, 1993). Flohr (2000) presents evidence for the hypothesis that the normal functioning of the NMDA-synapses (*N*-methyl-D-aspartate) is a necessary condition for consciousness. For a further hypothesis see Crick (1994) and Crick and Koch (1998).

Recently, researchers have been trying to put these results together in order to construct models of how the brain produces consciousness (cf. Metzinger, 2000). The neurosciences have much advanced in the last two decades, and their progress is generally regarded as fascinating. However, it is not yet possible to specify necessary and sufficient conditions for consciousness. When certain conscious states or functions are assigned to certain brain structures, or to certain microprocesses, this should at best be taken as the claim that these structures or microprocesses are *involved in*, but probably not sufficient for, producing consciousness. The whole brain mechanism sufficient for consciousness may be much more complex than anybody now assumes.

The cross-cultural perspective

Is consciousness culture dependent? Can we find in other cultures: (1) different views of *what consciousness is*; and/or (2) conscious states or processes of a quite different *kind*?

The view of consciousness now dominant in the Western culture (Europe, North America) is much influenced by the natural sciences, which suggest to considering consciousness as dependent on the brain, i.e. as a natural, biological product. By contrast, in preindustrialized societies consciousness was regarded as something that can come in contact with, or under the influence of, spirits, and can be altered by certain religious rituals, often with the help of drugs (Bourguignon, 1973). The practice called *shamanism* includes rituals that produce a state of trance, in which the shaman is insensitive to the surroundings but said to be in contact with spirit beings, often in order to heal somebody.

Some aberrant conscious states which modern science explains as *pathological* (e.g. epilepsy) were in classical antiquity thought to be of supernatural origin. In the Middle Ages in Europe, some altered conscious states were regarded to be due to diabolic possession. Even today, in segments of modern societies, one can found beliefs in demonic possession, and practices of exorcism.

The altered kind of consciousness most interesting to psychology and philosophy is probably the states as reported by *mystics*, and aimed at by various forms of *meditation*. In his famous *Varieties of religious experience*, William James (1902) dealt with mystical and religious experiences, characterized them in detail, and speculated about their origin. Recently, some researchers concerned with mystics (e.g. Forman, 1998; Rao, 2002) argued that Western psychology and philosophy could learn a lot from traditions that use meditation as a technique to achieve special states of consciousness.

Roughly, during meditation the mental processes slow down. One tries to concentrate on one single object (which may be a physical object, a word, or a question), and not to pay attention to sensations, images, and thoughts. As a result of much exercise, some people manage to realize a state of inner stillness where all thoughts and sensations have stopped although they are not asleep or unconscious. Such a state is called *pure consciousness* (Forman, 1990, 1998).

There is another mystical state closely associated with pure consciousness: a perceived unity between one's own consciousness and the objects around one. People who experienced that *mystical unity* described it with the help of statements like the following: "No sense of time; no separation between myself and the rest of the world; no sense of an 'observer'; everything became a unified whole". *Transpersonal psychology* calls this state *cosmic consciousness* (Tart, 1998). See Walsh (1998) for a classification and phenomenological characterization of "transpersonal" states as reported from different cultures.

It seems that states of pure consciousness and perceived unity between oneself and the world can be more or less intense. Many people say they had felt a flavor of that unity, but very few seem to have had deep and repeated experiences of that kind. When one speaks of a "mystical experience", one usually means a very deep state, which carries with it a kind of conviction and importance. It is difficult to express in words where that personal significance and importance comes from. Mystical experiences are said to be *ineffable*. As a consequence of mystical unity, people reported to feel less attached to their desires and emotions. Many people's lives change enormously after such an event.

However, not all people consider mystical experiences, or similar altered states of consciousness, as desirable. Such states seem to be experienced as desirable in a cultural context that provides an interpretation for them and evaluates them as something valuable, and as a personal advance. Without such a context, in untrained individuals, or even in novice meditators, such experiences may raise feelings of irritation, and even depersonalization (Castillo, 1990). It may well be that the same states some persons strive for are experienced as disturbing if they come unprepared, or produced by the use of drugs. It should be noted that many mystical traditions emphasize that spiritual growth requires moral development, in addition to exercises in meditation.

Mystical experiences are reported from all cultures. They are called "*turiya*" (the "fourth condition") in the *Upanishads*, "*purusha*" in Samkhya philosophy, and "*samadhi*" in Buddhism. Quite similar experiences are described in the Christian tradition (e.g. by Teresa of Avila, or Meister Eckhart), in Jewish mysticism, and in Islamic mysticism (Sufism).

Interestingly, in some of these traditions (e.g. in the Christian, but not in the Buddhist), the mystical unity has been experienced as a union with God. The interpretation of mystical states seems to depend on the belief system provided by the corresponding culture.

Based on the literature on mysticism, Forman (1998) concludes that the contemporary scientific view of consciousness—according to which consciousness is a property or aspect of certain mental states, such as perceptions or thoughts—must be wrong. When any mental state is absent there might still be something left, namely *pure consciousness*. This is an interesting point, which psychology and philosophy should take into account. However, Forman goes even further and suggests that consciousness may be *nonlocalized*, like an energy field, and can therefore not be an effect or an aspect of the brain. Obviously, this does not follow from the assumption that some people have really experienced pure consciousness.

So far, we have considered differences between mystic traditions, on the one hand, and modern psychology and philosophy, on the other. In a comprehensive cross-cultural analysis, Ramakrishna Rao (1998, 2002) compares the *West* with the *East*. In the Western tradition, from the Presocratics to modern science and analytical philosophy, the emphasis has been mainly on the outward, the physical, and the pervasive approach has been rational and intellectual. In contrast, the central focus in the Eastern tradition is on the inward, on subjectivity, and rationality is regarded as secondary compared to spiritual experience.

Of course, Rao knows that neither the East nor the West is homogeneous. The Western culture has also dealt with subjective experience; there is Christian mysticism. Many people in the West have now learned to use meditation for their health and well being, or for some spiritual goal. Moreover, there is phenomenology, and the recent philosophical debates over subjectivity and qualia. Within the Eastern culture, there are differences, too. The Chinese tradition, especially Confucianism, has been mainly concerned with man in society and has put aside metaphysical questions, whereas in India the emphasis has been on inner experience, spirituality, and the corresponding metaphysics. Note also that academic psychology as now taught in India and China is fairly similar to psychology at Western universities. When Rao speaks of the Eastern view, we have to keep in mind that he mainly refers to salient features of the Hindu and the Buddhist thought. Thus, the differences we consider in the following are differences in emphasis and in the dominant trends.

In the Western tradition: (1) consciousness is regarded as part of the mind, or as a property of certain states of the mind; (2) conscious states are conceived as *intentional*, i.e. as having a content or object; (3) the goal is seeking *rational understanding* of consciousness and mind.

In the Eastern tradition, as represented by the Indian view: (1) consciousness is not regarded part of the mind but as something that *transcends the mind* of an individual person; (2) consciousness, in contrast to the mind, is believed to be *nonintentional*; (3) the goal is developing *practical methods and exercises* that help to realize higher mental states with tangible benefits.

This characterization of the Western view seems to be correct. Although contemporary psychologists, in contrast to philosophers, do not talk much about intentionality, they conceive a conscious state as having a sensory quality, or a propositional content, or an object. But what does is mean that, according to the Eastern view, consciousness is something that transcends the mind?

This view goes back to the oldest Indian philosophical systems (Yoga practices combined with Samkhya metaphysics; see Mohanty, 1993; Rao, 2002). According to Samkhya-Yoga thinkers, our being is governed by two "principles", which are called *"purusha"* and *"prakriti"*. *Prakriti* is matter, and *purusha* has been translated as "consciousness". There is a separate *purusha* for each person. However, *purusha* is not the mind of a person. The mind is considered as consisting of a subtle form of matter. But without *purusha* the mind would remain "dark". *Purusha* is the "light" that illuminates the mind, so that we experience what we call our subjective inner life. The mind may also be regarded as an instrument that connects purusha to the world of matter. So far, *prurusha* seems to correspond to Descartes' *'res cogitans'*. However, *prurusha* is said not to interact with the (physical) mind. It only reflects the contents of the mind. *Purusha* itself cannot normally be perceived. Only in the state of *"samadhi"*, as reached by mystics, *purusha* reflects itself instead of the contents of the mind, and is experienced as pure consciousness.

Although this view bears at least some similarity to Cartesian dualism with its pluralism of individual minds, Advaita Vedanta (based on the *Upanishads*) is clearly holistic with respect to consciousness. Here the notion of many purushas, one for each person, is declared as false. There is only one supreme consciousness, the *"Atman"* (with capital A). It is claimed that what we consider our individual self, the *"atman"*, is really the same as the *Atman*. The supreme consciousness is the only reality, and it is the same in all beings. That truth is revealed to mystics in the state of *"turiya"* (or *samadhi*).

Clearly, this metaphysics deviates from the view that is now dominant in Western science. Remember, however, that German philosophy, some centuries ago, also held the notion of a holistic spirit or consciousness. We also know that Schopenhauer had read the *Upanishads*, which decisively influenced his thinking. Still, there is an important difference. In the West, the striving for "higher" states of consciousness has never been regarded as the central goal in the life of a person. And if nowadays some Europeans and North Americans engage in meditation, it is largely because of the influence of persons like Yogananda, Krishnamurti, or Daisetz Suzuki (1955), who brought this tradition from the East to the West.

Let us now turn to the second question: Do cultural factors influence conscious processes, for example, perception and thinking? And can such effects be experimentally demonstrated? Nisbett and his colleagues have addressed that problem (Nisbett, 2003; Nisbett & Masuda, 2003). They compared the performance of subjects from East Asia (China and the cultures it strongly influenced, especially, Japan and Korea) with that of Westerners. The Eastern and the Western tradition differ in social practices for more than two thousand years. The Chinese have always been engaged in complex *social relations*, with the extended family, the village, and the representatives of the state. Thus, they have learned to coordinate their actions with those of other people, and to perceive themselves as part of a larger context. In contrast, the ancient Greeks had less complex role relations and social constraints, and valued *individualism* and *autonomy*. It has now been claimed that such social factors might have led to differences in cognitive styles, the Western thought being rather analytic, the Eastern thought rather holistic. There is some evidence for this view. For example, the ancient Greek thinkers were inclined to focus on the object and to explain its behavior with reference to its properties (Aristotle). The Chinese, on the other hand, recognized the influence of fields, understood much about magnetism, and found out the true cause of the tides (cf. Nisbett, 2003). Here are some experimental results based on these considerations:

- In experiments on causal attribution, East Asian subjects used more *contextual information* than American subjects. More specifically, American subjects tended to explain murders and sports events by ascribed traits and abilities, i.e. characteristics of the individual, whereas Chinese subjects explained the same events with reference to contextual variables (Lee, Hallahan, & Herzog, 1996; Morris & Peng, 1994). This holds even for the explanation of physical events: Chinese subjects referred to *fields* as an explanatory factor, whereas American subjects rather concentrated on salient properties of the object (Peng & Knowles, 2003).
- Confronted with two *contradictory propositions*, both supported by evidence, Chinese subjects were more comfortable than American subjects. The Chinese subjects tried to find truth in both, whereas the American subjects tended to reject one proposition (Peng & Nisbett, 1999).
- Chiu (1972) found differences between Chinese and American children in classification tasks. When shown triplets of objects, e.g. a cow, a chicken and a piece of grass, the American children perceived the cow and the chicken as belonging together ("both are animals"). The Chinese children instead put the cow and the grass together ("the cow eats the grass"). The researchers interpreted this as *rule-based classification* in the American subjects and classification with respect to *family resemblance* in the Chinese subjects.
- In studies on perception, East Asians attended more to the *field* and Westerners more to *salient objects*. When asked to detect changes in

pictures, American students were better in detecting changes in salient objects, whereas Japanese students were better in recognizing changes in the background.

Interestingly, Nisbett and his research group were not the first to experimentally study the influence of cultural factors on cognitive processes. More than seven decades ago, the Russian psychologist Luria, who is known for his contributions to neuropsychology and psychology of language, asked quite similar questions and carried out (together with Vygotsky) a field experiment with subjects from Uzbekistan and Kirghizia (Luria, 1986). As a consequence of the October revolution in Russia, deep socioeconomic and cultural changes were going on in these countries. This made it possible to study and compare groups with extreme cultural differences (e.g. illiterate peasants from secluded villages, people with little education (short courses), and students with three years' education).

Luria found differences in elementary cognitive processes. For example, the educated subjects recognized geometrical properties of visual stimuli (e.g. circle, square), and similarities between them, and they used them in classification tasks. By contrast, the illiterate peasants, when asked to classify things, ignored geometrical aspects and treated the stimuli as concrete things (e.g. a circle as a coin or as the moon). Furthermore, they were not inclined to perceive as belonging together things that fall under the same concept (e.g. an axe and a hammer—both being tools). They rather put together things associated in practical situations (e.g. an axe and a piece of wood). The illiterate peasants also had difficulty with *deductive reasoning*. That is, they reasoned correctly when they talked about their practical problems. Confronted with syllogisms, however, they had difficulty in accepting inferences as valid if the premises did not represent anything they had experienced. Luria concluded that many results so far considered as laws of human perception and thinking were actually the product of culture and education. This corresponds exactly to what Nisbett and colleagues now claim.

Is it possible to integrate approaches from different cultures, with fruitful consequences for all parties concerned? Rao (2002) and Forman (1998) are convinced it is possible, and argue for such an endeavor (e.g. of integrating the Indian and the Western perspective, or the scientific and the mystic tradition). Rao hopes for an "East–West confluence" in consciousness studies. Forman holds that mysticism provides deep insight into the phenomenon of consciousness, since it is concerned with consciousness *in itself*. Nisbett believes that West and East will move in the direction of each other and contribute to a "world where social and cognitive aspects of both regions are represented but transformed" (2003, p. 229). For an integration of Zen Buddhism and neuroscience, see Austin (1998).

Of course, the idea of a confluence of traditions can only be approved, although, in some cases, it will probably not be easy to integrate elements from different cultures. Sometimes such elements appear to be incompatible.

Roughly, an integration will probably be fruitful if the different views *complement* each other, and if they do not contain *incompatible theoretical* or *methodological* elements. For example, the following two theoretical assumptions are clearly incompatible: (1) consciousness is a property of physical systems (especially brains), and there are no nonphysical beings (the "naturalist" view as held by many contemporary scientists); (2) human consciousness is sometimes under the control of (nonphysical) spirit beings.

Consider the above examples under this viewpoint. In the studies of Luria and in those of Nisbett and his Asian colleagues, culture was taken as an *independent variable*. The researchers used quantitative and qualitative methods, which complemented each other. The results were interpreted in accordance with the methodological criteria of (Western) science, which were, in this case, accepted and used by the Western researchers as well as by their Eastern colleagues.

Similarly, physiological studies of meditation with (EEG, neuroimaging; for an overview see Austin, 1998, chapter 19) create no conflict between theoretical assumptions, or methodological principles. Here, too, the object under consideration is investigated with a coherent canon of methods.

Consider, next, Nisbett's idea of learning cognitive styles from other cultures. For example, Westerners could learn to pay more attention to the background of the perceptual field, or learn to use explanatory approaches that stress situational factors instead of concentrating on mere properties of the focal object. Such a proposal is quite in accordance with the view of modern physics. Thus, there is *mutual enrichment*, and no "clash" of different approaches.

Now compare this with the ideas of Rao and Forman. They want to integrate results achieved with methods of (Western) science, on the one hand, and results based on meditation and mystics, on the other (which is a very different project to studying meditation with physiological methods). This may be possible, too, but it raises special problems. It presupposes that science and mystics are regarded on a par, i.e. as equal partners. Most scientists are not prepared to accept such a view. Many of them despise any kind of mystics. Tart (1998) complains about the prejudices of scientists against research that takes meditation seriously. (He calls this disapproving attitude "scientism", and holds that it was not the attitude of genuine science.) Mystics, on the other hand, have usually claimed that their approach is superior to logic and (Western) rationality, and that discursive thinking is an obstruction on the way to the deepest truth.

If we put aside prejudice and misappreciation, there actually seem to be some fundamental differences. Science and mystics are based on different *criteria of knowledge* and procedures of achieving knowledge. Science rests on *observation* and *empirical testing* of hypotheses. "Observation" here means acts of perception that can be made by *any person* with intact sense organs. The result of such observation can be *described* and *communicated* to other people.

In contrast, relatively few people seem to have had mystical experiences. These experiences are said to be *ineffable*. There are techniques that can be used to achieve such states as pure consciousness or mystical unity. However, no guarantee is given that a subject who uses these methods will ever reach his or her goal. Tart (1998, p. 673) estimates that it probably requires about 5000 hours of meditation to become a "trained observer" in that field. Even then, it is possible that a person fails to experience pure consciousness or mystical unity. However, advocates of mystical traditions would not regard this as evidence against the claim that mysticism offers the deepest insights.

This is not to say that science should ignore meditation and mystics. I rather wanted to point out that a "confluence of traditions" requires more than studying other religions, other forms of life, and perhaps some exotic rituals of other cultures. Beyond that, cultural studies may confront us with the challenge to reflect, and perhaps modify, some principles of our own knowledge and rationality.

References

Atkinson, R. C., & Shiffrin, R. M. (1968). Human memory: A proposed system and its control processes. In K. W. Spence & J. W. Spence (Eds.), *Advances in the psychology of learning and motivation research and theory* (Vol. 2). New York: Academic Press.

Austin, J. H. (1998). *Zen and the brain: Toward an understanding of meditation and consciousness*. Cambridge, MA: MIT Press.

Baars, B. J. (1983). Conscious contents provide the nervous system with coherent, global information. In R. J. Davidson, G. E. Schwartz, & D. Shapiro (Eds.), *Consciousness and self-regulation. Advances in research and theory* (Vol. 3). New York: Plenum Press.

Baars, B. J. (1988). *A cognitive theory of consciousness*. New York: Cambridge University Press.

Baars, B. J. (2003). Introduction. Treating consciousness as a variable: The fading taboo. In B. J. Baars, W. P. Banks, & J. B. Newman (Eds.), *Essential sources in the scientific study of consciousness* (pp. 1–10). Cambridge, MA: MIT Press.

Bobrow, D. G., & Norman, D. A. (1975). Some principles of memory schemata. In D. G. Bobrow & A. Collins (Eds.), *Representation and understanding* (pp. 131–149). New York: Academic Press.

Boring, E. G. (1950). *A history of experimental psychology*. New York: Appleton-Century-Crofts.

Bourguignon, E. (Ed.). (1973). *Religion, altered states of consciousness, and social change*. Columbus, OH: Ohio State University Press.

Brentano, F. V. (1874/1973). *Psychologie vom empirischen Standpunkt* (Vol. 1). (Ed. Oskar Kraus). Hamburg: Meiner. (Original work published 1874).

Bühler, C., & Allen, M. (1982). *Einführung in die humanistische Psychologie*. Stuttgart: Klett.

Castillo, R. J. (1990). Depersonalization and meditation. *Psychiatry, 53,* 158–168.

Chiu, L.-H. (1972). A cross-cultural comparison of cognitive styles in Chinese and American Children. *International Journal of Psychology, 7*, 235–242.

Crick, F. (1994). *The astonishing hypothesis*. New York: Scribner's.

Crick, F., & Koch, C. (1998). Consciousness and neuroscience. *Cerebral Cortex, 8*, 97–107.

Forman, R. K. C. (Ed.). (1990). *The problem of pure consciousness: Mysticism and philosophy*. New York: Oxford University Press.

Forman, R. K. C. (1998). What can mysticism teach us about consciousness? In S. R. Hameroff, A. W. Kaszniak, & A. C. Scott (Eds.), *Toward a science of consciousness II: The second Tucson discussions and debates* (pp. 53–70). Cambridge, MA: MIT Press.

Flohr, H. (2000). NMDA receptor-mediated computational processes and phenomenal consciousness. In T. Metzinger (Ed.), *Neural correlates of consciousness: Empirical and conceptual questions* (pp. 245–258). Cambridge, MA: MIT Press.

Frith, C. D. (1981). Schizophrenia: An abnormality of consciousness. In G. Underwood & R. Stevens (Eds.), *Aspects of consciousness* (Vol. 2, pp. 149–168). New York: Academic Press.

Frith, C. D. (1992). *The cognitive neuropsychology of schizophrenia*. Hillsdale, NJ: Lawrence Erlbaum Associates Inc.

Gadenne, V. (1996). *Bewusstsein, Kognition und Gehirn: Einführung in die Psychologie des Bewusstseins*. Bern: Huber.

Gadenne, V., & Oswald, M. (1991). *Kognition und Bewusstsein*. Berlin: Springer.

Gazzaniga, M. S. (1985). *The social brain*. New York: Basic Books.

Herzog, M. (1992). *Phänomenologische Psychologie*. Heidelberg: Asanger.

Jackendoff, R. (1987). *Consciousness and the computational mind*. Cambridge, MA: MIT Press.

James, W. (1890). *The principles of psychology*. New York: Holt.

James, W. (1902). *The varieties of religious experience*. New York: Longmans, Green.

Jung, G. (1933). Syneidesis, Conscientia, Bewusstsein. *Archiv für die gesamte Psychologie, 89*, 526–540.

Kim, J. (1996). *Philosophy of mind*. Boulder, CO: Westview Press.

Kolb, B., & Wishaw, I. Q. (1996). *Fundamentals of human neuropsychology*. New York: Freeman.

Kornhuber, H. H., & Deecke, L. (1965). Hirnpotentialänderungen bei Willkürbewegungen und passiven Bewegungen des Menschen: Bereitschaftspotential und reafferente Potentiale. *Pflügers Archiv für die gesamte Physiologie des Menschen und der Tiere, 284*, 1–17.

Lee, F., Hallahan, M., & Herzog, T. (1996). Explaining real life events: How culture and domain shape attributions. *Personality and Social Psychology Bulletin, 22*, 732–741.

Libet, B. (1985). Unconscious cerebral initiative and the role of conscious will in voluntary action. *Behavioral and Brain Sciences, 8*, 529–566.

Llinás, R., & Ribary, U. (1993). Coherent 40-Hz-oscillation characterizes dream state in humans. *Proceedings of the National Academy of Science, USA, 90*, 2078–2081.

Luria, A. R. (1986). *Die historische Bedingtheit individueller Erkenntnisprozesse*. Weinheim: VCH-Verl.-Ges.

Mandler, G. (1975). Consciousness: Respectable, useful, and probably necessary. In

R. Solso (Ed.), *Information processing and cognition*. Hillsdale, NJ: Lawrence Erlbaum Associates Inc.

Mandler, G. (1985). *Cognitive Psychology*. Hillsdale, NJ: Lawrence Erlbaum Associates Inc.

Metzinger, T. (Ed.). (2000). *Neural correlates of consciousness: Empirical and conceptual questions*. Cambridge, MA: MIT Press.

Miller, G. A. (1962). *Psychology: The study of mental life*. New York: Harper and Row.

Mohanty, J. N. (Ed.). (1993). *Essays on Indian philosophy*. Delhi: Oxford University Press.

Morris, M. W., & Peng, K. (1994). Culture and cause: American and Chinese attributions for social and physical events. *Journal of Personality and Social Psychology, 67*, 949–971.

Moruzzi, G., & Magoun, H. W. (1949). Brainstem reticular formation and activation of the EEG. *Electroencephalography and Clinical Neurophysiology, 1*, 455–473.

Nagel, T. (1971). Brain bisection and the unity of consciousness. *Synthese, 22*, 396–413.

Neisser, U. (1967). *Cognitive psychology*. New York: Appleton-Century-Crofts.

Nisbett, R. E. (2003). *The geography of thought: How Asians and Westerners think differently . . . and why*. New York: Free Press.

Nisbett, R. E., & Masuda, T. (2003). Culture and point of view. *Proceedings of the National Academy of Sciences, 100*, 11163–11170.

Penfield, W., & Rasmussen, T. (1950). *The cerebral cortex of man*. New York: Macmillan.

Peng, K., & Knowles, E. (2003). Culture, ethnicity, and the attribution of physical causality. *Personality and Social Psychology Bulletin, 29*, 1272–1284.

Peng, K., & Nisbett, R. E. (1999). Culture, dialectics, and reasoning about contradiction. *American Psychologist, 54*, 741–754.

Pöppel, E., Held, R., & Frost, D. (1973). Residual visual function in patients with lesions of the central visual pathways. *Nature, 256*, 489–490.

Rao, K. R. (1998). Two faces of consciousness. *Journal of Consciousness Studies, 5*, 309–327.

Rao, K. R. (2002). *Consciousness studies: Cross-cultural perspectives*. Jefferson, NC: McFarland.

Rosenthal, D. M. (1993). Thinking that one thinks. In M. Davies & G. Humphreys (Eds.), *Consciousness: Psychological and philosophical essays* (pp. 197–223). Oxford: Blackwell.

Shallice, T. (1972). Dual functions of consciousness. *Psychological Review, 79*, 383–393.

Sperry, R. W. (1971). The great cerebral commissure. In N. Chalmers, R. Crawley, & S. P. R. Rose (Eds.), *The biological bases of behavior* (S. 219–231). London: Harper.

Spiegelberg, H. (1972). *Phenomenology in psychology and psychiatry: A historical introduction*. Evanston, IL: Northwestern University Press.

Spiegelberg, H. (1994). *The phenomenological movement*. Dordrecht, the Netherlands: Kluwer.

Suzuki, D. (1955). *Studies in Zen*. New York: Delta.

Tart, C. T. (1998). Transpersonal psychology and methodologies for a comprehensive science of consciousness. In S. R. Hameroff, A. W. Kaszniak, & A. C. Scott (Eds.), *Toward a science of consciousness II: The second Tucson discussions and debates* (pp. 669–675). Cambridge, MA: MIT Press.

Valenstein, E. (Ed.). (1980). *The psychosurgery debate*. San Francisco: Freeman.

Varela, F. J. (1996). Neurophenomenology: A methodological remedy for the hard problem. *Journal of Consciousness Studies, 3*, 330–349.

Varela, F. J. (1998). A science of consciousness as if experience mattered. In S. R. Hameroff, A. W. Kaszniak, & A. C. Scott (Eds.), *Toward a science of consciousness II: The second Tucson discussions and debates* (pp. 31–44). Cambridge, MA: MIT Press.

Walsh, R. (1998). States and stages of consciousness: Current research and understandings. In S. R. Hameroff, A. W. Kaszniak, & A. C. Scott (Eds.), *Toward a science of consciousness II: The second Tucson discussions and debates* (pp. 677–686). Cambridge, MA: MIT Press.

Weiskrantz, L. (1986). *Blindsight: A case study and implications*. Oxford: Oxford University Press.

4   Culture

John W. Berry and Harry C. Triandis

Psychology has had a longstanding concern with the meaning of the concept of "culture" (Jahoda, 1992). For many, understanding culture is essential to any complete understanding of human behaviour (Triandis et al., 1980–1981), whereas for others, culture has been largely ignored. The chapter traces the origins of psychology's concern for culture, and how various meanings of the concept have been employed in the discipline.

Early history

Students of psychological processes in antiquity and the Middle Ages usually contrasted the assumed universal psychological processes found in their location with "inferior" psychological processes found among "inferior" groups (Jahoda & Krewer, 1997). The exception was Herodotus (460–359 BC) who realized that people in all cultures are ethnocentric. They see themselves as the centers of the world, and processes that are common in their location are "good", whereas processes that are different are "bad". In fact, Herodotus provided a surprisingly modern account of psychological processes. He argued that there were differences in the fertility of soils in ancient Greece, and humans gravitated toward the fertile soils. To hold these fertile soils people had to fight, so they developed war-like attributes. Those who did not like fighting moved to the Athens area, because that was not fertile. As a result, a highly heterogeneous population consisting of people from all over Greece was formed in Athens. These people had different ways of perceiving the world, but as they did not like to fight they debated with considerable frequency in order to reach agreements. Democratic behavior patterns and institutions were generated as a result of these debates. Thus, Herodotus had both the insight that people in all cultures are ethnocentric and he formulated the ecology–culture–personality causal chain that is one of the ways modern psychology deals with culture (Berry, 1976, 1979, 2003).

During the Renaissance (fifteenth and sixteenth centuries), the universality of psychological processes was assumed, but increasing diversity became apparent, as trade and exploration resulted in meeting diverse peoples. It was assumed that groups went through an evolution from "savage" to "civilized". This assumption continued until the twentieth century (e.g. Wundt, 1900–1914). The concept of culture as shared norms and customs or shared mentalities was used to explain the diversity among the people encountered. This concept is found also in the twentieth century, with Geertz (1973) defining culture as "shared meanings".

By the eighteenth century, Vico (1744/1948) used the concept of culture to include language, myth, art, custom, religion, and so on. Culture interacted with "mind" to produce, what researchers in the twentieth century called "context-specific competencies" (Laboratory of Comparative Human Cognition, 1983) and "multiple realities" (Shweder, 1990). By the end of the eighteenth century cultural relativism argued that psychological processes depend on time and place (Herder, 1784/1969). Linguistic analyses were incorporated in a *Völkerpsychologie*, which started with Wilhelm von Humboldt and, via Lazarus and Steinthal, ended with Wilhelm Wundt's ten-volume opus on the subject (Wundt, 1900–1914). Most of this work was theoretical and did not have a long-term impact on psychology.

The empirical developments were started with the *Observateurs de l'homme*, who formulated detailed manuals for how to collect data in other cultures. However, practical difficulties made data collection rare.

By the nineteenth century, Tylor provided a broad definition of culture: ". . . the complex whole which includes knowledge, belief, art, morals, law, custom, and many other capabilities and habits acquired by man as a member of society" (1871, p. 1). At the end of the nineteenth century, expeditions were undertaken to obtain "mental measurements" (Rivers, 1901, 1905). The Darwinian evolution framework was already important in psychology and has remained so (Campbell, 1975).

The twentieth century

An important influence on social psychology in the middle of the twentieth century was Kluckhohn's (1954) "Culture and behavior" chapter in the *Handbook of social psychology* and Klineberg's (1954) text, which used much cultural material.

Herskovits (1955), who defined culture as the human-made part of the environment, provided an influential definition. Based on that definition, Triandis (1972) distinguished objective and subjective culture. Objective culture includes concrete and observable elements such as artifacts, institutions, and structures. Categorizations, evaluations, beliefs, attitudes, stereotypes, expectations, norms, ideals, roles, tasks, and values were identified as elements of subjective culture. Psychological methods were proposed to study these constructs, and examples were provided for the study of stereotypes, roles, and values with data from Greece, India, Japan, and the USA.

The twentieth century has been characterized by multiple definitions of culture. Among the most interesting are the following: "culture is to society what memory is to individuals" (Kluckhohn, 1954). It includes what "has worked" in the experience of a society, so that it was worth transmitting to future generations. Sperber (1996) used the analogy of an epidemic. A useful idea (e.g. how to make a tool) is adopted by more and more people and becomes an element of culture. Barkow, Cosmides, and Tooby (1992) distinguished three kinds of culture: metaculture, evoked culture, and epidemiological culture. They argue that "psychology underlies culture and society, and biological evolution underlies psychology" (p. 635). The biology that has been common to all humans as a species distinguishable from other species results in a "metaculture" that corresponds to pan-human mental contents and organization. Biology in different ecologies results in "evoked culture" (e.g. hot climate leads to light clothing), which reflects domain-specific mechanisms that are triggered by local circumstances, and leads to within group similarities and between groups differences. What Sperber describes Barkow et al. call "epidemiological culture".

Klineberg (1980) discussed several topics important before 1960. For example, is thought influenced by language? The so-called Whorfian hypothesis was the focus of much interest before 1960 and even as early as 1994 a weak version of the hypothesis received some empirical support. An important achievement of early cross-cultural psychology was the demonstration that even a basic process such as perception is influenced by culture (Segall, Campbell, & Herskovits, 1966). Much of the work up to 1978 or so was summarized by the first edition of the *Handbook of cross-cultural psychology* (Triandis, 1980–1981, General Editor), which included volumes with co-editors on Perspectives (William W. Lambert), Methodology (John Berry), Basic processes (Walter Lonner), Developmental psychology (Alastair Heron & Elke Kroeger), Social psychology (Richard Brislin) and Psychopathology (Juris Draguns).

Some discussions of culture have focused on specific elements or processes. For example, Triandis (1994) stressed shared standard operating procedures, unstated assumptions, tools, norms, values, habits about sampling the environment, and the like. As perception and cognition depend on the information that is sampled from the environment and are fundamental psychological processes, this culturally influenced sampling of information is of particular interest to psychologists. Cultures develop conventions for sampling information from the environment (Triandis, 1989), and also implicit agreements about how much to weigh the sampled elements. For example, people in hierarchical cultures are more likely to sample clues about hierarchy than clues about aesthetics. Triandis (1989) argued that people in individualist cultures sample with high probability elements of the personal self (e.g. "I am busy, I am kind") and internal processes (such as attitudes, beliefs, personality) as predictors of behavior. People from collectivist cultures tend to sample mostly elements of the collective self (e.g. "my family thinks I am too busy, my co-workers think I am kind") and aspects of the external environment (such as group memberships, norms, social pressures, roles) as predictors of behavior (Trafimow, Triandis, & Goto, 1991; Triandis, 1995; Triandis, McCusker, & Hui, 1990).

Contemporary views

There are many definitions of culture (Kroeber & Kluckhohn, 1952), but there are certain aspects that almost all researchers see as characteristics of culture. First, culture emerges in adaptive interactions between humans and environments. Second, culture consists of shared elements. Third, culture is transmitted across time periods and generations. Each of these aspects of culture will now be considered in turn.

Interactions with environments

As people interact with others in their physical and social environments they reach agreements about how to behave together. This view of culture as adaptive to environmental context has a long history (Jahoda, 1995). At present (e.g. Berry, 2003), it considers that culture is both constrained and shaped by a group's habitat, leading to the use of the term *ecocultural* to describe it. People develop language, writing, tools, skills, and definitions of concepts. They determine ways of organizing information, symbols; evaluations; patterns of behavior; intellectual, moral, and aesthetic standards; knowledge; religion; social patterns (e.g. marriage, kinship, inheritance, social control, sports); systems of government; systems of making war; and expectations and ideas about correct behavior that are more or less effective (functional) in adapting to their ecosystem.

One way to think of cultural evolution is to think of Darwinian mechanisms (Campbell, 1965). That is, people try this and that and some of what they tried works, so they select it for transmission to their children and friends. Elements of culture that have been effective (e.g. resulted in solutions to everyday problems of existence that were satisfying), became shared and were transmitted to others (e.g. the next generation of humans).

These elements often reflect unstated assumptions and result in standard operating procedures for solving the problems of everyday life. Thus, these elements become aspects of culture. However, circumstances keep changing, and what was functional in one historic period (e.g. having six children when infant mortality was very high) can become dysfunctional in another historic period. But members of cultures do not shed easily the dysfunctional elements. Thus, many elements of culture are dysfunctional (Edgerton, 1992). For instance, Friedl (1964) described a phenomenon called "lagging emulation": as lower-status people acquire enough wealth, they emulate the obsolete customs of higher-status people. One could argue that this is not functional, but we must remember that people can derive satisfaction from some behaviors even when these behaviors are no longer functional. Many of our behaviors, clothes, features of our houses, etc. are no longer functional.

Common symbols, such as linguistic conventions, flags, or insignia make social interaction smoother. They are also elements of culture. Common ways of dealing with social problems are also helpful. For instance, if several people disagree, in the West one way of deciding what to do is to vote. That is an adaptive way of resolving conflict. In Japan the custom is to talk until there is agreement by consensus. In other cultures people who disagree are expelled from the group, or voluntarily leave the group, or are killed.

Human-like creatures hunted and gathered food on the face of the earth for more than 100,000 years, but only in the last 10,000 years did humans cultivate the land and live in fixed communities. So, today, when we study some of the remaining hunting-gathering people, such as the peoples of the Kalahari desert (De Vore & Konner, 1974; Draper, 1973; Eibl-Eibesfeldt, 1974; Truswell, Kennelly, Hansen, & Lee, 1972) we are studying cultural adaptations made for the first 99 per cent of human existence. Viewed within this timeframe modern cultures are evolving very rapidly. Many "inventions", such as voting, occurred only "yesterday" (2500 years ago).

Shared elements

As interaction normally requires a shared language and the opportunity to interact, one can conveniently use: (1) shared language; (2) same time; and (3) place as clues for identifying cultures. People who share a language, a time period and a geographic region are likely to be able to interact, and thus to belong to the same culture. However, interactions can also take place among individuals who do not share a language (e.g. via interpreters), or time (e.g. reading a book written centuries earlier), or place (e.g. via satellite). When this is the case, some elements of culture diffuse from one culture to another. In fact, diffusion and acculturation are two important ways in which cultures influence each other (see below). Furthermore, what has worked in one historic period is often used in other historic periods.

Common fate and other factors, resulting in easy interaction among individuals, can also result in the formation of cultures or subcultures. Thus nations, occupational groups, social classes, genders, "races", religions, tribes, corporations, clubs, and social movements may become the bases of specific subcultures.

How many cultures are there? Hundreds of thousands is probably a correct answer. Although there are thousands of cultures, fortunately there are similarities among the different kinds of culture. For example, Europe and North America, when viewed from a global perspective, are relatively similar; Africa South of the Sahara, South Asia, East Asia, Polynesia, and the American Indians have more elements of culture in common than elements that are different. Anthropologists talk about "cultural regions" such as Africa South of the Sahara. Of course, there are thousands of cultures in Africa, yet they have something in common, so we can consider Africa South of the Sahara as a cultural region. Even within culture there is a tremendous variation in personalities, yet there is something that most Frenchmen have in common so we can call France (with a distinct language, history, food, dress, etc.) a culture that is different from, say, Germany.

Nevertheless, considering culture, one should avoid thinking of nationality, religion, "race", or occupation as the criteria that define culture. The use of a single criterion is likely to lead to confusion, as would happen if all people who eat pizza were placed in one category. Culture is a complex whole, and it is best to use many measures to discriminate one culture from another. Most modern states consist of many cultures; most corporations have unique subcultures; most occupations have distinct subcultures.

Cultures are in constant flux, but the change tends to be slow. Some elements of culture do not change. For instance, whether people drive to the right or left usually does not change. Other elements change slowly, requiring one or two generations before there is a major transformation. Still other elements change quickly. For instance, when something was called "cool" it referred to temperature until about 1950, but after 1960 in the USA it also meant "good".

Transmission to others

For there to be continuity, cultural elements are transmitted to a variety of others, such as the next generation, co-workers, colleagues, family members, and a wide range of publics through a process of *enculturation*. A distinction has been made between three forms of cultural transmission: *vertical, horizontal,* and *oblique* (Berry, Poortinga, Segall, & Dasen, 2002). Vertical transmission takes place from parents to offspring, and thus parallels that of genetic forms of transmission. These two are usually entwined, so that the relative contributions to behavior in the second generation cannot easily be allocated to either genetic or cultural transmission, or to their interaction. In horizontal transmission, human behavior is influenced by peers (within generations) and is more of a mutual process than is parent–child (vertical) cultural transmission. Finally, oblique transmission takes place when social institutions (e.g. schools, media) that already pre-exist an individual in a society influence the developing individual. These latter two forms are entirely cultural, and have no genetic aspects.

Another form of transmission takes place from outside a person's own cultural group, as a result of direct contact (such as colonization, migration) or indirect influence (such as telemedia, or books). This form of cultural transmission is termed "acculturation" (Chun, Balls-Organista, &

Marin, 2003; Sam & Berry, 2006), and is responsible both for changing existing behaviors and introducing new ones. Thus, rather than providing a basis for cultural continuity (as enculturation does), acculturation serves as a cultural source of discontinuity, and even disruption in some cases.

Functions of culture

Recent reviews of the literature, such as Lehman, Chiu, and Schaller (2004) emphasize that culture has functions such as allowing people to understand their position in the cosmos. This reminds us of Katz (1960), who identified four functions of attitudes. Cultures have parallel functions. Katz identified four functions: (1) The *adjustment* function allows people to maximize their rewards and minimize the penalties. Cultures provide norms which provide guidance for behavior and maximize the chances that people will receive appropriate rewards. (2) The *ego-defensive* function allows the individual to protect the self from uncomplimentary truths. As members of all cultures are ethnocentric (Triandis, 1994), they compare themselves to other cultures in ways that increase their self-esteem. (3) The *value expressive* function, allows people to derive pleasure by expressing their basic values. Values are a central element of culture. (4) The *knowledge* function allows people to understand their position in the universe and to predict events. The epistemic function of culture is emphasized by Lehman et al. (2004), who review empirical research supporting it. Religion is an aspect of culture and certainly provides an understanding of the position of humans in the cosmos.

Biology constrains the development of culture. Certain aspects of culture develop more readily and other aspects develop with great difficulty, because biology interacts with the development of culture.

Emic and etic aspects of culture

Humans have very similar biologies. Psychological processes that are linked to biology or physiology are often universal. Moreover, because humans live in fairly similar social structures and physical environments, this also creates major similarities in the way they form cultures. For example, values are an important aspect of culture and their structures seem to be universal (Schwartz, 1992). Universal aspects of culture are called *etic*. Because there are biological and cultural universals, these provide a basis for the existence of psychological universals.

However, humans live in different environments and make a living in different ways, which results in both biological and cultural differences in the expression of these underlying similarities. Cultural elements that are unique to a particular culture are called *emic*. Pike (1967), developed these terms, inspired by the difference between phon*etics* and phon*emics* (see Triandis, 1964, and Berry, 1999, for details).

Some students of culture assume that every culture is unique. In some sense every *object* in the world is unique. However, science is an attempt to understand the world in as simple or as parsimonious a way as possible. The glory of science is that very diverse phenomena can be understood as being similar. For example, Newton "showed that the same force that pulls an apple to Earth keeps the Moon in its orbit and accounts for the revolutions of the then recently discovered moons of Jupiter in their orbits about that distant planet" (Sagan, 1980, p. 69). Thus the core issue is whether one is interested in the specific (emic) elements of culture and/or the elements that are broadly shared (etic) elements.

Many of the elements of culture, such as ideas, patterns of behavior, and standards of evaluation, are specific to each culture, but they are often of limited interest. Many cross-cultural psychologists find of greater interest the common or etic elements observed in cultural patterns. But, as argued by Pike, emics can be systematically related to etics. For instance, the concept of "social distance" is an etic. In all cultures some people feel close to other people and others feel far. Members of the same family feel close to each other and far from people on another continent. But the way that concept is expressed is different from culture to culture. In the Northern states of the USA, in 1900, the distance between American whites and African–Americans was large, and a reliable clue was the rejection of black people from the neighborhood. In the year 2000 that clue is no longer reliable or valid as a measure of social distance. Nowadays, a better clue might be rejection from a club, or job discrimination. In India, the same idea is expressed by rejecting people from one's kitchen, because the concept of ritual pollution includes the idea of not allowing people of a lower caste to touch one's earthenware. Thus an underlying etic can be stated by different emic expressions. We can ask people in different cultures to tell us where a particular emic behavior is located on a social distance scale that ranges from "to marry" to "to kill". Then we can obtain the scale value of the emic behavior in each culture (Triandis, 1992). When we present a particular social stimulus, for instance "an African–American physician" to people from different cultures, we can ask them to tell us what behaviors they are likely to use toward that stimulus person. They usually generate emic behaviors, but if we know the scale value of each emic behavior on the etic scale, we can compare cultures. We can, for example, say that an African–American physician is more acceptable in one culture than in another culture (Triandis, 1967).

In short, when we study cultures for their own sake we may well focus on emic elements, but when we compare cultures we have to work with the etic cultural elements.

Culture outside or inside the person

Up to about 1950, the dominant view of culture in anthropology was that it was outside the person; after that time many people emphasized that culture was also inside the person (Shweder & LeVine, 1984, p. 7). In other words, a recent view is that the internalization of aspects of culture has influenced all psychological processes; this is a view held by those who call themselves "cultural psychologists" (e.g. Cole, 1996). In contrast, those identifying as "cross-cultural psychologists" now accept both perspectives (e.g. Berry, 2000). Recent reviews of the literature, such as Lehman et al. (2004), have sections that review empirical studies supporting both perspectives. In short, culture is both outside the person (a set of practices shared by the group, and existing prior to any particular individual), and inside the person (influencing a person's behavior by providing interpretive perspectives for making sense of reality, as a result of enculturation). However, in the early stages of the development of cross-cultural psychology, the view of culture as being outside the person view was dominant. At that time, culture was considered as a kind of experimental treatment (Strodtbeck, 1964).

Indigenous and cultural psychologists have advocated the view that culture is inside the person. They try to develop a psychology that is satisfactory for understanding a particular culture. Indigenous psychologists do this by identifying categories and linguistic elements that are more or less unique in a particular culture. For example, the Japanese have a concept called *amae*. It means something like "indulgent dependency" (Doi, 1973), one interpretation of which is "to tolerate the other person's dependence". This concept does not exist as a single word (monoleximic) in other languages. Monoleximics tell us that the idea is used frequently in a culture (Zipf, 1949), so that means that it is really important in that culture. The judgment that *amae* is important in Japan is in agreement with expert analyses of Japanese psychology (Doi, 1986). In short, indigenous psychologists have a way of getting at the most important ways of thinking in a particular culture.

Cultural psychologists study most intensively a particular culture and look for the way psychological processes are influenced by culture. Ethno-psychologists look for different theories of the mind in various ethnic groups (Lillard, 1998).

It is probable that both views (the outside- and inside-the-person views) are going to be productive in future research, with one view being better able to explain some psychological phenomena and the other view being more able to explain others. Multimethod research that uses both perspectives and looks for convergence across findings may prove most useful (Triandis, 2000).

Culture as arbitrary elements or as a configuration

Culture has been discussed both as an arbitrary code (D'Andrade & Romney, 1964), and as consisting of a configuration of cultural elements that is organized into a meaningful framework. For instance, Triandis

(1996) proposed that "cultural syndromes" can be identified, such as individualism, collectivism, hierarchy, equality, tightness (or uncertainty avoidance). Masculinity (Hofstede, 1980, 2001), in which cultural elements are interrelated so as to form coherent wholes, centered around the importance of the individual, the collective, rank, equality, close observance of norms, or gender differentiation.

Culture is "superorganic" (Kroeber, 1917), because individuals come and go and cultures remain more or less stable. For example, observations of behavior of people in Corfu, Greece, in 1950 and 2000 showed considerable similarities. Young people walked up and down, in particular streets of that town, at specified hours. The functions of this activity, locally called *"sergyani"* and found in all the countries of the Mediterranean (e.g. *"corso"* in Italy and Spain), were for the young people to determine who was attractive and worth courting. In the case of this behavior pattern, although spanning 50 years, and with different members, the culture had changed relatively little.

Concluding comment on the meaning of culture

Since the problem of an adequate definition is difficult to solve (e.g. see Shweder & LeVine, 1984), it is best to approach it this way: There are many definitions of the concept and they are all valid. However, depending on what a particular investigator wishes to study, it may be optimal to adopt one or another of the more limited definitions. For example, if the investigator is a behaviorist, Skinner's definition (culture is a set of schedules of reinforcement) may be quite satisfactory; if the investigator is a cognitive psychologist, a definition that emphasizes information processing may be optimal.

Theoretical orientations to culture–behavior relationships

Three theoretical orientations to the relationships between culture and behaviour have been proposed (Berry et al., 2002): *absolutism, relativism,* and *universalism.* The *absolutist* position is one that assumes that human phenomena are basically the same (qualitatively) in all cultures: "honesty" is "honesty", and "depression" is "depression", no matter where one observes it. From the absolutist perspective, culture is thought to play little or no role in either the meaning or display of human characteristics. Assessments of such characteristics are made using standard instruments (perhaps with linguistic translation) and interpretations are made easily, without alternative culturally based views taken into account. This orientation resembles the *imposed etic* (Berry, 1999) approaches to cross-cultural research.

In sharp contrast, the *relativist* approach assumes that all human behaviour is culturally patterned, It seeks to avoid ethnocentrism by trying to understand people "in their own terms". Explanations of human diversity are sought from within the cultural context in which people have developed. Assessments are typically carried out employing the values and meanings that a cultural group gives to a phenomenon. Comparisons are judged to be problematic and ethnocentric, and are thus virtually never made. This orientation resembles the *emic* approach.

A third perspective, one that lies somewhere between the first two positions, is that of *universalism*. Here it is assumed that basic psychological processes are common to all members of the species (i.e. constituting a set of psychological givens), and that culture influences the development and display of them (i.e. culture plays different variations on these underlying themes). Assessments are based on the underlying process, but measures are developed in culturally meaningful versions. Comparisons are made cautiously, employing a wide variety of methodological principles and safeguards (Triandis & Berry, 1980), whereas interpretations of similarities and differences are attempted that take alternative culturally based meanings into account. This orientation resembles the *derived etic* approach.

Whereas few today advocate a strictly absolutist or imposed etic view, the relativist/emic position has given rise to both "indigenous psychology" (Kim & Berry, 1993), and to "cultural psychology" (Shweder, 1990). And the derived etic view has given rise to a "universalist psychology" (Berry et al., 2002). A mutual compatibility between the emic and derived etic positions has been noted by many: For example, Berry et al. (2002) and Berry and Kim (1993) have claimed that indigenous psychologies, while valuable in their own right, serve an equally important function as useful steps on the way to achieving a universal psychology.

The impact of culture on psychology

A major theme has been that psychological processes are probably shared features of our species, but that behavioral expression must be understood in the context of the culture in which a person develops. There are indeed psychological universals (Lonner, 1980). Some deal with phenomena that are at a high level of abstraction, and serve as a basis for making cross-cultural comparisons. Others are at intermediate and low levels of abstraction where they are more enveloped by culture, making comparisons more difficult. Thus, there are both universalistic and a context specific views of the development of cognition (Laboratory of Comparative Human Cognition, 1983), of perception (Segall et al., 1966), of learning (Brislin & Horvath, 1997; Tweed & Lehman, 2002), affective meaning (Osgood, May, & Miron, 1975), emotion (Kitayama & Markus, 1994; Mesquita, 2001), facial expression of emotion (Ekman, 1992), motivation (Markus & Kitayama, 1991), thinking (Nisbett, 2003), personality (e.g. McClelland, 1961) and other basic processes (Berry, Dasen, & Saraswathi, 1997a), communication (e.g. Gudykunst, 1991) and social behavior (Berry, Segall, & Kagitcibasi, 1997c; Fiske, 1990; Miller, 1984). Many theoretical perspectives that include culture, such as evolutionary approaches, and the stress on indigenous psychologies (Berry, Poortinga, & Pandey, 1997b) evolved after 1980. In fact, up to that point most cross-cultural psychology was concerned with methods (Triandis & Berry, 1980). As the field matured, multi-method approaches were developed that found consistencies among ethnographic, survey, and experimental methods (e.g. Nisbett, 2003). After 1980, much research (e.g. Triandis & Suh, 2002) used a theoretical framework that focused on individualism and collectivism (Triandis, 1995) and the presence of an independent or relational or interdependent self (Kagitcibasi, 1996; Markus & Kitayama, 1991) in a particular form of culture. Behavior can be conceived as a consequence of both culture and the definition of the situation (Triandis, 1995). Other conceptions have examined culture-sensitive taxonomies of activities (Cole, 1995) or action in action-in-context (Eckensberger, 1995).

Much pre-1980 psychology was shaped by the fact that the participants, the researchers, and editors of the major journals were members of Western individualistic cultures. A universal psychology will require expansion to include the perspectives that are found in all cultures; this view is the hallmark and rationale for cross-cultural psychology. Future work will undoubtedly include the discovery of additional aspects of culture (and their organization into cultural syndromes). This elaboration of cultural variation will require psychologists to take culture into account in their work in ever more complex ways.

References

Barkow, G., Cosmides, L., & Tooby, J. (Eds.). (1992). *The adapted mind: Evolutionary psychology and the generation of culture*. New York: Oxford University Press.

Berry, J. W. (1976). *Human ecology and cognitive style*. Beverly Hills, CA: Sage.

Berry, J. W. (1979). A cultural ecology of human behavior. In L. Berkowitz (Ed.), *Advances in experimental social psychology* (Volume 12, pp. 177–207). New York: Academic Press.

Berry, J. W. (1999). Emics and etics: A symbiotic conception. *Culture & Psychology*, *5*, 165–171.

Berry, J. W. (2000). Cross-cultural psychology: A symbiosis of cultural and comparative approaches. *Asian Journal of Social Psychology*, *3*, 197–205.

Berry, J. W. (2003). Origin of cross-cultural similarities and differences in human behavior: An ecocultural perspective. In A. Toomela (Ed.), *Cultural guidance in the development of the human mind* (pp. 97–109). Westport, NJ: Ablex.

Berry, J. W., Dasen, P. R., & Saraswathi, T. S. (1997a). *Handbook of cross-cultural psychology* (Vol. 2). Boston, MA: Allyn & Bacon.

Berry, J. W., & Kim, U. (1993). The way ahead: From indigenous psychologies to a universal psychology. In U. Kim & J. W. Berry (Eds.), *Indigenous psychologies* (pp. 277–280). Newbury Park, CA: Sage.

Berry, J. W., Poortinga, Y., & Pandey, J. (1997b). *Handbook of cross-cultural psychology* (Vol. 1). Boston, MA: Allyn & Bacon.

Berry, J. W., Poortinga, Y. H., Segall, M. H., & Dasen, P. R. (2002). *Cross-cultural psychology: Research and applications.* New York: Cambridge University Press.

Berry, J. W., Segall, M. H., & Kagitcibasi, C. (1997c). *Handbook of cross-cultural psychology* (Vol. 3). Boston, MA: Allyn & Bacon.

Brislin, R. W., & Horvath, A. M. (1997). Cross-cultural training and multicultural education. In J. W. Berry, M. H. Segall, & C. Kagitcibasi (Eds.), *Handbook of Cross-Cultural Psychology* (Vol. 3, pp. 327–370). Boston, MA: Allyn & Bacon.

Campbell, D. T. (1965). Variation and selective retention in socio-cultural evolution. In J. R. Barringer, G. Blanksten, & R. Mack (Eds.), *Social change in developing areas* (pp. 19–49). Cambridge, MA: Schenkman.

Campbell, D. T. (1975). On the conflicts between biological and social evolution and between psychology and moral tradition. *American Psychologist, 30,* 1103–1126.

Chun, K., Balls-Organista, P., & Marin, G. (Eds.). (2003). *Acculturation: Advances in theory, measurement and applied research.* Washington, DC: American Psychological Association.

Cole, M. (1995). Culture and cognitive development: From cross-cultural research to creating systems of cultural mediation. *Culture & Psychology, 1,* 25–54.

Cole, M. (1996). *Cultural psychology: A once and future discipline.* Cambridge, MA: Harvard University Press.

D'Andrade, R., & Romney, A. K. (1964). Summary of participants' discussion: Transcultural studies in cognition. *American Anthropologist, 66,* 230–242.

De Vore, I., & Konner, M. J. (1974). Infancy in hunter–gatherer life: An ethnographic perspective. In N. F. White (Ed.), *Ethology and psychiatry* (pp. 113–141). Toronto: University of Toronto Press.

Doi, T. (1973). *The anatomy of dependence.* Tokyo: Kodansha International.

Doi, T. (1986) *The anatomy of conformity: The individual versus society.* Tokyo: Kadansha.

Draper, P. (1973). Crowding among hunter–gatherers. The !Kung bushmen. *Science, 182,* 301–303.

Eckensberger, L. H. (1995). Activity or action: Two different roads towards an integration of culture into psychology? *Culture and Psychology, 1,* 67–80.

Edgerton, R. (1992). *Sick societies: Challenging the myth of primitive harmony.* New York: Free Press.

Eibl-Eibesfeldt, I. (1974) The myth of the aggression free hunter and gatherer society. In R. L. Holloway (Ed.), *Primate aggression, territoriality and xenophobia: A comparative perspective.* New York: Academic Press.

Ekman, P. (1992). Facial expression of emotion: New findings, new questions. *Psychological Science, 3,* 34–38.

Fiske, A. P. (1990). *Structures of social life: The four elementary forms of human relations.* New York: Free Press.

Friedl, E. (1964) Lagging emulation in post-peasant society. *American Anthropologist, 66,* 569–586.

Geertz, C. (1973). *The interpretation of cultures.* New York: Basic Books.

Gudykunst, W. (1991) *Bridging differences.* Newbury Park, CA: Sage.

Herder, J. G. (1784/1969). Herder's Werke (5 volumes). Berlin: Aufbau.

Herodotus. *The histories.* New York: Norton.

Herskovits, M. J. (1955). *Cultural anthropology.* New York: Knopf.

Hofstede, G. (1980). *Culture's consequences*. Beverly Hills, CA: Sage.

Hofstede, G. (2001). *Culture's consequences*. Thousand Oaks, CA: Sage.

Jahoda, G. (1992). *Crossroads between culture and mind*. London: Harvester Wheatsheaf.

Jahoda, G. (1995). The ancestry of a model. *Culture & Psychology*, *1*, 11–24.

Jahoda, G., & Krewer, R. (1997). *History of cross-cultural and cultural psychology*. In J. W. Berry, Y. H. Poortinga, & J. Pandey (Eds.), *Handbook of cross-cultural psychology* (pp. 1–42). Boston, MA: Allyn & Bacon.

Kagitcibasi, C. (1996). *Family and human development across cultures: A view from the other side*. Hillsdale, NJ: Lawrence Erlbaum Associates Inc.

Katz, D. (1960). The functional approach to the study of attitudes. *Public Opinion Quarterly*, *24*, 163–204.

Kim, U., & Berry, J. W. (1993). *Indigenous psychologies*. Newbury Park, CA: Sage.

Kitayama, S., & Markus, H. R. (Eds.). (1994) *Emotion and culture: Empirical studies of mutual influence*. Washington, DC: American Psychological Association.

Klineberg, O. (1954). *Social psychology*. New York: Holt.

Klineberg, O. (1980). Historical perspectives: Cross-cultural psychology before 1960. In H. C. Triandis & W. W. Lambert (Eds.), *Handbook of Cross-Cultural Psychology, Volume 1* (pp. 31–68). Boston, CA: Allyn & Bacon.

Kluckhohn, K. (1954). Culture and behavior. In G. Lindzey (Ed.), *Handbook of social psychology, Volume 2* (pp. 921–976). Cambridge, MA: Addison-Wesley.

Kroeber, A. L. (1917). The superorganic. *American Anthropologist*, *19*, 163–213.

Kroeber, A. L., & Kluckhohn, C. (1952). *Culture: A critical review of concepts and definitions*. Cambridge, MA: Peabody Museum.

Laboratory of Comparative Human Cognition (1983). Culture and cognitive development. In P. H. Mussen (Ed.), *Handbook of child psychology* (Vol. 1, pp. 295–356). New York: Wiley.

Lehman, D. R., Chiu, C., & Schaller, M. (2004). Psychology and culture. *Annual Review of Psychology*, *55*, 689–714.

Lillard, A. (1998). Ethnopsychologies: Cultural variations in theories of mind. *Psychological Bulletin*, *123*, 3–32.

Lonner, W. J. (1980). The search for psychological universals. In H. C. Triandis & W. W. Lambert (Eds.), *Handbook of cross-cultural psychology* (Vol. 1, pp. 143–204). Boston, MA: Allyn and Bacon.

Markus, H., & Kitayama, S. (1991). Culture and self: Implications for cognition, emotion and motivation. *Psychological Review*, *98*, 224–253.

McClelland, D. C. (1961). *The achieving society*. Princeton, NJ: Van Nostrand.

Mesquita, B. (2001). Emotions in collectivist and individualist contexts. *Journal of Personality and Social Psychology*, *80*, 68–74.

Miller, J. G. (1984). Culture and the development of everyday social explanation. *Journal of Personality and Social Psychology*, *46*, 961–978.

Nisbett, R. (2003). *The geography of thought*. New York: Free Press.

Osgood, C. E., May, W., & Miron, M. (1975). *Cross-cultural universals of affective meaning*. Urbana, IL: University of Illinois Press.

Pike, K. L. (1967). *Language in relation to a unified theory of the structure of human behavior*. The Hague: Mouton.

Rivers, W. H. R. (1901). Primitive color vision. *Popular Science Monthly*, *59*, 44–58.

Rivers, W. H. R. (1905). Observations on the senses of the Todas. *British Journal of Psychology*, *1*, 321–396.

Sagan, C. (1980). *Cosmos*. New York: Random House.

Sam, D. L., & Berry, J. C. (Eds.). (2006). *Cambridge handbook of acculturation psychology*. Cambridge, UK: Cambridge University Press.

Schwartz, S. H. (1992). Universals in the content and structure of values: Theoretical advances and empirical tests in 20 countries. In M. Zanna (Ed.), *Advances in Experimental Social Psychology* (Vol. 25, pp. 1–66). New York: Academic Press.

Segall, M. H., Campbell, D. T., & Herskovits, M. J. (1966). *Influence of culture on visual perception*. Indianapolis, IN: Bobbs-Merrill.

Shweder, R. A. (1990). Cultural psychology—what is it? In J. W. Stigler, R. A. Shweder, & G. Herdt (Eds.), *Cultural psychology* (pp. 1–46). Cambridge, MA: Cambridge University Press.

Shweder, R. A., & LeVine, R. A. (1984). *Culture theory*. Cambridge, MA: Cambridge University Press.

Sperber, D. (1996). *Explaining culture: A naturalistic approach*. Oxford, UK: Blackwell.

Strodtbeck, F. (1964). Considerations of meta-method in cross-cultural studies. *American Anthropologist, 66*, 223–229.

Trafimow, D., Triandis, H. C., & Goto, S. (1991). Some tests of the distinction between private self and collective self. *Journal of Personality and Social Psychology, 60*, 640–655.

Triandis, H. C. (1964). Cultural influences upon cognitive processes. In L. Berkowitz (Ed.), *Advances in experimental social psychology* (pp. 1–48). New York: Academic Press.

Triandis, H. C. (1967). Towards an analysis of the components of interpersonal attitudes. In C. Sherif & M. Sherif (Eds.), *Attitudes, ego involvement and change* (pp. 227–270). New York: Wiley.

Triandis, H. C. (1972). *The analysis of subjective culture*. New York: Wiley.

Triandis, H. C. et al. (Eds.). (1980–81). *Handbook of cross-cultural psychology*. Boston, MA: Allyn & Bacon.

Triandis, H. C. (1989). The self and social behavior in different cultural contexts. *Psychological Review, 96*, 269–289.

Triandis, H. C. (1992). Cross-cultural research in social psychology. In D. Granberg & G. Sarup (Eds.), *Social judgment in intergroup relations: Essays in honor of Muzafer Sherif* (pp. 229–244). New York: Springer Verlag.

Triandis, H. C. (1994). *Culture and social behavior*. New York: McGraw-Hill.

Triandis, H. C. (1995). *Individualism and collectivism*. Boulder, CO: Westview Press.

Triandis, H. C. (1996) The psychological measurement of cultural syndromes. *American Psychologist, 51*, 407–415.

Triandis, H. C. (2000). Dialectics between cultural and cross-cultural psychology. *Asian Journal of Social Psychology, 3*, 185–195.

Triandis, H. C., & Berry, J. W. (1980). *Handbook of cross-cultural psychology* (Vol. 1). Boston, MA: Allyn & Bacon.

Triandis, H. C., McCusker, C., & Hui, C. H. (1990). Multimethod probes of individualism and collectivism. *Journal of Personality and Social Psychology, 59*, 1006–1020.

Triandis, H. C., & Suh, E. M. (2002). Cultural influences on personality. *Annual Review of Psychology, 53*, 133–160.

Truswell, A. S., Kennelly, B. M., Hansen, J. D. L., & Lee, R. B. (1972). Blood pressure in !Kung bushmen in northern Botswana. *American Heart Journal, 84,* 5–12.

Tweed, R. G., & Lehman, D. R. (2002). Learning considered within a cultural context. *American Psychologist, 57,* 89–99.

Tylor, E. B. (1871). *Primitive culture.* New York: Harper.

Vico, G. (1744/1948). *The new science* (T. G. Bergin & M. H. Fish, Trans.). Ithaca, NY: Cornell University Press.

Wundt, W. (1900–1914). *Völkerpsychologie.* Leipzig: Engelmann.

Zipf, G. K. (1949). *Human behavior and the principle of least effort.* Cambridge, MA: Addison-Wesley.

5   (Individual) Development

Martin Pinquart and Rainer K. Silbereisen

Working in the field of developmental psychology poses the general question of what development means, what kind of process it is, what are the basic mechanisms of development, and what factors lead to development? The search for a conceptualization of the course of human development has been a long one, approached from many different theoretical perspectives. Concepts of human development imply worldviews about human nature and environments that create a human life course (Reese & Overton, 1970). There has been, and still is, pluralism of concepts and ideas about development, although at certain times and in particular areas some concepts and theories have dominated. The history of the concept of development, therefore, cannot be described as a linear process that has led to a specific view on human development now accepted by all developmentalists. For this reason, we will rather describe selected lines of conceptualizing human development. After briefly characterizing historic roots of the concept of development in philosophy and biology, we will discuss general models or families of theories about human development (Reese & Overton, 1970), namely, mechanistic, organismic, dialectic and contextual models of human development. We will then discuss recent developments in the field of life-span developmental psychology and developmental systems approaches. Finally, we will draw some conclusions about the development of concepts of development, and on the implications of these concepts for research methodology and intervention. Overall, the main focus of this chapter will be on concepts of human *individual* development ("ontogeny"). Where necessary for a better understanding of individual development, we will also refer to development of the human species ("human phylogeny") and to the development of single psychological processes (microgenesis; e.g. Li, 2003). As our focus is on psychological development, we will not discuss the use of the concept of development in other sciences, such as biology or sociology.

The term "development" has affinities to other terms, such as "socialization" and "maturation". Socialization refers to the process by which persons acquire knowledge, skills, and dispositions with the help of instruction, explanation, observation, and reinforcement. Its meaning is often focused on what is required to function well within a society and its rules. The term "maturation" describes the genetically driven unfolding of bio-logical structures and functions, and is a main topic of biology, rather than psychology (Montada, 2003). Socialization and maturation are sources of individual development, but individual development cannot be restricted to the effect of socialization or maturation.

Scientific and philosophical roots of concepts about development

With regard to the roots of developmental psychology, we refer to the historical overviews by Cairns (1998), Lerner (2002), and Reinert (1976). The first general ideas about human development were formed by philo-sophers more than two thousand years ago, although no elaborated con-cepts of human development were provided by these authors. For example, Plato (427–347 BC) suggested that the individual is born with innate ideas, with pre-existing knowledge. At birth, the body "traps" a particular soul. As the soul resides in the realm of ideas, it enters the body with these ideas at birth. He believed that the soul was divided into three layers (desires and appetites, spirit, reason), and that people exercise the attributes of each layer successively over their lifetime. Aristotle (384–322 BC) referred to phylogeny when also suggesting three layers of the soul, namely a plant-like layer (related to the life functions of reproduction and nourishment), an animal-like layer (associated with functions such as locomotion, sensation, and perception), and a human-like layer (associated with thinking and reasoning). Plants would only have the first layer, animals the first and second, and humans have all three layers.

The idea of a homunculus was wide-spread in the medieval Christian era (e.g. John Calvin, 1509–1564). This miniature, full-grown adult, containing sin and basic depravity, was suggested to be present in a newborn's head from birth. Similar to Plato's view of development, children would not have to develop except in size because they already had preformed adults within them. From this perspective, there was no need for a specific concept or theory of development. Locke (1632–1704), however, rejected the idea that the mind is composed of innate ideas. He considered that the mind at birth was a blank table (*"tabula rasa"*) and that any knowledge the mind obtained was derived from experience.

The interest in individual development reached a first peak with Jean-Jacques Rousseau's (1712–1778) educational novel *Emile* (Rousseau, 1762). Rousseau developed a philosophy of nature about human development, although not yet based on systematic observation method. He suggested a universal sequence of four steps that would be based on the nature of mankind. The first step of development would be the formation of the human body in the first 3 years of life. As a second step, Rousseau suggested the formation of sensory activity from years 4 to 12. The third step was characterized by the formation of mind and judgment (years 13 to 15). In the final step, individuals would develop their emotional life and morality at 16 years and older. Before that age, individuals would have no moral feelings and consequently would not be ready for participation in society. Rousseau believed in natural maturational processes and viewed environmental and cultural influences as negative for the child as they would interfere with the natural course of development.

Fifteen years later, the philosopher Johann Nikolas Tetens (1777) published an important book about human development. He pushed the search for general developmental laws to the forefront of developmental thinking, suggesting the emergence of new structures and functions in the course of individual development by evolution as general hypothesis. According to Tetens, lifelong development comprised an initial increase to a maximum and temporal stability, followed eventually by decline. He saw development as influenced by individual aptitude and differential environmental forces, such as culture, education, and other persons who serve as models. With these thoughts, Tetens was a forerunner of the concept of life-span developmental psychology that was elaborated in the second half of the twentieth century.

In the nineteenth century, scientific and historical thinking about individual human development dominated, and was characterized by terms such as preformation, evolution, and epigenesis. As described in the following, these concepts saw development as a lawful and well-ordered process that shows a specific sequence in time, although they differed regarding possible causes and individual processes of development.

Following the tradition of Plato, *preformationism* claims that development is the unfolding of characteristics that are wholly predetermined at the outset of development, to a final form. According to this view, parts or the interrelations of parts of the organism may change, but the essential properties are preset and predetermined. Thus, development cannot bring about novel properties, so that main characteristics would be stable from embryogenesis to adulthood (Gould, 1977). In developmental psychology, such nativist views were, amongst others, proposed by Gesell (1948) who described psychological and physical development in childhood as a succession of endogenous preformed stages.

Contrary to the concept of preformationism, *evolution* theorists did not see development as predetermined and in particular highlighted the emergence of new characteristics. General laws of development were suggested by Herbert Spencer (1820–1903) and Charles Darwin (1809–1882). Spencer (1852, 1862) suggested a general law of evolution, characterized by change from an indefinite and incoherent homogeneity to a definite and coherent heterogeneity. This idea was further elaborated in the work of Heinz Werner (1957), but overall Spencer's theory tended to be overshadowed by the work of Charles Darwin.

Darwin's (1859) evolution theory of the survival of the fittest was developed in the mid-nineteenth century. The term "evolution" relates to development during phylogeny and means the transformation of organisms in terms of their form and way of life, showing differences between descendants and ancestors. Darwin proposed a theory of evolution in which the development of species occurs in gradual, continual, and adaptive steps. According to Darwin, heterogeneity of species is based on transformations over millions of years.

In evolution theory, development was conceptualized as transformation from a uniform origin to a large number of varieties. If an animal has characteristics that fit to its environment, it will survive and reproduce and pass on to its offspring those characteristics that enabled it to meet the demands for survival. Although Darwin pointed out the function of physical structures of species for survival in his early work (1859), he later emphasized that behavior also has survival value (Darwin, 1872). Darwin (1871) further suggested that there is substantial similarity and continuity between the adult and the child of a given species, although dissimilarity and discontinuity also exist. Thus, ahistoric views of the adult form of a given species were called into question, and scientific interest was raised as to how a present form or psychological phenomenon has developed from earlier forms during life (Richards, 1982).

Darwin's theory is the first major scientific view of (phylogenetic) development. Evolutionary theory prepared the way for a scientific analysis of change and continuity, between human and animal, and between child and adult (e.g. Peters, 1965). The focus on the function of behavior for survival or for adaptation, in general, was applied in the work of Hall (1904), Freud (1905), Skinner (1938), Piaget (1950), and many others.

According to the concept of *epigenesis*, new characteristics are brought about through progressive transformations in development. The course of development was suggested to be determined by the recapitulation concept, which is the belief that individuals in their development repeat the history of the development of their species. The German zoologist Ernst Haeckel (1868) first stated that ontogeny recapitulates phylogeny. He believed that an embryo's ontogenetic progression mirrored the phylogenetic history of its species (the evolution of its species). By recapitulation, he believed that the mechanism of evolution was a change in the timing of developmental events such that there occurred a universal acceleration of development that pushed ancestral (adult) forms into the juvenile stages of descendants (Gould, 1977; Lerner, 2002). Haeckel's principle of recapitulation encouraged the idea that development (ontogeny) is a simple cumulative increase in capacities, rather than a complex, dynamic, and nonlinear pattern of change. The recapitulation principle was later applied to psychological development in childhood and adolescence by Hall (1883). He believed that psychological changes characterizing childhood were a repetition of the sequence of changes in human beings during evolution. For example, very early childhood was assumed to correspond to an ape-like ancestor of the human race. The years of 6–12 would represent the reenactment of the more advanced prehistoric forms of humankind, possibly a species that had managed to survive by hunting and fishing. In adolescence, environmental influences on development would become more important than nature. The recapitualist theory, however, was not generally accepted by his students and colleagues. Amongst others, Thorndike (1904) had already suggested that the cognitive capacity of 2- to 3-year-old children exceeds the capacity of all other species. Nonetheless, the ideas by Haeckel (1868) and Hall (1883) inspired an increasing scientific interest in individual development.

Finally, it is worth considering the work of the embryologist Karl Ernst von Baer (1792–1876), who suggested general principles of ontogenetic (developmental) change. Von Baer proposed that development proceeds in successive stages from the more general to the more specific, from relatively homogeneous stages to increasingly differentiated hierarchically organized structures (von Baer, 1828, 1837). He described development as differentiation of organization in which novel developments could occur at any point in development. Similar to Spencer (1852), he saw development as a continuous process of differentiation and organization, rather than a mechanical repetition of ancestral forms (recapitulatism). Von Baer's view, although not being immediately accepted because of its inconsistency with the broadly held beliefs in biology of the nineteenth century, did influence later developmental concepts, such as modern system models, transactional theory, and developmental psychobiology (Cairns, 1998).

Traditional models of psychological development

In general terms, individual development means intraindividual change. In order to differentiate development from other processes of change, such as learning, forgetting, or mood swings, individual development (or ontogeny) is broadly defined as age-associated change. However, individual concepts of development usually elaborate this definition according to a number of specific criteria. First, concepts of development differ in assumptions regarding the form of development. For example, development may be conceptualized as quantitative and/or qualitative change, as relatively uniform or differential, or as directed to a final state versus open-ended. Second, although all concepts of ontogeny agree that psychological development starts with conception (or with birth), they differ regarding the time when development ends. Third, concepts differ concerning the postulated causes of development, namely on the role of nature, nurture, individual activity, and of the interplay of these factors. Finally, they explicitly or implicitly differ as far as research methodology and practice (e.g. education, prevention) are concerned.

Concepts and theories about human development have been formulated at different theoretical levels (Eckensberger & Silbereisen, 1980). At the highest (most general) level, there are meta-theories or general models and worldviews about development, such as the mechanistic and organismic model as elaborated by Reese and Overton (1970). At the next level are models about general developmental processes, such as Piaget's equilibration model of cognitive structures, which are still too general to be falsified by empirical data. At the third and fourth level, theories become more specific and testable, such as specific theories about social role taking. Theories and models at the general level often inspire the development of more specific theories. In the following paragraphs, therefore, and due to the number of highly specific theories being too large to be summarized in a chapter, we will focus mainly on the two most general levels of theories.

Reese and Overton have written a series of seminal essays on ways in which theory and methods are influenced by philosophical issues pertinent to the study of human development. They suggest that developmental theories which were influential up to the 1960s can be traced back to two fundamental philosophical models (metatheories) that provide the basis for many extant assumptions about human development, that is, the mechanistic model and the organismic model (e.g. Reese & Overton, 1970). Two additional metatheories that became influential in Western developmental psychology starting in the 1970s and thereafter, dialectic and contextual models, will be discussed subsequently.

Mechanistic models of development

The history of the mechanistic model stems from the time of John Locke (1632–1704) and David Hume (1711–1776), although Locke himself was less restrictive than the mechanistic (behavioristic) model of development in suggesting that, in addition to learning, humans have an inherent function of reflection, which is composed of the process of comparing, distinguishing, judging, and willing (Reese & Overton, 1970). Although the mechanistic model of behaviorism is mainly based on learning theory, there are also influences of Darwin's evolution theory. For example, in his book *About behaviorism* Skinner (1974), who was one of the most important proponents of this model, wrote a chapter about inborn behavior that he saw as the prerequisite for conditioning processes. He also suggested that phylogenetic evolutionary processes, which influence the gene pool of species, would be similar to processes of operant conditioning in that trial and error determine the success of behavior (Skinner, 1966). Thus, genes that promote behavior that is reinforced by the environment are more likely to be widespread in evolution.

The mechanistic model emerged in the work of William Preyer (1841–1897) on the role of stimulus–experience relations in child development, the work of John B. Watson (1878–1958), Bloomfield F. Skinner (1904–1990), Donald M. Baer (1931–2002), and Sidney W. Bijou (1908). Within this (behavioristic) mechanistic model of development, developmental theories have usually been refinements or extensions of more general learning theories.

The basic metaphor employed for the mechanistic model is that of the machine: Activity is viewed as a result of external or peripheral forces. Psychological functions as complex phenomena are seen as reducible to more simple phenomena governed by efficient causes, namely basic stimulus–response connections as defined by the principles of classical and operant conditioning, and the learning history of the "machine". The mechanistic model of development proposes first, that behavioral development is controlled by forces outside the individual (although the individual may actively try out new behaviors). Development is not seen as resulting from change in the structure of the organism itself. It is, instead, causally explained by specific learning processes, namely stimulus-stimulus or stimulus-reaction contingencies. Differential developmental outcomes of the same "stimulus" can only be explained by previous learning history. Early proponents of the mechanistic–behavioristic models saw the individual as passive, because development (learning) is shaped by environment. For example, Watson (1924, p. 82) proposed: "Give me a dozen healthy infants, well-formed, and my own specified world to bring them up in and I'll guarantee to take any one at random and train him to become any type of specialist I might select—doctor, lawyer, artist, merchant—chief and yes, even beggarman and thief, regardless of his talents; penchants, tendencies, abilities, vocations, race of his ancestors".

Second, the concept of development is reduced to a concept of change in the elements of the behavioral repertoire. Development is conceptualized as quantitative change (e.g. quantitative increase in knowledge), additive, and continuous. The appearance of qualitative change is considered either as epiphenomenal or as reducible to quantitative change, as the organism does not exhibit basic qualitative changes. However, qualitatively different operations may cause development, such as different learning processes that are switched on or off according to environmental stimulation and learning history.

Third, the mechanistic model is normative neutral, in that no specific final goal or end point of development is suggested: Psychological development may include increase and decrease, and no optimal developmental sequence can be derived from that model. In addition, as people grow up in different learning environments, their psychological development may differ.

Fourth, as basic learning principles are suggested to be causes of developmental change, the model views development as something that can be explained by elementary processes, such as reinforcements or learning history.

Fifth, in general terms, behavioristic–mechanistic models define development as change in behavior. For example, Bijou and Baer (1961, p. 1) defined psychological development as "progressive changes in the way an organism's behavior interacts with the environment. An interaction between behavior and environment means simply that a given response may be expected to occur or not, depending on the stimulation the environment provides". However, developmental psychology may refer to changes over periods of weeks, months, or years, whereas learning psychology is concerned with changes over shorter periods (Zigler, 1963). Thus, although developmental change may be correlated with age, it is not caused by age or by age-associated maturational processes.

In this model, the term "development" is often used only in descriptive terms. Nonetheless, other proponents of the model used the term "development" as an exploratory concept rather than a descriptive term. For example, Baer (1970) viewed development as change in behavior that requires programming, that is, being presented with a sequence of experiences in optimal order. In the 1950s and 1960s behaviorist views on human development were dominant in the United States. Later, behaviorist theorists split into two groups, one following Skinner's concept of operant conditioning, and a second which used imitation as key mechanism for the acquisition of complex patterns of behavior (e.g. Sears, Maccoby, & Levin, 1957).

Whereas early behavioristic concepts saw the developing individual as a passive respondent to stimuli (e.g. Watson, 1913), later revisions emphasized that the individual is always in an interactive relationship with the environment, although they still focus on individual adjustment toward the environment rather than on the active role of the individual (Bijou, 1992). Revisions also emphasized that associations between the environment and behavior are influenced by specific contexts or setting conditions. Thus, Bijou (1992) defined his theory of behavior analysis as a combination of mechanism and contextualism, but from our perspective view, the mechanistic model is still dominant.

The mechanistic–behavioristic model stimulated many psychological interventions. Starting in the 1950s, the concept and principles of the behavioristic mechanistic model of development have been applied to child behavior therapy, preschool education, classroom management, the treatment of retarded and developmentally disabled children, parent training, adolescent delinquency, and many other fields.

As individuals are seen as inherently passive, Lerner (2002) also subsumed monocausal nature explanations of development under the mechanistic model. In this research, however, development is not explained by environmental stimulation, as does behaviorism, but by genetic inheritance. For example, some behavioral genetic researchers explain developmental phenomena mainly by the effects of genes (Rowe, 1994). However, as behavior–genetic concepts of passive, evocative, and active genotype–

environment correlation have shown that the separation between influences of nature and nurture can no longer be maintained (Plomin, 1986), mono-causal nature explanations of development have lost importance.

Organismic models of development (active organism models)

At the beginnings of developmental psychology in the late nineteenth and early twentieth century, many researchers followed an organismic view of human development. According to Reese and Overton (1970), the basic metaphor employed for the organismic model, the organism, is drawn from biology. Individuals are represented as an organized entity, a configuration of parts that gain their meaning and function from the whole in which they are embedded. The organismic model relates to the philosopher Leibniz and evolved in psychology in the early work of G. Stanley Hall (1846–1924) and James M. Baldwin (1861–1934) through Sigmund Freud (1856–1939), Arnold Gesell (1880–1961), Pierre Janet (1859–1947), Jean Piaget (1896–1980), Erik Erikson (1902–1994), and others.

First, this meta-theoretical model is rooted in an image of human beings as spontaneously active and its corollary epistemological position of constructivism. Constructivism means that the individual actively participates in the construction of the known reality, so that the locus of developmental dynamics lies within the individual. Individuals are thereby seen as active, for example, by forming cognitive schemata. Developmental change cannot be explained by material cause, but material factors may inhibit or facilitate change.

As a second characteristic of the organismic model, development is characterized as qualitative change, although quantitative change may also be observed. In development, the basic configurations of parts change, as well as the parts themselves. As organization changes to the extent that new system properties (new structures and functions) emerge and become operational, a new level of organization is reached that exhibits basic discontinuity with the previous level, and is, therefore, qualitatively different from them. Thus, development can be defined as changes in the form, structure, or organization of the system. Whereas according to the mechanistic model, development (behavior change) can be observed directly, change in the organization of the structure of behaving or thinking, which defines development according to the organismic model, cannot be directly observed, but has to be inferred from observed behavior.

Third, within this view, development is thought to be goal-directed (leading to higher states that are superior, such as more flexible or broader) and teleological in character (directed toward a final state). The general function of development is postulated by the theory in advance and acts as a principle of ordering change. End states or goals of development are defined by concepts such as maturity, ego integrity, genital sexuality, or formal operations. Structure–function relations develop and these changes are, in a final sense, unidirectional (Lerner, 2002; Reese & Overton, 1970). The search for general developmental laws led to suggestions for rules of sequences of developmental stages.

Fourth, whereas mechanistic models do not use the concept of development to explain an individually present state or present abilities, in organismic models the concept of development is used to explain existent structures or performances.

Fifth, some organismic models emphasize the high importance of early experiences for later development (e.g. Busemann, 1927; Freud, 1917) similar to assumptions from ethology (e.g. the concept of critical periods, Lorenz, 1935). For example, Freud (1917) believed in the irreversibility of early experiences by claiming that the origins of neuroses go back to the child's initial encounters with the adult world. However, available research shows that early experiences do not have a dominant role on their own and that a reversal of negative early effects may be possible. Not all negative effects may be surmountable, however, as is the case with regard to severe and long deprivation (Schaffer, 2000).

Despite similarities of the representatives of the organismic model, there are differences in the hypothesized form of change, for example, succession of stages (Gesell, 1946), differentiation and integration (Werner, 1957) and in proposed end states, such as maturity in terms of cognitive functioning (Piaget, 1955; Werner, 1957) or maturity in terms of sexual functioning (Freud, 1905).

Stage theories

The most widely used concepts of development that follow the organismic model are stage theories. They suggest that people pass through unchangeable sequences of qualitatively different phases, periods, levels, or stages of development (e.g. Erikson, 1959; Freud, 1905; Gesell, 1946; Kohlberg, 1958, 1976; Kroh, 1922; Piaget, 1955). Stage concepts provide descriptions of the stages themselves and suggest mechanisms by which the individual progresses through these stages.

The idea that psychological development follows an ordered sequence can be traced back to Aristotle, who suggested the stages of infancy, boyhood, and young manhood, to Rousseau (1762), who suggested five stages of development, and to stage conceptions in evolutionary biology (e.g. von Baer, 1828, 1837). However, these early divisions of childhood and adolescence into distinctive stages were based on the description of behaviors that were foremost in a given age period, rather than suggesting stages of development of a particular form of behavior and the processes that result in these changes.

Compared to these descriptive approaches, psychological stage theories in the narrower sense have major conceptual orientations to theory building. To a stage theorist, there are universal stages of development applicable to all humans. It is assumed that all persons pass through a series of qualitatively different levels (stages) of organization in a fixed order, so that it would be theoretically impossible for someone to skip a stage. According to these models, only two sources of interindividual differences can occur: (1) people may differ in the rate of progression through the stages (in how fast they develop); and (2) they may differ in the final stage they reach (how far they develop). All stage theories focus on an interaction between nature and nurture in accounting for behavioral development, although some put more emphasis on such an interaction (e.g. Piaget, 1950) than others (Freud, 1905; Gesell, 1948).

Theoretically, passing into a qualitatively different stage may be seen as a completely abrupt change or as gradual change. However, no stage theorist assumes abrupt transition. Stage transition is not seen as an all-or-none process, and it is suggested that people progress gradually from one stage to another. Although, in general, most behaviors that represent a stage are expected to begin and end their development at the same time, absolute concurrence is not a theoretical requirement of a developmental stage. Thus, people may show behavior representative of more than one stage of development at the same time. For example, certain sequences may take the form of a staggered progression (e.g. horizontal décalage; Piaget, 1950). Although the main focus of stage theorists is on qualitative change, stage theorists also maintain that there are continuous elements in development.

As one of the earliest examples of stage theories, Freud (1905) believed that the location of the libido and modes of psychosexual gratification at a particular point in the person's development follow a sequence of invariant stages. The first erogenous zone in development would be the oral zone, followed by the anal zone and the genital zone. He postulated five stages in psychosexual development: the oral, anal, phallic, latency, and genital stages. The emergence of these stages was considered as primarily maturationally determined, but the effects of these stages on individual psychosexual functioning were said to be dependent on the specifics of that person's experience. Psychoanalytic theory delineates two major mechanisms through which early events influence later behavior: fixation and regression. A blocking of an infant's attempts to obtain appropriate stimulation may result in a fixation for the rest of that person's life, so that the individual will attempt to obtain the gratification missed earlier. Unlike the typical organismic stage model, regression (which is the movement back through earlier stages) was seen as possible and, in some cases, even frequent. According to Freud, the first five years of life are the most crucial for adult psychosexual functioning in that the forms of development after childhood would be determined during this period. As Freud's conception was mainly derived from clinical case studies, and as the central concepts, such as libido, were difficult to measure, Freud (1905) provided only very limited empirical support for his model.

With regard to cognitive development, Piaget (1950) suggested four stages: sensorimotor stage, preoperational stage, concrete operational stage, and formal operational stage. He proposed a general, biology-based adaptive tendency that applies to the organism throughout its development. According to Piaget, the progressive interaction of the person with his or her environment in form of two processes of assimilation and accommodation is central for the successive development of mental structures. The concept of assimilation and accommodation were originally introduced into developmental psychology by James M. Baldwin (1895). Assimilation is a process by which children try to interpret new experiences in terms of their existing models of the world, of the schemes they already possess. For example, a young child who sees a flying bat for the first time may try to assimilate it into one of his or her schema of flying birds and may think of it as a "birdie". As truly novel objects and experiences may be difficult to interpret in terms of existing schemes, the child may be inclined to seek a better understanding of his or her observations. Accommodation, the complement of assimilation, is the process of modifying existing cognitive structures to account for new experiences. The child may recognize that the bat has no feathers and is no bird, and invent a new name for this new creature.

Individuals were suggested to strive for a cognitive equilibrium, that is, for a balance between assimilation and accommodation (Piaget, 1975). In the process of so doing, the available cognitive schemata are applied to new situations (reproductive assimilation). However, when the available cognitive schema is not adequate to assimilate new information, a disequilibrium results that necessitates a return to accommodation (the change in cognitive structures leading to higher cognitive functioning) and a repetition of the sequence. In the course of such cognitive development, mental structures were said to become increasingly flexible allowing a child to represent information symbolical and to manipulate it mentally. In this way, Piaget viewed cognitive development as the outcome of organism–environment interactions and, thus, as an active, self-generated process.

In his stage model on moral development, Kohlberg (1958) suggested three levels of moral reasoning (preconventional level, conventional level, and postconventional level), each consisting of a further two stages. This concept was later revised to five stages (Kohlberg, 1976), however, as in empirical studies no individuals could be found for Stage 6. The stages were described as: Stage 1, heteronomous morality and individualism; Stage 2, instrumental purpose and exchange; Stage 3, mutual interpersonal expectations, relationships, and interpersonal conformity; Stage 4, social systems and conscience; and Stage 5, social contract or utility and individual rights. In this model, the focus on the individual's social perspective was suggested to move toward increasingly greater scope and greater abstraction. The motor of development was seen in role taking abilities, that is, the increasing cognitive ability to understand another person's perspective.

When comparing the concepts of development by Freud, Piaget, and Kohlberg, they are similar in viewing development as proceeding through a series of qualitatively different levels of organization. Whereas the concepts by Freud and Piaget explicitly focus on psychological development in childhood and adolescence, Kohlberg's model also includes developmental progression in adulthood. As in childhood and adolescence, maturation processes play an important role for psychological development and as many new social demands are similar for all children in most developed countries (e.g. entering the school around age 6), stage theories can easily be applied to that age range. However, for the description of psychological development in adulthood, the description of a fixed sequence of stages that would lead to the same outcome in all individuals would be less adequate, given the heterogeneity of demands and associated individual changes. Thus, the stage theory for the whole life-span developed by Erik Erikson (1959), and probably the widest known, provided a synthesis between classical stage theory and an explicit differential orientation to development.

According to Erikson, psychosocial development involves the development of the ego's emerging capabilities to meet social demands, and the person's attempts to resolve the emotional crises provoked by these changing demands. If the ego develops the appropriate capabilities, the crisis will be successfully solved resulting in healthy development. Erikson (1959) proposed eight stages of psychosocial development or ego development. The emergence of each stage of development is fixed in accordance with a maturational timetable. As each stage involves the development of a specific ego capability, a person has only limited time to develop each stage-specific capability. Within each stage of development, Erikson suggested an emotional crisis occurs which he conceptualized as a bipolar trait dimension in opposing directions (e.g. trust versus mistrust in infancy). Within each stage, therefore, a person develops a feeling (or attitude) that lies between the endpoints of each feeling (attitude) dimension. In his later work, however, Erikson reviewed his ideas of a fixed order of stages and emphasized the recurrence and reworking of earlier stages during later stages of development (Erikson; Erikson, & Kivnick, 1989). The suggestion that development across the life-span can be conceptualized as dealing with age-associated demands is also found in other theoretical concepts, such as Havighursts's (1948) concept of developmental tasks that arise from age-associated biological changes (e.g. puberty, menopause), social demands (e.g. age-norms for entering and leaving school), and individual aspirations and values. However, compared to Erikson's theory, the concept of developmental tasks is less specific with regard to potential developmental outcomes, and did not suggest a direction and final state of development, as stage theories did.

Freud's (1905) stage model of psychosexual development, Kohlberg's (1976) model on moral development, Piaget's (1970) theory of cognitive development, and Erikson's stage theory (1959) are still widely used today, despite some critiques, revisions, and further development, for example, in contemporary ego-psychology (e.g. Loevinger, 1997) and among neo-Piagetians (e.g. Pascual-Leone & Johnson, 1999). However, many developmental changes cannot be described as a sequence of steps or stages that follow on each other, such as for example, the development of attitudes and interests for which the directions of change vary considerably between individuals (e.g. Evans, 2001). Similarly, as some individuals are to retrace steps (Colby, Kohlberg, Gibbs, & Lieberman, 1983) and, with regard to Erikson's model, as some stages may even reoccur for many individuals at later age (Erikson et al., 1989), the suggested universal nature of stages does not hold well universally. Many stage theories are too restrictive for describing and explaining the large interindividual variability that can be observed beyond childhood and adolescence. In addition, although stage theories see the outcomes of development as resulting from an interaction between organismic characteristics and characteristics of experience, these assumptions could often not be made more specific due to limited available scientific knowledge at the time of theory development.

Spiral models

Spiral models of individual development emerged in the context of stage models. This concept was first elaborated by Siegert (1891) and was further developed by Busemann (1927) and Gesell (1954). For example, Busemann (1927) assumed that children develop not according to a smooth upward curve of physical and mental progress, but rather by an irregular course of "favorable and unfavorable phases", so that the impression of periodicity is given. He conceptualized development in childhood and adolescence as sequence of phases of excitement and compensatory calming. Phases of excitement or critical phases were expected at the ages 3, 6, 9, 12 or 13, 16 or 17, and perhaps at 19 or 20, followed by phases of calming. In phases of excitement, development would speed up, so that these are times of increased growth and vulnerability for emotional disturbances (a suggestion related to the concept of critical periods). Correlations between the appearance of the excitation phases and rapidity in anatomical growth led him to suggest a maturational basis for the observed behavioural spiral. Although Busemann's spiral conception did not receive much theoretical and empirical attention, spiral views of development have been applied by other developmentalists, such as Kohlberg, Piaget and Riegel (against the backdrop of a dialectic model of development; see later). For example, according to Kohlberg (1958, 1976), at each level of moral development, the first stage is relatively rigid, whereas the second stage is more flexible by the inclusion of more perspectives. Similarly, Piaget's (1975) equilibration model of development entails an initial state of harmonious existence within a system, the emergence of some disruption in that state because of perturbations in the organism–environment relation, followed by a movement toward restoring the initial state of harmony at a higher stage.

Differentiation and integration models

Differentiation and integration models conceptualize development from an organismic point of view. The view that development proceeds from a lack of differentiation to increasing differentiation, integration, and hierarchical organization can be traced back to Goethe's theory of metamorphosis (Goethe, 1790/1998), which described an increasing differentiation and subordination of parts within the whole with regard to the development of plants. Similarly, the idea was anticipated by the work of the biologist and philosopher Herbert Spencer (1852, 1862) and the psychologist James M. Baldwin (1915).

The main proponent of this model in developmental psychology was Heinz Werner, who formulated the orthogenetic principle as heuristic law: Wherever development occurs it proceeds from a state of relative globality and lack of differentiation to a state of increasing differentiation, articulation, and hierarchical integration (Werner, 1957, p. 126). In this model, Werner focuses on the emergence of an increasing person–environment differentiation. The process of hierarchical integration involves qualitative reorganization of the previously established levels of organization. If "one assumes that the emergence of higher levels of operations involves hierarchic integration, it follows that lower-level operations will have to be reorganized in terms of their functional nature so that they become subservient to higher functioning" (Werner, 1957, p. 139). Thus, earlier developments will become subsumed under later ones, and will be subordinated to later developments (Langer, 1970). Development is characterized as directional and unilinear and as including elements of discontinuity and continuity. The tendency for global characteristics to become differentiated into specific characteristics describes discontinuity, whereas the tendency for earlier developments to be subsumed under later ones (hierarchical organization) shows continuity of development. Werner also argued that any developmental process tends toward stabilization, thus adding a teleological (goal-directed) component to his concept.

Concepts of differentiation and integration are used in recent theories and fields of research, such as Developmental Systems Theory (e.g. Ford & Lerner, 1992; Gottlieb, 1991) and developmental psychopathology (Cicchetti & Cohen, 1999). However, as the orthogenetic principle describes change directed toward higher level of functioning, it is less useful for describing declines (Schmidt, 1970) that are a focus of life-span developmental psychology (see later).

Canalization and funnel models

These models emerged in evolutionary biology (e.g. Waddington, 1942) and developmental psychology (e.g. Harris, 1943). They conceptualize development as reduction of the variability or scope of behavior and as stabilization of behavior. They assume that the range of human behavior or potential behavior is very broad and plastic at birth and then becomes increasingly reduced in scope, fixed in form, and shaped to conform to social norms or other demands, thus becoming more adaptive. The concept of canalization was put forward by Holt (1931) to describe how prenatal conditioning narrows the initially diffuse or random nature of motor activity in the embryo or fetus. Holt described behavior at development as learning to narrow down originally diffuse pathways to a definitive neural reflex arc. Similarly, Kuo (1976) described canalization as a broadly applicable principle characterizing the narrowing of the initially large range of behavior potentials, correlated with a decrease in plasticity. According to Kuo, canalization can be based on physiologic and anatomic changes and experience. The concept of canalization has been applied from an organismic perspective, but also from the perspective of developmental systems theory: Gottlieb (1991) suggested that canalization can take place at all levels of the developing system (genes–physiological processes–experience–environment). Thus, normatively occurring experience in concert with genetic and other activities can canalize development. Canalizing contributes to the stabilization of behavior of successive generations. For example, as the range of a particular behavior is canalized in the parental generation, children will learn to show this narrowed scope of behavior. The concept of canalization also relates to processes of selecting developmental goals or pathways and to the age-associated reduction of plasticity that have been elaborated in modern life-span developmental psychology (e.g. Baltes, 1987).

Stratification models

This concept, the philosophical roots of which go back to Plato, is based on models of personality consisting of different layers (e.g. Freud, 1923/1960; Lersch, 1938; Thiele, 1940). With regard to personality development, this model suggests that the lowest layer develops first, followed by the higher layers. Thus, stratification models conceptualize development as overlay of the new over old. Pre-existing characteristics are often not totally replaced, but overlaid, so that they may emerge again later under certain (normal or pathological) circumstances. For example, according to Freud (1923/1960), the id develops first, followed by the ego and the superego. Amongst others, the id was suggested to be manifest in dreams and in other situations that are not under control of the ego.

Overcoming some limitations of the organismic model

According to the organismic model, development is described as a relatively uniform, goal-directed process that leads to definite end states or goals of development (the concept of predetermined epigenesis). Although organismic theories assume some interactions between the organism and the environment, they characterize these interactions as being of low variety. In his probabilistic–epigenetic concept, Schneirla (1902–1968) focused on the dynamic interaction between nature and nurture factors. Similar to organismic model of development, he saw ontogenetic development as involving qualitative discontinuity, at least in part. However, he suggested the reciprocal interaction of two factors to make up successive developmental changes, of maturation (growth and differentiation of the physical and physiological systems of an organism), and experience (all stimuli that act on the organism throughout the course of life). Experience may change the organism and vice versa. The nature and timing of interactions between maturation and experience are central in determining behavioral development. As the nature and timing of this interaction cannot be predicted in advance for every organism within a species, human development has a probabilistic element (Schneirla, 1957). Similarly, Gottlieb (1970, p. 123) proposed a probabilistic epigenetic organismic view in that the behavioral development of individuals within a species does not follow an invariant or inevitable course, and that the sequence or outcomes of individual behavioral development are probabilistic: Whereas the unidirectionality of structure–function relationships is a main assumption of predetermined epigenesis in organismic models of development, Gottlieb suggested bidirectional structure–function relationships, in that not only structure can influence function, but function (e.g. exposure to stimulation) can modify the development of the structures that are involved in these events. The concept of probabilistic epigenesis integrates assumptions from the organismic and the contextualistic model of development (see later).

The dialectic models of development

Dialectic materialism of the nineteenth century has influenced the third meta-theoretical approach to developmental psychology, dialectic models. This approach has not been included in the seminal work by Reese and Overton (1970), in part because important work by Soviet developmentalists from the 1920s and 1930s had not been translated into English before the late 1980s, and because the main work of the most important Western proponent of this concept, Klaus F. Riegel, was published only in the second half of the 1970s.

Dialectic models of human development have their philosophical roots in the work of Georg Wilhelm Friedrich Hegel (1770–1831) on ideational change and of Karl Marx (1818–1883). Marx himself was influenced by Darwin's theory of evolution (Padover, 1978), although his work was mainly on social change. The dialectic model of individual development was elaborated in the Soviet Union by Lev S. Vygotsky (1896–1934) and his successors Alexander R. Luria (1902–1977) and Alexei N. Leontiev (1904–1979), and in the West by Klaus F. Riegel (1925–1977). The basic metaphor of the dialectic model is contradiction or conflict (Riegel, 1975a, 1976): Conflicts were seen as the source of development.

After the October Revolution in 1917, dialectic developmental psychology was developed in the Soviet Union by Vygotsky, Luria, and Leontiev. Their concept can be characterized as sociocultural in that it stressed the social and cultural origins of individual development, and the idea that instrumental activities (goal-directed activities) are established by social life. According to Vygotsky, the person is an active agent of his or her own development. The development of thinking is neither controlled by maturational processes nor by social interaction and learning. Rather, social interaction provides sociocultural means that are actively taken up by the child if they correspond to his or her level of development, are slowly interiorized, and finally transformed into new available means for problem solving.

Vygotsky's concept of the "zone of proximal development" became well known in modern educational psychology: Some goals are available to the developing person through taking actions already in his or her repertoire and by utilizing available means. Thus, the field that exists within the child can be divided into a "zone" within which the child can fend for him- or herself, and a "zone" within which the child requires education or instruction. The potential level of development is determined by children's problem solving under the guidance of their parents, teachers, or older children. If the stimulation fits the current developmental level, the child can reach a higher level than would be expected according to his or her age. Thus, "the zone of proximal development of the child is the distance between actual development, determined with the help of independently solved tasks, and the level of the potential child's development, determined with the help of tasks solved by the child under the guidance of adults and in cooperation with his more intelligent partners" (Vygotsky, 1933, p. 42). By engaging in actions within a zone, Vygotsky believed that the child develops through a process in which he or she transcends his or her present level of development. The concept of the zone of proximal development shows that schooling or education depends on the child's level of understanding, and vice versa.

In Western psychology, Riegel (1975a, 1976) proposed that dialectical philosophy could be used to devise a unique theory of development, that is, one that does not focus only on the organism (e.g. genes, maturationally guided progression through stages), or on the environment (e.g. as source of stimulation, as suggested by behaviorist models of development). According to Riegel, dialectical theory of development is focused on the relations between developing organisms and their changing environments. He suggested that such relations involve continual conflicts among variables from several levels of the organization of life phenomena (from inner biological through individual psychological and physical–environmental to sociocultural influences). In other words, each level is influenced by other levels, and development is brought about by contradictions that create discordances and conflicts. Through the actions of individuals, synchronicity will be re-established and thereby progress achieved. As synchronicity is achieved, new discrepancies emerge producing a continuous flux of contradictions and changes (Riegel, 1976). Riegel described three dialectic laws of developmental change based on Marxist and Hegelian theory: (1) the unity and opposition of contradictory principles and their resolution through synthesis; (2) the possibility of transforming basic quantitative change into qualitative change; and (3) the negation of a negation, or the continual process of replacing the old by the new. Some dialectic psychologists represent the individual as developing through a continuous process of thesis, antithesis, and synthesis (Wozniak, 1975), a perspective that emphasized the continuous nature of change and the fact that change occurs at multiple levels (Riegel, 1975a, 1976). The dialectic model saw crises or catastrophes as essential and constructive steps through which developmental progression alone becomes possible. Based on the dialectic laws, it was suggested that both continuity and discontinuity can occur in individual development.

Lerner (2002) suggested that Riegel's view of change may be widely compatible with the organismic model. As the nature of dialectic change is always in the same direction, that of a synthesis between two "conflicting" opposites, this view shows many similarities with organismic models. However, Riegel argued against organismic concepts of development that suggest a discrete final stage of development. For example, whereas Piaget proposed that after the stage of formal operations no new cognitive structure would emerge, Riegel suggested that the dialectic resulted in a fifth, open-ended stage of cognitive development. Contrary to conceptions of a unidirectional progression from lower to higher stages of development, Riegel emphasized that individuals may switch back and forth between different levels of cognition (Riegel, 1975b p. 376), thus clearly differing from organismic models.

The dialectic model of Riegel has not remained a conception of prime focus among modern developmental psychology, partly because of the early death of its founder and partly because thoughts on the interplay of different levels of organization of life phenomena were further elaborated in the contextual model of human development. However, the attention to Riegel's ideas encouraged the interest of developmentalists in the role of individual–context relations for human development. Some ideas, such as the interdependence of short-term and long-term changes and the influence they exert upon each other (Riegel, 1975a) are a recent focus of developmental psychology (e.g. Li, 2003). Today, the work of Vygotsky is more widely discussed than the work by Riegel. For example, some contemporary theorists have adapted Vygotsky's zone of proximal development to conceptualize the link between the active individual and his or her context (e.g. Valsiner, 1998). However, other aspects of Vygotsky's work have been criticized. For example, although Vygotsky stated that in ontogenesis two lines of development—the cultural and the natural line—come into contact and transform each other, he did not specify the natural line of development (Wertsch & Tulviste, 1992).

Contextual models of development

Contextual models of development are the fourth family of theories. They are derived in part from pragmatic philosophers such as Charles S. Peirce (1839–1914) and George Herbert Mead (1863–1931), and the work of William James (1842–1910) and John Dewey (1859–1952). According to Pepper (1942), the main metaphor of contextualism is the historic event. Every behavior and incident in the world can be viewed as a historic event, so that change and newness are accepted as fundamental. Contextualism turns attention to the external contexts of psychological development, but also to the internal "context" (affective processes, motivation, other skills or schemata). It focused on the interaction of contexts (e.g. on the coordination, interaction, or fusion of aspects of the organism and external context; Tobach & Greenberg, 1984), and on opportunities and constraints for change promoted by organism and external context.

According to James (1890), the meaning of a mental event is inseparable from the context of its occurrence, which is itself in flux. Development was viewed by James as continuous, composed of quantitative differences rather than qualitative distinct stages. Mental reaction on every given thing was considered to be a result of our individual experience of the world to date. Like Darwin, James viewed the human mind as active and functional, involved continuously in the process of adapting to a changing ecology. As the significance of an event is inseparable from the context in which it occurs and as contexts are themselves continuously changing, James, as well as Peirce (1992) suggested that the course of development therefore has an element of chance (e.g. Peirce's "tychism", a theory that conceives chance as an objective reality). As in the first six decades of the twentieth century organismic and (in the USA in the 1950s and 1960s) mechanistic concepts became dominant views of development, early proponents of developmental contextualism had little influence on developmental psychology for decades. However, from the 1970s onwards, many psychologists have rediscovered contextual thinking.

The contextual model assumes constant levels of change at all levels of analysis, and that change in one level promotes change in all levels (Lerner, 2002). As any change is related to changes at other levels, any target change must be conceptualized in the context of the other changes within which it is embedded. These changing relations constitute the basic process of human development. The individual and the social environment are viewed as mutually influential, as involved in a dynamic interaction. All contextualistic models focus on the dynamic interplay of nature, nurture, and activities of the developing individual, and they exclude any notion of final cause.

Bronfenbrenner (1979, 1986, 1999) proposed an ecological–contextual systems model of the lifelong adjustment individuals make to the environment in which they develop. He conceptualized the ecological environment (or context) in which human development occurs as a set of "nested structures". Bronfenbrenner refers to the macrosystem as a cultural "blueprint" that partially determines the social structures and activities that occur in the more immediate system levels. Components of the macrosystem include political structures and institutions, material resources, opportunity structures (e.g. access to educational opportunities) and shared knowledge and cultural beliefs. Developmental outcomes are also influenced by interactions within microsystems, that is, the immediate settings that contain the developing person (such as the family, school, or workplace). Mesosystems encompass the interrelations among two or more microsystems, each of which contains the developing person (e.g. relations between the child's peer group and family), and exosystems encompass linkages between two or more settings, at least one of which does not contain the developing person. Events from exosystems influence individual development indirectly, mediated by microsystems (e.g. parental work stress may influence parenting behavior). Finally, chronosystems incorporate the time dimension of Bronfenbrenner's model, including the succession of ecological systems over the life course (e.g. kindergarden–school–workplace) and the impact of social change on the ecological systems. Whereas Bronfenbrenner originally focused on the interplay between change in external contexts and the developing individual, later reformulations were extended to a bio-ecological model. Thus, according to Bronfenbrenner and Morris (1998, p. 996), especially in its early phases but also throughout the life course, human development takes place through processes of progressively more complex reciprocal interaction between an active, evolving biopsychosocial human organism and the persons, objects, and symbols in its immediate external environment.

Whereas the organismic model of development follows a universalistic conception of developmental processes that would be similar or even identical across cultures, contextualistic concepts emphasize that there are also meaningful cultural differences. A relevant theoretical framework is the "developmental niche", which emerged from research on cultural differences in naive parenting theories, parenting practices, and child outcomes. Super and Harkness (1986, 2002) identified three subsystems of a developmental niche; the physical and social settings, the historically constituted customs and practices of child rearing, and the psychology of the caretaker, particularly parental ethnotheories that are shared by the community. They suggested three organizational aspects of the niche that create developmental outcomes: contemporary redundancy (the mutually reinforcing repetition of similar influences from several parts of the environment during the same period of development), thematic elaboration (repetition and cultivation of core symbols and systems of meaning), and chaining, which is the linking of disparate elements of the environment because no single element of the environment would be sufficient to produce a particular outcome.

A useful approach for understanding the significance of the person–context relations for individual development is the goodness-of-fit perspective (e.g. Thomas & Chess, 1977): If a child's individual characteristics fit the demands of a particular setting, adaptive outcomes emerge. For example, in the transition to school, a highly active and distractible child will have problems in adapting to the new demands to sit still and concentrate over longer periods of time. The child is then likely to be criticized by his or her teachers, which may further impair performance and motivation to comply to the new demands. Person–environment fit and associated positive developmental outcomes can be increased by helping the child to learn self-control and by providing more time to adapt to the new demands.

According to a pure contextualistic paradigm, relations between parts and continuity of development may exist at one time but not at another, so that there would be no prediction possible from one point in life to the next (Overton, 1984; Pepper, 1942). However, according to Lerner (2002), a world view that stressed only the chaotic, dispersive and disorganized character of life would not readily lend to the derivation of a theory of development. If development is conceptualized as being more than change of whatever form and direction, there must be systematic and successive changes in the organization of the organism. Thus, as a solution to this dilemma, Lerner (2002) suggested a combination of contextualistic and organismic thinking (see, later on Developmental Systems Approaches).

Recent views on human development

In the third part of our chapter, we review two recent approaches to developmental psychology, the life-span approach and developmental systems approaches.

Life-span developmental psychology

The life-span tradition of developmental psychology is present in each of the four models or families of developmental theories. Although major historical precursors of developmental psychology were life-span centered (Carus, 1808; Quetelet, 1835; Tetens, 1777), and the first textbooks on human development with a focus on the entire life-span had been published already in the 1920s and 1930s (Bühler, 1933; Hollingworth, 1927; Pressey, Janney, & Kuhlen, 1939), an explicit attempt to conceptualize developmental psychology as life-span psychology only began in the 1960s and 1970s (for overview, see Baltes, 1979; 1987). Baltes (1979) identified two directions of the expansion of concepts that originally emerged in child development towards life-span development. The first is the application of constructs from child development to other age periods. For example, Bühler (1933) applied the stage model of development to the whole life-span. The second, and in our view more important, expansion is the identification of new facets of behavioral development that emerge beyond childhood and adolescence. This is more than the introduction of the study of development of new classes of behavior (e.g. wisdom, time perspective; Baltes, 1979) as it also includes the emergence of new theoretical assumptions about development in general.

According to life-span developmental psychology, ontogenetic development is a lifelong process, and no age period holds supremacy in determining subsequent development. It involves processes of change that do not originate at birth but lie in later periods of the life-span. Life-long development is a system of diverse patterns of change that differ in terms of timing (onset, duration, termination), direction, and order. Thus, life-span psychology does not limit the concept of development to growth or increase in general functional capacity, as was the case with most organismic stage models, spiral models, stratification models, and models of differentiation and hierarchic integration. This broader focus raised questions as to whether concepts about development that have been developed with regard to childhood and adolescence are applicable for individual development across the whole life-span. For example, life-span developmental research has shown limitations of the applicability of Werner's (1957) orthogenetic principle of development as increasing differentiation: Whereas cognitive research on younger adults found two factors of intellectual abilities (one related to speed, accuracy, and processing of information, and one to acquired knowledge), in very old age, a characteristic de-differentiation of cognitive abilities appears, based on an increasing dominance of biological constraints (e.g. Ghisletta & Lindenberger, 2003).

Life-span developmental psychology defines development as multidirectional, as a joint expression of features of growth (gain) and decline (loss) at all points of the life-span. No developmental change during the life course is pure gain. Adaptation implies not only advances in adaptive capacity but also losses in adaptivity for alternative pathways. For example, in childhood we gain competency in our native language but lose the capacity to be as fluent as a native speaker in other languages. Typical examples of gains in old age are increases in expert knowledge in different domains.

According to life-span psychology, successful development can be defined as the maximization of gains and the minimization of losses. Ontogenetic development involves the coordinated and competitive allocation of resources into distinct functions (growth, maintenance inclusive recovery, and regulation of loss). Life-span developmental changes involve a shift from the allocation of resources to growth (which is more typical in childhood) toward an increasingly larger share allocated to maintenance and management of loss.

According to life-span psychology, the course of psychological development is not completely predetermined, either within or across domains. Variable components are reflected in interindividual differences, intraindividual modifiability, and cross-cultural as well as historical differences. The concept of plasticity is an index of the individual potential for change in adaptive capacity. It reflects how flexible and robust the individual may be in dealing with challenges. There is always developmental plasticity across the entire life-span, although plasticity declines with age-associated changes of the nervous system and dementia in old age.

According to life-span developmental theory, individual development occurs within social, physical, cultural, and historical contexts. It is assumed that human development is a complex, dynamic phenomenon in which biological and intrapsychological factors interact with social–interactive, societal, cultural, historical, and ideosyncratic events and experiences. A three-factor model of these influences includes normative age-graded influences (biological/maturational and age-associated social norms, such as normatively determined school entry), historically graded influences (historical–cultural events or changes, such as wars, economic crises that affect members of certain age-cohorts in similar ways), and non-normative events that do not follow any predictable patterns (e.g. illness, loss of confidants). The focus on age-graded influences has already been typical for organismic concepts of human development (e.g. stage models) and the interest in history-graded and non-normative influences had previously been stated by proponents of the dialectic model of development. For example, Riegel (1975b) has emphasized the role of critical life events and social change for individual development, and Luria (1976) wrote on the role of social change for cognitive development. Contextualistic models of individual development, such as Bronfenbrenner's (1986) suggestion of a chronosystem (which is the changing environment that influences individual development) have also referred to history-graded influences on human development. History-graded and non-normative influences on development are a central focus of life-span development because it is very unlikely that environmental influences would be stable across longer periods of time.

Age-graded influences lead to interindividual similarities in development, historically graded influences lead to differences even between adjacent cohorts, and non-normative events increase interindividual differences between persons of the same cohort. Ontogeny is not universal. According to Baltes (1987), the nature of psychological ontogeny is always newly created for any given birth cohort or cultural setting. Baltes (1997) underscored the link between evolutionary and life-span perspectives. As processes of natural selection apply mainly to characteristics that emerge before and during the reproductive phase, and as the much shorter life-span in early human evolution did not allow selection pressures to work for characteristics that emerge in later life, benefits resulting from evolutionary selection show a negative age-correlation. In the postreproductive mature adult, these processes lose importance and the social and cultural contexts, such as medical technology, become more important for the content and direction of development.

As individuals are co-producers of their development, Baltes and Baltes (1980) described the course of development as an active process consisting of selective optimization of adaptive capacity with compensation: Individuals invest time and energy to attain their goals and seek an optimal relationship between their effort and the outcome of their behavior (optimization). A feature of life-span development is the age-related increase in specialization (elective selection) of motivational and cognitive resources. Selection is due to biological, psychological, and environmental factors. If limits or thresholds of capacity are exceeded during the course of development for a given individual, he or she may give up an activity or goal that that is no longer possible (loss-based selection) or use compensatory and/or substitute strategies to maintain his or her goal or activity. For example, before a developmental deadline such as the "biological clock" for child-bearing is reached, individuals increase their effort for goal attainment, but in the case of failure and passing the deadline, they switch to goal disengagement and self-protective strategies, such as downgrading the importance of the failed goal and increased investment in the pursuit of alternative goals (Heckhausen, Wrosch, & Fleeson, 2001). Developmental advance is due to processes of optimization, which is the active striving for goal attainment.

Developmental systems approaches (biocultural co-constructive theories)

Advances in the identification of biological, social/cultural, and psychological influences in human development [e.g. the human genome project (Sham, 2003); cognitive neuroscience (Nelson, Bloom, Ameral, Cameron, & Pine, 2002)] call for complex developmental theories that take into account the interplay between biological, psychological, and social influences on individual development. This progress led to co-constructive concepts of development, such as Developmental Systems Theory (Ford & Lerner, 1992), the Dynamic Systems Approach (Thelen & Smith, 1994), Wapner's holistic, systems-oriented perspective (Wapner & Demick, 1998), and—with main focus on phylogenesis—the developmental psychobiological systems view (Gottlieb, 2002).

All developmental systems approaches agree in that development can only be understood as the multiple, mutual, and continuous interaction of all levels of the developing system, from the molecular to the behavioral to the cultural. According to this developmental contextualism, development occurs in a multilevel context. "Development is not a concept that is pertinent to any single level of organization. Rather it is a concept that pertains to a property of a system" (Lerner, 1995, p. 362). The theories assume reciprocal causal relationships between variables at each level of analysis.

Changes in the dynamic organization of variables between and within levels constitute the basic nature of human development. Thus, they characterize human development as an open, self-regulating and self-constructing system. For example, van Geert conceptualized development as:

> A process that incorporates and transforms a host of processes and influences that each have their unique sources, laws and forms and integrates them into a phenomenon that is more than just the sum of its parts. That is, development integrates the biological condition of growth and change with external sociocultural influences, support and education, with the subject's own activity, motives and goals, with the formal, structural and historical properties of the contents and skills that become part of the subject's mental and behavioral equipment.
>
> (van Geert, 1998, p. 144)

The complexity of the interplay of changes of these contexts leads to a probabilistic character of development, and the same change in one context (e.g. onset of puberty) can have different effects on each individual, depending upon the interplay with the other developmental contexts. This complexity of the interrelated processes calls for the inclusion of knowledge from other developmental sciences, such as developmental neurobiology.

Individuals are seen as co-constructors of their development, because they engage in specific contexts or they alter their actual and potential environments. Developmental systems approaches focus on changes across the whole course of life of an individual, rather than on childhood and adolescence as many organismic theories do. They describe differential developmental processes as well as changes that are similar for most or even all individuals.

No instance of continuity or discontinuity is necessarily excluded within developmental systems approaches. As a pure contextualist view of development does not allow specific hypotheses about the course of individual development, to be derived developmental systems approaches formulate additional assumptions that reduce the theoretically indefinite number of combinations within a dynamic system. For example, Ford and Lerner (1992), and Wapner and Demick (1998) synthesize features of contextual and organismic models by describing development as a process moving from a lack of differentiation and integration to a differentiated and hierarchic integration of organismic functioning according to Werner's (1957) orthogenetic principle. Thelen and Smith (1994) referred to order principles of entropy change from systems theory (Prigogine, 1978). Thus, developmental systems approaches can be described as an integration or "compromise" position derived from several different philosophical models or world views in order to model the complexity of human development (Lerner, 2002).

Despite many similarities, there are differences between developmental systems approaches with regard to specific assumptions. As there is no single, ideal developmental pathway for a given person, all theories assume relative plasticity of development, but differ in assumptions regarding age-associated change in plasticity. For example, Ford and Lerner (1992) stated that plasticity varies across the lifetime (based on genetic factors or age-associated environmental boundaries), whereas Thelen and Smith (1994) suggested only small age differences in plasticity in that greater effort would be needed for promoting change in old age. As these theories are still in progress, it is too early to estimate which of them will have the strongest impact on the future of developmental psychology.

Developmental systems approaches also provide a theoretical framework for integrating the levels of development of species (phylogeny), of the single individual (ontogeny), and of psychological processes within the individual (microgenesis). Individual development throughout life is seen as a dynamic process of cumulative by moment-to-moment experiences and activities taking place at the behavioral, cognitive, and neurobiological levels on the microgenetic time scale. These microgenetic events are influenced by social interactions in the proximal developmental contexts and by long-range culture–gene–co-evolution during phylogeny. However, given the high complexity of interrelated processes, it is difficult to specify the individual interactions between contexts (e.g. how a particular gene influences neurological changes) and to derive testable specific hypotheses regarding individual development from developmental systems approaches.

Conclusions

A multitude of different concepts about human development have emerged in developmental psychology. Almost all general models show some relations to Darwin's evolution theory, although these ties are weak for the behaviorist mechanistic model. The philosophical roots of these concepts are more specific. Whereas for decades, different meta-theories have been developed independently or in dissociation from each other, recent developmental systems approaches try to integrate some core assumptions of previously developed concepts or meta-theories and knowledge from developmental biology, developmental neuroscience, and related disciplines (e.g. Gottlieb, 2002). The proposed characteristics of development, such as whether development is described as a continuous and/or discontinuous process, vary considerably between meta-models and between more specific theories. These differences were not only based on the different general theoretical background, but also on the constraints of the variables considered relevant by the researcher's theory or meta-theory, for example, when focusing on the accumulation of knowledge versus the emergence of new cognitive structures.

Making concepts of development more complex allows weaknesses of previous views of development as a uniform, goal directed process, which shows little or no interindividual variability (e.g. stage theories), or as change that is completely under the control of the environment (behavioristic model) to be overcome. However, as developmental theories have to explain and predict behavioral change, the increasing complexity also makes it more difficult to derive specific hypotheses concerning individual development.

To model the interplay of biological, psychological and sociocultural processes in detail, more scientific knowledge is needed about the mechanisms that relate genes to physiological processes of the CNS, brain development to behavioral change, and behavioral development to changes in the immediate environment and at societal level. Here, progress in developmental neuroscience will help the elaboration of concepts about human development. Medical progress (e.g. regarding the survival of premature newborns), increase in average life-expectancy, and changes of human living conditions call for research on the latitudes and limits of human adaptability which will also expand our understanding of individual development. Of no lesser importance is a better understanding of the ways in which social and cultural change influences individual development (Pinquart & Silbereisen, 2004).

Whereas according to the mechanistic–behavioristic and contextualistic perspective, suggested influences on individual development could be easily observed or otherwise measured (e.g. via questionnaires), such methods would not be sufficient when including the measurement of biological change. Thus, a broadening of the focus to developmental science (including developmental biology, developmental neuroscience, developmental psychology, etc.) would be needed, which has implications for the training of developmentalists or, at least, for the need for interdisciplinary scientific work.

Concepts about human development also relate to research methodology and the application of developmental psychological knowledge (Table 5.1). According to the mechanistic–behavioristic model, single-subject designs that relate the rate or quality of individual change to environmental characteristics (e.g. different reinforcement plans) were an adequate method for studying development (e.g. Bijou, 1992). As long as development was conceptualized as a unidirectional, goal-directed process with low levels of or even no interindividual variability (e.g. in stage theories), cross-sectional studies were regarded as sufficient to study psychological development (e.g. Gesell, 1940). Given the proposed openness of development, and possibilities to move forward and backward between different levels of development, dialectic models of development call for a measure of individual change, which is the case for longitudinal studies. In addition, as individual development is conceptualized as interaction with one's sociocultural environment, knowledge about individual development can be gained from cross-cultural research (e.g. Luria, 1976) and cohort-sequence designs. Contextualistic models and developmental systems approaches call for a combination of longitudinal multi-level measurements of biological processes,

Table 5.1 Comparison of main concepts of individual development

Concept/ model	Main scientific roots	Definition of development	Proposed influences on development	Suggested research methodology	Consequences of intervention
Mechanistic (behavioristic)	Locke, Hume, learning theories	Development = quantitative change of behavior (based on learning processes), no end state suggested, life-long development	Active environment (stimuli and reinforcements from environment). Individual is seen as passive	Single-subject designs, learning experiments	Course of development is changeable by new learning experiences
Organismic	Leibniz, Darwin	Development = (relatively) uniform, goal-directed change in form, structure, and organization of behavior (e.g. toward higher stages, differentiation and integration). Models are often restricted to development in childhood and adolescence	Individuals are seen as active, interaction of maturation and experience. Specific assumptions in single theories	Cross-sectional studies	Limited latitude of change (plasticity)
Dialectic	Hegel, Marx, Darwin	Development = an open process leading from one form of contradiction to a new one. Life-long development	Conflicts as source of development. Interaction between individual activity and sociocultural environment	Study of change (e.g. longitudinal research), cross-cultural research, cohort-sequential research	Stimulation of conflicts and individual activity for conflict solving

continues overleaf

Table 5.1 continued

Concept/ model	Main scientific roots	Definition of development	Proposed influences on development	Suggested research methodology	Consequences of intervention
Contextual	Peirce, Mead, Darwin	Development = an open process (differential development). Life-long development	Changing relations between biological, psychological, and social processes	Longitudinal research, measures at multiple levels (biology, behavior, environment), cross-cultural research, person-centered approach	Diverse starting points of interventions (at biological, psychological, and social level), results of interventions are difficult to anticipate
Life-span approach	Tetens, Carus, Quetelet, Darwin	Development = life-long multidirectional process containing gains and losses. Relatively open process (but decline of plasticity in old age)	Interplay of biology, environment (culture), and individual activity	Longitudinal and cohort-sequential studies across the whole life-span	Multilevel interventions (e.g. training of competence in old age, environmental change, genetic engineering)
Developmental systems approach	Peirce, Mead, Darwin, Schneirla (Prigogine, Werner)	Development = change in the dynamic organization of variables between and within systems of development (e.g. genes, neurobiological processes, behavior, environment), probabilistic (open) process, life-long process	Interplay of biology, environment, and individual activity. Individuals as co-constructors of their development	Longitudinal studies, measures at multiple levels (biology, behavior, environment), person-centered approach	Multilevel interventions (e.g. training of competence, environmental change, programs for promotion of positive development)

psychological processes, and changing social contexts. Complex statistical methods, such as structural equation or growth curve modelling, are required for testing reciprocal relationships of variables over time. Similarly, cross-cultural research is suggested for the study of the impact of culture on individual development. Further, the focus on interindividual variability in developmental processes calls for a person-centered, holistic approach of data analysis, rather than studying average associations between variables across the whole population (Magnusson, 1999). As the complexity of factors that may influence human development is probably too high to be measured within one study, it is necessary to reduce the complexity, for example, by focusing on two contexts, as is the case with cohort-sequential designs (Schaie & Baltes, 1975). The life-span focus of developmental psychology not only calls for longitudinal research on adulthood and old age, but also for long-term longitudinal studies that follow individuals from (early) childhood to (very) old age. For example, studies that were originally focused on a smaller time interval (such as childhood and adolescence) have been continued or resumed into old age (e.g. Friedman, Tucker, & Schwartz, 1995).

Concepts of human development have also important implications for psychosocial interventions. Such interventions may be directed toward the reduction or amelioration of developmental problems (e.g. promoting the trajectory from a maladaptive pathway back to a better adjusted developmental path), the prevention of problems from occurring, and the promotion of positive, healthy development.

According to the mechanistic model, psychological development was considered as highly malleable by new learning experiences, so that providing new learning experiences is an adequate intervention (e.g. training of competence in retarded children, classroom management to reinforce students' adaptive behavior, parental training for improving competence to raise children; Bijou, 1992). According to stage theories, the latitude of intervention-based change is seen as restricted, so that interventions could only slightly speed up normative progression, or help reach the developmental stage expected by the age of the respondent. These theories usually considered one dominant form of intervention, as one central factor was proposed as causing development (e.g. promoting cognitive conflicts of an optimal intensity as a means for increasing the level of cognitive or moral development; e.g. Piaget, 1975). Similar to cognitive stage theories, dialectic models of development suggest the promotion of (dialectic) conflicts as modes for intervention, although the result of the intervention is seen as relatively open and less predictable.

Life-span developmental approaches would suggest interventions across the whole life-span, such as interventions to improve competence or changes in the environment of the developing individual. As some age-associated declines and forms of illness that emerge in old age seem difficult to influence with traditional forms of intervention, it may even be necessary to think about gene insertions in sex cells or embryos to correct hereditary diseases or genetic risk factors for impaired individual development (Baltes, 1997).

Contextualistic and developmental systems approaches suggest that interventions can happen at all levels or systems that are involved in a particular behavior (e.g. on the level of genes, neurobiological processes, behavior, or environment), also some systems may be more open to change than others. Because interventions mesh in a complex interplay of variables, the relationship between intervention and outcomes is a probabilistic one. As developmental systems include biological, psychological, and social processes, interventions may presuppose the cooperation of specialists from these fields. Because change at one level is expected to influence changes at other levels, developmental systems approaches also recommend multilevel interventions. For example, as preventing or correcting negative development would not be sufficient to promote healthy, competent development and success in life, researchers and practitioners are increasingly interested in interventions aimed at promoting positive development. These programs intervene at the psychological (behavioral) level, for instance, by helping to develop positive values and social competencies, as well as at the social–environmental level, for example by stimulating positive family communication, building supportive neighbourhoods, giving people useful roles in the community, and promoting constructive use of time (Catalano, Berglund, Ryan, Lonczak, & Hawkins, 2002).

In this chapter we focused on the history of the concept of individual development (ontogeny). Thus, the conceptual history of related concepts, such as phylogeny, were beyond our scope. Similarly, we could not characterize conceptual and theoretical advances in individual fields of developmental psychology, such as cognitive development or social development. Nonetheless, the present chapter shows how philosophical and scientific views about human development were elaborated and applied in the field of developmental psychology, how different concepts about development relate to each other, and how these conceptualizations of individual development relate to specific research methodologies and strategies for psychosocial intervention.

References

Baer, D. M. (1970). An age-irrelevant concept of development. *Merrill-Palmer Quarterly, 16*, 238–245.

Baldwin, J. M. (1895). *Mental development in the child and the race*. New York: Macmillan.

Baldwin, J. M. (1915). *Genetic theory of reality, being the outcome of genetic logic, as issuing in the aesthetic theory of reality called pancalism*. New York: Putnam.

Baltes, P. B. (1979). Entwicklungspsychologie unter dem Aspekt der gesamten Lebensspanne: Einige Bemerkungen zur Geschichte und Theorie. [Developmental psychology from a life-span perspective: Some comments regarding history and theory]. In L. Montada (Ed.), *Brennpunkte der Entwicklungspsychologie* (pp. 42–60). Stuttgart: Kohlhammer.

Baltes, P. B. (1987). Theoretical propositions of life-span developmental psychology: On the dynamics between growth and decline. *Developmental Psychology, 23,* 611–626.

Baltes, P. B. (1997). On the incomplete architecture of human ontogeny: Selection, optimization, and compensation as foundation of developmental theory. *American Psychologist, 52,* 366–380.

Baltes, P. B., & Baltes, M. M. (1980). Psychological perspectives on successful aging: The model of selective optimization with compensation. In P. B. Baltes & M. M. Baltes (Eds.), *Successful aging: Perspectives from the behavioral sciences* (pp. 1–34). New York: Cambridge University Press.

Bijou, S. W. (1992). Behavior analysis. In R. Vasta (Ed.), *Six theories of child development: Revised formulations and current issues* (pp. 61–83). London: Kingsley.

Bijou, S. W., & Baer, D. M. (1961). *Child development: A systemic and empirical theory* (Vol. 1). New York: Appleton-Century-Crofts.

Bronfenbrenner, U. (1979). *The ecology of human development.* Cambridge, MA: Harvard University Press.

Bronfenbrenner, U. (1986). Ecology of the family as a context for human development. *Developmental Psychology, 22,* 723–742.

Bronfenbrenner, U. (1999). Environments in developmental perspective: Theoretical and operational models. In S. L. Friedman & T. D. Wachs (Eds.), *Measuring environment across the life span: Emerging methods and concepts* (pp. 3–28). Washington, DC: American Psychological Association.

Bronfenbrenner, U., & Morris, P. A. (1998). The ecology of developmental processes. In R. M. Lerner (Ed.), *Handbook of child psychology* (5th ed., Vol. 1, pp. 993–1028). New York: Wiley.

Bühler, C. (1933). *Der menschliche Lebenslauf als psychologisches Problem* [Human life course as psychological problem]. Leipzig: Hirzel.

Busemann, A. (1927). Die Erregungsphasen der Jugend [Excitement stages in adolescence]. *Zeitschrift für Kinderforschung, 33,* 115–137.

Cairns, R. B. (1998). The making of developmental psychology. In W. Damon & R. M. Lerner (Eds.), *Handbook of child development* (Vol. 1, pp. 25–106). New York: Wiley.

Carus, F. A. (1808). *Psychologie. Zweiter Teil: Spezialpsychologie.* [Psychology. Second part: Special psychology]. Leipzig: Barth & Kummer.

Catalano, R. F., Berglund, M. L., Ryan, J. A., Lonczak, H. S., & Hawkins, J. D. (2002). Positive youth development in the United States: Research findings on evaluations of positive youth development programs. *Prevention & Treatment, 5,* 1–104.

Cicchetti, D., & Cohen, D. J. (1999). Perspectives on developmental psychopathology. In D. Ciccetti & D. J. Cohen (Eds.), *Developmental psychopathology* (Vol. 1, pp. 3–20). New York: Wiley.

Colby, A., Kohlberg, L., Gibbs, J., & Lieberman, M. (1983). A longitudinal study of moral judgement. *Monographs of the Society for Research in Child Development, 48,* 1–124.

Darwin, C. (1859). *The origin of species by means of natural selection or the preservation of favoured races in the struggle for life.* London: Murray.

Darwin, C. (1871). *Descent of men.* London: Murray.

Darwin, C. (1872). *The expression of emotions in man and animals.* London: Murray.

Eckensberger, L., & Silbereisen, R. K. (1980). Handlungstheoretische Perspektiven für die Entwicklungspsychologie: Soziale Kognition [Action theoretical perspectives of developmental psychology: Social cognition]. In L. Eckensberger & R. K. Silbereisen (Eds.), *Entwicklung sozialer Kognitionen* (pp. 11–45). Stuttgart: Klett-Cotta.

Erikson, E. H. (1959). Identity and the life cycle. *Psychological Issues, 1,* 50–100.

Erikson, E. H., Erikson, J. M., & Kivnick, H. Q. (1989). *Vital involvement in old age: The experience of old age in our time.* New York: Norton.

Evans, E. M. (2001). Cognitive and contextual factors in the emergence of diverse belief systems: Creation versus evolution. *Cognitive Psychology, 42,* 217–266.

Ford, D. H., & Lerner, R. M. (1992). *Developmental systems theory.* Newbury Park, CA: Sage.

Freud, S. (1905). *Drei Abhandlungen zur Sexualtheorie* [Three contributions to the sexual theory]. Leipzig: Franz Deuticke.

Freud, S. (1917). *Allgemeine Neurosenlehre* [General teaching about neuroses]. Leipzig: Heller.

Freud, S. (1923/1960). *The ego and the id.* New York: Norton.

Friedman, H. S., Tucker, J. S., & Schwartz, J. E. (1995). Psychosocial and behavioral predictors of longevity: The aging and death of the "Termites". *American Psychologist, 50,* 69–78.

Gesell, A. (1940). *The first five years of life.* New York: Harper & Row.

Gesell, A. (1946). The ontogenesis of infant behavior. In L. Carmichael (Ed.), *Manual of child psychology* (pp. 295–331). New York: Wiley.

Gesell, A. (1948). *Studies in child development.* Westport, CT: Greenwood.

Gesell, A. (1954). The ontogenesis of infant behavior. In L. Carmichael (Ed.), *Manual of child psychology* (pp. 335–373). New York: Wiley.

Ghisletta, P., & Lindenberger, U. (2003). Age-based structural dynamics between perceptual speed and knowledge in the Berlin Aging Study: Direct evidence for ability dedifferentiation in old age. *Psychology and Aging, 18,* 696–713.

Goethe, J. W. (1790/1998). *Versuch die Metamorphose der Pflanzen zu erklären* [Attempt to explain the methamorphosis of plants]. Hermannsburg: Albers.

Gottlieb, G. (1970). Conceptions of prenatal behavior. In L. R. Anderson, E. Tobach, D. S. Lehrman, & J. S. Rosenblatt (Eds.), *Development and evolution of behavior* (pp. 111–137). San Francisco, CA: Freeman.

Gottlieb, G. (1991). Experiential canalization of behavioral development: Theory. *Developmental Psychology, 27,* 4–13.

Gottlieb, G. (2002). *Individual development and evolution.* Mahwah, NJ: Lawrence Erlbaum Associates, Inc.

Gould, S. J. (1977). *Ontogeny and phylogeny.* Cambridge, MA: Harvard University Press.

Hall, G. S. (1883). The contents of children's minds. *Princeton Review, 2,* 249–272.

Hall, G. S. (1904). *Adolescence.* New York: Appleton.

Haeckel, E. (1868). *Natürliche Schöpfungsgeschichte: Gemeinverständliche wissenschaftliche Vorträge über die Entwicklungslehre im allgemeinen und diejenige von Darwin, Goethe und Lamarck im Besonderen* [The history of creation: scientific papers about general developmental theory, and the theories of Darwin, Goethe, and Lamarck in particular]. Berlin: Reimer.

Harris, D. B. (1943). Relationships among play interests and delinquency in boys. *American Journal of Orthopsychiatry, 13,* 631–638.

Havighurst, R. J. (1948). *Developmental tasks and education.* New York: David McKay.

Heckhausen, J., Wrosch, C., & Fleeson, W. (2001). Developmental regulation before and after a developmental deadline: The sample case of "biological clock" for childbearing. *Psychology & Aging, 16,* 400–413.

Hollingworth, H. L. (1927). *Mental growth and decline: A survey of developmental psychology.* New York: Appleton.

Holt, E. B. (1931). *Animal drive and learning process.* New York: Holt.

James, W. (1890). *The principles of psychology* (Vol 1). New York: Dover.

Kohlberg, L. (1958). *The development of modes of moral thinking and choice in the years ten to sixteen.* Unpublished doctoral dissertation. University of Chicago.

Kohlberg, L. (1976). Moral stages and moralization: The cognitive–developmental approach. In T. Lickona (Ed.), *Moral development and behavior: Theory, research, and social issues* (pp. 31–53). New York: Holt, Rinehart & Winston.

Kroh, O. (1922). *Subjektive Anschauungsbilder bei Jugendlichen* [Subjective opinions of adolescents]. Göttingen: Vandenhoek & Ruprecht.

Kuo, Z. Y. (1976). *The dynamics of behavior development.* New York: Plenum.

Langer, J. (1970). Werner's comparative organismic theory. In P. H. Mussen (Ed.), *Carmichael's manual of child psychology* (Vol. 1, pp. 733–772). New York: Wiley.

Lerner, R. M. (1995). The place of learning within the human development system: A developmental contextual perspective. *Human Development, 38,* 361–366.

Lerner, R. M. (2002). *Concepts and theories of human development.* Mahwah, NJ: Lawrence Erlbaum Associates Inc.

Lersch, P. (1938). *Der Aufbau des Charakters* [The construction of character]. Leipzig: Barth.

Li, S.-C. (2003). Biocultural orchestration of developmental plasticity across levels: The interplay of biology and culture in shaping the mind and behavior across the life span. *Psychological Bulletin, 129,* 171–194.

Lorenz, K. (1935). Der Kumpan in der Umwelt des Vogels [The mate in the bird's environment]. *Journal für Ornithologie, 83,* 137–213.

Luria, A. R. (1976). *Cognitive development: Its cultural and social foundations.* Cambridge, MA: Harvard University Press.

Loevinger, J. (1997). Stages of personality development. In R. Hogan & J. A. Johnson (Eds.), *Handbook of personality psychology* (pp. 199–208). San Diego, CA: Academic Press.

Magnusson, D. (1999). Holistic interactionism: A perspective for research on personality development. In L. A. Pervin & O. P. John (Eds.), *Handbook of personality: Theory and research* (pp. 219–247). New York: Guilford.

Montada, L. (2003). Fragen, Konzepte, Perspektiven [Questions, concepts, perspectives]. In R. Oerter & L. Montada (Eds.), *Entwicklungspsychologie* (pp. 3–53). Weinheim: Beltz.

Nelson, C., Bloom, F. E., Ameral, D., Cameron, J. L., & Pine, D. (2002). An integrative, multidisciplinary approach to the study of brain-behavior relations in the context of typical and atypical development. *Development & Psychopathology, 14,* 499–520.

Overton, W. F. (1984). World views and their influence on psychological theory and research: Kuhn–Lakatos–Lauden. In H. W. Reese (Ed.), *Advances in child development and behaviour* (Vol. 18, pp. 194–226). New York: Academic Press.

Padover, S. K. (1978). *The essential Marx: The non-economic writings.* New York: New American Library.

Pascual-Leone, J., & Johnson, J. (1999). A dialectical constructivist view of representation: Role of mental attention, executives, and symbols. In I. E. Sigel (Ed.), *Development of mental representation: Theories and applications* (pp. 169–200). Mahwah, NJ: Lawrence Erlbaum Associates Inc.

Peirce, C. (1992). The doctrine of necessity examined. In N. Houser & C. Kloesel (Eds.), *The essential Peirce: Selected philosophical writings 1867–1893* (Vol. 1, pp. 298–311). Bloomington, IN: Indiana University Press.

Pepper, S. C. (1942). *World hypotheses: A study in evidence.* Berkeley, CA: University of California Press.

Peters, R. S. (Ed.). (1965). *Brett's history of psychology.* Cambridge, MA: MIT Press.

Piaget, J. (1950). *Introduction à l'épistémologie génétique.* Paris: Presses Universitaires de France.

Piaget, J. (1955). Perceptual and cognitive (or operational) structures in the development of the concept of space in the child. *Acta Psychologica, 11,* 41–46.

Piaget, J. (1970). *Science of education and the psychology of the child.* Trans. D. Coltman. Oxford: Orion.

Piaget, J. (1975). *L'équilibration des structures cognitives.* Paris: Presses Universitaires de France.

Pinquart, M., & Silbereisen, R. K. (2004). Human development in times of social change: Theoretical considerations and research needs. *International Journal of Behavioral Development, 28,* 289–298.

Plomin, R. (1986). *Development, genetics, and psychology.* Hillsdale, NJ: Lawrence Erlbaum Associates Inc.

Pressey, S. L., Janney, J. E., & Kuhlen, R. G. (1939). *Life: A psychological survey.* New York: Harper.

Prigogine, I. (1978). Time, structure, and fluctuation. *Science, 201,* 777–785.

Quetelet, A. (1835). *Sur l'homme et le développement de ses facultés* [On men and the development of his faculties]. Paris: Bachelier.

Reese, H. W., & Overton, W. F. (1970). Models of development and theories of development. In L. R. Goulet & P. B. Baltes (Eds.), *Life-span developmental psychology* (pp. 115–145). New York: Academic Press.

Reinert, G. (1976). Grundzüge einer Geschichte der Entwicklungspsychologie [Essential features of the history of developmental psychology]. In H. Ballmer (Hrsg.), *Die Psychologie des 20. Jahrhunderts* (Vol. 1, pp. 862–896). Zürich: Kindler.

Richards, R. J. (1982). Darwin and the biologizing of moral behavior. In W. R. Woodward & M. G. Ash (Eds.), *The problematic science: Psychology in nineteenth-century thought* (pp. 43–64). New York: Praeger.

Riegel, K. (1975a). Toward a dialectical theory of development. *Human Development, 18,* 50–64.

Riegel, K. (1975b). From traits and equilibrium toward developmental dialectics. In W. J. Arnold (Ed.), *Nebraska symposium on motivation* (pp. 349–407). Lincoln, NE: University of Nebraska Press.

Riegel, K. (1976). The dialectics of human development. *American Psychologist, 31,* 689–700.

Rousseau, J. J. (1762). *Emile ou de l'éducation.* Amsterdam: Néaulme.

Rowe, D. C. (1994). *The limits of family influence: Genes, experience, and behavior.* New York: Guilford.

Schaffer, H. R. (2000). The early experience assumption: Past, present, and future. *International Journal of Behavioral Development, 24,* 5–14.

Schaie, K. W., & Baltes, P. B. (1975). On sequential strategies in developmental research: Description or explanation. *Human Development, 18,* 384–390.

Schmidt, H. D. (1970). *Allgemeine Entwicklungspsychologie* [General developmental psychology]. Berlin: Deutscher Verlag der Wissenschaften.

Schneirla, T. C. (1957). The concept of development in comparative psychology. In D. B. Harris (Ed.), *The concept of development: An issue in the study of human behavior* (pp. 78–108). Minneapolis, MN: University of Minnesota Press.

Sears, R. R., Maccoby, E. E., & Levin, H. (1957). *Patterns of child rearing.* Evanston, IL: Row Petterson & Co.

Sham, P. (2003). Recent developments in quantitative trait loci analysis. In R. Plomin & J. C. De Fries (Eds.), *Behavioral genetics in the postgenomic era* (pp. 41–54). Washington, DC: American Psychological Association.

Siegert, F. (1891). *Die Periodicität in der Entwicklung der Kindesnatur: Neue Gesichtspunkte für Kinderforschung und Jugenderziehung* [Periodicity in child's nature: New aspects for child research and youth education]. Leipzig: Voigtländer.

Skinner, B. F. (1938). *The behavior of organisms.* New York: Appleton.

Skinner, B. F. (1966). The ontogeny and phylogeny of behavior. *Science, 153,* 1205–1215.

Skinner, B. F. (1974). *About behaviorism.* New York: Random House.

Spencer, H. (1852, 1891). Developmental hypothesis. In H. Spencer (Ed.), *Essays, scientific, political & speculative* (pp. 1–7). London: Williams and Norgate.

Spencer, H. (1862). *First principles.* London: Williams and Norgate.

Super, C. M., & Harkness, S. (1986). The developmental niche: A conceptualization of the interface of child and culture. *International Journal of Behavioral Development, 9,* 545–569.

Super, C. M., & Harkness, S. (2002). Culture structures the environment for development. *Human Development, 45,* 270–274.

Tetens, J. N. (1777). *Philosophische Versuche über die menschliche Natur und ihre Entwicklung* [Philosophical experiments about human nature and its development]. Leipzig: Weidemanns Erben und Reich.

Thelen, E., & Smith, L. B. (1994). *A dynamic systems approach to the development of cognition and action.* Cambridge, MA: MIT Press.

Thiele, R. (1940). *Person und Character* [Person and character]. Leipzig: Thieme.

Thomas, A., & Chess, S. (1977). *Temperament and development.* New York: Brunner/Mazel.

Thorndike, E. L. (1904). The newest psychology. *Educational Review, 28,* 217–227.

Tobach, E., & Greenberg, G. (1984). The significance of T. C. Schneirla's contribution to the concept of levels of integration. In G. Greenberg & E. Tobach (Eds.), *Behavioral evolution and integrative levels* (pp. 1–7). Hillsdale, NJ: Lawrence Erlbaum Associates Inc.

Valsiner, J. (1998). The development of the concept of development: Historical and epistemological perspectives. In W. Damon & R. M. Lerner (Eds.), *Handbook of child development* (Vol. 1, pp. 189–232). New York: Wiley.

van Geert, P. (1998). We almost had a great future behind us: The contribution of non-linear dynamics to developmental-science-in-the-making. *Developmental Science, 1*, 143–159.

von Baer, K. E. (1828, 1837). *Über Entwickelungsgeschichte der Thiere: Beobachtung und Reflexion. Erster + Zweiter Theil* [On the developmental history of animals: Observation and reflection. First + second part]. Königsberg.

Vygotsky, L. S. (1933). Play and its role in the mental development of the child. *Voprosy Psikhologii, 12*, 62–76 (in Russian).

Waddington, C. H. (1942). Canalization in development and the inheritance of acquired characters. *Nature, 150*, 563–564.

Wapner, S., & Demick, J. (1998). Developmental analysis: A holistic, developmental, systems-oriented perspective. In W. Damon (Ed.), *Handbook of child psychology* (Vol. 1, pp. 761–805). New York: Wiley.

Watson, J. B. (1913). Psychology as the behaviorist views it. *Psychological Review, 20*, 158–177.

Watson, J. B. (1924). *Behaviorism*. Chicago: Chicago University Press.

Werner, H. (1957). The concept of development from a comparative and organismic point of view. In D. B. Harris (Ed.), *The concept of development* (pp. 125–147). Minneapolis, MN: University of Minnesota Press.

Wertsch, J. V., & Tulviste, P. (1992). L. S. Vygotsky and contemporary developmental psychology. *Developmental Psychology, 28*, 548–557.

Wozniak, R. H. (1975). A dialectic paradigm for psychological research: Implications drawn from the history of psychology in the Soviet Union. *Human Development, 18*, 18–34.

Zigler, E. (1963). Metatheoretical issues in developmental psychology. In M. H. Marx (Ed.), *Theories in contemporary psychology* (pp. 341–369). New York: Macmillan.

6 Passion and *qing*: Intellectual histories of emotion, West and East

James R. Averill and Louise Sundararajan

Histories of emotion are of two kinds: The first explores emotions as lived in everyday life (e.g. Stearns, 2000); the second, which is the focus of this chapter, explores ideas about emotions, that is, explicit theories and teachings. Theories about emotions are not always congruent with the way emotions are experienced. It is reasonable to assume, however, that over time a dialectical relation exists between ideas and realities of emotion, such that each helps shape the other (Parkinson, 1995).

Given that the focus of the chapter is on the history of ideas, the question arises: Whose ideas? We juxtapose the history of Western thought about emotion with an equally venerable tradition—East Asian, particularly Chinese. Paranjpe (2002) has noted a twofold gap when comparisons are made between non-Western ("indigenous") and contemporary Western ("scientific") approaches to psychology. First, indigenous approaches typically draw on ancient texts and traditions, which are often dismissed as irrelevant to a modern, empirically based science. Second, indigenous approaches are more closely allied with the humanities than with the sciences. We try to bridge these two gaps by drawing on ancient as well as modern texts, and on literary as well as scientific traditions.

We review, first, the ways emotions have been conceived at different periods of Western history, from ancient Greece to modern times; we then survey Chinese history over a similar span of time. Our purpose in juxtaposing these two histories is not simply to add an international flavor to the chapter but rather, by mapping the development of thought without limitations imposed by time or geography, to provide a potent catalyst for new ideas and approaches. We therefore conclude the chapter by describing six antinomies of emotion—seemingly conflicting ideas that might help set the stage for a history of emotion in the twenty-first century.

Western theories of emotion

We divide the Western history of ideas about emotion into four epochs: The classical age of Greece and Rome, beginning around the fifth century before the Christian era (BCE); the medieval period, from about 400 to

1500; the early modern period, beginning with the Renaissance and scientific revolution; and the twentieth century, following the founding of psychology as a scientific discipline. This is not to suggest that our knowledge of emotions has progressed in a linear fashion, from ancient to modern times. On the contrary: Similar themes recur throughout history, albeit in different guises. We focus on a few of those recurrent themes. Our intent is not to be complete, which would be impossible in a short chapter. We review just enough theories to provide a Gestalt of Western ideas about emotion. If the Gestalt has good form (*Prägnanz*), closure might be possible despite inevitable gaps.

Western concepts of emotion

Western history represents more than a temporal sequence; it also involves changes in language, geography, religion, and cultural orientation. This diversity is reflected in the terms that have been used to denote emotions.

The ancient Greek term for emotion was *pathē*, which could refer to any object, animate or inanimate, that was undergoing ("suffering")—change through the action of an external agent. A rock, for example, could suffer the blow of a hammer. Emotions in the contemporary sense were one category of *pathē* a person might suffer; diseases were another category. Hence, from *pathē* we get such medical terms as "pathology", "pathogen", and "idiopathy", as well as such emotional terms as "pathetic", "empathy", and "antipathy".

A strict Latin rendering of *pathē* would be *morbos*, literally, "disease". However, Cicero (106–43 BCE), who was one of the persons most responsible for transmitting Greek thought to the Roman world, rejected such a literal translation (Lang, 1972). He considered the more turbulent emotions to be disorders of the soul (*perturbationes animi*) and not disease in a strict sense. Nevertheless, a variation on the Greek root became common, namely, *passio* (from the past participle of the Latin verb *pati*, which means to suffer). Hence, the emotions, or at least the more turbulent emotions, came to be knows as "passions".

Another Latin term for emotion was *affectus*, from which we get the modern English term "affect". Historically, "affect" and its cognates had a more inclusive and positive connotation than "passion" and its cognates.

Turning to modern European languages, emotion and its cognates are commonly used in French and German as well as English, particularly in the psychological literature. Etymologically, emotion stems from the Latin, *e + movere*, which originally meant to move out, to migrate, or to transport an object. Metaphorically, it was sometimes used to describe physical conditions, such as turbulent weather, or psychological states involving turmoil. It did not, however, become a common term for human emotions until about the middle of the eighteenth century.

In French, *sentiment* also refers to emotional phenomena generally, with a connotation similar to the English "feeling". The French term *émotion* refers primarily to less cultured emotions that humans might share with infrahuman animals. In German, *Gefühl* and *Emotion* are common lay terms that correspond roughly to "feeling" and "emotion". *Affekt* and, occasionally, *Gemütsbewegung* are also found in the psychological literature. For related terms in other Indo-European languages, see Buck (1949).

The above terminological differences reflect more than multiple ways of expressing the same concept; they also reflect subtle differences in connotation and theoretical implication. Therefore, although we use "emotion" in a generic sense to denote the broad and heterogeneous class that includes such states as anger, fear, love, sympathy, and the like, we also indicate the more specific terms used by an author when a difference in connotation is implied.

The classical period: The primacy of reason

Perhaps the most notable characteristic of the classical period was a questioning attitude, epitomized by Socrates, and a conviction that the world could be understood through rational inquiry. Of course, not everyone shared this view, as the antics of Greek gods amply attests, not to mention the fact that Socrates was condemned to death in 399 BCE, ostensibly for casting doubt on the gods and corrupting the youth of Athens through his questioning. Nevertheless, theories of emotions (*pathē*) during this period can only be understood against the backdrop of generally high esteem accorded reason.

We owe to Plato (427–347 BCE), Socrates's most illustrious disciple, one of the most enduring images of the relation between emotion and reason. In the *Phaedrus* (pp. 246b, 253d, trans. 1961), Plato imaged a charioteer (Reason) attempting to control two unruly steeds, each representing a different class of emotion. One steed, the "spirited emotions" epitomized by anger, guarded against threats to the self, either from enemies without or impulses from within; if not reined in, however, this steed could itself usurp reason's authority. The other steed represented the baser passions (sex, greed, etc.), which also need the guidance of reason lest they threaten the good of the whole. It is an image that evokes not only the supremacy of reason, but of inherent intrapsychic conflict. A similar image was invoked over two millennia later by Freud, with the ego serving as charioteer, and the superego and id as the two steeds.

In a manner less allegorical, but still for reasons more symbolic than factual (Averill, 1974), Plato localized rational thought in the head, the spirited emotions in the region about the heart, and the baser passions in the torso below the midriff, as far from reason as they could be.

Like Plato, Aristotle (ca. 384–322 BCE) envisioned a threefold division of the psyche; unlike Plato, he interpreted the psyche in a more naturalistic fashion, specifically, as the capacity of a living body to engage in certain activities. To use one of Aristotle's own analogies, if the eye had a psyche, its psyche would be seeing. Each organism has a psyche appropriate to its kind. Plants, for example, have the capacity to grow and reproduce; animals have, in addition, the capacity to perceive and move about; and humans have the capacity for rational thought.

The emotions are "located" in the sensitive faculty, common to humans and infrahuman animals. Aristotle's most general definition of emotion was simply "feelings accompanied by pleasure or pain" (*Nicomachean ethics*, 1105b21, trans. 1947). Of course, not all pleasures are alike; nor are all pains—different emotions arise depending on the eliciting event and the corresponding response. For example, anger is "an impulse, accompanied by pain, to a conspicuous revenge for a conspicuous slight directed without justification towards what concerns oneself or towards what concerns one's friends" (*Rhetoric*, 1378a30, trans. 1941).

The emotions have their proper place—according to Aristotle—provided they are experienced in moderation and in accordance with reason:

> For instance, both fear and confidence and appetite and anger and pity and in general pleasure and pain may be felt both too much and too little, and in both cases not well; but to feel them at the right times, with reference to the right objects, towards the right people, with the right motive, and in the right way, is what is both intermediate and best, and this is characteristic of virtue
>
> (*Nicomachean ethics*, 1106b20, trans. 1947)

It is clear that Aristotle left the relation between emotion and reason ambiguous. On the one hand, the emotions are treated as automatic responses to provocations that are perceived intuitively, at the sensory level of the psyche. On the other hand, as the above quotations suggest, emotions are inextricably linked to "higher" thought processes.

The above ambiguity was resolved by the Stoics. Stoicism was founded by Zeno of Citium (c. 340–265 BCE) and was named after the open colonnade (*stoa*) in Athens where he taught. Stoicism flourished for over 500 years, ultimately becoming the dominant civic philosophy of the Roman Empire. Much of the writings of the early Stoics have been lost, so we draw here primarily on the work of the Roman Stoic, Lucius Annaeus Seneca (4 BCE–65 CE).

The Stoics rejected the Platonic and Aristotelian division of the human psyche into parts; rather, they conceived it to be unitary, characterized by reason. This meant that the emotions, too, must be part of the rational faculty. Or, as Seneca put it, reason and passion are not distinct, but are "only the transformation of the mind toward the better or worse" (Seneca, *On anger*, I. viii. 3). Take anger: "while it is the foe of reason, it is nevertheless born only where reason dwells" (Seneca, *On anger*, I. iii. 4). And so it is with the other emotions. Only a being capable of making correct (rational) judgments is susceptible to false judgments; and emotions are just that—false judgments. It follows that the emotions are not commendable in moderation, as Aristotle asserted. To say that it is acceptable to be moderately emotional is equivalent to saying that it is acceptable to be moderately wrong. For the Stoics, emotions were literally pathologies of the mind. To the extent possible, they should be cured, not moderated. The ways such "cures" might be effected compare favorably to contemporary cognitive–behavioral therapies (Nussbaum, 1994).

Among the objections to the Stoic thesis that emotions are "born only where reason dwells" is the fact that dumb animals and children before the age of reason seem to show signs of emotion; so, too, do Stoic philosophers when confronted, say, with life-threatening danger, even though such philosophers have presumably learned to refrain from making irrational judgments.

To defend the notion that emotions are (irrational) judgments, Seneca— following the lead of earlier Stoics—made a historically important distinction between two kinds of assessment: (1) an initial appraisal that a thing is good or bad; and (2) a secondary appraisal that it is appropriate to react, either overtly or covertly, to that initial assessment. Fear, for example, involves an assessment that (1) danger threatens and that (2) it is appropriate to avoid the danger. The initial assessment might lead to a "first movement", such as pallor or trembling; this automatic reaction is, however, preliminary to the emotion itself, which involves the additional assessment that one should flee.

Lest this answer appears to beg the question, note that some contemporary theories observe a similar distinction, but make the opposite identification. That is, the real emotion is identified with an immediate reaction that may last for only moments; subsequent cognitive elaborations leading to coping responses are dismissed as secondary elaborations. This reconceptualization of "first movements" as the real emotions has obvious implications for theories of emotion.

The medieval period: Volition rivals reason

The medieval period reflects the confluence of two main streams of thought, Greco-Roman and Judeo-Christian. The merger was not easy. As described above, the Greeks and Romans generally considered reason to be the regnant faculty of the human mind. The Judeo-Christian tradition placed greater value on faith in god as revealed by the scripture. The idea that human reason is capable of comprehending an omniscient god was considered by early Christians as akin to blasphemy; yet, people of good will might believe or have faith in that which they could not fully comprehend. The will was thus elevated to a status commensurate with reason, although it, too, was recognized as limited. People cannot always do what they will, any more than they can rationally comprehend what they believe: Ultimately, faith depends on the grace of god.

The shift from the classical to medieval world views is well illustrated by the altered conception of "first movements". Recall that the Stoics denied that initial stirrings to a provocative stimulus (e.g. pallor when faced with danger) were emotions *per se*; rather, they became emotions only when given assent. Under the influence of early church fathers, first movements became temptations, incipient emotions in their own right.

The early medieval period is best epitomized by St Augustine's (354–430) entreaty to god: "Grant me chastity and continency—but not yet" (*Confessions*, VIII, 7, trans. 1948). Augustine recognized a broad class of emotional phenomena—the affections (*affectiones*)—of which the passions are a subcategory. It is appropriate to experience affections, he argued, provided they are appropriately directed. Referring to the Stoic ideal of imperturbability, Augustine suggested that people who "are not roused or stirred, moved or swayed by any emotion (*affectu*) at all, . . . rather suffer a total loss of humanity than attain true tranquility. For it does not follow that if a thing is hard, it must be right, or that if it is inert, it must be healthy" (*The city of God*, XIV, ix, trans. 1966). Only the subset of affections called passions are contrary to nature and hence to be avoided.

It is to Augustine that we owe what is called the "principle of interiorization", namely, that the soul has direct knowledge of itself: "Seek not abroad, turn back into thy self, for in the inner man dwells the truth" (*De vera religione*, cited by Ellenberger, 1970, p. 450). As far as the emotions are concerned, when Augustine turned inward, what he found was seemingly unfathomable: "Man is a great deep, Lord. You number his very hairs and they are not lost in your sight: but the hairs of his head are easier to number than his affections and the movements of his heart" (*Confessions*, IV, 14, trans. 1948).

How might the multiplicity of emotions be reduced to a more manageable number, one easily grasped by humans? Earlier, the Stoics had addressed this question by recognizing four fundamental emotions: desire, joy, fear, and grief. Augustine went a step further and reduced these four to a single underlying principle: love (*amor*): "[T]he love that is bent on obtaining the object of its love is desire, while the love that possesses and enjoys its object is joy; the love that avoids what confronts it is fear, and the love that feels it when it strikes is grief" (*The city of God*, XIV, vii, trans. 1966). The goal of reducing various emotions to the vicissitudes of an underlying drive or motivational force has been a recurrent theme in Western theories of emotion. We will meet it again, for example, in the *conatus* of Spinoza and the libido of Freud.

Augustine's life coincided roughly with the disintegration of the Roman Empire in the West. The ensuing middle ages have been described by some historians (e.g. Elias, 1978) as a period of emotional instability and the uninhibited expression of primitive impulses, reflecting a harsh and precarious existence. Other historians (e.g. Rosenwein, 1998) have questioned this interpretation, noting that emotions that seem "uncivilized" by modern standards were actually well attuned to and helped reinforce the political culture of the time. Be that as it may, by the thirteenth century, the political and intellectual climate of Europe was beginning to change, as reflected in the writings of St Thomas Aquinas (1225–1274). It was largely through Aquinas that the work of Aristotle was reintroduced to the Latin West, initially under the influence of Arabic sources.

Like Aristotle, Aquinas recognized three levels of the soul: the intellectual (uniquely human), sensitive (common to human and animals), and vegetative (common also to plants). The sensitive level included not only the ability to perceive objects but also to intuit their potential for benefit or harm, and to respond accordingly. To illustrate the process, Aquinas used the example of a lamb frightened by a wolf (*Summa theologiae*, 1a. 78. 4, trans. 1970). The lamb apprehends the wolf not simply as an animal of a certain size, color, etc.; it also recognizes the wolf as a "natural enemy" that portends harm, and hence the lamb experiences fear and flees.

In humans, with the power to reason and will, another complexity is added. A shepherd, for example, might decide to remain and protect his sheep in spite of the danger. Following a by now familiar tradition, Aquinas referred to volitions at the intellectual level as affects rather than passions (*Summa theologiae*, 1a. 82. 5, trans. 1970). With regard to the passions proper, Aquinas made another historically important distinction, namely, between irascible and concupiscible emotions. This distinction was implicit in Plato's division between the spirited and appetitive elements of the psyche, and it was made explicit by Aristotle, but not treated in a systematic fashion. Aquinas made it central to his classification of emotions (*Summa theologiae*, 1a. 81. 2, trans. 1970).

Briefly, an object of emotion can be appraised not only as beneficial or harmful, but also as easy or difficult to obtain or avoid. If the object can be obtained or avoided without difficulty, the result is a concupiscible emotion, such as love or joy. If difficulties exist, the result is an irascible emotion. Anger (*ira*), from which the category receives its name, is the epitome of an irascible emotion, but other emotions, such as hope and despair, also belong to the category.

The distinction between concupiscible and irascible emotions is of more than historical interest. Some later theorists (e.g. Descartes, but especially since Darwin) have focused primarily on concupiscible emotions, that is, on straightforward impulses to action, whether of biological ("instincts"; McDougall, 1936) or psychological (Frijda, 1986) origin. Other theorists (e.g. Dewey, 1894, 1895; Hebb, 1946; Mandler, 1984; Oatley, 1992) contend that emotions arise only when impulses are blocked or interrupted; that is, emotions are inherently irascible. Freudian psychoanalysis would also fall within the latter tradition, as will be discussed shortly.

The early modern period: Mechanism contra humanism

The early modern era is marked by an emphasis on the sciences and humanities. Both trends originated in the Renaissance. Although of a common origin, the sciences and humanities have diverged over the centuries, resulting in what C. P. Snow (1963) has described as two cultures. Each "culture" also has had considerable impact on theories of emotion. Science has resulted in the mechanization of emotion; the humanities in a humanization of emotion.

The mechanization of emotion

Descartes (1596–1650) epitomizes the scientific approach. Descartes professed to reject all teaching on emotion that came before. With hindsight, of course, his rejection of tradition was not as radical as he believed. Most importantly, he retained the fundamental distinction between actions and passions, as well as the notion that emotions are common to humans and infrahuman animals. The way he combined these two ideas was, however, unique.

Emotions, according to Descartes (1649/1968), are actions of the body that, when impressed on the mind, result in passions of the soul. More specifically, "animal spirits" (especially fine-grained substances) that arise about the heart and course through the veins, result in passions of the soul when they impact on the pineal gland, a small organ near the center of the brain. The entire process was conceived by Descartes to be strictly mechanical. The body of a dog, say, to the extent that it was similar to the body of a human, responded in a similar manner. Dogs, however, could not suffer passions of the soul, for the obvious reason (to Descartes) that they had no soul. By contrast, Descartes maintained that actions of the soul, which consist of deliberate, rational thought, are uniquely human and cannot be explained in strictly mechanical terms.

With regard to function, Descartes speculated that emotions helped to sustain motions of the body in the absence of external stimulation. Thus, the sight of a bear might cause a person to flee. But once the bear was out of sight, something else was needed so that the person did not stop running until safety was reached. The animal spirits, impacting on the pineal gland, served that purpose.

Descartes' mechanization of the emotions was given a mentalistic twist by the British Empiricists, especially Hume (1711–1776). According to Dixon (2003), Hume was the first to use the term "emotion" regularly (albeit not consistently) to refer to the passions. Dixon further traces the use of "emotion" as it came to be preferred over "passion", first among the Scottish moral philosophers (e.g. Thomas Brown) and later by such notables as Bain, Spencer, Darwin, and James. We will have more to say about the last two theorists—Darwin and James—in a later section.

Dixon maintains that the contemporary concept of emotion is overly inclusive and has masked the subtleties in earlier conceptions (e.g. "passions", "affections", "sentiments"), especially with regard to the relation of emotions to reason, intellect, and will. In particular, he claims that the view of the emotions "as a set of morally disengaged, bodily, non-cognitive and involuntary feelings, is a recent invention" (Dixon, 2003, p. 3). This may be true, but mechanization is not the only recent invention as far as the emotions are concerned.

The humanization of emotion

We have seen how, in the long sweep of Western history, the emotions have typically been treated as a reflection of the animal in human nature or, if recognized as human, then as irrational, misguided judgments. But there is a third alternative, namely that emotions are a hallmark of humanity; that which sets humans apart from infrahuman animals and complex but lifeless automata.

Two theorists epitomize the humanist movement at the beginning of the modern period: Desiderius Erasmus (1466–1536) and Jean-Jacques Rousseau (1712–1778). Erasmus was a Renaissance scholar whose work preceded the major advances that have come to be known as the Scientific Revolution. Nevertheless, he was wont to poke fun at the pretensions of those, including himself, who placed too high a value on the fruits of reason. One of his most popular works, *Praise of folly* (1508/1989), was a satire in which emotion (folly) proves superior to reason as a source of wisdom.

Rousseau lived more than two centuries after Erasmus, and thus had a greater opportunity to witness both the advantages and disadvantages of scientific progress. He saw mostly disadvantages. His novel *Emile* depicts the ideal education of a young man and woman, an education focused, at least in the early years, on the cultivation and refinement of emotions (Rousseau, 1762/1911). But Rousseau was somewhat of an anomaly for the time in which he lived. For the most part, the eighteenth century is known as the Enlightenment, the motto of which, in Kant's (1784/1986, p. 263) words, was *Sapere aude!*—dare to reason! Rousseau, however, was not alone in his critique of reason, and a reaction ultimately set in as the advancement of science led not to greater prosperity and freedom for the majority, but to concentrations of wealth in the hands of a few, and to urban slums, child labor, degradation of the environment, and other social ills. Thus, the eighteenth-century Enlightenment gave way to the nineteenth-century Romanticism.

Romanticism was more a literary and social movement than a scientific one. Yet its influence on the science of emotion can still be felt. Existentialism, for example, is part of that legacy (cf. Solomon, 1976); so, too, is the human potential movement in psychology (e.g. Maslow, 1971; Rogers,

1961) and its latest incarnation, "positive psychology", which emphasizes the more functional aspects of emotion (Snyder & Lopez, 2002).

Bridging the divide

The division between mechanistic and humanistic orientations is overly simplistic. Many theorists do not fall easily into one group or the other. Benedict Spinoza (1632–1677), a younger contemporary of Descartes, is an early—and still relevant (Damasio, 2003; Frijda, 2000)—example. Spinoza was much influenced by the advancement of science in his day, to which he contributed in a minor way as a lens grinder for scientific instruments and by conducting experiments in optics. Spinoza's influence, however, has been greater in the humanities than in the sciences. Among other things, he is considered one of the founders of hermeneutics (Curley, 1994), which involves the interpretation of texts and, in an extended sense, the interpretation of behavior conceived in narrative terms.

Spinoza's (1677/1967) analysis of emotion is contained in his *Ethics*. As the title of Part Four of this work suggests, Spinoza considered the emotions to be a form "*Of human bondage*". Freedom from that bondage is to be gained through reason, but not reason in the sense of a separate faculty distinct from the emotions. In contrast to Descartes, Spinoza rejected any dualism between mind and body, reason and emotion. There exists but a single substance, he argued, of which the mental and physical are but two aspects or manifestations. Like the convex and concave sides of an arc, the two aspects do not interact, although a change in one necessarily involves a change in the other. Analogously, a change in thought is necessarily associated with a change in the body, and vice versa.

Spinoza recognized three broad domains of emotion: desire, joy, and sadness. Desire reflects the tendency (conatus) of each individual to persevere in his or her own being. Joy is the passion that occurs when one's being is enhanced; sorrow, when it is diminished. Specific emotions arise when one or more of these basic passions is conjoined with an idea of an external cause. For example, lust is the immoderate desire for sexual intercourse; love is joy accompanied by the idea of an eliciting object; and hatred is sorrow accompanied by the idea of its provocation. Spinoza described numerous other, more complex emotions; but he did not try to be exhaustive; indeed, he recognized "that so many variations can arise, that no limits can be assigned to their number" (*Ethics*, Part III, Prop. LIX, Note). This is not as picturesque as saying that the emotions are more numerous than the hairs on a man's head (Augustine), but the idea is similar.

If emotions are a kind of human bondage, as Spinoza believed, the question arises: How do we break those bonds? According to Spinoza (1677/1967), an emotion "ceases to be a passion, as soon as we form a clear and distinct idea of it" (*Ethics*, Part V, Prop. III). Specifically, if we change our thoughts (increase our knowledge) about the causes of an emotion, the emotion is necessarily transformed from a more passive to a more active state.

Spinoza's conception of emotion as inadequate knowledge is reminiscent of the Stoics and has similar implications for the treatment of emotional disorders. Looking forward rather than backwards in history, the philosopher Nietzsche could assert with reference to Spinoza, "I have a forerunner, and what a forerunner!" (quoted by Moreau, 1996). Freud, who in turn regarded Nietzsche as a forerunner, has also been described as a "crypto-Spinozist" (Neu, 1977). We will have more to say about Freud shortly.

Twentieth-century developments

In the preceding historical sketches, we took one or at most a few figures to represent entire epochs or movements. That clearly neglects the diversity of opinion that existed at any particular time. When we turn to twentieth-century developments, we try to capture some of that diversity. Specifically, we describe briefly seven current approaches to emotion: evolutionary, psychodynamic, dimensional, phenomenological, psychophysiological, behaviorist, and social constructionist. Each approach represents continuities with the past, as though the contents of the previous 2500 years were poured into the twentieth century, with some new ingredients added. We present the approaches in no particular order of importance.

Evolutionary approaches

Probably no earlier thinker has influenced twentieth-century ideas about emotions more than Darwin. His theory of evolution seemed to give scientific legitimacy and rationale to the long tradition of treating the emotions as common to human and infrahuman animals (cf. Plato, Aristotle, Aquinas, and Descartes). After Darwin, many theorists came to view emotions as instinctive reactions bequeathed to us through natural selection. Early in the century, William McDougall was a prominent advocate of this position. His *An introduction to social psychology*, first published in 1908, went through 23 editions during his lifetime, the last in 1936, two years before his death—and it is still in print. Despite its title, this is more a book on emotion than on social psychology. And although McDougall's "hormic psychology" (as it came to be called) went out of fashion during the mid-decades of the century, many of the issues he raised have regained prominence—and controversy—in the fields of sociobiology and evolutionary psychology.

Darwin's *Expression of emotion in man and animals* (1872/1965) also gave impetus to one of the dominant topics for empirical research during the twentieth century, namely, expressive reactions (Ekman, 1984). Darwin argued that many emotional expressions are without adaptive value, being remnants of an evolutionary past or even the adventitious products of an overly excited nervous system. Subsequent research has indicated that expressive reactions have greater functional significance than Darwin assumed. As Fridlund (1992) has pointed out, Darwin made his arguments, in part, to counter the generally accepted belief that human and animal features are products of special creation, put there by a god for the benefit of humankind. Darwin might have been wrong as far as expressive reactions are concerned but the general thrust of his argument remains valid: Many anatomical and behavioral features of humans are inexplicable in terms of "intelligent design" (the contemporary version of the creationist thesis), but are readily explicable as non-functional—even, in some instances, dysfunctional—remnants of our evolutionary past.

Darwin also gave new meaning to the idea of basic emotions. As long as there have been classifications of emotion, some have been considered more basic than others. For example, Aquinas included hope and courage among the basic emotions; Descartes included wonder; and Hume gave a prominent place to pride. Following Darwin, however, "basic" came to be used almost exclusively in a biological sense. In subtle ways, this has biased much of twentieth-century thinking about emotions. Most academic psychologists consider themselves to be "basic scientists". It is only natural, therefore, that they should focus on emotions that are also considered "basic", that is, biologically primitive.

Psychodynamic approaches

As it spans the twentieth century, the psychodynamic approach involves many noteworthy figures: Freud, Jung, Adler, Rank, and Horney, to mention a few early representatives, as well as later ego-psychologists and object-relation theorists. Among the latter, John Bowlby deserves special mention for his influential work on vicissitudes of attachment (as opposed to sex) as a foundation for later emotional development, including separation anxiety, love, and grief (see Bowlby, 1969, 1973, 1980). Despite the diversity of theorists within the psychodynamic tradition, we limit our remarks to a few observations on Freud's approach to emotion.

Freud, it has often been noted, had two intertwined theories. One, his "metatheory", was modeled after late nineteenth-century physics and was couched in terms of causal mechanisms, energy distribution, cathexes, and the like. His "clinical theory", by contrast, was couched more broadly in terms of wishes, conflicts, subterfuges, and purposive behavior. The nature of this distinction has importance beyond Freud, so we expand on it briefly.

Bruner (1986) has described two approaches to understanding human behavior, the "paradigmatic" and the "narrative", which help clarify Freud's two theories. The paradigmatic approach is scientific in the traditional sense; that is, it relies on general principles, cause-and-effect relations, logic, and objective data. The narrative approach is hermeneutic in an extended sense: It seeks meaning in the stories people tell about themselves; revealing often hidden intentions and desires; the goal is less to explain behavior in an objective sense than to establish possibilities for new experiences. Put somewhat differently, "paradigmatic truth" sees a correspondence between theoretical constructs and some external reality, whereas "narrative truth" establishes coherence in the seemingly incongruent aspects of a person's life.

Using Bruner's terms, Freud's "metatheory" was paradigmatic; his "clinical theory", narrative. Bruner's distinction can also be applied cross-culturally. To anticipate discussion later in this chapter, Western approaches to emotion generally have tended toward the paradigmatic, whereas Chinese approaches have tended toward the narrative. But our concern at the moment is with Freud.

Although strongly influenced by Darwin, Freud's concept of instinct—or, more accurately, drive (*Trieb*)—was so broad as to lose much of its biological implication. For example, in conformity with social strictures libido can, according to Freud, be transformed into an indefinite variety of emotional syndromes. Among the possibilities are transformations idiosyncratic to an individual, namely, hysterical reactions. In Freud's (1917/1963) own words, a hysterical reaction is "a freshly constructed individual affect" (p. 396). Obviously, not all emotionally arousing situations are idiosyncratic to the individual. Drawing on the view, common in his time, that experiences oft repeated could ultimately become inherited (a view, incidentally, shared by Darwin), Freud (1917/1963) described widely shared emotions (i.e. those recognized as standard within a culture) as hysterical reactions that had become part of our biological inheritance. The idea that acquired characteristics can be inherited has been discredited; however, Freud's ideas regarding the malleability of emotional syndromes under social influence continue to be important.

Earlier, we cited Neu's (1977) description of Freud as a crypto-Spinozist. This description extends beyond the similarity between Spinoza's *conatus* and Freud's libido, each of which could be transformed into an indefinite variety of specific emotions. More fundamentally, Freud, like Spinoza, believed the way to ameliorate a maladaptive emotion (passion, hysterical reaction) is through increased understanding of its causes; as Freud described the goal of psychoanalytic treatment, "Where id was, there ego shall be" (1933/1965, p. 71). Finally, with regard to method, as a founder of hermeneutics, Spinoza anticipated the kind of "narrative truth" implicit in Freud's clinical theory and advocated explicitly by many contemporary psychoanalysts (e.g. Spence, 1982).

Dimensional approaches

Darwin was a biologist and naturalist; Freud was a neurologist and physician: Neither held an academic position. The most prominent academic psychologist at the turn of the twentieth century was Wilhelm Wundt (1832–1920). Wundt originally viewed feelings (*Gefühle*), the presumed building blocks out of which complex emotional experiences are constructed, as an attribute of sensation. Specifically, in addition to quality and intensity, sensations could vary in feeling tone, from pleasant to unpleasant. In 1896, however, Wundt separated feelings from sensations, treating them as a distinct class of elements within consciousness. This was equivalent to an internationally prominent chemist announcing a new class of physical elements, distinct from those contained in the familiar periodic table.

Feelings, Wundt (1897) now suggested, could be ordered within a dimensional space formed by three bipolar factors: pleasantness–unpleasantness (*Lust–Unlust*), excitement–inhibition (*Erregung–Hemmung*), and tension–relaxation (*Spannung–Lösung*). This tridimensional theory of feeling quickly became the subject of controversy. Introspective reports under controlled conditions suggested that the dimensions of excitement–inhibition and tension–relaxation could be "reduced" to bodily sensations, or else they were confounded with feelings of pleasantness–unpleasantness, or they were associated with other sensory attributes through past experience (Titchener, 1908). Only pleasantness–unpleasantness seemed to remain as an unalloyed dimension of feelings. But additional research suggested that it, too, might be reducible to organic sensations (Nafe, 1924).

Wundt's tridimensional theory does not depend, however, on introspection, nor on an identification of emotions with feelings. Facial expressions (Schlosberg, 1954) and the connotative meaning of words (Osgood, 1969) also suggest that emotions can be arrayed in a three-dimensional space roughly equivalent to that proposed by Wundt. More recently, Russell (2003) has made a similar proposal, referring to the dimensions as "core affects". Time will tell whether history repeats itself with regard to the fate of this newer tridimensional theory.

Phenomenological / existentialist / cognitive approaches

A different approach to feelings of emotion can be traced to Wundt's contemporary, Franz Brentano (1838–1917). Brentano was an Aristotelian and Thomistic (Aquinas) scholar. The distinguishing characteristic of mental phenomena, Brentano (1874/1971) argued, is that they take an object. When angry, for example, a person must be angry at something; when afraid, afraid of something; when in love, in love with someone; and so forth. The object need not actually exist; in a sense, it is created (actualized) in the act of becoming angry, frightened, or in love. Technically, the directedness of mental phenomena is known as intentionality.

Brentano's major contribution to the psychology of emotion was through his students, among them Husserl, the founder of phenomenology, and Scheler, who applied phenomenological principles to the analysis of emotion. Contrary to Wundtian introspection, the goal of "phenomen-ological reduction" is not to break consciousness down into elements, but to analyze it without presuppositions. Through vicissitudes that need not concern us here, phenomenology became allied with existentialism, and the latter's emphasis on freedom of choice. We will limit our few remarks to Sartre (1905–1960).

For Sartre (1948) emotions are ways of "magically" transforming the world to fit our needs and desires. To illustrate, Sartre retells Aesop's fable of the fox and grapes. When the fox realizes that the grapes are out of his reach, he concludes they are sour. In phenomenological terms, the sour grapes are the intentional object, a product of the fox's frustration and disappointment. An important implication of Sartre's analysis is that emotions are a matter of choice, and hence we are responsible for what we do or think while in an emotional state (Solomon, 1976).

In addition to existential phenomenology, Bretano's influence is perhaps most evident today in appraisal theory, introduced by Magda Arnold. Arnold (1960) acknowledged Sartre's "careful phenomenological analysis" but criticized "his fascination with the way in which emotion changes the world" (p. 170). She therefore undertook her own phenomenological analysis. An emotion, she concluded, is "the felt tendency toward anything intuitively appraised as good (beneficial) or away from anything appraised as bad (harmful)" (p. 182). By appraisal, Arnold meant a sense judgment, that is, an immediate, non-intellectual assessment of the potential benefit or harm a perceived object might have for the individual. This process occurs on the animal as well as the human level. Recall the example by Aquinas, cited earlier, of a lamb becoming frightened when it recognizes a wolf as a natural enemy. Indeed, Arnold's approach, including her classification of emotions, owes much to Aquinas, as well as to Brentano and his followers.

Contemporary appraisal theory addresses two main issues: The first issue concerns the ways in which appraisals help distinguish among different emotions, or, in phenomenological terms, the link between an emotion and its intentional object. For example, anger and envy may both lead to aggression and have similar physiological accompaniments; what distin-guishes them is how the person appraises the instigation—as an unjustified affront in the case of anger or an unfavorable comparison with the self in the case of envy. The link between an emotion and its object, it might be noted, is conceptual, not contingent; for example, appraising an event as an unjustified affront is part of what we mean by anger. However, empirical research can help identify the dimensions along which appraisals vary (Roseman, 1991).

The second issue addressed by appraisal theory concerns the processes or "steps" that lead from the initial rudiments of perception and memory to a full-blown emotional experience (e.g. Lazarus, 1991; Scherer, 2001). With this issue, the study of emotion becomes thoroughly embedded in contem-porary cognitive psychology.

Psychophysiological and neurocognitive approaches

Another early critic of Wundt was William James (1842–1910). In an 1887 letter to Carl Stumpf, James compared Wundt's prodigious corpus of writings to a worm: When cut to pieces by criticism, each piece wiggles off in a new direction (in H. James, 1920, p. 67). James could have said the same about his own theory of emotion, the central thesis of which is that "bodily changes follow directly the perception of the exciting fact, and that our feeling of the same changes as they occur *is* the emotion" (1890, vol. 2, p. 449, emphasis in original). When cut to pieces on physiological and conceptual grounds (e.g., Cannon, 1927), James's theory simply wiggled off in different directions, for example, the two-factor theory of Schachter (1964), the facial feedback theory of Tomkins (1981), and the somatic marker theory of Damasio (1994). According to Schachter's two-factor theory, physiological arousal provides an undifferentiated quale to emotional experience, whereas cognitive appraisals differentiate among emotions; according to Tomkin's facial feedback theory, proprioceptive feedback from the richly innervated facial musculature helps differentiate among emotions; and according to Damasio's somatic marker theory, physiological reactions to emotional events provide information, without necessarily entering into conscious awareness, for further reasoning and action.

James considered his theory to be an original insight. It wasn't. In addition to Descartes and Spinoza, Titchener (1914) quotes from 18 authors (e.g. Malebranche, LaMettrie, Cabanis, Bichat, Lamarck, Lotze) who had previously articulated a position similar to that of James. "All in all" Titchener concluded, "James's acceptance of the complete novelty of his theory must, I believe, be left to stand as something of a curiosity in the history of psychology" (p. 446).

James was generally quite careful in giving credit to others, as indicated by his inclusion of the Danish physician Carl Lange in what is now known as the James–Lange theory. But given the pre-Jamesian theories documented by Titchener, it is hardly surprising that post-Jamesian theories should also proliferate. There is, after all, an irrefutable grain of truth to the idea that bodily changes contribute to the experience of emotion. A grain of truth, however, does not make a loaf, and James's theory is only a partial explanation, at best. James seemed to recognize this fact: In his *Varieties of religious experience* (1902/1961), one of the most provocative early twentieth-century works on emotion (not just religious), James found few occasions to refer to his own prior theory.

In recent decades the psychophysiological study of emotion has shifted from an emphasis on peripheral responses (visceral changes and expressive reactions) to an emphasis on central neural mechanisms. This shift, which reflects Cannon's (1927) views more than James's, is due, in part, to the development of increasingly sophisticated technologies (e.g. neuroimaging) to trace the activity of the brain during emotional episodes. As a result a new discipline, cognitive neuroscience (Lane & Nadel, 2000; Panksepp, 1998), is emerging, where "cognitive" means everything "mental", emotions included.

As exciting and promising as these developments are, two cautions are in order: First, neurocognitive studies are necessarily limited to short-term emotions or to part processes (such as the recognition of facial expressions) that can be studied under constrained laboratory conditions. The danger is that limitations imposed by methodology will impose limits on ideas about emotion. Second, we must be careful not to fall into what Uttal (2001) has called a "new phrenology", replacing the question, "What?" with the more tractable question, "Where?"

Behavioral approaches

Behaviorism was initiated by John Watson (1919) who, by his own admission, was more comfortable doing research with animals than with humans. But unlike later ethologists (e.g. Tinbergen, Lorenz), Watson was more interested in learned than in inherited patterns of behavior. In this respect, he and other early behaviorists had their Russian counterparts, especially Pavlov (1926/1960). Behaviorism also owed a debt to psychoanalysis: If the major determinants of behavior occur below the surface of awareness, as Freud maintained, then conscious experience could not provide a firm foundation on which to build a science of psychology.

Although no longer considered fundamental on theoretical grounds, a distinction is commonly drawn between classical (Pavlovian) and instrumental (Skinnerian) conditioning. Except for a few "basic" emotions or primary drives, most behaviorists assumed emotions to be classically conditioned responses. This is yet another incarnation of the ancient distinction between passions (classically conditioned) and actions (instrumentally conditioned). Skinner, undoubtedly the most influential behaviorist of the last half of the century, broke with this tradition by interpreting emotions instrumentally, that is, in terms of what a person does rather than how a person feels or responds physiologically. Skinner (1963/1988) was particularly critical of the postulation of feelings as causes of behavior. Instead, he suggested that feelings be analyzed as another form of behavior: To illustrate, a hallucination is a clear example of an experience that a person does; Skinner argued that veridical perceptions are no different in principle, and neither are emotional feelings.

Social constructionist approaches

Emotions do not exist only in the heart or mind of the autonomous individual. With few exceptions (e.g. some fears to immediate dangers), emotions are inherently social phenomena and can only be understood as part of the culture in which they have meaning. This is a central tenet of social constructionist approaches (Harré, 1986). Like most contemporary approaches, social constructionism has its roots in the nineteenth century and earlier. Conceptually, it is related to the sociology of knowledge (e.g. Marx, Mannheim) as applied to everyday life (Berger & Luckmann, 1966); empirically, it draws on cultural differences in emotional syndromes (e.g. as documented by anthropologists) and on individual differences in the way emotions are experienced and expressed (see earlier discussion of Freud and the psychodynamic tradition).

More specifically, from a social constructionist approach, emotions are organized patterns of responses, no one component of which (whether feelings, thoughts, or behavioral reactions) is necessary or sufficient for the whole. To say that emotional responses are organized implies principles of organization. For some components, such as certain facial expressions, and even for some simple emotional syndromes, such as sudden fright, the primary organizing principles may have been hard-wired into the nervous system during evolution, as Darwin suggested. From a social-constructionist perspective, however, the primary organizing principles for most emotions are implicit beliefs or folk-theories of emotion.

Social constructionism also views emotional episodes as unfolding over time, sometimes lasting for hours, days, or even months or years (as in the case of grief or love). For all but the briefest episodes, emotional responses are constructed "on line", drawing on the person's unique talents, past experiences, and current concerns, as well as on the exigencies of the situation. In the process, a great deal of improvisation on culturally specified norms is possible, even inevitable.

Concluding observations on twentieth-century ideas about emotion

The above seven approaches might seem like the work of the blind men of Indostan, each of whom examined one part of an elephant and concluded that the whole must be like the part. The analogy, however, is misleading. Each approach considers the emotional elephant in its entirety, but from a different angle. Thus, the approaches are not mutually exclusive; indeed, over the century they have intersected and enriched one another in many ways. However, like viewing an elephant with clear vision, but from different angles, the approaches do not allow easy synthesis into a single perspective.

This raises another issue. When reviewing the near (twentieth century) history of emotion, details loom large. If this chapter were being written in the twenty-fourth century, how many of those details would then seem relevant? Obviously, this rhetorical question cannot be answered with any certainty. However, a hint of an answer can be gained by taking into account psychology's long history as well as its short past. Issues that have survived the tests of centuries are liable to remain important in the future.

Eastern theories of emotion

Unlike our overview of Western theories, which straddled diverse cultures from ancient Greece and Rome to modern Europe and America, we now focus on a single culture, namely, China. This limitation is due partly to space, but it also reflects our own expertise (Louise Sundararajan, *née* Kuen-Wei Lu, was educated in Taiwan as well as the United States).

The overview of Chinese theories requires a somewhat lengthy introduction because of the unfamiliar intellectual terrain we are now entering. In the West, philosophy and, more recently, science have been major sources of ideas about the emotions; this is not as true in China. Although the early texts came out of philosophical schools at a similar time as the Greco-Roman period in Western history, the successors to Confucius (551–479 BCE) were schooled in poetry more than in philosophical enquiry. By contrast, although literature, especially poetry, has influenced Western theories of emotion (cf. Romanticism), that influence has been mostly indirect and tangential.

Chinese concepts of emotion

Broadly conceived as a kind of feeling, *qing* (*ch'ing*) is the term closest in meaning to "emotion". In its original sense, as documented in pre-Han texts (500–200 BCE), *qing* meant "genuine", "the facts", or "what essentially is" (Graham, 1986, p. 63). As something genuine, *qing* and *xing* (nature) are overlapping concepts. *Qing* is often used in combination with *gan* to mean emotion in a more narrow sense (*gan qing* or *qing gan*). *Gan* is a verb meaning "affect"/"stir" or "affected"/"moved". In still other combinations, *qing* can refer to mood (*qing xu*), personality or natural inclinations (*xing qing*), and circumstance or condition (*qing kuang*).

In early Chinese philosophy, the broad definition of *qing* as feelings in general was not a concern. At stake was not so much the distinction between mental agony, say, and a toothache, but between a thing and its mental representation—its name/concept. In this philosophical context, the notion of *qing* gains importance because of its emphasis on experience in general. Hansen (1995) notes that *qing* serves as the "authentic standard" (p. 197). The implication is that without the "reality input" (p. 198) of *qing*, names/concepts may become decoupled from experience. As a fundamental part of human nature, *qing* are presumed to be prior to culture. Thus, the seven "basic" *qing*—joy, anger, sadness, fear, love, hate, desire—are what humans are capable of "without learning" (Graham, 1986, p. 64). That feelings constitute the core of being genuine is an assumption that runs deep in Chinese thought. Even the twentieth-century Chinese scholar Hsu Fu-kuan (1990) claims that "emotions are what is true in life" (p. 451).

What are the critical questions posed by the notion of feelings? One question is how the concept of emotion informs the experience of emotion.

This is the question that drives formulations such as: "the experience of emotion is a perceptual act, guided by conceptual knowledge about emotion" (Barrett, 2005, p. 256). The Chinese, however, are not concerned with the construction of meaning out of experience so much as the question of experience as mental representation, a concern best expressed by the semiotics of Charles Peirce (Colapietro, 1989): How does the mind present its constructed meaning to itself? This question is manifest in the self-reflexive tendency of the Chinese to render emotions the object of reflection. It is also manifest in the Chinese preoccupation with the different modes of emotion representation (experience proximate imagery versus experience distant conceptualization), as well as in their laborious deliberations over the different functions of emotion expression (to replicate or to explicate the experience). Examined in the following pages are these issues and concerns that drive the intellectual history of *qing*.

In presenting Western histories of emotion, we drew on the notion of a Gestalt or good form (*Prägnanz*) to fill in the gaps. We do something similar in presenting Chinese histories, but instead of speaking of a Gestalt we invoke the notion of "evocative image" (*xing*) to reinforce the shift in emphasis from a more cognitive-centered to a more affect-centered orientation.

We will have more to say about *xing* shortly. For the moment, we simply note that the image Westerners have of Chinese affective life is often incomplete, if not actually misleading. For example, the anthropologist Potter (1988) reports that when Chinese villagers are asked how they feel about a particular event, a typical response might be, "How I feel doesn't matter". Potter calls this attitude the "image of irrelevant affect". Below, we offer a far different image, an affect central landscape the contours of which have been shaped by three schools of thought—Confucianism, Taoism, and Buddhism.

Emotion in Confucian thought

Whether or not we agree with some modern scholars that Confucius (551–479 BCE) is more legend than reality (Brooks & Brooks, 1998), his teachings are real, especially as transmitted by Hsün Tzu (ca. 313–238 BCE), Mencius (372–298 BCE), and the neo-Confucianists of the twelfth century, such as Chu Hsi (1130–1200).

"In Confucianism we perceive a consistent and all pervading emphasis on the affective life of human beings. This emphasis on the feeling, emotional aspect of life was considered of primary importance in sustaining people in a human form of existence" (Berry, 2003, p. 96). Another pan-Chinese belief that finds an eloquent expression in Confucian philosophy is the profound "intercommunion of Heaven, earth, and humanity" (Berry, 2003, p. 97). This affective bond between ourselves and other things was the foundation for the "feeling of commiseration" or the "unbearing mind"

(Fung, 1966, p. 283)—principles of sympathy that Mencius claimed to be innate, hence "the beginning of humanity". For illustration, Mencius gave the hypothetical scenario of a child falling into the well:

> Now, when men suddenly see a child about to fall into a well, they all have a feeling of alarm and distress, not to gain friendship with the child's parents, nor to seek the praise of their neighbors and friends, nor because they dislike the reputation [of lack of humanity if they did not rescue the child]. From such a case, we see that a man without the feeling of commiseration is not a man . . . The feeling of commiseration is the beginning of humanity.
>
> (Chan, 1969, p. 65)

In light of this affect-central perspective, the greatest contribution of Confucius to the Chinese civilization lies in his aesthetic vision of government (Hall & Ames, 1987) and his promotion of poetry (Sundararajan, 2002).

Confucian poetics

The text that sets the tone for centuries of Chinese literary thought is the book of poetry *The she king* (1971), or the *Odes*, which was an anthology of over 300 poems allegedly edited by Confucius and included in his curriculum. The uniqueness of the *Odes* can be captured through one of its genres called "*xing*". *Xing* literally means "stirring" or "arousing". The arousing of one's affectivity by poetry is considered by Confucius to be the fundamental first step, on the heels of which the rest of the Confucian program—rites and music—will ensue and complete the self-cultivation process:

> Aroused [*xing*] by the Odes;
> Established by the rites;
> Brought into perfect focus by music.
>
> (*Analects*, 8/8, in Fang, 1954, p. ix)

In Chinese poetics, *xing* is a technical term that refers to one of the two types of indirect expression of emotions: *bi* (comparison) and *xing* (evocative image) (Wixted, 1983, p. 238). *Bi* is metaphor or simile, whereas *xing* has no Western counterpart (Yu, 1987), although cognate ideas can be found in the Indian tradition of *dhvani* (Hogan, 1996). The major difference between these two tropes has traditionally been understood along the divide between explicitness and covertness. As metaphor or simile—such as "My love is a red, red rose"—*bi* is explicit in its signification. "Evocative image", by contrast, does not have a clear connection between its source and target, thus it signifies in a "covert", "latent", or "concealed" way. Here is an evocative image from the *Odes*:

> Kwan-kwan go the ospreys,
> On the islet in the river.
> The modest, retiring, virtuous, young lady:
> For our prince a good mate she.

(The she king, 1971, p. 1)

The connection between the ospreys and the prince's sexual feelings is obscure, at best.

How does "evocative image" work? It works by the mechanism of priming. Owen (1992) claims that "Because the mechanism by which affective image [*xing*] functions is latent, its operations are interior and thus it works on the affections (*ch'ing* [*qing*]) directly, unmediated by the understanding" (p. 256). Thus the literary critic Chung Hung's (469–518) definition of this term: "When meaning lingers on, though writing has come to an end, this is an 'evocative image' [*xing*]" (Wixted, 1983, p. 238).

Hsu (1990) claims that *xing*-based poetry is "purely expressive of emotions", and thus is representative of what is unique about Chinese poetry (p. 105). Yet how can a covert type of expression be most expressive of emotions? This makes sense when we realize that the best way, from the Chinese perspective, to convey what it is like to have certain emotional experience is to replicate, not explicate, that experience. Thus when moved by the stimuli, the poet uses imageries to evoke resonating moods and imageries in the reader; the reader/critic in turn can convey his/her understanding of the poem through resonating imagery (Yu, 1987).

As theory of emotion, the Confucian poetics makes three bold claims: (1) emotions entail not simply reactions to the vicissitudes of life but also actions initiated by the individual, as evidenced by the importance given to deliberate attempts to be "aroused" by poetry; (2) emotions are semiotic signs that inhabit the intersubjective space of a community of the mind; (3) better suited than symbolic thought, as exemplified by the use of metaphor (*bi*), for the illumination of emotions are the subsymbolic, non-propositional processes of associative reasoning (Smith & Neumann, 2005), as exemplified by the use of imagery (*xing*). A cognate perspective is found in Western mysticism, which is well articulated by Rudolf Otto's claim (1923/1970) that mystical experiences have no need for explications and explanations, but "can be firmly grasped, thoroughly understood, and profoundly appreciated, purely in, with, and from the feeling itself" (p. 34).

Emotion refinement

Within the Western tradition, the regulation of emotion has been a consistent theme; within the Confucian tradition, it is more appropriate to speak of emotion refinement than regulation. One major difference between refinement and regulation is that the former does not necessarily imply the control of something bad, whereas the latter does. In Confucianism, the assumption is generally made that human nature is intrinsically good, and that, by extension, the emotions (*qing*) are too. There are, of course, exceptions to this generalization. Hsün Tzu (ca. 313–238 BCE), for one, held that human nature is not all good, and hence some aspects of *qing* require regulation. According to Hsün Tzu's formulation: "*Nature* is the tendency which is from Heaven. *Qing* is the substance of our nature. *Desire* is the response of *qing* in us" (*Hsün-tzu*, ch. 24, adapted from Graham, 1986, p. 65, italics added). Desire needs regulation for two reasons: (1) it is one step removed from the source (human nature); and (2) it is a response to temptation, and hence corruptible. Thus, Hsün Tzu claimed that desires need to be kept in check as not to proliferate unnecessarily: "The desires of man's *qing* are few, but everyone thinks that in his own qing the desires are many, which is a mistake" (*Hsün-tzu*, ch. 18, adapted from Graham, 1986, p. 65).

According to Hsün Tzu, the most important means of emotion regulation is *li* (rituals). He claimed that, as paraphrased by Fung: "the *li* provide regulation for the satisfaction of man's desires . . . But in the sense of ceremonies and rituals, the *li* . . . give *refinement* and purification to man's emotions" (*Hsün-tzu*, ch. 19, in Fung, 1966, p. 147, emphasis added). Note that even in Hsün Tzu's system, "regulation" tends to acquire the additional meaning of refinement: "The sacrificial rites are the expression of man's affectionate longing. They represent the height of piety and faithfulness, of love and respect. They represent also the completion of propriety and *refinement* . . ." (p. 149, emphasis added).

Overall in the Confucian system it is difficult to make a compelling argument for the elimination or control of something intrinsically bad in emotions. For instance, desire is not intrinsically bad in the *Analects* of Confucius. To Confucius a desire is good or bad depending on whose desire it is, a virtuous or a petty person's. The main thrust therefore is on refinement, or self-cultivation. In its vision of the ideal state of emotions, refinement sets goals above and beyond regulation. The benchmarks of emotion refinement include more elusive goals such as creativity, growth and development. A case in point is Wang Fu-chih's (1619–1692) vision of allowing emotions full sway: "Overcoming the restrictions of each of the four emotional activities [joy, anger, sadness, happiness], one allows these four emotions full sway; and moving freely within these four emotions, one prevents one's own emotions from being clogged up . . . The freedom of movement that man's emotions enjoy knows no bounds" (cited in Wong, 1978, p. 142).

Emotion refinement differs from emotion regulation also in the locus of regulation: Refinement is from within the emotion system; regulation is from without. In emotion regulation, automatically activated feelings are controlled or overridden by reason or cognition, by behavioral (e.g. relaxation) techniques, or even by drugs. By contrast, emotion refinement capitalizes on the mutual inhibition and constraint among multiple desires and motivations within the affective sphere. This principle of internal regulation that ensures the due proportion of things in their dynamic interaction is called harmony (Lu, 2004). In the *Tso Chuan*, Zen Tsu (died 493 BCE) is quoted as saying "Harmony is like soup. There being water and heat, sour flavoring and pickles, salt and peaches . . . The salt flavoring is the other to the bitter, and the bitter is the other to the salt. With these two 'others' *combining in due proportions* and a new flavor emerging, this is what is expressed in 'harmony'" (Fung, 1962, pp. 107–108, emphasis added). The same applies to the emotional stew, in which multiple desires interacting with one another may, if guided by the principle of harmony, congeal into a personality marked by four emotional tones: *wen, jou, tun, hou*, which are feelings and thoughts "moderate, gentle, sincere, and deep" (Liu, 1962, p. 67). Hsu (1990) explains that emotions that strive against inextricable ties and inexpressible pains would eventually coagulate into a mild and gentle disposition: "Thus mild and gentle comportment has the compressed structure of sincere and deep emotions" (p. 448; for further details, see Sundararajan, 2002).

Harmony is the central theme of the classical text *Chung yung* (*The doctrine of the mean*, 1971; Tu, 1989), attributed to K'ung Ch'i, the grandson of Confucius. The first term of the title, *chung*, refers to balance and moderation that ensure the due proportion of things; the second term, *yung*, refers to the ordinary or commonplace, in which the Tao is supposed to reside. This notion has far reaching implications for emotion refinement.

Self-reflexivity and second-order awareness

Confucius allegedly said in the *Chung yung*, "The path [*Tao*] is not far from man" (ch. 13, *The doctrine of the mean*, 1971, p. 393). As the Tao is immanent, rather than transcendent like the Christian God, such that all forms of life necessarily follow the Tao, the difference between the uninitiated and the sage is in levels of consciousness—the former follows the Tao unknowingly, whereas the latter knowingly. The main thrust of the Confucian pedagogue was therefore to raise consciousness to a second-order awareness so that people will know that they know, or in the words of Fung (1966), "to give people an understanding that they are all, more or less, actually following the Way [*Tao*], so as to cause them to be conscious of what they are doing" (p. 175).

The centrality of second-order awareness in traditional China is manifest in the proliferation of the so-called "second-order desires"; that is, the ability to evaluate one's own desires. Of particular importance is a second-order desire known as savoring (Sundararajan, in press; Sundararajan & Averill, in press). One of the earliest references to savoring is found in the

Chung yung, which states that "There is no body but eats and drinks. But they are few who can distinguish flavors" (*The doctrine of the mean*, 1971, p. 387). The knowing involved in savoring is a second-order awareness: In contrast to the first-order experience of tasting the flavors in food, savoring entails knowing that one knows the flavors so as to be able to manipulate the experience by prolonging it, making fine discriminations, etc. Furthermore, as a second-order awareness, savoring is different from the garden variety of self-reflections: It is experience proximate, more akin to the Buddhist practice of mindfulness than to the experience distant type of self reflections such as self-analysis or self-understanding.

One of the most important theorists of savoring is Ssu-k'ung T'u (837–908) (Owen, 1992; Sundararajan, 2004), whose notion of savoring differs from the typical Western formulation as well as the Indian *rasa*. The Western formulation entails relishing a positive experience in the here and now (Bryant, 1989); the Chinese savoring includes negative experiences as well, and has a relatively wider scope of temporality that extends to both the aftertaste of an experience (Eoyang, 1993), and the subtle incipient phase of things (Sundararajan, 2004). Lastly, whereas *rasa* seeks to transcend the individual self (Dehejia, 1996), savoring in the Chinese tradition is a means of refining, not eliminating, the idiosyncratic tastes of the individual.

Emotion in Taoist thought

In Confucianism, the Tao (Way) is a system of moral truths; in Taoism, it is nature (heaven) in the most fundamental sense—eternal, nameless, indescribable. As a way of life, the Tao implies simplicity, tranquility, and non-action (*wei wei*) or letting nature take its course. Lao Tzu (ca. sixth century BCE) is considered the founder of both philosophical and popular Taoism. Although the so-called popular Taoism has much to say about emotion in traditional Chinese medicine (see, for example, Wu, 1982), it is not reviewed here due to limitation of space. In this chapter, we concentrate on classical Taoist thought.

Whereas a central theme in Confucianism is suffering (Tu, 1984), that in Taoism is freedom. This keynote of freedom is articulated by the claim by Chuang Tzu (born ca. 369 BCE) that the sage has no emotions. In his own words: "[The sage] has the shape of a man, but without *qing*" (*Chuang-tzu*, ch. 5). This enigmatic statement has generated much speculation throughout Chinese history. Presented below are three major perspectives on the question of freedom and emotions.

Beyond culture

The first perspective is found in the dialogue between Chuang Tzu and Hui Shih. When queried by Hui Shih as to how the sage could be without *qing*,

Chuang Tzu replied that "judging between right and wrong is what I mean by *qing*. What I mean by being without *qing* is that a man does not inwardly harm himself by likes and dislikes, but instead constantly follows the spontaneous and does not add to what is natural in him" (adapted from Graham, 1986, p. 62). This discussion is obviously an extension of the nature versus culture debate that looms large in Taoism. The Taoist back-to-nature position intends to recover the original innocence in emotions by divesting of *qing* all the vestiges of "conceptualization, convention, society, and language" (Hansen, 1995, pp. 200–201). This proposition has far reaching implications: The relatively simple and intuitive appraisals are privileged as the hallmarks of spontaneity, and genuineness; the more cognitively elaborate appraisals are distrusted for their calculativeness and value judgments. The former was referred to by the neo-Confucianist Chou Tun-yi (1017–1073) as "vacuous in quiescence and straightforward in movement" (Fung, 1966, p. 290), as exemplified by the immediate impulse to save the proverbial child falling into the well. Fung (1966) explains that if one does not act on one's first impulse, but pauses instead to think the matter over before coming to the child's rescue, "he is motivated by secondary selfish thoughts and thereby loses both his original state of vacuity in quiescence and the corollary state of straightforwardness in movement" (p. 272).

Disperse emotion with reason

The second perspective is that the sage has no emotions because her mind is like a mirror. This interpretation also finds support in the text of the *Chuang-tzu* (ch. 7): "The mind of the perfect man is like a mirror. It does not move with things, nor does it anticipate them. It responds to things, but does not retain them. Therefore the perfect man is able to deal successfully with things but is not affected by them" (Fung, 1966, p. 287). This is the rational approach, or what is referred to in Taoism as "dispersing emotion with reason". One way to attain a mind that approximates "the emptiness of a mirror and the evenness of a balance" (Fung, 1962, p. 183) is to take an objective perspective, as advocated by the philosopher and literary critic Wang Fu-chih (1619–1692): "those who are not reduced to helplessness by *ch'ing* [*qing*], they recognize that when they are sad, things can still be happy, but this does not alter the fact that they are themselves sad; when they are happy, things can still be sad, but this does not alter the fact that they are themselves happy" (Wong, 1978, pp. 128–129).

The romantic spirit

The third attempt to answer the koan posed by the *Chuang-tzu* is to modify the original statement from having no emotions to having emotions but without ensnarement. This was the exegesis of Wang Pi (226–249) on the *Chuang-tzu*: "That in which the sage is superior to ordinary people is the spirit. But what the sage has in common with ordinary people are the emotions . . . and therefore cannot respond to things without joy or sorrow. He responds to things, yet is not ensnared by them. It is wrong to say that because the sage has no ensnarement, he therefore has no emotions" (Fung, 1966, p. 238). How does one have emotions without ensnarement? The answer from neo-Taoism of the third and fourth centuries is *feng liu.*

Feng liu means literally "wind and stream" and is rendered by Fung (1966) as "the romantic spirit" (p. 231). According to the neo-Taoists, *feng liu* derives from *tzu-jan* (spontaneity, naturalness), and is in opposition to morals and institutions (Fung, 1966, p. 240). Its essential quality is "to have a mind that transcends the distinctions of things and lives in accord with itself, rather than with others" (Fung, 1966, p. 291). The main source on *feng liu* is *Shih-shuo hsin-yü* (Mather, 1976), or *Shih-shuo* for short. The colorful anecdotes of the neo-Taoists as recorded in the *Shih-shuo* suggest an alternative approach to theory, an experience proximate approach in which one lives one's theory instead of constructing it intellectually.

Whereas authenticity is a main concern of the Confucian tradition (Sundararajan, 2002), novelty constitutes the key element of *feng liu.* In the following episode from the *Shih-shuo* (ch. 23), the neo-Taoist Liu Ling (ca. 221–300) was considered *feng liu* not because of his nudity, but because of his novel take on it: Liu had a habit of going completely naked in his room. To his critics he said, "I take the whole universe as my house and my room as my clothing. Why, then, do you enter here into my trousers?" (Fung, 1966, p. 235).

And it is novelty in a radical way: One is to transcend all given norms, from the biologically given sensory experiences to the socially given codes of conduct. The result is what may be called a cult of spontaneity, characterized by a paradoxical combination of impulsivity, on the one hand, and "a more subtle sensitivity for pleasure and more refined needs than sheerly [*sic*] sensual ones . . ." on the other (Fung, 1966, p. 235). Thus individuals of *feng liu* "acted according to pure impulse, but not with any thought of sensuous pleasure" (Fung, 1966, p. 235). A good example of refined sensitivity is the artist Wang Hui-chih (died ca. 388). One night, when awakened by a heavy snowfall, Wang Hui-chih thought of his friend Tai K'uei. "Immediately he took a boat and went to see Tai. It required the whole night for him to reach Tai's house, but when he was just about to knock at the door, he stopped and returned home" (*Shih-shuo*, ch. 23, Fung, 1966, p. 235). To those who were puzzled by his action, Wang's explanation was: "I came on the impulse of my pleasure, and now it is ended, so I go back. Why should I see Tai?" (Fung, 1966, p. 236).

Paradoxes abound in Taoism

The immediacy/impulsivity celebrated by the neo-Taoists may best be understood as "mediated immediacy" or controlled impulsivity, just as *bonsai* is not raw but cultivated nature. The key to the "refined pleasure" of Wang seems to lie in the virtuosity of his controlled processing that selectively activated one impulse (paying someone a visit) and inhibited the other (seeing someone), thus defying the ordinarily tight coupling of theses action tendencies in the goal-oriented thinking that Taoism never tires of disparaging.

With the "romantic spirit", the question of ensnarement of emotions is no longer whether to have emotion or not, but: How are emotions to be expressed, with refined sensitivity and rare insight, or not. Emotions are no longer the problem, since it is insight and sensitivity that count.

Emotion in Chinese Buddhist thought

With Confucianism and Taoism the floor plan is laid. The Buddhist influence since the first century CE added a few wings, but did not change the basic architecture of Chinese thought. Buddha, the "enlightened one", is the name given to Siddhartha Gautama (563–483 BCE) from North India, whose teaching centered on enlightenment and compassion as means to end suffering. From India, Buddhism spread to Southeast Asia (Burma, Thailand, etc.) and northward to the Far East (Tibet, China, Korea and Japan). By the third century CE, many Buddhist concepts were aligned with those of Taoism, and a recognizable school of Chinese Buddhism emerged.

With its conceptualization of emotions far more psychological and analytical than the Chinese indigenous variety, Buddhism expanded not only the Chinese vocabulary of emotions but also insights into the nature of emotions. The following are some Buddhist notions of emotions that we shall mention but not explore, due to limitation of space: passion (*klesa*, or *fan-nao*), with a pejorative coloring (Galik, 1980) not found in the indigenous *qing*; suffering (*dukkha*, or *ku*), and emptiness (*sunyata*, or *kong*). In addition, there are the wrong cognitive sets responsible for our suffering—delusion and ignorance (de Silva, 1995), and a more fine-grained analysis of desire into the notions of "contact" and "clinging". Contact (*phassa*) refers to the notion that due to ignorance we are attached to things we experience through our senses. Clinging (*upadana*) refers to an adhesiveness, or fixation—the holding onto the object of desire (de Silva, 1995).

There is a tendency under the Buddhist influence to dichotomize human nature and feelings along the divide of good and bad. For instance, the Confucian philosopher Li Ao (died ca. 844) stated that "The feelings are the evil that is in the [human] nature" (Fung, 1953, vol. 2, p. 420). Fung (1953) points out that what Li called "nature" is akin to the Buddhist notion of the "original mind", while his concept of feelings resembles the Buddhist notion of the "Passions" (*fan nao* or *klesa*) (vol. 2, p. 414). The notion of impermanence of things and the corresponding ideal of detachment or not "clinging" also help to add another nuance to the "mind as a mirror" metaphor. The neo-Confucianists, under the influence of

Buddhism, "argue that there is nothing wrong with the emotions per se; what is important is simply that they should not be a permanent part of the person who sometimes expresses them . . . This is quite different from the ordinary man, whose anger, being a part of him . . . still remains after those objects have passed away . . ." (Fung, 1953, vol. 2, p. 526).

According to Abrams (1976, p. 48), there are two antithetical metaphors of mind: mirror ("comparing mind to a reflector of external objects") and lamp (comparing mind "to a radiant projector which makes a contribution to the objects it perceives"). The mind as a lamp is the line of thinking that benefited the most from the Buddhist influence. As a radical rendition of the lamp metaphor, the Buddhist perspective, in a nutshell, is that the world is a projection of the mind such that different states of consciousness result in different "mental worlds" (*jing* or *jing-jie*) or *Visaya* in Sanskrit. The notion of emotion as having the power to reveal the "world" one is in shares some affinities with Heidegger's notion of "mood" (Smith, 1981). But whereas the Heideggerian mood is characterized by "thrownness", that is, one finds oneself always already in a mood-disclosed world, the Chinese *jing-jie* or "mental world" is supposedly a matter of attainment in spiritual development or self cultivation on the part of the individual (Yeh, 2000, vol.1). One of the first literary critics who developed a theory of the "mental world" is Ssu-k'ung T'u (837–908), whose masterpiece is a collection of twenty-four poems (*Erh-shih-ssu Shih-p'in*) (Ssu-k'ung T'u, 1992) that delineated as many categories of the mental world or "modes of being" supposedly characteristic of great poetry (Sundararajan, 2004).

Twentieth-century developments

Recent history is characterized by three trends. The first is a continuation of the best in Confucian poetics, with its emphasis on the authenticity of *qing*, and the semiotic approach to emotions as signs that are best communicated through "evocative images", which enable the reader to participate in the "mental world" of the writer through resonance and association. This trend is exemplified by the literary critic and philosopher Wang Kuo-wei (1877–1927; see Yeh, 2000, vols 1 & 2). Although influenced by Western philosophy, especially by Schopenhauer, Wang's literary criticism (1977) is primarily Confucian and Buddhist in persuasion, and best known for its significant contribution to the further development of the notion of the "mental world". His now classic definition of the term is as follows: "The world [*jing-jie*] does not refer to scenes and objects only; joy, anger, sadness, and happiness also form a *world* in the human heart. Therefore, poetry that can describe true scenes and true emotions may be said to have a *world*; otherwise, it may be said not to have a *world*" (Wang, 1977, p. 4, emphasis in original).

The second trend in contemporary Chinese research is an analysis of indigenous emotional syndromes, using approaches based on Western social sciences. Examples include filial piety (e.g. Ho, 1998), the Chinese notion of face (e.g. Jia, 2001), and studies of indigenous forms of emotional disorders (e.g. Tseng, 1975).

The third trend involves laboratory and field studies of presumably pan-cultural aspects of emotion, such as the evolution of behavior, peripheral physiological changes, expressive reactions, neurocognitive mechanisms, and social influence. For the most part, this research is indistinguishable from that being conducted in the West. Thus, much of what we said earlier about twentieth-century trends in the West could be applied *mutatis mutandis* to twentieth-century trends in the East. Even the psychodynamic approach, which is perhaps the most culturally specific of the approaches we reviewed earlier, has its East Asian counterparts (see, for example, Doi's (1973) analysis of the Japanese emotion of *amae*).

Discussion: Six antinomies of emotion

Histories of ideas are important, if for no other reason than to satisfy one of the most fundamental of human emotions: curiosity. But histories of ideas gain added importance when they raise issues or provide guideposts for future research. With this in mind, we present six antinomies of emotion. An antinomy consists of two conflicting or incompatible beliefs, each reasonable in its own right. We make no pretense at resolving these antinomies. We present them, rather, as a way of summarizing some of the salient points from our historical reviews, and as goads to further thought.

I. The antinomy between action and passion: Emotions are things we do, versus emotions are things that happen to us. An emotion is a passion, something that seems to happen to a person; however, unlike tripping over a chair, or coming down with the flu, an emotion is also an action, some-thing a person does. The connotation of passivity—of being acted upon—was well articulated by Plato and Aristotle, and it has remained central to Western theories of emotion, even when changes in terminology (e.g. from "passion" to "emotion") have tended to mask the original connotation of "suffering" or undergoing change. The passion versus action conundrum is less acutely felt in the Chinese tradition, primarily for two reasons. First, the Chinese term, *gan* (to be affected), that implies the patient role has a positive connotation in the context of intersubjectivity, where the self functions as a tuning fork that needs to be affected and in turn affects others to keep the interconnected web of life going (or, as the Chinese put it, to keep the cosmic *qi* circulating). Second, the Chinese predilection for self-reflexivity yields a large stock of second-order desires (such as savor-ing), which, as self-initiated rather than reactive emotions, help to restore to passion its beleaguered sense of agency.

II. The antinomy between the extraordinary and the ordinary: Emotions are intense, episodic occurrences, versus emotions are an ever-present back-ground to all experience. Western history is often woven around the exceptional deeds of "great" men and women, whereas Chinese history, following the *Doctrine of the mean*, puts a premium on the commonplace, where the Tao is supposed to reside. This difference in emphasis is reflected in our presentation of Western and Eastern histories of emotion—our Western history focused on specific individuals (e.g. Aristotle, Augustine, Descartes, Spinoza, Darwin, Wundt), whereas our Eastern history focused on general movements (Confucianism, Taoism, and Buddhism). This difference in orientation is not limited to historical accounts. In literature, for example, it is the difference between the drama of epic poetry in the West and the subtlety of *haiku* in the East. And on the level of emotional experience, Western theories tend to emphasize episodic perturbations, whereas Chinese analyses favor the rippling eddies of affect, both in the pre-perturbation phase, as evidenced by attention to "the subtle" (Sundararajan, 2004), and in the post-stimulus phase, as evidenced by savoring the after taste of an event.

This difference in emphasis has far reaching implications. The Chinese notion of emotion as a pervasive, ongoing process that evolves continuously and does not have a clear demarcation of beginning and end implies that "refinement" is part of emotion, rather than a post-emotion development as is assumed by the episodic perspective. This is an important point, so let us phrase it differently. The regulation of emotion has long been a concern of Western theorists. Often, this has involved increased understanding of the causes of emotion (e.g. the Stoics, Spinoza, psychoanalysis). In the Chinese tradition, the emphasis is more on savoring than abstract knowledge, on refinement more than regulation (e.g. Ssu-k'ung T'u).

III. The antinomy between intuitive and intellectual judgments: Emotional appraisals are immediate and unpremeditated, versus emotional appraisals are basically rational. Appraisal theory—the basic idea of which is that emotions depend on judgments—dominates much of contemporary psychology. Paralleling the contemporary distinction between early perceptual processing of stimuli and latter conceptual processing, the Stoics made the distinction between "first movements"—those initial impulses to action when a threat is first appraised, and "second movements"—more complex appraisals, the kind only a rational being could make (albeit mistakenly). The rationality of emotional appraisals is receiving increased attention among contemporary theorists (e.g. Solomon, 1976; de Sousa, 1987). But the most radical advocates were the Stoics, who claimed that the intuitive "first movements" were not emotions at all. By contrast, the Chinese tend to privilege intuitive appraisals. Both Confucianism and Taoism frown at the complex appraisals, because of their contamination by the intellect. The Chinese view experience-distant intellectualizing tendencies as posing the danger of distorting the intent of emotions. Intuition, by contrast, seldom raises a red flag for the Chinese thinkers, who take it for granted that the most valid kind of reasoning is reasoning with the heart.

IV. The antinomy between nature and culture: Emotions are innate responses common to humans and animals, versus emotions are part of our cultural heritage. What would emotional life be if it were divorced of language and culture? Throughout history, West and East, this question has yielded conflicting answers, depending on presuppositions about what it means to be human. On one side, the seventeenth-century philosopher Thomas Hobbes famously suggested that, without the benefits of society, human existence would be "solitary, poor, nasty, brutish, and short". On the other side, we have seen how that paragon of eighteenth-century Romanticism, Rousseau, argued that society oppresses and distorts human nature. In contrast to either of these extreme positions, nature and culture are not terms impervious to each other in China, where the cultivation of nature is highly prized, from *bonsai* to the making of a Confucian gentleman. Thus it is not considered contradictory for a Chinese to tout the innateness of *qing* on the one hand, and to insist on its refinement through *li* (propriety), on the other.

V. The antinomy between feeling and emotion: Emotions are a kind of subjective experience, versus emotions are a kind of behavior. Although the terms "feeling" and "emotion" are often used interchangeably, they are not synonymous. Feelings are only one of the multiple components (e.g. feelings, physiological change, overt behavior) of an emotional syndrome. In the West, the assertion that emotions are feelings has often been a stopping point, letting the part stand for the whole. The Chinese notion of *qing* also places emphasis on subjective experience, similar in some respects to the "embodied view of emotional processing" (Barrett, 2005) in contemporary psychology. However, covert feelings accessed through the priming of imagery (*xing*) seem to involve information processing strategies distinctly different from talking about "feelings" in the West. Not surprisingly, Kleinman (1986) found that Chinese patients are not good at analyzing, differentiating or talking about their "inner feelings"—tasks that entail the elaboration and retrieval of memory in contradistinction to the pre-attentive priming capitalized by the *xing* tradition.

VI. The antinomy between emotional stereotypy and emotional creativity: Emotions are fixed and few in number, versus emotions are flexible and indefinite in number. Many theorists view emotions as fixed patterns of response, impervious to change except for their external expression. But some (e.g. Augustine, Spinoza) have also recognized that emotions are indefinite in number and subtle in variety, which implies the possibility for creative change. Although not absent, the seeming contradiction between emotion and creativity is more muted within Eastern traditions. For example, the notion, espoused by Ssu-k'ung T'u and others, that emotion should be savored, not explained, results in the privileging of "endocepts", that is, imageries that are pregnant with highly suggestive ideas but are incomplete in terms of their explicitness as concepts. Whereas the Western notion of endocepts takes the incompleteness of a concept in imagery as a way station in the creative process (Arieti, 1976), in Chinese poetics it is a matter of conscious choice and rigorous discipline for the individual not to drift into the mode of conceptualization (for more on East–West differences in emotions and creativity; see Averill, Chon, & Hahn, 2001; Sundararajan & Averill, in press).

Concluding observations

The above antinomies could easily be multiplied, but we leave that to the interests of the reader. Moreover, each antinomy can be found within a cultural tradition, as a contrast between major and minor themes. But what is a minor theme in one culture might be a major theme in another. In presenting the antinomies, therefore, we have focused on differences between rather than within cultures. This makes it more difficult to dismiss either pole of an antinomy as of secondary importance. Also, as stated earlier, we make no pretense of solving the antinomies. Indeed, they are not meant to be solved. Their existence helps ensure the diversity and richness of ideas that provide the foundation for future developments.

In concluding, it is worth reiterating that our history of Western theories incorporated ideas from different countries as well as times (Greece, Rome, Germany, Britain, France, the United States, among others), whereas our history of Eastern ideas has focused primarily on one country—China. If we had included other East Asian countries—Japan and Korea—the diversity of ideas discussed would have been greater. And, needless to say, equally rich intellectual traditions exist in the countries of South Asia, especially India.

As psychology becomes increasingly international, it is important that it does not become homogenized. Especially in an area such as emotion, a diversity of ideas and approaches is essential. More than most psychological phenomena (e.g. memory or perception), emotions embody deeply held but often contradictory views of what it means to be human. As we have seen, for example, emotions are often depicted as alien forces that lead a person astray; yet, a person devoid of emotion is viewed as shallow, at best, and little better than a beast or automaton, at worst. In a rapidly changing world, the last thing psychology needs do is narrow the meaning of what it means to be human.

References

Abrams, M. H. (1976). *The mirror and the lamp*. Oxford: Oxford University Press.

Aquinas, T. (1970). *Summa theologiae* (Vol. 11, *Man* 1a. 75–83) (T. Suttor, Trans.). New York: McGraw-Hill/Blackfriars.

Arieti, S. (1976). *Creativity: The magic synthesis*. New York: Basic Books.

Aristotle (1941). Rhetoric (W. R. Roberts, Trans.). In R. McKeon (Ed.), *The basic works of Aristotle* (pp. 1318–1451). New York: Random House.

Aristotle (1947). Nicomachean ethics (W. D. Ross, Trans.). In R. McKeon (Ed.), *The basic works of Aristotle* (pp. 935–1112). New York: Random House.

Arnold, M. B. (1960). *Emotion and personality* (2 volumes). New York: Columbia University Press.

Augustine (1948). Confessions (J. G. Pilkington, Trans.). In J. W. Oates (Ed.), *Basic writings of Saint Augustine* (Vol 1). New York: Random House.

Augustine (1966). *The city of God* (Vol. 4). (P. Levine, Trans.). Cambridge, MA: Harvard University Press.

Averill, J. R. (1974). An analysis of psychophysiological symbolism and its influence on theories of emotion. *Journal for the Theory of Social Behavior, 4*, 147–190.

Averill, J. R., Chon, K. K., & Hahn, D. W. (2001). Emotions and creativity, East and West. *Asian Journal of Social Psychology, 4*, 165–183.

Barrett, L. F. (2005). Feeling is perceiving: Core affect and conceptualization in the experience of emotion. In L. F. Barrett, P. M. Niedenthal, & P. Winkielman (Eds.), *Emotion and consciousness* (pp. 255–284). New York: Guilford.

Berger, P. L., & Luckmann, T. (1966). *The social construction of reality*. Garden City, NY: Doubleday.

Berry, T. (2003). Affectivity in classical Confucian tradition. In W. M. Tu, & M. E. Tucker (Eds.), *Confucian spirituality* (pp. 96–112). New York: Crossroad.

Bowlby, J. (1969). *Attachment and loss. Vol 1: Attachment*. London: Hogarth Press.

Bowlby, J. (1973). *Attachment and loss. Vol II: Separation: Anxiety and anger*. New York: Basic Books.

Bowlby, J. (1980). *Attachment and loss. Vol III: Loss: Sadness and depressions*. New York: Basic Books.

Brentano, F. (1971). Psychology from the empirical standpoint. (D. B. Terrell, Trans.). London: Routledge and Kegan Paul (Original work published 1874).

Brooks, E. B., & Brooks, A. T. (1998). *The original analects: Sayings of Confucius and his successors*. New York: Columbia University Press.

Bruner, J. S. (1986). *Actual minds, possible worlds*. Cambridge, MA: Harvard University Press.

Bryant, F. B. (1989). A four-factor model of perceived control: Avoiding, coping, obtaining, and savoring. *Journal of Personality, 57* (4), 773–797.

Buck, C. D. (1949). *A dictionary of selected synonyms in the principal Indo-European languages*. Chicago: University of Chicago Press.

Cannon, W. B. (1927). The James–Lange theory of emotions: A critical examination and an alternative theory. *American Journal of Psychology, 34*, 106–124.

Chan, W-T. (Trans.) (1969). *A source book in Chinese philosophy*. Princeton, NJ: Princeton University Press.

Colapietro, V. M. (1989). *Peirce's approach to the self: A semiotic perspective on human subjectivity*. Albany, NY: SUNY Press.

Curley, E. (1994). Notes on a neglected masterpiece: Spinoza and the science of hermeneutics. In G. Hunter (Ed.), *Spinoza: The enduring questions* (pp. 64–99). Toronto: University of Toronto Press.

Damasio, A. R. (1994). *Descartes' error: Emotion, reason, and the human brain*. New York: Putnam.

Damasio, A. R. (2003). *Looking for Spinoza: Joy, sorrow, and the feeling brain*. Orlando, FL: Harcourt.

Darwin, C. (1965). *The expression of the emotions in man and animals*. Chicago: University of Chicago Press (Original work published 1872).

de Silva, P. (1995). Theoretical perspectives on emotions in early Buddhism. In J.

Marks & R. T. Ames (Eds.), *Emotions in Asian thought* (pp. 109–120). Albany, NY: SUNY Press.

de Sousa, R. (1987). *The rationality of emotion.* Cambridge, MA: MIT Press.

Dehejia, H. V. (1996). *The advaita of art.* Delhi: Motilal Banarsidass.

Descartes, R. (1968). The passions of the soul. In E. S. Haldane & G. R. T. Ross (Trans.), *The philosophical works of Descartes* (Vol. 1). Cambridge, UK: Cambridge University Press (Original work written 1649).

Dewey, J. (1894). The theory of emotion. I. Emotional attitudes. *Psychological Review, 1,* 553–569.

Dewey, J. (1895). The theory of emotion. II. The significance of emotions. *Psychological Review, 2,* 13–32.

Dixon, T. (2003). *From passions to emotions: The creation of a secular psychological category.* Cambridge, UK: Cambridge University Press.

Doi, T. (1973). *The anatomy of dependence.* Tokyo: Kodansha International.

Ekman, P. (1984). Expression and the nature of emotion. In K. Scherer & P. Ekman (Eds.), *Approaches to emotion* (pp. 319–343). Hillsdale, NJ: Lawrence Erlbaum Associates Inc.

Elias, N. (1978). *The history of manners* (Vol. 1) (E. Jephcott, Trans.). New York: Pantheon Books.

Ellenberger, H. F. (1970). *The discovery of the unconscious.* New York: Basic Books.

Eoyang, E. C. (1993). *The transparent eye.* Honolulu: University of Hawaii.

Erasmus, D. (1989). *Praise of folly* (R. M. Adams, Ed. & Trans.). New York: Norton. (Original work published 1508).

Fang, A. (1954). Introduction. In E. Pound, *Shih-ching/The classic anthology defined by Confucius* (pp. ix–xvi). Cambridge, MA: Harvard University Press.

Freud, S. (1963). Introductory lectures on psycho-analysis. Part 3. In J. Strachey (Ed. and Trans.), *The standard edition of the complete psychological works of Sigmund Freud* (Vol. 15, pp. 243–576). London: Hogarth Press (Original work published 1917).

Freud, S. (1965). *New introductory lectures on psychoanalysis* (J. Strachey, Trans.). New York: Norton. (Original work published 1933).

Fridlund, A. (1992). Darwin's anti-Darwinism in the *Expression of the emotions in man and animals.* In K. Strongman (Ed.), *International review of studies on emotion.* (Vol. 2, pp. 117–137). New York: Wiley.

Frijda, N. H. (1986). *The emotions.* Cambridge, UK: Cambridge University Press.

Frijda, N. H. (2000). Spinoza and current emotion theory. In Y. Yovel (Ed.), *Desire and affect: Spinoza as psychologist* (pp. 235–264). New York: Little Room Press.

Fung, Y-l. (1953). *A history of Chinese philosophy* (Vols 1 & 2), (D. Bodde, Trans.). Princeton, NJ: Princeton University Press.

Fung, Y-l. (1962). *The spirit of Chinese philosophy* (E. R. Hughes, Trans.). Boston: Beacon.

Fung, Y-l. (1966). *A short history of Chinese philosophy* (D. Bodde, Ed.). New York: Free Press.

Galik, M. (1980). The concept of creative personality in traditional Chinese literary criticism. *Oriens Extremus, 2,* 183–202.

Graham, A. C. (1986). *Studies in Chinese philosophy and philosophical literature.* Albany, NY: SUNY Press.

Hall, D. L., & Ames, R. T. (1987). *Thinking through Confucius.* Albany, NY: SUNY Press.

Hansen, C. (1995). Qing (emotions) in pre-Buddhist Chinese thought. In J. Marks & R. T. Ames (Eds.), *Emotions in Asian thought* (pp. 181–209). Albany: SUNY Press.

Harré, R. (Ed.) (1986). *The social constructions of emotions.* New York: Basil Blackwell.

Hebb, D. O. (1946). On the nature of fear. *Psychological Review, 53,* 259–276.

Ho, D. Y. F. (1998). Filial piety and filicide in Chinese family relationships: The legend of Shun and other stories. In U. P. Gielen & A. L. Comunian (Eds.), *The family and family therapy in international perspectives* (pp. 134–149). Italy: Edizioni Lint Trieste S. R. L.

Hogan, P. C. (1996). Towards a cognitive science of poetics: Anadavardhana, Abhinavagupta, and the theory of literature. *College Literature, 23*(1), 164–178.

Hsu, F. K. (1990). *Chung-kuo wen-hsüeh lun-chi* [Collected essays on Chinese literature]. Taipei: Hsüeh-sheng shu-chü.

James, H. (Ed.) (1920). *The letters of William James* (Vol. 1). Boston: Atlantic Monthly Press.

James, W. (1890). *The principles of psychology* (Vol. 2). New York: Henry Holt and Company.

James, W. (1961). *Varieties of religious experience.* New York: Collier Books (Original work published 1902).

Jia, W. (2001). *The remaking of the Chinese character in the 21st century: The Chinese face practices.* Westport, CT: Greenwood Press.

Kant, I. (1986). What is enlightenment? (L. W. Beck, Trans.). In E. Behler (Ed.), *The German library. Vol. 13: Immanuel Kant: Philosophical writings* (pp. 263–269). New York: Continuum (Original work published 1784).

Kleinman, A. (1986). *Social origins of distress and disease: Neurasthenia, depression and pain in modern China.* New Haven, CT: Yale University Press.

Lane, R. D., & Nadel, L. (Eds.). (2000). *Cognitive neuroscience of emotion.* New York: Oxford University Press.

Lang, F. R. (1972). Psychological terminology in the Tusculans. *Journal of the History of the Behavioral Sciences, 8,* 419–436.

Lazarus, R. S. (1991). *Emotion and adaptation.* New York: Oxford University Press.

Liu, J. J. Y. (1962). *The art of Chinese poetry.* Chicago: University of Chicago Press.

Lu, R. R. (2004). *Zhung-guo gu-dai xiang-dui guan-xi si-wei tan-tao* [Investigations of the idea of relativity in ancient China]. Taipei: Shang ding wen hua.

Mandler, G. (1984). *Mind and body: Psychology of emotion and stress.* New York: Norton.

Maslow, A. H. (1971). *The farther reaches of human nature.* New York: Viking Press.

Mather, R. (Trans.) (1976). *Shih-shuo hsin-yü: A new account of tales of the world.* Minneapolis, MN: University of Minnesota Press.

McDougall, W. (1936). *An introduction to social psychology* (23rd ed.). London: Methuen.

Moreau, P.-F. (1996). Spinoza's reception and influence. In D. Garrett (Ed.), *The Cambridge companion to Spinoza* (pp. 408–433). New York: Cambridge University Press.

Nafe, J. (1924). An experimental study of the affective qualities. *American Journal of Psychology, 35,* 507–544.

Neu, J. (1977). *Emotion, thought, and therapy: A study of Hume and Spinoza and the* relationship of philosophical theories of the emotions to psychological theories of therapy. Berkeley, CA: University of California Press.

Nussbaum, M. C. (1994). *The therapy of desire: Theory and practice in Hellenistic ethics*. Princeton, NJ: Princeton University Press.

Oatley, K. (1992). *Best laid schemes: The psychology of emotion*. Cambridge, UK: Cambridge University Press.

Osgood, C. E. (1969). On the whys and wherefores of E, P, and A. *Journal of Personality and Social Psychology, 12*, 194–199.

Otto, R. (1970). *The idea of the holy* (J. W. Harvey, Trans.). London: Oxford University (Original work published 1923).

Owen, S. (1992). *Readings in Chinese literary thought*. Cambridge, MA: Harvard University Press.

Panksepp, J. (1998). *Affective neuroscience: The foundations of human and animal emotions*. New York: Oxford University Press.

Paranjpe, A. C. (2002). Indigenous psychology in the post-colonial context: An historical perspective. *Psychology and Developing Societies, 14*, 27–43.

Parkinson, B. (1995). *Ideas and realities of emotion*. London, UK: Routledge.

Pavlov, I. P. (1960). *Conditioned reflexes* (G. V. Anrep, Trans. & Ed.). New York: Dover Publications. (Original work published 1926).

Plato (1961). Phaedrus (R. Hackworth, Trans.). In E. Hamilton & H. Cairns (Eds.), *The collected dialogues of Plato* (pp. 475–525). New York: Pantheon Books.

Potter, S. H. (1988). The cultural construction of emotion in rural Chinese social life. *Ethos, 16*, 181–208.

Rogers, C. R. (1961). *On becoming a person*. Boston: Houghton Mifflin.

Roseman, I. J. (1991). Appraisal determinants of discrete emotions. *Cognition and Emotion, 5*, 161–200.

Rosenwein, B. H. (1998). Controlling paradigms. In B. H. Rosenwein (Ed.), *Anger's past* (pp. 234–247). Ithaca, NY: Cornell University Press.

Rousseau, J.-J. (1911). *Emile* (B. Foxley, Trans.). New York: E. P. Dutton (Original work published 1762).

Russell, J. A. (2003). Core affect and the psychological construction of emotion. *Psychological Review, 110*, 145–172.

Sartre, J.-P. (1948). *The emotions: Outline of a theory* (B. Frechtman, Trans.). New York: Philosophical Library.

Schachter, S. (1964). The interaction of cognitive and physiological determinants of emotional states. In L. Berkowitz (Ed.), *Advances in experimental social psychology* (Vol. 1). New York: Academic Press.

Scherer, K. R. (2001). Appraisal considered as a process of multi-level sequential checking. In K. R. Scherer, A. Schorr, T. Johnstone (Eds.), *Appraisal processes in emotion: Theory, methods, research* (pp. 92–120). New York: Oxford University Press.

Schlosberg, H. (1954). Three dimensions of emotion. *Psychological Review, 61*, 81–88.

Seneca (1963). On anger. In J. W. Basore (Trans.), *Moral essays* (Vol. 1. pp. 106–355). Cambridge, MA: Harvard University Press (Original work written ca. 50 CE).

Skinner, B. F. (1988). Behaviorism at fifty. In A. C. Catania & S. Harnad (Eds.), *The selection of behavior: The operant behaviorism of B. F. Skinner* (pp. 278–292). New York: Cambridge University Press (Original work published 1963).

Smith, E. R., & Neumann, R. (2005). Emotion processes considered from the perspective of dual-process models. In L. F. Barrett, P. M. Niedenthal, & P. Winkielman (Eds.), *Emotion and consciousness* (pp. 287–311). New York: Guilford.

Smith, Q. (1981). On Heidegger's theory of moods. *The Modern Schoolman, LVIII (4)*, 211–235.

Snow, C. P. (1963). *The two cultures: And a second look*. New York: Cambridge University Press.

Snyder, C. R., & Lopez, S. J. (Eds.). (2002). *Handbook of positive psychology*. New York: Oxford University Press.

Solomon, R. C. (1976). *The passions*. Garden City, NY: Doubleday Anchor.

Spence, D. P. (1982). *Narrative truth and historical truth: Meaning and interpretation in psychoanalysis*. New York: Norton.

Spinoza, B. de (1967). *Ethics* (J. Gutman, Ed., W. H. White & A. Hutchinson, Trans.). New York: Hafner Publishing Company (Original work published 1677).

Ssu-k'ung T'u (1992). *Erh-shih-ssu Shih-p'in* [The twenty-four categories of poetry] (S. Owen, Trans.). In S. Owen, *Readings in Chinese literary thought* (pp. 299–357). Cambridge, MA: Harvard University Press (Original work in the ninth century).

Stearns, P. N. (2000). History of emotions: Issues of change and impact. In M. Lewis & J. M. Haviland-Jones (Eds.), *Handbook of emotions* (pp. 16–29). New York: Guilford Press.

Sundararajan, L. (2002). The veil and veracity of passion in Chinese poetics. *Consciousness and Emotion, 3*, 197–228.

Sundararajan, L. (2004). Twenty-four poetic moods: Poetry and personality in Chinese aesthetics. *Creativity Research Journal, 16*, 201–214.

Sundararajan, L. (in press). The plot thickens—or not: Protonarratives of emotions and the principle of savoring. *Theoria et Historia Scientarium*.

Sundararajan, L. & Averill, J. R. (in press). Creativity in the everyday: Culture, self, and emotions. In R. Richards (Ed.), *Everyday creativity and new views of human nature*. Washington, DC: American Psychological Association.

The doctrine of the mean (J. Legge, Trans.) (1971). In J. Legge, *The Chinese Classics* (Vol. I, pp. 382–434). Taipei: Wen Shih Chi (Translation first published 1893).

The she king/The book of poetry (J. Legge, Trans.) (1971). In J. Legge, *The Chinese Classics* (Vol. IV). Taipei: Wen Shih Chi (Translation first published 1893).

Titchener, E. B. (1908). The tridimensional theory of feeling. *American Journal of Psychology, 19*, 213–231.

Titchener, E. B. (1914). A historical note on the James–Lange theory of emotions. *American Journal of Psychology, 251*, 427–447.

Tomkins, S. S. (1981). The quest for primary motives: Biography and auto-biography of an idea. *Journal of Personality and Social Psychology, 41*, 306–329.

Tseng, W. S. (1975). The nature of somatic complaints among psychiatry patients: The Chinese case. *Comprehensive Psychiatry, 16*, 237–245.

Tu, W. M. (1984). Pain and suffering in Confucian self-cultivation. *Philosophy East and West, 34*(4), 379–388.

Tu, W. M. (1989). *Centrality and commonality*. Albany: SUNY Press.

Uttal, W. R. (2001). *The new phrenology*. Cambridge, MA: MIT Press.

Wang, K. W. (1977). *Poetic remarks in the human world (Jen chien tz'u hua)*. (Ching-I Tu, Trans.). Taipei: Chung Hwa.

Watson, J. B. (1919). *Psychology from the standpoint of a behaviorist.* Philadelphia: Lippincott.

Wixted, J. T. (1983). The nature of evaluation in the *Shih-p'in* (Gradings of poets) by Chung Hung (AD 469–518). In S. Bush & C. Murck (Eds.), *Theories of the arts in China* (pp. 225–266). Princeton, NJ: Princeton University Press.

Wong, S-K. (1978). *Ch'ing* and *Ching* in the critical writings of Wang Fu-chih. In A. A. Rickett (Ed.), *Chinese approaches to literature from Confucius to Liang Ch'i-ch'ao* (pp. 121–150). Princeton, NJ: Princeton University Press.

Wu, D. Y. H. (1982). Psychotherapy and emotion in traditional Chinese medicine. In A. J. Marsella & G. M. White (Eds.), *Cultural conceptions of mental health and therapy* (pp. 285–301). Dordtrecht, Netherlands: D. Reidel.

Wundt, W. (1897). *Outlines of psychology* (C. H. Judd, Trans.). New York: Gustav E. Stechert.

Yeh, C. Y. (2000). *Wang Kuo-wei chi ch'i wen-hsüeh p'i-p'in* [Wang Kuo-wei and his literary criticism] (Vols. 1 & 2). Taipei: Kuei-kuan T'u-shu.

Yu, P. (1987). *The reading of imagery in the Chinese poetic tradition.* Princeton, NJ: Princeton University Press.

7 Mental imagery

*Simona Gardini, Cesare Cornoldi, and
Rossana De Beni*

Anything could exist in the mind which
was not previously present in the senses
(Thomas Aquinas)

State of the concept of mental image

When we speak of mental images we refer to representations of objects in
our mind. Typically, mental images refer to visual representations, but we
could also imagine the sound of a river, the scent of a daisy, the softness of
wool, the taste of a piece of chocolate cake, and thus produce also auditory,
olfactory, tactile, and gustative mental images. However, the literature
on imagery has taken into consideration almost exclusively visual mental
images, so this is what we shall focus on in this chapter. According to a
constructive view of mental imagery (e.g. Cornoldi, De Beni, Giusberti, &
Massironi, 1998), a mental image is less modality specific than the corresponding perception. Furthermore, the content of the mental images evoked
may consist of more layers than the corresponding sensory perception. Thus
we could imagine a dear friend or the long hours before obtaining a result
of an exam with deep emotional involvement, and hence produce a specific
emotional mental image, but also reconstructed it as a mental image
involving many modalities simultaneously.

The imagery process is strongly related to memory, thinking and perception. A number of different interpretations of the concept of mental images
have been proposed. Holt (1964) observed that a mental image refers to all
the subjective awareness experiences with an almost-sensitive modality that
is not only perceptual. Differently from perception, imagery is a mental
process, difficult to ascribe to an exact stimulus situation (Cornoldi, 1976).
Kosslyn (1980, 1994) defined mental images as representations of objects
that we can see through the mind's eye in the absence of the perceptual
stimulus. Richardson (1999) proposed considering mental images as complex mental products, inner representations where information on the
actual perceptual appearance of objects can be described and transformed.

Intons-Peterson and McDaniel (1991) claimed that mental images might be created by the interaction between visual representation and the subject's knowledge, suggesting that images could be defined as "knowledge-based" products. Mental images may be considered as a means of knowing the world, as suggested by the famous sentence of Aristotle: "Are objects of memory only those that fall under the imagination".

In the cognitive scientific lexicon, imagery indicates a different process with respect to the imagination. Imagery refers to the controlled and voluntary production of mental images, regarding facts or objects very similar to the perceptual ones, whereas imagination refers to fantasy processes (McKellar, 1957). In this chapter, we refer to the imagery process and not to the imagination.

The beginning of the imagery process is perceptual experience, which allows us to represent the object in our knowledge system. Information of what we have experienced is registered in our memory system and then retrieved every time we need it. In many circumstances of our life, the retrieval of mental images from memory represents a useful tool, as, for example, when we orient ourselves in a familiar environment using a visual mental map, or when—before leaving for a holiday—we imagine the optimal luggage arrangement in the trunk of the car. The large use of imagery in everyday life and the close relationship between imagery and other cognitive processes justify the interest toward this topic.

Historical development of imagery

The interest towards the study of mental imagery dates back to ancient times. Aristotle postulated the "figural theory" of images and considered them as having a key role in the memory process. A mental image was defined as an inner representation of the real object, like a copy of a specific scene of life. The nature of the images was considered figural and not symbolic, and their use was considered to facilitate the retrieval of specific objects stored in memory. Aristotle's "figural theory" seems to be the antecedent of the analogical view of imagery, which considers mental images as real perceptual representations of the objects in our mind (e.g. Kosslyn, 1980, 1994; Shepard & Metzler, 1971). If Aristotle assigned a central role to imagery in both thinking and retrieval processes, about two thousand years later, Cartesius, although sharing the consideration that mental images were learned through experience and were figural representations of objects, denied the relation between mental images and thinking.

Even though interest towards mental images started a long time ago, imagery was considered a central topic of experimental psychology only from the 1970s, with the advent of cognitive psychology. Prior to this period, especially in the USA, the behaviourist approach considered the study of imagery as being beyond the range of psychological investigation and mental events not directly observable through an experimental methodology. This attitude towards mental concepts was less rigid in Europe, where many important psychological theories, as for example those of Bartlett and Piaget, included a specific reference to mental imagery. Piaget and Inhelder (1966) attributed to the image a preparatory role in the development of intelligence, one that anticipates mental operations although not a real expression of logical thinking. In the USA, Holt (1964) re-established interest in the mental phenomena within the psychological domain and questioned the ostracism toward the study of inner processes.

The advent of cognitive science signalled a new era in the research of imagery processes. Interest towards mental events returned to be a central topic of psychology and different experimental paradigms were applied to the investigation of higher cognitive processes, such as imagery. Individual reports and subjective introspective experiences were again considered objects of interest and the imagery process was considered an intermediary between stimulus and response, to the same extent as other cognitive processes, such as memory (Paivio, 1971).

Mental images may be created almost continually in our mind and represent a basic element of thinking (Singer & Antrobus, 1972). The distinction between imagery and thinking has been the object of reflection of many philosophers. For example, around the seventeenth century, classical British empiricism (see texts reported by Herrnstein & Boring, 1973) considered every form of thinking as a manipulation of simple images derived from sensorial activities. Berkeley (1871) considered every operation of the mind as based on experience, so that ideas about things and events in reality could be represented by their images. Locke identified an image as the idea of the corresponding object, thus ideas and images were mental figures of things. This was considered particularly true for simple ideas. Complex ideas were produced from the reasoning activity and did not maintain the figural properties of the objects. Ideas were stored in memory and represented in an abstract modality, such as the linguistic format. Berkeley, however, did not accept the mind's faculty of abstraction. He postulated that the idea of a certain object, for example of a man, would always refer to a particular exemplar of man. Mental images and percepts would be phenomena of the same type (i.e. ideas), and the former would derive from the combination of perceptual representations stored in memory. Hume (1739) affirmed that every idea derives from sensorial impressions and considered the idea as a weak image of the real object. In some sense, empiricism considered the phenomenological properties of mental images as distinguished from real perceptions. Hobbes (1685/1999) affirmed that mental images of objects absent in the perceptual field are not so clear as the visual objects, but vague and weak, and were not considered as real pictures in the mind.

In the history of psychology, the debate between the so-called "symbolist" position sustained by Wundt and Titchener and the "conceptualistic" one sustained by the Würzburg School showed two different points of view on the relationship between imagery and thinking. The symbolists affirmed that thinking works through the combination of symbols, which could have a verbal or imaginative nature. Wundt and Titchener maintained that thinking is the result of associative processes based on sensations and images. The conceptualistic perspective highlighted the existence and importance of studying higher cognitive processes, including thinking, without reference to sensory images. Although the Würzburg School maintained that thinking differs from the use of mental images, its approach had the effect of increasing the interest for different complex processes.

A different debate concerning the existence and the role of mental images in cognitive activity re-appeared in the first phases of the cognitive psychology era. Pylyshyn (1973, 1981) refused the idea of images as having an independent format with specific functional properties, and affirmed that they were part of the conceptual and propositional systems of knowledge. A unique amodal format existed either for images or for words. Propositionalists (e.g. Pylyshyn, 1973, 1981) attributed to mental image a like-description and symbolic format, without any sensorial property, on which the processing occurred in a sequential manner; the relationships between elements were explicitly explained. The propositional format interested both the information in long-term memory and the conscious representations. Contrarily, the analogical or pictorial view (e.g. Shepard & Metzler, 1971) maintained that mental images were very similar to the percepts, with a specific modality format, in which the information was presented in parallel and the relations between the elements were implicit. These two extreme positions were then integrated by intermediate models that considered the information in long-term memory as being represented in a more abstract and propositional format, whereas conscious mental images maintained more sensorial properties (Kosslyn, 1980; Marschark & Cornoldi, 1990), which were, however, in many respects different from the perceptual representation. This discussion is once again in progress, but many studies have focused more on the imagery processes and image characteristics *per se*, suggesting different interpretations of the image formats.

Cultural variability and the evolution of research paradigms on imagery

The research on mental images showed on occasions a different development in North America and Europe. The methodology used in North America to investigate imagery processes was very similar to that applied to perception. The studies of Kosslyn (see 1994 for a review) are an example of an approach linked to an analogical representation of the mental images. The European tradition considered the imagery processes as linked to the cognitive activities of the mind, such as memory, problem solving, and thinking, and further considered the introspective method as a valid method of investigation.

Since the 1960s, an impressive body of evidence has showed that imagery can be investigated applying different controlled experimental procedures. Brooks (1968) introduced the *selective interference* paradigm. He presented participants with two tasks simultaneously, examining to what extent one would disrupt the other. In one of these tasks, the participants had to memorize an outlined letter and then to decide if, starting from a certain point, the corners were posed on the external or internal part of the letter. A verbal task required them to listen to a sentence and, for each word, to state whether it was or was not a noun. Brooks established two response conditions: (1) a visual one, requiring participants to cross, on paper, the letter "y" for the positive response or the letter "n" for the negative answer; and (2) a verbal one, requiring the participants to say "yes" or "no". Results showed that the visual response created more interference (by increasing the mean response times) with the visual task (analysing the position of the corners of the letter), and that the verbal response interfered more with the verbal task (noun or not-noun). These data showed that verbal and imagery processes involve different mechanisms.

The investigation of imagery processes and their characteristics must take into account the problem that the observer is the same as the observed and that the only channel to know these directly is the introspective method (Cornoldi, 1976). In this respect, imagery tasks can be divided into two categories: (1) direct tests that are based on the introspective report of individuals, which however can also include a quantitative evaluation of the subjective experiences; and (2) indirect tasks, based on quantitative scores obtained by the individual's performance on tasks that involve the imagery process.

Considering the first, an investigation of mental images of this type would be the study of vividness ratings of images. The vividness of a mental image represents a measure of the extent to which an individual has generated a clear, distinct, accurate and bright representation. At the end of the nineteenth century, Galton (1883) created the first test to measure the vividness of mental images. Galton sent a questionnaire-letter to a group of scientists. He asked them to imagine an object, for example the table where they had had breakfast that morning, and then to consider some of the characteristics of the image, such as the "illumination" (image clearness, weakness, or similarity to the real object), the clarity of the borders (border definition) and the colour. This study showed that there was a large amount of individual difference between individuals according to their employment and area of research. Many individuals involved in mechanical science, who were often involved in visualization, gave high visual vividness scores, whereas scientists of other fields gave lower vividness ratings. Successively, Marks (1973) elaborated the Vividness of Visual Images Questionnaire (VVIQ) to establish the individual evaluation of the vividness of visual mental images. This test is accomplished in two ways: either with open or closed eyes. The subject is required to judge, on a 5-point scale, the vividness of four scenes and, for each scene, four different situations. This test is usually used to investigate the individual differences in visual imagery ability. Cornoldi et al. (1992) found that a higher vividness rating of visual mental images corresponded to better recall, and that certain characteristics played an important role on the vividness rating.

The subjective impressions regarding the quality and properties of images led to a classification of an individual's images into different categories. The primitive representations that are associated with sensory experiences could also be included in the domain of mental images. For example, when fixing a red square for a certain time and then moving gaze on a grey surface, it is possible to see an image of a square in the complementary green colour. Eidetic images are very detailed images, also called "photographic" representations. Individuals describe eidetic images like a photograph in front of the eyes (Allport, 1924). However, the eidetic image should not be considered as a copy of the stimulus, because also in this case the imagery system maintains a critical influence (Paivio, 1971). Eidetic images are usually present only among particular individuals, mainly children.

At a higher cognitive level, a distinction is made between mental images deriving from memory and images of the imagination (Griffitts, 1927). The first refers to images that we could evoke from memory, such as the image of a boat. The second refers to fantasy images, created by combining elements stored in memory in new and unreal ways; for example, creating an image of a car with wings. This distinction is not always so clearly defined because images from memory are not always exact reproductions of the equivalent perceptual experiences, whereas fantasy images could be created on the bases of visual memory traces. Griffitts (1927) distinguishes between concrete and verbal imagery. The image of a letter, for example an "A", could be considered an imagery process more than a verbal one, distinguishing between verbal imagination with visual characteristics and inner elaboration of discourse (inner speech). However, this image represents a verbal stimulus and can be distinguished from the image of a shape without a verbal implication. As already discussed, a taxonomy of mental images also includes the existence of common vs. bizarre or unusual images, single vs. interactive, prototypical vs. exemplar (Kosslyn, 1994), personal–impersonal vs. specific–general (Helstrup, Cornoldi, & De Beni, 1997), contextual vs. autobiographical vs. episodic–autobiographical (De Beni & Pazzaglia, 1995) mental images. From the same word it is possible to generate different types of image. The theoretical distinctions between these categories of image are supported by quantitative measures, revealed by differences in the generation and maintenance times, in recall performance and in qualitative measures, such as vividness and goodness (Cornoldi, De Beni, & Pra Baldi, 1989; De Beni & Pazzaglia, 1995; Helstrup et al., 1997). Cocude and Denis (1988) measured the generation and maintenance times of visual mental images. They found that nouns with high imagery value correlated with shorter generation times; however, imagery value did not affect maintenance times, suggesting a functional distinction between the generation and maintenance processes. Cocude, Charlot, and Denis (1997) compared the generation and maintenance processes between a normal and a depressed population. They found that generation times for the depressed group were longer than for the normal one; however, there were no significant differences between the duration times of the two groups, confirming the conclusion of previous research on the distinction between generation and maintenance processes.

The indirect tests investigate imagery through the use of visuo-spatial tests. Classical examples of these procedures are tests requiring the mental manipulation of shapes. Shepard and Metzler (1971) created a *mental rotation* task in which they showed participants pairs of three-dimensional configurations formed by cubes, asking them which two pictures in each pair represented the same object (although rotated differently) and which represented different objects. The two pictures could differ, either as regards the angular degree of the rotation or one could be a rotated version of the mirror image of the other. Results showed a linear relationship between the degree of rotation of the two configurations and the time required to perform the task. This result confirms the analogy between imagery and perception.

The *mental scanning* paradigm requires imagining an object and either inspects or computes some mental operation on the object. Kosslyn, Ball, and Reiser (1978) invited participants to learn a map of an island with different landmarks located at different distances from one another. Individuals had to imagine themselves moving from one landmark to another. Results showed that the more distance between locations, the more time was required to imagine moving between them, accordingly to an analogical view. De Beni and Giusberti (1990) found that instructions given to subjects and/or how instructions were understood played a critical role in the performance of this task. They found that not all individuals reported using the same methods in moving through the imagined environment: For example, in imaging moving from one room to another of their own home, one subject reported following a particular route, whereas others described passing directly from one room to another without visualizing intermediate points. These data suggested the importance of the cognitive strategies used in the performance of the scanning task. In particular, these findings suggested that mental imagery is not necessarily constrained by perceptual limitations.

The *mental synthesis* task (Brandimonte, Hitch, & Bishop, 1992; Finke, Pinker, & Farah, 1989) evaluates the ability of people to mentally assemble different figures and to represent them in a new configuration. This procedure showed that within the imagery modality it is possible to combine single elements to produce a new configuration. The Mental Clock Test (Paivio, 1971) requires participants to imagine two different clock faces. The task is to decide in which of the two clock faces, the clock hands form the greater angle.

The findings from these research paradigms have shown that different mental operations and transformations can be executed on mental images, and that mental images can maintain some visual–spatial properties similar to real perceptual objects.

The relationship between imagery and perception

Mental images have been considered similar to perceptual representation in our mind. A debate is still running on the hypothesis that imagery and perception share common mechanisms. Neisser (1976) sustained the idea that mental images and percepts have in common certain elaboration processes.

The analogical view sustains the identity between perception and imagery and is supported by data obtained comparing cognitive performance in a task adopting an imagery and perceptual processing. Some results found assuming an imagery processing confirmed an effect found in the perceptual field. For example, the mental rotation task of three-dimensional visuo-spatial configurations (Shepard & Metzler, 1971) or the dot-localization task using imagined stimuli, showed that visual mental images are subjected to the constraints of the physical world.

Sometimes, the terms used to describe a mental image are the same used for percepts, like those indicating shape, size, colour, and orientation of point of view. Furthermore, the content of a mental image, or the elements that constitute it, are based on a previous sensorial experience. Different studies showing the similarity between perception and imagery followed a methodology similar to the one used in the selective interference paradigm. Some studies (e.g. Segal & Fusella, 1970) showed the similarity between the visual characteristics of mental images and percepts. They demonstrated that auditory and visual mental images could interfere with the detection of visual and auditory perceptual stimuli.

A different line of research evidenced that in certain cases the image could have a preparatory role toward the perception of stimuli. The image can thus either interfere or prime the detection of the percept. Farah (1985), using a detection task during which subjects imagined a particular stimulus, discovered that when the image matched the stimulus the detection was better than when it did not, and the effect was particularly strong when the image and the stimulus were in the same position.

To establish if an event has really happened or it is the fruit of imagination (reality monitoring process) is not always possible and clear. This effect demonstrates the similarity of the subjective impression derived from imagery and from perceptual experience and that perception and imagery might share some level of processing. Subjects are usually more likely to mention perceptual and contextual details for perceived events, while report more reasoning considerations for imagined events.

One interesting field of investigation as regards the relationship between imagery and perception is the replication in the imagery modality of certain phenomena or effects of illusion obtained in the perceptual modality. This area is particularly open to criticism. Under imagery conditions different visual illusions may be obtained, such as the Mueller–Lyer illusion (Heller, Brackett, Wilson, Yoneama, Boyer, & Steffen, 2002), and the Ponzo, Hering and Wundt illusion among higher imagers individuals (Wallace, 1984). However, Intons-Peterson, and McDaniel (1991) reported a series of asymmetries between imagery and perception regarding the distance and magnitude estimations, relative contrast (brightness), structural factors, mental rotation and the role of knowledge. Giusberti, Cornoldi, De Beni, and Massironi (1992) considered the different subjective experiences linked to imagery and perception and found that visual images and visual percepts differed in vividness ratings, and that the visual perception involved more automatic and pre-attentive processes; on the other hand, visual images generation implied the involvement of controlled and non-automatic processes. Further studies by the same authors revealed that, when participants do not know the perceptual effect and/or the image is not based on a preceding perceptual experience, the visual illusion is not present at the mental imagery level. For example, the "pop-out" effect was examined by contrasting the representations of a reversed or inclined letter in a matrix made with the same letter under three different conditions, perceptual, memory perceptual and imagery. In the first two conditions, it was the inclined letter to "pop out", and it did so clearly, producing the most vivid representation; in the imagery representation, the reversed letter appeared more vividly than the inclined one. Giusberti, Cornoldi, De Beni, and Massironi (1998) confirmed the asymmetry between perception and imagery by using the Ebbinghaus and Ponzo illusions. Studies carried out on totally congenitally blind people suggested that not only could an analogical interpretation of imagery process exist, but that blind people seem to form mental representations using other sensory modalities (Cornoldi, Bertuccelli, Rocchi, & Sbrana, 1993). Thus, given the existence of contradictory results emerging from different studies, the conclusions in this particular field are as yet difficult to draw. However, the distinction proposed by Cornoldi et al. (1998) between a visual trace, sharing characteristics with perception, and a generated image, with different properties, seems able to take into account the different findings.

Some studies revealed that common neural patterns have been activated during perceptual and imagery tasks (Kosslyn, 1994; Kosslyn et al., 1999). Kosslyn et al. (1993) compared the brain areas involved in the same task but performed in a visual and an imagery modality. In the first case, individuals saw the perceptual stimulus (an uppercase letter) in a grid and had to decide if an "x" presented in the grid was located on the letter; in the imagery task, subjects were required to imagine the uppercase or a lowercase letter in the grid and execute the same task. Kosslyn et al. found that the areas involved in the two tasks were very similar and, when the activation for the perception condition was subtracted from the mental imagery one, the primary visual area showed an increase in activation. Moreover, mental images of small objects activated more the posterior portion of the visual cortex, whilst mental images of large objects involved more the anterior parts of the visual cortex. These findings suggested a topographical organization of visual areas during an imagery task. In a positron emission tomography (PET) study, Kosslyn et al. (1999) found that in the visual discrimination of the properties of stripes, the visual areas, in particular area 17, were activated and that the application of transcranial magnetic stimulation (rTMS) impaired the task performance.

A neuropsychological study by Bisiach and Luzzatti (1978) presented a unilateral neglect patient with right parietal lesion who demonstrated a deficit on the visual perception of left hemispace and in the formation of mental images of the same portion of space. However, Behrmann, Winocur, and Moscovitch (1992) and Jankowiak et al. (1992) described cases of an intact imagery function in visual agnosia patients, suggesting that some visual mechanisms involved in object recognition are not required during imagery. Goldenberg, Muellbacher, and Nowak (1995) reported the case of a patient with severe damage to the primary visual cortex but preserved imagery function and thus suggested the existence of areas of preserved visual cortex responsible for the generation of mental images.

The use of an integrated perspective, including experimental designs, neuropsychological data and neuroimaging data, seems to be useful in understanding the dynamic of the relationship between imagery and perception.

The role of imagery in memory process

In the past, many philosophers described the strong relationship between memory and imagery. In more recent times, within the field of experimental psychology, Paivio (1971) began to study the role of imagery in human thought and memory. He proposed that a possible way to investigate imagery functioning could be based on the study of memory performance. Paivio started with a series of studies on the paired-associate recall of nouns and adjectives. He discovered that when the pairs were composed of a concrete noun before an abstract noun (or an adjective), the recall was better than when the order was reversed. More generally, concrete nouns increased the memory recall compared to abstract ones. Paivio, Yuille, and Madigan (1968) investigated the role of different indexes of verbal stimuli, such as meaningfulness, concreteness, imagery value, and familiarity, on memory. The verbal associative meaningfulness indicates the mean number of verbal associations that a word would elicit in a given period of time. The imagery value refers to the facility with which words prime a mental image. The concreteness is related to the extent to which words refer to a tangible object, person, or material. Paivio et al. (1968) demonstrated that stimulus imagery value was strongly related to recall when meaningfulness was kept constant. Instead, meaningfulness did not produce any effect when the imagery value was controlled. Results confirmed the importance of imagery mechanisms on memory recall of nouns. Different studies confirmed that imagery is independent from familiarity and meaningfulness. Furthermore, imagery value and concreteness were shown to correlate not only with memory, but also with other cognitive tasks (Paivio, 1971).

Paivio (1971, 1991) proposed the dual coding theory. Following this model an experience can be represented in a modality-specific format corresponding to that of the original event. By consequence, a verbal system is responsible for the encoding and processing of verbal stimuli, and a non-verbal system is responsible for the encoding of information regarding objects and events presented in the environment. The two representational systems are independent. The starting points are separate; logogens are the basic units for verbal stimuli, whereas imagens are the basic units for imagery material. The two systems of processing then continue towards two different systems in long-term memory. In some cases, certain referential connections between the two processes occur, producing a double encoding of material, both in the verbal and in the imagery system.

The case of concrete nouns would offer an example of stimuli that undergo a double encoding. In fact, concrete nouns with a high imagery value would be processed by both systems and this could explain the memory recall advantage of this noun category (Paivio et al., 1968).

Paivio's neo-mentalist approach to the study of the relationship between imagery and memory processes also considered material characteristics, facilitative effects of imagery instructions on memory, and individual differences in imagery ability. De Beni and Moè (2003) showed that individual differences in imagery ability influenced the beneficial effect of imagery strategies in memory recall: High imagers benefited from imagery strategies whereas poor imagers benefited more from rehearsal or verbal strategies in the memorization of passages. These results suggested that the general assumption that imagery strategies benefit memory performance is dependent on individual differences in imagery ability.

The art of memory (Yates, 1967) affirmed that the use of good and well-elaborated images improves memory performance. The use of imagery processes for memory improvement has been investigated using a paradigm that requires the generation of mental images of a list of nouns, and their subsequent recall. However, research showed that different types of image can be generated, and that these may have different implications on memory. Cornoldi, De Beni, and Pra Baldi (1989) considered the effects of different types of mental image on memory recall performance. By comparing memory performance after the generation of general (i.e. the prototypical image of an object), specific (the image of an exemplar of an object category) and autobiographical (the image of an object relating to me) mental images, they showed that the recall of general and specific mental images did not differ, but the autobiographical mental images produced a better recall with respect to the other two types of image. Helstrup et al. (1997) reported that the most remembered nouns were associated with the mental generation of specific and personal images. De Beni and Pazzaglia (1995) differentiated, within the self-referred mental images, between the personal images (in which an individual imagines her- or himself together with an object) and the episodic autobiographical (representing a particular episode of the life, spatially and temporally defined, connected with an object). The personal images that were rated as either good or not good were remembered equally well, and the episodic autobiographical images judged as good were recalled better than those judged poorly. The episodic autobiographical mental images allowed an improvement in memory performance with respect to the contextual images. In general, the episodic autobiographical attribute had a specific influence on the increase of recall for the particular format of the image (i.e. complexity and richness in details) and for the characteristics of the generation process (i.e. those that required a longer generation time compared to other categories of images).

Concerning the differentiation in types of image, a possible categorization can regard the distinction between single (generating a mental image of a single object) versus interactive (creating a mental image in which different elements to remember interact each other) mental images. Interactive images improve memory retrieval of elements contained in the image more than the generation of a single image of them. A further important distinction of types of image is between common and bizarre images. The first ones represent objects as we know them in the real world, whereas the second one contains an impossible and strange representation of the object. An example of a bizarre image could be the image of a table, which is walking. Cornoldi, Cavedon, De Beni, and Pra Baldi (1988) found that the generation of bizarre representations improved memory recall of item in a list of nouns if subjects are allowed to evoke the type of image they prefer for each noun. Further studies (Einstein, McDaniel, & Lackey, 1989) reported that recall was influenced by the distinctiveness of the materials. In fact, authors found that when in a list of words all the stimuli were imagined in the bizarre modality, the recall was not better than when using common images; when the bizarre and common mental images were generated alternatively in the same list of words, the bizarre images produced a better memory performance. These findings indicated that bizarreness *per se* does not produce an increase in memory performance but needs to be accompanied by distinctiveness.

The use of memory strategies, and/or mnemonics based on mental imagery, to improve memory performance has been considered useful since the times of the ancient Roman philosopher Cicero, who used image-based strategies to remember his public speeches. Since then, the use of imagery strategies to improve memory has been investigated in an experimental setting, such as recall of lists of words or passages. Mnemonics consist of different strategies with which to organize the material to improve memory retrieval. Some of the principal mnemonics, like the loci's method, keyword, and chaining of images techniques are based on the use of mental imagery. De Beni, Moè. and Cornoldi (1997) found an improvement of text memory performance using the loci's mnemonics when the materials were presented orally rather than in a written format (effect of oral presentation), suggesting that the use of imagery processes is facilitated when it is not simultaneously performed a visual processing.

The process of mental generation of images

The possibility of "seeing" an object with our mind's eye generally seems to require that we have first experienced it in the perceptual world. This happens especially when the mental generation regards images of memory. We could also create original and totally new representations in our mind, not based on real perceptual representations. Images of memory can be generated on the basis of information retrieved from long-term memory. Cornoldi et al. (1998) called this type of mental image "generated image", and distinguished it from a representation directly derived from a recent experience or from a well-learned sensory pattern, called "a visual trace" (Table 7.1). According to their constructive view, generated images are the result of the combined synthesis of long-term memory information coming from different sources and may be penetrated by beliefs, emotions, and conceptual knowledge. Contrarily, visual traces share many properties with visual percepts.

In accordance with Kosslyn's analogical view (1980, 1994), the mental generation of images requires the retrieval of associative memories (stored in the posterior, superior temporal regions) and of perceptual and conceptual characteristics of objects. The visual buffer, supposedly located in the occipital lobe, is the temporary store where images are generated either on the basis of information loaded by the perceptual view (eyes) or on the basis of information stored in long-term visual memory (Figure 7.1).

According to this model, all real objects we have experienced have left a visuospatial representation in our memory. During the perceptual process, the visual information forms a retinotopic representation in the visual area of the occipital lobe and the information is then stored in the temporal lobe as a memory representation of objects. The format of the memory representation of objects is independent from their spatial orientation, giving us the possibility of recognizing a learned object also from a different perspective. The image generation process can be defined as the activation of early retinotopic representations by higher-level object memory representations, via back projection (Farah, 1995). If the object is not easily retrieved, a top-down processing starts on the stored information, involving the dorsolateral prefrontal cortex (Damasio, 1985).

Table 7.1 Main distinctions between a visual trace and an image
generated from long-term memory information

	Visual trace	Generated image
Access	Directly access	Generated
Attention	Very low (often pre-attentive)	High level
Represented object	Phenomenic object	Constructed object
Perception analogy	Almost complete	Partial
Main characteristics	Sensorial–phenomenic properties	Selected perceptual–conceptual properties
Role of long-term memory	Marginal	Substantial
Process penetrability	Almost none	Substantial
Modality of loss	Same as sensorial information	Same as elaborated information
Interference	Visual similarity representations requiring similar processes	Different processing requiring attention
Capacity limitations	Limits of storage	Limits of storage and operator
Memory variation related to age development	Minimal	Substantial

The generation of images seems to be a sequential operation that moves from the retrieval of the global shape of an object to the subsequent enrichment of its details. In line with this suggestion, more time is necessary to form images of objects with a greater numbers of parts, that is, more complex objects (Kosslyn, 1980). An important question regarding image generation is whether what is retrieved first is its inner protomodel, the template representation, or the specific representation of an exemplar belonging to the category of an object. For example, if we imagine a setter (or even a specific exemplar of a setter, like our uncle's setter), do we first retrieve the general shape of a dog and then add the details of a setter, or do we immediately retrieve the specific image of this breed (exemplar) of dog? If we assume that we have the mental representation of a setter in our long-term memory, it is possible to directly retrieve his image. But the time required to generate the image of a specific exemplar of a certain category is longer than the time necessary to retrieve the prototypical or general representation of it. This is particularly true for the generation of autobiographical images (De Beni & Pazzaglia, 1995). This could be due to the fact that the generation of an autobiographical image requires the preceding generation of a general image or also to the fact that the search of an autobiographical representation of the object maybe "contained" in a different memory store (with episodic autobiographical systems).

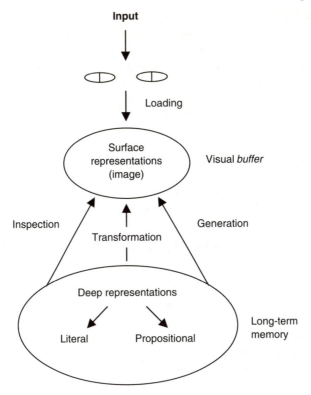

Figure 7.1 Representation of the imagery buffer model (adapted from Brandimonte, 1998).

During the generation of mental images, central operations, which work on the information stored in memory, are also involved. Images can be created with the retrieval of propositional descriptions from memory, or with the activation of frame and scene descriptions, or by forming visual percepts. Images represent the interpretation of the perceptual shapes, elaborated by the superior conceptual structures of the semantic long-term memory.

Farah (1984) revised the Kosslyn model adding a number of components: (1) a *describe* component, which permits to describe the contents of the visual buffer (visual to verbal translation); (2) a *copy* component that is required when the contents of the visual buffer must be reconstructed (visual to motor translation); (3) a *match* component involved when the contents of the visual buffer must be compared with the contents of long-term visual memory to recognize objects; and (4) a sensory process that *encodes* visually presented stimuli and *detects* activation in the visual buffer. These cognitive components are supposed to be involved both in visual perception and in visual imagery, except for the generation process (specific for visual imagery). This model recognizes the multicomponential structure of the imagery process, and could explain the different neuropsychological imagery deficits (Farah, 1984).

Baddeley (1986) proposed a multicomponent working memory model. He theorized the existence of a central executive system involved in reasoning, decision making, and the control of two slave systems: the phonological loop and the visual–spatial sketch pad. The former would be involved in temporary retention and processing of verbal material and the latter would be responsible for the retention and processing of visual–spatial stimuli. Series of studies using a dual-task paradigm found that during mental image generation not only the visual–spatial working memory system, but also the central attention resources are involved in imagery (see the review in Denis, Logie, Cornoldi, De Vega, & Engelkamp, 2001).

Neuroanatomical correlates of imagery process

Considering imagery as a multicomponent process composed by image generation, maintenance, rotation, and inspection suggests that different anatomical neural areas are involved in these different imagery sub-processes.

Some of the main issues investigated in studying the neural correlates of imagery regard the hemispheric specialization of imagery function and the involvement of the primary visual cortex in imagery.

With respect to hemispheric specialization, initial studies reported a pre-dominant right hemisphere involvement in imagery (Springer & Deutsch, 1981). Farah (1984) reported that neuropsychological patients with intact left inferior–temporal and occipital areas were able to generate mental images. Kosslyn, Holtzman, Farah, and Gazzaniga (1985) assigned a differ-ent role to right and left hemisphere in image generation. The right would be responsible for the formation of global and skeleton images, whilst the left would be implicated in the addition of details to the prototypical and global images. Goldenberg, Podreka, Steiner, and Willmes (1987) suggested that the left hemisphere activation during imagery task could be attributed to the verbal format of stimuli administered during the generation session. Tippet (1992) supported the main involvement of the left hemisphere in image generation, but he attributed to the posterior regions of both hemispheres a different contribution to image generation. Further data (Kosslyn, Maljkovic, Hamilton, Horowitz, & Thompson, 1995) indicated that the right hemisphere was responsible for generating mental images using the metric position of different parts stored in memory, whereas the left hemi-sphere would be advantaged for mental image generation starting from stored descriptions. More recent studies reported a left hemisphere special-ization for visual mental image generation (Trojano & Grossi, 1994). Milivojevic, Johnson, Hamm, and Corballis (2003) attributed a different function to the right and left hemispheres in relation to simple or complex mental transformations. The right hemisphere would be more involved in simpler (single mental rotation) mental transformation and the left one in more complex transformations. In conclusion, few studies supported a specialization of the right hemisphere in mental imagery, whereas most agree for a left hemispheric specialization.

Another important consideration regarding the neuroanatomical correlates of imagery regards the involvement of the primary cortical areas in correspondence to mental images of different sensory modality. Neurophysiological changes in the visual, acoustic and somatosensory areas were respectively observed during imagery evocated by pictures, sounds or tactile sensations (Fallgatter, Mueller, & Strik, 1997). Some studies found activation of V1 during imagery task (Kosslyn et al., 1993; Thompson et al., 2001), while other studies did not find its involvement (D'Esposito et al., 1997; Knauff et al., 2000). The involvement of the primary visual cortex could be related to the requirement of inspection of details with high resolution during imagery (Kosslyn & Thompson, 2003). Mellet, Tzourio, Denis, and Mazoyer (1998) denied the hypothesis that the primary visual area is activated by high-resolution tasks reporting no activation in this area during these types of task. However, the authors highlighted a difference of activation in the primary visual cortex during the learning modality: They found a significant deactivation during image generation of visually learned stimuli, suggesting a possible top-down modulation. Lambert, Sampaio, Scheiber, and Mauss (2002) found activation in the calcarine sulcus and in the occipito-parietal region during a mental image generation task in correspondence to animal nouns. They suggested that the use of a unique semantic category (e.g. animal) might facilitate the activation of the visual components. Ishai, Haxby, and Ungerleider (2002) investigated the different activation occurring in the generation of visual images of famous faces in either one of two cases: (1) retrieving the images from short-term memory (individuals saw the images before generating that specific image); or (2) generating the images from long-term memory (individual did not see an image prior to generation). During the visual perception of famous faces, the inferior occipital gyri, lateral fusiform gyri, the superior temporal sulcus, and the amygdala were activated. The visual imagery condition activated the bilateral calcarine (including the primary visual cortex), hippocampus, precuneus, intraparietal sulcus, and the inferior frontal gyrus. The activation in these regions was larger when the visual images were generated from short-term memory than from long-term memory. Knauff, Kassubek, Mulack, and Greenlee (2000) did not find activation of the primary visual cortex during a visual imagery task with complex configurations, and reported a more critical involvement of the visual association cortex, and of the parietal cortex, suggesting the importance of the spatial subsystems and higher visual areas. Despite the controversial results regarding the involvement of V1 in imagery, the role of visual associative areas has been suggested (Cabeza & Nyberg, 2000).

Some studies supported the validity of the dichotomy between the dorsal or occipito-parietal ("where" pathway) and the ventral or occipito-temporal ("what" pathway) in imagery domain. A number of different PET studies highlighted the activation of the dorsal pathway, related to the spatial information processing, during imagery spatial tasks (Cabeza & Nyberg, 2000). Cohen et al. (1996) found activation of the superior parietal lobe during Mental Rotation Test performance. Vingerhoets, de Lange, Vande-maele, Deblaere, and Achten (2002) reported the activation of bilateral superior parietal lobule, visual extrastriate cortex and prefrontal area during mental rotation of hand and tools.

Some neural regions, associated with other cognitive processes, such as language, memory, and reasoning, appeared to be involved during imagery (Denis, 2002; Mellet et al., 1998). The involvement of the prefrontal cortex in imagery (Cabeza & Nyberg, 2000) could be related to the role of working memory in imagery (Jonides et al., 1993), and to the retrieval of infor-mation from long-term memory (Ishai, Ungerleider, & Haxby, 2000). The precuneus, located in the mesial parietal cortex, has been considered to be involved both in imagery and memory retrieval. This structure has been associated with mental image generation of stored percepts (D'Esposito et al., 1997; Kosslyn et al., 1993). During a reasoning task involving mental imagery, Knauff, Mulack, Kassubek, Salih, and Greenlee (2002) found the activation of occipito-parietal-frontal areas, including prefrontal cortex, cingulate gyrus, superior and inferior parietal cortex, precuneus, and visual association cortex, suggesting the involvement of spatial imagery processes during reasoning. Findings obtained from the neuroimaging field confirmed the high degree of interaction between imagery and other cognitive func-tions, such as memory.

References

Allport, G. W. (1924). Eidetic imagery. *British Journal of Psychology*, *15*, 99–120.

Baddeley, A. (1986). *Working memory*. Oxford: Oxford University Press.

Behrmann, M., Winocur, G., & Moscovitch, M. (1992). Dissociation between mental imagery and object recognition in a brain damaged patient. *Nature*, *359*, 636–637.

Berkeley, G. (1871). *Works*. London: Campbell Fraser.

Bisiach, E., & Luzzatti, C. (1978). Unilateral neglect of representational space. *Cortex*, *14*, 129–133.

Brandimonte, M. A. (1998). Memoria e immaginazione. In R. Job (Ed.), *I processi cognitivi:modelli e ricerca in psicologia*. Roma: Carocci.

Brandimonte, M. A., Hitch, G. J., & Bishop, D. V. (1992). Influence of short-term memory codes on visual image processing: Evidence from image transformation tasks. *Journal of Experimental Psychology: Learning, Memory, and Cognition, 18*, 157–165.

Brooks, L. R. (1968). Spatial and verbal components of recall. *Canadian Journal of Psychology*, *22*, 349–368.

Cabeza, R., & Nyberg, L. (2000). Imaging Cognition II: An empirical review of 275 PET and fMRI studies. *Journal of Cognitive Neuroscience, 12*, 1–47.

Cocude, M., Charlot, V., & Denis, M. (1997). Latency and duration of visual mental images in normal and depressed subjects. *Journal of Mental Imagery, 21*, 127–142.

Cocude, M., & Denis, M. (1988). Measuring the temporal characteristics of visual images. *Journal of Mental Imagery, 12*, 89–101.

Cohen, M. S., Kosslyn, S. M., Breiter, H. C., DiGirolamo, G. J., Thompson, W. L., & Anderson, A. K. et al. (1996). Changes in cortical activity during mental rotation: A mapping study using functional MRI. *Brain, 119*, 89–100.

Cornoldi, C. (1976). *Memoria e immaginazione*. Bologna, Italy: Casa Editrice Patron.

Cornoldi, C., Bertuccelli, B., Rocchi, P., & Sbrana, B. (1993). Processing capacity limitations in pictorial and spatial representations in the totally congenitally blind. *Cortex, 29*, 675–689.

Cornoldi, C., Cavedon, A., De Beni, R., & Pra Baldi, A. (1988). The influence of the nature of material and of mental operations on the occurrence of the bizarreness effect. *Quarterly Journal of Experimental Psychology, 40A*, 73–85.

Cornoldi, C., De Beni, R., & Pra Baldi, A. (1989). Generation and retrieval of general, specific and autobiographic images representing concrete nouns. *Acta Psychologica, 72*, 25–39.

Cornoldi, C., De Beni, R., Cavedon, A., Mazzoni, G., Guisberti, F., & Marucci, F. (1992). How can a vivid image be described: Characteristics influencing vividness judgments and the relationship between vividness and memory. *Journal of Mental Imagery, 16*, 89–107.

Cornoldi, C., De Beni, R., Giusberti, F., & Massironi, M. (1998). Memory and imagery: A visual trace is not a mental image. In M. Conway, S. Gathercole, & C. Cornoldi (Eds.), *Theories of memory, Volume II* (pp. 87–110), Hove, UK: Psychology Press.

Damasio, A. R. (1985). Prosopagnosia. *Trends in Neurosciences, 8*, 132–135.

De Beni, R., & Giusberti, F. (1990). Explicit and tacit knowledge on mental imagery: A metacognitive study. *Ricerche di Psicologia, 14*, 57–75.

De Beni, R., & Moè, A. (2003). Presentation modality effects in studying passages: Are mental images always effective? *Applied Cognitive Psychology, 17*, 309–324.

De Beni, R., Moè, A., & Cornoldi, C. (1997). Learning from texts or lectures: Loci mnemonics can interfere with reading but not with listening. *European Journal of Cognitive Psychology, 9*, 401–415.

De Beni, R., & Pazzaglia, F. (1995). Memory for different kinds of mental images: Role of contextual and autobiographic variables. *Neuropsychologia, 11*, 1359–1371.

Denis, M. (2002). Can the human brain construct visual mental images from linguistic inputs? In A. M. Galaburda, S. M. Kosslyn, et al. (Eds.), *The languages of the brain* (pp. 215–225). Cambridge, MA: Harvard University Press.

Denis, M., Logie, R., Cornoldi, C., De Vega, M., & Engelkamp, J. (Eds.). (2001). *Imagery, language and visuo-spatial thinking*, Hove, UK: Psychology Press.

D'Esposito, M., Detre, J. A., Aguirre, G. K., Stallcup, M., Alsop, D. C., Tippet, L. J., & Farah, M. J. (1997). A functional MRI study of mental image generation. *Neuropsychologia, 35*, 725–730.

Einstein, G., McDaniel, M., & Lackey, S. (1989). Bizarre imagery, interference, and distinctiveness. *Journal of Experimental Psychology: Learning, Memory, and Cognition, 15*, 137–146.

Fallgatter, A. J., Mueller, T. J., & Strik, W. K. (1997). Neurophysiological correlates of mental imagery in different sensory modalities. *International Journal of Psychophysiology, 25*, 145–153.

Farah, M. J. (1984). The neurological base of mental imagery: A componential analysis. *Cognition, 18*, 241–269.

Farah, M. J. (1985). Psychophysical evidence for a shared representational medium for mental images and percepts. *Journal of Experimental Psychology: General, 114*, 91–103.

Farah, M. J. (1995). Current issues in the neuropsychology of image generation. *Neuropsychologia, 33*, 1455–1471.

Finke, R. A., Pinker, S., & Farah, M. J. (1989). Reinterpreting visual patterns in mental imagery. *Cognitive Science, 13*, 51–78.

Galton, F. (1883). *Inquiries into human faculty and its development.* London: Macmillan.

Giusberti, F., Cornoldi, C., De Beni, R., & Massironi, M. (1992). Differences in vividness ratings of perceived and imagined patterns. *British Journal of Psychology, 83*, 533–547.

Giusberti, F., Cornoldi, C., De Beni, R., & Massironi, M. (1998). Perceptual illusions in imagery. *European Psychologist, 3*, 281–288.

Goldenberg, G., Muellbacher, W., & Nowak, A. (1995). Imagery without perception: A case study of anosognosia for cortical blindness. *Neuropsychologia, 33*, 1373–1382.

Goldenberg, G., Podreka, I., Steiner, M., & Willmes, K. (1987). Patterns of regional cerebral blood flow related to memorizing of high and low imagery words: An emission computer tomography study. *Neuropsychologia, 25*, 473–485.

Griffitts, C. H. (1927). Individual differences in imagery. *Psychological Monographic, 37*, 172.

Heller, M. A., Brackett, D. D., Wilson, K., Yoneama, K., Boyer, A., & Steffen, H. (2002). The haptic Mueller–Lyer illusion in sighted and blind people. *Perception, 31*, 1263–1274.

Helstrup, T., Cornoldi, C., & De Beni, R. (1997). Mental images: Specific or general, personal or impersonal? *Scandinavian Journal of Psychology, 38*, 189–197.

Herrnstein, R. J., & Boring, E. G. (Eds.). (1973). *A source book in the history of psychology.* Cambridge, MA: Harvard University Press.

Hobbes, T. (1685/1999). *Human nature and de corpore politico.* New York: University Press (Original work published 1685).

Holt, R. R. (1964). Imagery: The return of the ostracized. *American Psychologist, 19*, 254–264.

Hume, D. (1739). *A treatise on human nature.* London: Noon.

Intons-Peterson, M., & McDaniel, M. (1991). Symmetries and asymmetries between imagery and perception. In C. Cornoldi & M. A. McDaniel (Eds.), *Imagery and cognition* (pp. 47–76). New York: Springer.

Ishai, A., Haxby, J. V., & Ungerleider, L. G. (2002). Visual imagery of famous faces: Effects of memory and attention revealed by fMRI. *Neuroimage, 17*, 1729–1741.

Ishai, A., Ungerleider, L. G., & Haxby, J. V. (2000). Distributed neural systems of the generation of visual images. *Neuron, 28*, 979–990.

Jankowiak, J., Kinsbourne, M., Shalev, R. S., & Bachman, D. L. (1992). Preserved visual imagery and categorization in a case of associative visual agnosia. *Journal of Cognitive Neuroscience, 4,* 119–131.

Jonides, J., Smith, E. E., Koeppe, R. A., Awh, E., Minoshima, S., & Mintun, M. A. (1993). Spatial working memory in humans as revealed by PET. *Nature, 363,* 623–625.

Knauff, M., Kassubek, J., Mulack, T., & Greenlee, M. W. (2000). Cortical activation evoked by visual mental imagery as measured by fMRI. *NeuroReport, 11,* 3957–3962.

Knauff, M., Mulack, T., Kassubek, J., Salih, H., & Greenlee, M. W. (2002). Spatial imagery in deductive reasoning: A functional MRI study. *Cognitive Brain Research, 13,* 203–212.

Kosslyn, S. M. (1980). *Image and mind.* Cambridge, MA: Harvard University Press.

Kosslyn, S. M. (1994). *Image and brain: The resolution of the imagery debate.* Cambridge, MA: MIT Press.

Kosslyn, S. M., Alpert, N. M., Thompson, W. L., Maljkovic, V., Weise, S. B., Chabris, C. F. et al. (1993). Visual mental imagery activates topographically organized visual cortex: PET investigations. *Journal of Cognitive Neuroscience, 5,* 263–287.

Kosslyn, S. M., Ball, T. M., & Reiser, B. J. (1978). Visual images preserve metric spatial information: Evidence from studies of image scanning. *Journal of Experimental Psychology: Human Perception and Performance, 4,* 47–60.

Kosslyn, S. M., Holtzman, J. D., Farah, M. J., & Gazzaniga, M. S. (1985). A computational analysis of mental image generation: Evidence from functional dissociations in split-brain patients. *Journal of Experimental Psychology: General, 114,* 311–341.

Kosslyn, S. M., Maljkovic, V., Hamilton, S., Horowitz, G., & Thompson, W. (1995). Two types of image generation: evidence for left and right hemisphere processes. *Neuropsychologia, 33,* 1485–1510.

Kosslyn, S. M., Pascual-Leone, A., Felician, O., Camposano, S., Keenan, J. P., Thompson, W. L., Ganis, G., Sukel, K. E., & Alpert, N. M. (1999). The role of Area 17 in visual imagery: Convergent evidence from PET and rTMS. *Science, 284,* 167–170.

Kosslyn, S. M., & Thompson, W. L. (2003). When is early visual cortex activated during visual mental imagery? *Psychological Bulletin, 129,* 723–746.

Lambert, S., Sampaio, E., Scheiber, C., & Mauss, Y. (2002). Neural substrates of animal mental imagery: Calcarine sulcus and dorsal pathway involvement-An fMRI study. *Brain Research, 924,* 176–183.

Marks, D. F. (1973). Visual imagery differences in the recall of pictures. *British Journal of Psychology, 64,* 17–24.

Marschark, M., & Cornoldi, C. (1990). Imagery and verbal memory. In C. Cornoldi & M. McDaniel (Eds.), *Imagery and cognition* (pp. 133–182). New York: Springer-Verlag.

McKellar, P. (1957). *Imagination and thinking.* London: Cohen.

Mellet, E., Tzourio, N., Denis, M., & Mazoyer, B. (1998). Cortical anatomy of mental imagery of concrete nouns based on their dictionary definition. *NeuroReport, 9,* 803–808.

Milivojevic, B., Johnson, B. W., Hamm, J. P., & Corballis, M. C. (2003). Non-identical neural mechanisms for two types of mental transformation: Event related potentials during mental rotation and mental paper folding. *Neuropsychologia*, *41*, 1345–1356.

Neisser, U. (1976). *Cognition and reality*. San Francisco, CA: Freeman.

Paivio, A. (1971). *Imagery and verbal processes*. New York: Holt, Rinehart, Winston.

Paivio, A. (1991). *Images in mind: The evolution of a theory*. Hertfordshire, UK: Harvester Wheatsheaf.

Paivio, A., Yuille, J. C., & Madigan, S. A. (1968). Concreteness imagery, and meaningfulness values for 925 nouns. *Journal of Experimental Psychology*, *76*.

Piaget, J., & Inhelder, B. (1966). *L'image mentale chez l'enfant*. Paris: P.U.F.

Pylyshyn, Z. W. (1981). The imagery debate: Analogue media versus tacit knowledge. *Psychological Review*, *88*, 16–45.

Pylyshyn, Z. W. (1973). What the mind's eye tells the mind's brain: A critique of mental imagery. *Psychological Review*, *80*, 1–24.

Richardson, J. T. E. (1999). *Cognitive psychology: A modular course*. Hove, UK: Psychology Press.

Segal, S. J., & Fusella, V. (1970). Influences of imaged pictures and sounds on detection of visual and auditory signals. *Journal of Experimental Psychology*, *83*, 458–464.

Shepard, R. N., & Metzler, J. (1971). Mental rotation of three dimensional objects. *Science*, *171*, 701–703.

Singer, J. L., & Antrobus, J. S. (1972). Daydreamer, imaginal processes, and personality: A normative study. In P. W. Sheehan (Ed.), *The function and nature of imagery* (pp. 175–202). New York: Academic Press.

Springer, S., & Deutsch, G. (1981). *Left brain, right brain*. San Francisco, CA: Freeman.

Thompson, W. L., Kosslyn, S. M., Sukel, K. E., & Alpert, N. M. (2001). Mental imagery of high- and low-resolution gratings activates area 17. *NeuroImage*, *14*, 454–464.

Thompson-Schill, S. L., Aguirre, G. K., D'Esposito, M., & Farah, M. J. (1999). A neural basis for category and modality specificity of semantic knowledge. *Neuropsychologia*, *37*, 671–676.

Tippet, L. J. (1992). The generation of visual images: A review of neuro-psychological research and theory. *Psychological Bulletin*, *112*, 415–432.

Trojano, L., & Grossi, D. (1994). A critical review of mental imagery defects. *Brain and Cognition*, *24*, 213–243.

Vingerhoets, G., de Lange, F. P., Vandemaele, P., Deblaere, K., & Achten, E. (2002). Motor imagery in mental rotation: An fMRI study. *NeuroImage*, *17*, 1623–1633.

Wallace, B. (1984). Apparent equivalence between perception and imagery in the production of various visual illusions. *Memory and Cognition*, *12*, 156–162.

Yates, F. A. (1967). *The art of memory*. London: Routledge & Kegan.

8   Intelligence

Robert J. Sternberg

There is no one history of the development of the concept of intelligence, but rather many histories, depending on who is doing the telling. For example, the largely laudatory histories recounted by Carroll (1982, 1993), Herrnstein and Murray (1994), and Jensen (1998, 2002) read very differently from the largely skeptical histories recounted by Gardner (1983, 1999), Gould (1981), and Sacks (1999). And, of course, there are differences within these groups of authors. For example, there is virtually no overlap in the historical data used by Carroll (1993) versus Gardner (1983) to support their respective theories of intelligence.

The emphasis in this chapter is on the history of the development of the concept of intelligence, particularly with reference to theories of intelligence. Readers interested primarily in contemporary work and in measurement issues might consult relevant chapters in Mackintosh (1998) or Sternberg (1982, 1994, 2000).

Perhaps the most fundamental question in the field of intelligence arises from the issue of how we should conceive of intelligence. Several different positions have been staked out (Sternberg, 1990). Many of the differences in ideology that arise in accounts of the history of the field of intelligence arise from differences in the model of intelligence to which an investigator adheres. To understand the history of the development of the concept of intelligence, one must understand the alternative epistemological models that can give rise to the concept of intelligence. But before addressing these models, consider simply the question of how psychologists in the field of intelligence have defined the construct on which they base their models.

Implicit theories of intelligence

One way to discover what intelligence is involves asking people. There are two obvious groups to ask: experts and laypersons.

Expert conceptions of the nature of intelligence

Historically, one of the most important approaches to figuring out what intelligence is has relied on the opinions of experts. Such opinions are sometimes referred to as *implicit theories*, to distinguish them from the more formal *explicit theories* that serve as the formal bases for scientific hypotheses and subsequent data collections.

Implicit theories (which can be of laypersons as well as experts) are important to the history of a field for at least three reasons (Sternberg, Conway, Ketron, & Bernstein, 1981). First, experts' implicit theories are typically what give rise to their explicit theories. Second, much of the history of intelligence research and practice is much more closely based on implicit theories than it is on formal theories. Most of the intelligence tests that have been used, for example, are based more on the opinions of their creators as to what intelligence is than they are based on formal theories. Third, people's everyday judgments of each other's intelligence always have been, and continue to be, much more strongly guided by their implicit theories of intelligence than by any explicit theories.

Intelligence operationally defined

E. G. Boring (1923), in an article in *The New Republic*, proposed that intelligence is what the tests of intelligence test. Boring did not believe that this operational definition was the end of the line for understanding intelligence. On the contrary, he saw it as a "narrow definition, but a point of departure for a rigorous discussion . . . until further scientific discussion allows us to extend [it]" (p. 35). Nevertheless, many psychologists, and especially testers and interpreters of tests of intelligence, have adopted this definition or something similar to it, despite the circularity of the definition.

The 1921 symposium

Probably the most well known study of experts' definitions of intelligence was one done by the editors of the *Journal of Educational Psychology* ("Intelligence and its measurement", 1921). Contributors to the symposium were asked to address two issues: (1) what they conceived intelligence to be and how it best could be measured by group tests; and (2) what the most crucial next steps would be in research. Fourteen experts gave their views on the nature of intelligence, with such definitions as the following: the power of good responses from the point of view of truth or facts (E. L. Thorndike); the ability to carry on abstract thinking (L. M. Terman); sensory capacity, capacity for perceptual recognition, quickness, range or flexibility of association, facility and imagination, span of attention, quickness or alertness in response (F. N. Freeman); having learned or ability to learn to adjust oneself to the environment (S. S. Colvin); ability to adapt oneself adequately to relatively new situations in life (R. Pintner); and the capacity to learn or to profit by experience (W. F. Dearborn).

Of course, there have been many definitions of intelligence since those represented in the journal symposium, and an essay even has been written on the nature of definitions of intelligence (Miles, 1957). One well-known set of definitions was explicitly published in 1986 as a follow-up to the 1921 symposium (Sternberg & Detterman, 1986).

Sternberg and Berg (1986) attempted a comparison of the views of the experts in 1986 with those of the experts in 1921. They reached three general conclusions.

First, there was at least some general agreement across the two symposia regarding the nature of intelligence. When attributes were listed for frequency of mention in the two symposia, the correlation was .50, indicating moderate overlap. Attributes such as adaptation to the environment, basic mental processes, higher-order thinking (e.g. reasoning, problem solving, and decision making) were prominent in both symposia.

Second, central themes occurred in both symposia. One theme was the one versus the many: Is intelligence one thing or is it multiple things? How broadly should intelligence be defined? What should be the respective roles of biological versus behavioral attributes in seeking an understanding of intelligence?

Third, despite the similarities in views over the 65 years, some salient differences could also be found. Metacognition—conceived of as both knowledge about and control of cognition—played a prominent role in the 1986 symposium but virtually no role at all in the 1921 symposium. The later symposium also placed a greater emphasis on the role of knowledge and the interaction of mental processes with this knowledge.

Definitions of any kind can provide a basis for explicit scientific theory and research, but they do not provide a substitute for these things. Thus it was necessary for researchers to move beyond definitions, which they indeed did. Many of them moved to models based on individual differences.

Lay conceptions of intelligence

In some cases, Western notions about intelligence are not shared by other cultures. For example, at the mental level, the Western emphasis on speed of mental processing (Sternberg et al., 1981) is not only not shared by many other cultures but the quality of work that is done very quickly might be viewed with suspicion. Indeed, other cultures emphasize depth rather than speed of processing. They are not alone: Some prominent Western theorists have pointed out the importance of depth of processing for full command of material (e.g. Craik & Lockhart, 1972).

Yang and Sternberg (1997a) have reviewed Chinese philosophical conceptions of intelligence. The Confucian perspective emphasizes the characteristic of benevolence and of doing what is right. As in the Western notion, the intelligent person spends a great deal of effort in learning, enjoys learning, and persists in life-long learning with a great deal of enthusiasm. The Taoist tradition, by contrast, emphasizes the importance of humility, freedom from conventional standards of judgment, and full knowledge of oneself as well as of external conditions.

The difference between Eastern and Western conceptions of intelligence may persist even in the present day. Yang and Sternberg (1997b) studied contemporary Taiwanese Chinese conceptions of intelligence, and found five factors underlying these conceptions: (1) a general cognitive factor, much like the *g* factor in conventional Western tests; (2) interpersonal intelligence; (3) intrapersonal intelligence; (4) intellectual self-assertion; and (5) intellectual self-effacement. In a related study, but with different results, Chen (1994) found three factors underlying Chinese conceptualizations of intelligence: nonverbal reasoning ability, verbal reasoning ability, and rote memory. The difference may be due to different subpopulations within China, to differences in methodology, or to differences in when the studies were done.

The factors uncovered in both studies differ substantially from those identified in American people's conceptions of intelligence by Sternberg et al. (1981): (1) practical problem solving; (2) verbal ability; and (3) social competence, although in both cases, people's implicit theories of intelligence seem to go quite far beyond what conventional psychometric intelligence tests measure. Of course, comparing the Chen (1994) to the Sternberg et al. (1981) study simultaneously varies both language and culture.

Chen and Chen (1988) varied only language. They explicitly compared the concepts of intelligence of Chinese graduates from Chinese-language versus English-language schools in Hong Kong. They found that both groups considered nonverbal reasoning skills as the most relevant skill for measuring intelligence. Verbal reasoning and social skills came next, and then numerical skill. Memory was seen as least important. The Chinese-language-schooled group, however, tended to rate verbal skills as less important than did the English-language-schooled group. Moreover, in an earlier study, Chen, Braithwaite, and Huang (1982) found that Chinese students viewed memory for facts as important for intelligence, whereas Australian students viewed these skills as of only trivial importance.

Das (1994), also reviewing Eastern notions of intelligence, has suggested that in Buddhist and Hindu philosophies, intelligence involves waking up, noticing, recognizing, understanding, and comprehending, but also includes such things as determination, mental effort, and even feelings and opinions in addition to more intellectual elements.

Differences between cultures in conceptions of intelligence have been recognized for some time. Gill and Keats (1980) noted that Australian university students value academic skills and the ability to adapt to new events as critical to intelligence, whereas Malay students value practical skills, as well as speed and creativity. Dasen (1984) found Malay students to emphasize both social and cognitive attributes in their conceptions of intelligence.

The differences between East and West may be due to differences in the kinds of skills valued by the two kinds of cultures (Srivastava & Misra, 1996). Western cultures and their schools emphasize what might be called "technological intelligence" (Mundy-Castle, 1974), and so things like artificial intelligence and so-called smart bombs are viewed, in some sense, as intelligent or smart.

Western schooling also emphasizes other things (Srivastava & Misra, 1996), such as generalization or going beyond the information given (Connolly & Bruner, 1974; Goodnow, 1976), speed (Sternberg, 1985), minimal moves to a solution (Newell & Simon, 1972), and creative thinking (Goodnow, 1976). Moreover, silence is interpreted as a lack of knowledge (Irvine, 1978). By contrast, the Wolof tribe in Africa views people of higher social class and distinction as speaking less (Irvine, 1978). This difference between the Wolof and Western notions suggests the usefulness of looking at African notions of intelligence as a possible contrast to US notions.

Studies in Africa in fact provide yet another window on the substantial differences. Ruzgis and Grigorenko (1994) have argued that, in Africa, conceptions of intelligence revolve largely around skills that help to facilitate and maintain harmonious and stable intergroup relations; intragroup relations are probably equally important and at times more important. For example, Serpell (1974, 1982, 1996) found that Chewa adults in Zambia emphasize social responsibilities, cooperativeness, and obedience as important to intelligence; intelligent children are expected to be respectful of adults. Kenyan parents also emphasize responsible participation in family and social life as important aspects of intelligence (Harkness & Super, 1983; Super & Harkness, 1982). In Zimbabwe, the word for intelligence, *ngware*, actually means to be prudent and cautious, particularly in social relationships. Among the Baoule, service to the family and community and politeness toward and respect for elders are seen as key to intelligence (Dasen, 1984).

Similar emphasis on social aspects of intelligence has been found as well among two other African groups—the Songhay of Mali and the Samia of Kenya (Putnam & Kilbride, 1980). The Yoruba, another African tribe, emphasizes the importance of depth—of listening rather than just talking—to intelligence, and of being able to see all aspects of an issue and of being able to place the issue in its proper overall context (Durojaiye, 1993).

The emphasis on the social aspects of intelligence is not limited to African cultures. Notions of intelligence in many Asian cultures also emphasize the social aspect of intelligence more than does the conventional Western or IQ-based notion (Azuma & Kashiwagi, 1987; Lutz, 1985; Poole, 1985; White, 1985).

It should be noted that neither African nor Asian notions emphasize exclusively social notions of intelligence. These conceptions of intelligence place much more emphasis on social skills than do conventional American conceptions of intelligence, and at the same time recognize the importance of cognitive aspects of intelligence. A study of Kenyan conceptions of intelligence (Grigorenko et al., 2001), found that there are four distinct terms constituting conceptions of intelligence among rural Kenyans: *rieko* (knowledge and skills), *luoro* (respect), *winjo* (comprehension of how to handle real-life problems), *paro* (initiative); only the first directly refers to knowledge-based skills (including, but not limited to, the academic).

It is important to realize, again, that there is no one overall US conception of intelligence. Indeed, Okagaki and Sternberg (1993) found that different ethnic groups in San José, California, had rather different conceptions of what it means to be intelligent. For example, Latino parents of schoolchildren tended to emphasize the importance of social-competence skills in their conceptions of intelligence, whereas Asian parents tended rather heavily to emphasize the importance of cognitive skills. Anglo parents also emphasized cognitive skills. Teachers, representing the dominant culture, emphasized cognitive- more than social-competence skills. The rank order of children of various groups' performance (including subgroups within the Latino and Asian groups) could be perfectly predicted by the extent to which their parents shared the teachers' conception of intelligence. In other words, teachers tended to reward those children who were socialized into a view of intelligence that happened to correspond to the teachers' own. Yet, as we shall argue later, social aspects of intelligence, broadly defined, may be as important as or even more important than cognitive aspects of intelligence in later life. Some, however, prefer to study intelligence not in its social aspect, but in its cognitive one.

Intelligence as arising from individual differences: The differential model

McNemar (1964) was one of the most explicit in speculating on why we even have a concept of intelligence and in linking the rationale for the concept to individual differences. He queried whether two identical twins stranded on a desert island and growing up together ever would generate the notion of intelligence if they never encountered individual differences in their mental abilities.

Perhaps without individual differences, societies would never generate the notion of intelligence and languages would contain no corresponding term. In fact, some languages, such as Mandarin Chinese, have no concept that corresponds precisely to the Western notion of intelligence (Yang & Sternberg, 1997a, 1997b), although they have related concepts that are closer, say, to the Western notion of wisdom or other constructs. Whatever may be the case, much of the history of the field of intelligence is based on an epistemological model deriving from the existence of one or more kinds of individual differences.

The seminal views of Galton and Binet

If current thinking about the nature of intelligence owes a debt to any scholars, it is to Sir Francis Galton and to Alfred Binet. These two investigators—Galton at the end of the nineteenth century and Binet at the beginning of the twentieth century—have had a profound impact on thinking about intelligence, an impact that carried down to the present day. Many present conflicts of views regarding the nature of intelligence can be traced to a dialectical conflict between Galton and Binet.

Intelligence is simple: Galton's Theory of Psychophysical Processes

Intelligence as energy and sensitivity

The publication of Darwin's (1859) *On the origin of species* had a profound impact on many lines of scientific endeavor, one of which was the investigation of human intelligence. The book suggested that the capabilities of humans were in some sense continuous with those of lower animals, and hence could be understood through scientific investigation.

Galton (1883; see also Galton, 1869) followed up on these notions to propose a theory of the "human faculty and its development". Because Galton also proposed techniques for measuring the "human faculty", his theory could be applied directly to human behavior.

Galton proposed two general qualities that he believed distinguish the more from the less intellectually able. His epistemological rooting, therefore, was in the individual differences approach. The first quality was *energy*, or the capacity for labor. Galton believed that intellectually gifted individuals in a variety of fields are characterized by remarkable levels of energy. The second general quality was *sensitivity*. Galton observed that the only information that can reach us concerning external events passes through the senses and that the more perceptive the senses are of differences in luminescence, pitch, odor, or whatever, the larger would be the range of information on which intelligence could act.

For seven years (1884–1890), Galton maintained an anthropometric laboratory at the South Kensington Museum in London where, for a small fee, visitors could have themselves measured on a variety of psychophysical tests. Examples of tests used were weight discrimination, pitch perception (the highest pitch one could perceive), and olfaction (distinguishing smells).

Cattell's operationalization of Galton's theory

James McKeen Cattell carried many of Galton's ideas to the USA. As head of the psychological laboratory at Columbia University, Cattell was in a good position to publicize the psychophysical approach to the theory and measurement of intelligence. In 1890, he proposed a series of 50 psychophysical tests. Two examples were how hard one could press a dynamometer (pressure gauge) and the least difference between two weights one could notice.

Wissler blows the whistle

A student of Cattell's, Clark Wissler (1901), decided to validate Cattell's tests. Using 21 of these tests, he investigated among Columbia University undergraduates the correlations of the tests with each other and with college grades. The results were devastating: Test scores neither intercorrelated much among themselves nor did they correlate significantly with undergraduate grades. The lack of correlation could not have been due entirely to unreliability of the grades or to restriction of range, because the grades did correlate among themselves. A new approach seemed to be needed.

Intelligence is complex: Binet's Theory of Judgment

In 1904, the Minister of Public Instruction in Paris named a commission charged with studying or creating tests that would insure that mentally defective children (as they then were called) would receive an adequate education. The commission decided that no child suspected of retardation should be placed in a special class for children with mental retardation without first being given an examination, ". . . from which it could be certified that because of the state of his intelligence, he was unable to profit, in an average measure, from the instruction given in the ordinary schools" (Binet & Simon, 1916a, p. 9).

Binet and Simon devised a test based on a conception of intelligence very different from Galton's and Cattell's. They viewed judgment as central to intelligence. At the same time, they viewed Galton's tests as ridiculous. They cited Helen Keller as an example of someone who was very intelligent but who would have performed terribly on Galton's tests.

Binet and Simon's (1916a, 1916b) theory of intelligent thinking in many ways foreshadowed later research on the development of metacognition (e.g. Brown & DeLoache, 1978; Flavell & Wellman, 1977; Mazzoni & Nelson, 1998). According to Binet and Simon (1916b), intelligent thought comprises three distinct elements: direction (knowing what needs to be done and how to do it), adaptation, and control.

What are some examples of the kinds of problems found on a Binet-based test (e.g. Terman & Merrill, 1937, 1973; Thorndike, Hagen, & Sattler, 1986)? In one version (1973), 2-year-olds are given a three-hold form board, into which they are required to place in the appropriate indentations circular, square, and triangular pieces. Another test requires children to identify body parts on a paper doll. Six years later, by age eight, the character of the test items changes considerably. By age eight, the tests include vocabulary, which requires children to define words; verbal absurdities, which requires recognition of why each of a set of statements is foolish; similarities and differences, which requires children to say how each of two objects is the same as and different from each other; and comprehension, which requires children to solve practical problems of the sort encountered in everyday life. At age fourteen, there is some overlap in kinds of tests with age eight, as well as some different kinds of tests. For example, in induction, the experimenters makes a notch in an edge of some folded paper and asks participants how many holes the paper will have when it is unfolded.

The early Binet and Simon tests, like those of Cattell, were soon put to a test, in this case by Sharp (1899). Although her results were not entirely supportive, Sharp generally accepted the view of judgment, rather than psychophysical processes, as underlying intelligence. Most subsequent researchers have accepted this notion as well.

Binet's work was to have far more influence than was Galton's. Binet set many trends that have been influential even up to the present day. The kinds of test items used by Binet are, for the most part, similar to those used in the present day. From the standpoint of modern test constructors, Binet "largely got it right". Indeed, a current test, the Stanford–Binet Intelligence Scale (fourth edition) (Thorndike et al., 1986) is a direct descendant of the Binet test. The Wechsler tests (e.g. Wechsler, 1991), although somewhat different in their conceptualization, owe a great deal to the conceptualization and tests of Binet.

An important aspect of Binet's theory has been lost to many. This was Binet's belief that intelligence is malleable and could be improved by "mental orthopedics". To this day, many investigators are interested in raising levels of mental functioning (see review by Grotzer & Perkins, 2000). But many other investigators, even those who use Binet-based tests, question whether intelligence is malleable in any major degree (e.g. Jensen, 1969, 1998).

Models of the nature of intelligence

A number of different types of models have been proposed to characterize intelligence. What are the main models, and how are they similar to and different from one another?

Psychometric models

The early efforts of intelligence theorists largely built upon the Binetian school of thought rather than the Galtonian school of thought. The most influential theorist, historically, and perhaps even into the present, was also among the first, a British psychologist named Charles Spearman.

Spearman's Two-factor Theory

Spearman (1904, 1927) proposed a two-factor theory of intelligence, a theory that is still very much alive and well today (e.g. Brand, 1996; Demetriou, 2002; Detterman, 2002; Gottfredson, 2002; Humphreys & Stark, 2002; Jensen, 1998, 2002; Kyllonen, 2002; Schmidt & Hunter, 1998). The theory posits a general factor (*g*) common to all tasks requiring intelligence and one specific factor (*s*) unique to each different type of task. Thus, there are two types of factors, rather than, strictly speaking, two factors.

Spearman (1904) got this idea as a result of looking at data processed by a statistical technique of his own invention, namely, *factor analysis*, which attempts to identify latent sources of individual (or other) differences that underlie observed sources of variation in test performance. Spearman observed that when he factor analyzed a correlation matrix, two kinds of factors appeared—the general factor common to all of the tests, and the specific factor unique to each particular test.

Spearman (1927) admitted to not being sure of what the psychological basis of *g* is, but suggested that it might be mental energy (a term that he never defined very clearly). Whatever it was, it was a unitary and primary source of individual differences in intelligence-test performance.

The theories of bonds and of connections

Theory of bonds

Spearman's theory was soon challenged, and continues to be challenged today (e.g. Gardner, 1983; Sternberg, 1999a, 1999b). One of Spearman's chief critics was British psychologist Sir Godfrey Thomson, who accepted Spearman's statistics but not his interpretation. Thomson (1939) argued that it is possible to have a general psychometric factor in the absence of any kind of general ability. In particular, Thomson argued that *g* is a statistical reality but a psychological artifact. He suggested that the general factor might result from the working of an extremely large number of what he called *bonds*, all of which are sampled simultaneously in intellectual tasks. Imagine, for example, that each of the intellectual tasks found in Spearman and others' test batteries requires certain mental skills. If each test samples all of these mental skills, then their appearance will be perfectly correlated with each other because they always co-occur. Thus, they will give the appearance of a single general factor, when in fact they are multiple.

Although Thomson did not attempt to specify exactly what the bonds might be, it is not hard to speculate on what some of these common elements might be. For example, they might include understanding the problems and responding to them.

Theory of connections

Thorndike, Bregman, Cobb, and Woodyard (1926) proposed a quite similar theory, based on Thorndike's theory of learning. They suggested that:

> ... in their deeper nature the higher forms of intellectual operations are identical with mere association or connection forming, depending upon the same sort of physiological connections but requiring *many more of them*. By the same argument the person whose intellect is greater or higher or better than that of another person differs from him in the last analysis in having, not a new sort of physiological process, but simply a larger number of connections of the ordinary sort.
>
> (Thorndike et al., 1926, p. 415)

According to this theory, then, learned connections, similar to Thomson's bonds, are what underlie individual differences in intelligence.

Thurstone's Theory of Primary Mental Abilities

Louis L. Thurstone, like Spearman, was an ardent advocate of factor analysis as a method of revealing latent psychological structures underlying observable test performances. Thurstone (1938, 1947) believed, however, that it was a mistake to leave the axes of factorial solutions unrotated. He believed that the solution thus obtained was psychologically arbitrary. Instead, he suggested rotation to what he referred to as *simple structure*, which is designed to clean up the columns of a factor pattern matrix so that the factors display either relatively high or low loadings of tests on given factors, rather than large numbers of moderate ones. Using simple-structure rotation, Thurstone and Thurstone (1941) argued for the existence of seven primary mental abilities: verbal comprehension, verbal fluency, number, spatial visualization, memory, inductive reasoning, and perceptual speed.

The argument between Spearman and Thurstone could not be resolved on mathematical grounds simply because, in exploratory factor analysis, any of an infinite number of rotations of axes is acceptable. As an analogy, consider axes used to understand world geography (Vernon, 1971). One can use lines of longitude and latitude, but really, any axes at all could be used, orthogonal or oblique, or even axes that serve different functions, such as in polar coordinates. The locations of points, and the distances between them, do not change in Euclidean space as a result of how the axes are placed.

Because Thurstone's primary mental abilities are intercorrelated, Spearman and others have argued that they are nothing more than varied manifestations of *g*: Factor analyze these factors, and a general factor will emerge as a second-order factor. Thurstone, of course, argued that the primary mental abilities were more basic. Such arguments became largely polemical because there neither was nor is any way of resolving the debate in the terms in which it was presented. Some synthesis was needed for the opposing thesis of *g* versus the antithesis of primary mental abilities.

Hierarchical theories

The main synthesis to be proposed was to be hierarchical theories—theories that assume that abilities can be ordered in terms of levels of generality. Rather than arguing which abilities are more fundamental, hierarchical theorists have argued that all of the abilities have a place in a hierarchy of abilities from the general to the specific.

Vernon's Theory of Verbal: educational and spatial: mechanical abilities

A more widely adopted model has been that of Vernon (1971), which proposes the general factor, *g*, at the top of the hierarchy. Below this factor are two group factors, *v : ed* and *k : m*. The former refers to verbal–educational abilities of the kinds measured by conventional tests of scholastic abilities. The latter refers to spatial–mechanical abilities (with *k* perhaps inappropriately referring to the nonequivalent term *kinesthetic*).

Cattell's Theory of Fluid and Crystallized Abilities

More widely accepted than any of the previous theories is that of Raymond Cattell (1971), which is somewhat similar to Vernon's theory. This theory proposes general ability at the top of the hierarchy, and two abilities immediately beneath it, fluid ability, or g_f, and crystallized ability, or g_c. Fluid ability is the ability to think flexibly and to reason abstractly. It is measured by tests such as number series and figural analogies. Crystallized ability is the accumulated knowledge base one has developed over the course of one's life as the result of the application of fluid ability. It is measured by tests such as vocabulary and general information.

More recent work has suggested that fluid ability is extremely difficult to distinguish statistically from general ability (Gustafsson, 1984, 1988). Indeed, the tests used to measure fluid ability are often identical to the tests used to measure what is supposed to be pure *g*. An example of such a test would be the Raven Progressive Matrices (Raven, Court, & Raven, 1992), which measures people's ability to fill in a missing part of a matrix comprising abstract figural drawings.

Horn (1994) has greatly expanded upon the hierarchical theory as originally proposed by Cattell. Most notably, he has suggested that *g* can be split into three more factors nested under fluid and crystallized abilities. These three other factors are: visual thinking (g_v), auditory thinking (g_a), and speed (g_s). The visual thinking factor is probably closer to Vernon's *k : m* factor than it is to the fluid ability factor.

Carrolls' Three-stratum Theory

Today, perhaps the most widely accepted hierarchical model is a model proposed by Carroll (1993), which is based on the reanalysis of (more than 450) data sets from the past. At the top of the hierarchy is general ability; in the middle of the hierarchy are various broad abilities, including fluid and crystallized intelligence, learning and memory processes, visual and auditory perception, facile production, and speed; at the bottom of the hierarchy are fairly specific abilities.

Guilford's Structure-of-Intellect Model

Although many differential theorists followed the option of proposing a hierarchical model, not all did. J. P. Guilford (1967, 1982; Guilford & Hoepfner, 1971) proposed a model with 120 distinct abilities (increased to 150 in 1982 and to 180 in later manifestations). The basic theory organizes abilities along three dimensions: operations, products, and contents. In the best-known version of the model, there are five operations, six products, and four contents. The five operations are cognition, memory, divergent production, convergent production, and evaluation. The six products are units, classes, relations, systems, transformations, and implications. The four contents are figural, symbolic, semantic, and behavioral. Because these dimensions are completely crossed with each other, they yield a total of $5 \times 6 \times 4$ or 120 different abilities. For example, inferring a relation in a verbal analogy (such as the relation between BLACK and WHITE in BLACK : WHITE :: HIGH : LOW) would involve cognition of semantic relations.

Guilford's model has not fared well psychometrically. Horn and Knapp (1973) showed that random theories could generate support equal to that obtained by Guilford's model when the same type of rotation was used that Guilford used—so-called "Procrustean rotation". Horn (1967) showed that equal support could be obtained with Guilford's theory, but with data generated randomly rather than with real data. These demonstrations do not prove the model wrong: They show only that the psychometric support that Guilford claimed for his model was not justified by the methods he used. In general, factor analysis can be subject to a variety of statistical problems and so results must always be interpreted with care (Horn & Knapp, 1973; Humphreys, 1962; McNemar, 1951).

Guttman's Radex Model

The last psychometric model to be mentioned is one proposed by Louis Guttman (1954). The model is what Guttman referred to as a radex, or radial representation of complexity. The radex consists of two parts.

The first part is what Guttman refers to as a simplex. If one imagines a circle, then the simplex refers to the distance of a given point (ability) from the center of the circle. The closer a given ability is to the center of the circle, the more central that ability is to human intelligence. Thus, *g* could be viewed as being at the center of the circle, whereas the more peripheral abilities such as perceptual speed would be nearer to the periphery of the circle. Abilities nearer to the periphery of the circle are viewed as being constituents of abilities nearer the center of the circle, so the theory has a hierarchical element.

The second part of the radex is called the circumplex. It refers to the angular orientation of a given ability with respect to the circle. Thus, abilities are viewed as being arranged around the circle with abilities that are more highly related (correlated) nearer to each other in the circle. Thus, the radex functions through a system of polar coordinates. Snow, Kyllonen, and Marshalek (1984) used nonmetric multidimensional scaling on a Thurstonian type of test to demonstrate that the Thurstonian primary mental abilities actually could be mapped into a radex.

Intelligence as arising from cognitive structures and processes

Cognitive structures

Piaget (1952, 1972), among others, has staked out an alternative position to the differential one. Piaget, who was never very interested in individual differences, viewed intelligence as arising from cognitive schemas, or structures that mature as a function of the interaction of the organism with the environment.

Equilibration

Piaget (1926, 1928, 1952, 1972), like many other theorists of intelligence, recognized the importance of adaptation to intelligence. Indeed, he believed adaptation to be its most important principle. In adaptation, individuals learn from the environment and learn to address the changes in the environment. Adjustment consists of two complementary processes: assimilation and accommodation. *Assimilation* is the process of absorbing new information and fitting it into an already existing cognitive structure about what the world is like. The complementary process, *accommodation*, involves forming a new cognitive structure in order to understand information. In other words, if no existing cognitive structure seems adequate to understand new information, a new cognitive structure must be formed through the accommodation process.

The complementary processes of assimilation and accommodation, taken together in an interaction, constitute what Piaget referred to as equilibration. *Equilibration* is the balancing of the two and it is through this balance that people either add to old schemas or form new ones. A *schema*, for Piaget, is a mental image or action pattern. It is essentially a way of organizing sensory information. For example, we have schemas for going to the bank, riding a bicycle, eating a meal, visiting a doctor's office, and the like.

Stages of intellectual development

Piaget (1972) suggested that the intelligence of children matures through four discrete stages, or periods of development. Each of these periods builds on the preceding one, so that development is essentially cumulative.

The first period is the *sensorimotor period*, which occupies from birth to roughly 2 years of age. By the end of the sensorimotor period, the infant has started to acquire object permanence, or the realization that objects can exist apart from him- or herself. In early infancy, the infant does not ascribe a separate reality to objects. Thus, if a toy is hidden under a pillow or behind a barrier, the infant will not search for the toy because as far as he or she is concerned, it no longer exists when it goes out of sight. By the end of the period, the infant knows that a search will lead to finding the object.

The second period is the *preoperational period*, which emerges roughly between ages 2 to 7. The child is now beginning to represent the world through symbols and images, but the symbols and images are directly dependent upon the immediate perception of the child. The child is still essentially egocentric: He or she sees objects and people only from his or her own point of view. Thus, to the extent that thinking takes place, it is egocentric thinking.

The third period is the *concrete-operational period*, which occupies roughly ages 7 to 11. In this period, the child is able to perform concrete mental operations. Thus, the child can now think through sequences of actions or events that previously had to be enacted physically. The hallmark of concrete-operational thought is reversibility. It is now possible for the child to reverse the direction of thought. The child comes to understand, for example, that subtraction is the reverse of addition and division is the reverse of multiplication. The child can go to the store and back home again or trace out a route on a map and see the way back.

This period is labeled as one of "concrete" operations because operations are performed for objects that are physically present. A major acquisition of the period is conservation, which involves a child's recognizing that objects or quantities can remain the same, despite changes in their physical appearance. Suppose, for example, that a child is shown two glasses, one of which is short and fat and the other which is tall and thin. If a preoperational child watches water poured from the short, fat glass to the tall, thin one, he or she will say that the tall, thin glass has more water than the short, fat one had. But the concrete-operational child will recognize that the quantity of water is the same in the new glass as in the old glass, despite the change in physical appearance.

The period of *formal operations* begins to evolve at around 11 years of age, and usually will be fairly fully developed by 16 years of age, although some adults never completely develop formal operations. In the period of formal operations, the child comes to be able to think abstractly and hypothetically, not just concretely. The individual can view a problem from multiple points of view and can think much more systematically than in the past. For example, if asked to provide all possible permutations of the numbers 1, 2, 3, and 4, the child can now implement a systematic strategy for listing all of these permutations. In contrast, the concrete-operational child will have essentially listed permutations at random, without a systematic strategy for generating all of the possible permutations. The child can now think scientifically and use the hypotheticodeductive method to generate and test hypotheses.

Vygotsky and Feuerstein's theories

Whereas Piaget has emphasized primarily biological maturation in the development of intelligence, other theorists interested in structures, such as Vygotsky (1978) and Feuerstein (1979), have emphasized the role of interactions of individuals more with the environment. Vygotsky suggested that basic to intelligence is *internalization*, which is the internal reconstruction of an external operation. The basic notion is that we observe those in the social environment around us acting in certain ways and we internalize their actions so that they become a part of ourselves.

Vygotsky (1978) gave as an example of internalization the development of pointing. He suggested that, initially, pointing is nothing more than an unsuccessful attempt to grasp something. The child attempts to grasp an object beyond his reach and, initially, is likely to fail. When the mother sees the child attempting to grasp an object, she comes to his or her aid and is likely to point to the object. He thereby learns to do the same. Thus, the child's unsuccessful attempt engenders a reaction from the mother or some other individual, which leads to his being able to perform that action. Note that it is the social mediation, rather than the object itself, which provides the basis for the child's learning to point.

Vygotsky also proposed the important notion of a *zone of proximal development*, which refers to functions that have not yet matured but are in the process of maturation. The basic idea is to look not only at developed abilities, but also at abilities that are developing. This zone is often measured as the difference between performance before and after instruction. Thus, instruction is given at the time of testing to measure the individual's ability to learn in the testing environment (Brown & French, 1979; Grigorenko & Sternberg, 1998; Feuerstein, 1980). The research suggests that tests of the zone of proximal development tap abilities not measured by conventional tests.

Related ideas have been proposed by Feuerstein (1979, 1980). Feuerstein has suggested that much of intellectual development derives from the mediation of the environment by the mother or other adults. From Feuerstein's point of view, parents serve an important role in development not only for the experiences with which they provide children, but also for the way they help children understand these experiences. For example, what would be important would be not so much encouraging children to watch educational television or taking children to museums, but rather, helping children interpret what they see on television or in museums.

By any standard, Piaget's contribution to the study of intelligence was profound. His theory stands alone in terms of its comprehensiveness in accounting for intellectual development. There is no competition in this respect. Yet the theory of Piaget has not stood the test of time without many scars (Siegler, 1996). Piaget's interpretations of data have proven to be problematical in many different respects. For example, there is evidence that infants achieve object permanence much earlier than Piaget had thought (e.g. Baillargeon, 1987; Bowers, 1967, 1974; Cornell, 1978). There is also evidence that conservation begins earlier than Piaget suspected (Au, Sidle, & Rollins, 1993). As another example, difficulties that Piaget attributed to reasoning appear in some instances actually to have been due to memory (e.g. Bryant & Trabasso, 1971).

Many investigators today question the whole notion of stages of development (e.g. Brainerd, 1978; Flavell, 1971). Some of them believe that development is simply much more domain specific than Piaget was willing to admit (e.g. Carey, 1985; Keil, 1989). As another example, children master different kinds of conservation problems at different ages, with the differences appearing in a systematic fashion (Elkind, 1961; Katz & Beilin, 1976; Miller, 1976), with conservation of number appearing before conservation of solid quantity, and conservation of solid quantity before weight.

Whatever questions investigators may have, Piaget remains one of the most influential psychologists of the twentieth century. The same can be said for Vygotsky.

Vygotsky's theory recognizes more completely than does Piaget's theory the important role of the social–cultural environment in intellectual development. And it also suggests how conventional tests may fail to unearth developing intellectual functions that give children added potential to succeed intellectually. Vygotsky's theory is rather vague, however, and much of the recent development has gone considerably beyond anything Vygotsky proposed. Perhaps if Vygotsky had not died tragically at an early age (38 years), he would have extensively amplified on his theory.

Cognitive processes

A related position is that of cognitive theorists (e.g. Anderson, 1983; Miller, Galanter, & Pribram, 1960; Newell & Simon, 1972), who seek to understand intelligence in terms of the processes of human thought and also the architecture that holds together these processes. These theorists may use the software of a computer as a model of the human mind, or in more recent theorizing, use the massively parallel operating systems of neural circuitry as a model (e.g. Rumelhart, McClelland, & the PDP Research Group, 1986). Much of the history of this field is relatively recent, simply because much of the "early" development of the field has occurred in recent times. The field today, for example, has advanced quite far beyond where it was 30 years ago. At the same time, the origins of the field go back to early in the twentieth century and even further back, depending upon how broad one is in labeling work as related to this approach.

The origins of the process-based approach in Spearman's Principles of Cognition

Although some psychologists in the nineteenth century were interested in information processing (e.g. Donders, 1868/1869), the connection between information processing and intelligence seems first to have been explicitly drawn by Charles Spearman (1923), the same individual known for initiating serious psychometric theorizing about intelligence.

Spearman (1923) proposed what he believed to be three fundamental qualitative principles of cognition. The first, *apprehension of experience*, is what today might be called the encoding of stimuli (see Sternberg, 1977). It involves perceiving the stimuli and their properties. The second principle, *eduction of relations*, is what today might be labeled inference. It is the inferring of a relation between two or more concepts. The third principle, *eduction of correlates*, is what today might be called application. It is the application of an inferred rule to a new situation. For example, in the analogy, WHITE : BLACK :: GOOD : ?, apprehension of experience would involve reading each of the terms. Eduction of relations would involve inferring the relation between WHITE and BLACK. And eduction of correlates would involve applying the inferred relation to complete the analogy with *BAD*. Tests that measure these attributes without contamination from many other sources, such as the Raven Progressive Matrices tests, generally provide very good measures of psychometric *g*.

The cognitive-correlates approach

Lee Cronbach (1957) tried to revive interest in the cognitive approach with an article on "the two disciplines of scientific psychology", and there were some fits and starts during the 1960s in an effort to revive this approach. But serious revival can probably be credited in large part to the work of Earl Hunt. Hunt (1978, 1980; Hunt, Frost, & Lunneborg, 1973; Hunt, Lunneborg, & Lewis, 1975) was the originator of what has come to be called the *cognitive-correlates approach* to integrating the study of cognitive processing with the study of intelligence (Pellegrino & Glaser, 1979).

The proximal goal of this research is to estimate parameters representing the durations of performance for information-processing components constituting experimental tasks commonly used in the laboratories of cognitive psychologists. These parameters are then used to investigate the extent to which cognitive components correlate across participants with each other and with scores on psychometric measures commonly believed to measure intelligence, such as the Raven Progressive Matrices tests. Consider an example.

In one task—the Posner and Mitchell (1967) letter-matching task—participants are shown pairs of letters such as "A A" or "A a". After each pair, they are asked to respond as rapidly as possible to one of two questions: "Are the letters a physical match?" or "Are the letters a name match?" Note that the first pair of letters provides an affirmative answer to both questions, whereas the second pair of letters provides an affirmative answer only to the second of the two questions. That is, the first pair provides both a physical and a name match, whereas the second pair provides a name match only.

The goal of such a task is to estimate the amount of time a given participant takes to access lexical information—letter names—in memory. The physical-match condition is included to subtract out (control for) sheer time to perceive the letters and respond to questions. The difference between name and physical match time thus provides the parameter estimate of interest for the task. Hunt and his colleagues found that this parameter and similar parameters in other experimental tasks typically correlate about −.3 with scores on psychometric tests of verbal ability.

The precise tasks used in such research have varied. The letter-matching task has been a particularly popular one, as has been the short-term memory scanning task originally proposed by S. Sternberg (1969). Other researchers have preferred simple and choice reaction-time tasks (e.g. Jensen, 1979, 1982). Most such studies have been conducted with adults, but some have been conducted developmentally with children of various ages (e.g. Keating & Bobbitt, 1978).

The cognitive-components approach

An alternative approach has come to be called the *cognitive-components approach* (Pellegrino & Glaser, 1979). In this approach, participants are tested in their ability to perform tasks of the kinds actually found on standard psychometric tests of mental abilities, for example, analogies, series completions, mental rotations, and syllogisms. Participants typically are timed and response time is the principal dependent variable, with error rate and pattern-of-response choices serving as further dependent variables. This approach was suggested by Sternberg (1977; see also Royer, 1971).

The proximal goal in this research is, first, to formulate a model of information processing in performance on the types of tasks found in conventional psychometric tests of intelligence. Second, it is to test the model at the same time as parameters for the model are estimated. Finally, it is to investigate the extent to which these components correlate across participants with each other and with scores on standard psychometric tests. Because the tasks that are analyzed are usually taken directly from psychometric tests of intelligence or are very similar to such tasks, the major issue in this kind of research is not whether there is any correlation at all between cognitive task and psychometric test scores. Rather, the issue is one of isolating the locus or loci of the correlations that are obtained. One seeks to discover what components of information processing are the critical ones from the standpoint of the theory of intelligence (Carroll, 1981; Pellegrino & Glaser, 1979, 1980, 1982; Royer, 1971; Sternberg, 1977, 1980, 1983; Sternberg & Gardner, 1983).

Consider the analogies task mentioned above. The participant might be presented with an analogy such as WHITE : BLACK :: GOOD : (A) BAD, (B) BETTER. The task is to choose the better of the two response options as quickly as possible. Cognitive-components analysis might extract a number of components from the task, using an expanded version of Spearman's theory (Sternberg, 1977). These components might include: (1) the time to *encode* the stimulus terms; (2) the time to *infer* the relation between WHITE and BLACK; (3) the time to *map* the relation from the first half of the analogy to the second; (4) the time to *apply* the inferred relation from GOOD to each of the answer options; (5) the time to *compare* the two response options; (6) the time to *justify* BAD as the preferable option; and (7) the time to *respond* with (A).

The cognitive-training approach

The goal of the *cognitive-training approach* is to infer the components of information processing from how individuals perform when they are trained. According to Campione, Brown, and Ferrara (1982), one starts with a theoretical analysis of a task and a hypothesis about a source of individual differences within that task. It might be assumed, for example, that components A, B, and C are required to carry out task X and that less able children do poorly because of a weakness in component A. To test this assertion, one might train less able participants in the use of A and then retest them on X. If performance improves, the task analysis is supported. If performance does not improve, then either A was not an important component of the task or participants were originally efficient with regard to A and did not need training, or the training was ineffective (see also Belmont & Butterfield, 1971; Belmont, Butterfield, & Ferretti, 1982; Borkowski & Wanschura, 1974).

The cognitive-contents approach

In the *cognitive-contents approach*, one seeks to compare the performances of experts and novices in complex tasks such as physics problems (e.g. Chi, Feltovich, & Glaser, 1981; Chi, Glaser, & Rees, 1982; Larkin, McDermott, Simon, & Simon, 1980), the selection of moves and strategies in chess and other games (Chase & Simon, 1973; De Groot, 1965; Reitman, 1976), and the acquisition of domain-related information by groups of people at different levels of expertise (Chiesi, Spilich, & Voss, 1979). The notion underlying such research can be seen as abilities being forms of developing expertise (Sternberg, 1998). In other words, the experts have developed high levels of intellectual ability in particular domains as results of the development of their expertise. Research on expert–novice differences in a variety of task domains suggests the importance of the amount and form of information storage in long-term memory as key to expert–novice differences.

Information-processing psychologists have not been terribly sensitive to individual differences or to contextual variables (see Neisser, 1976; Sternberg, 1997). Nevertheless, they have uncovered a great deal about the processes of the mind and how these processes interface with intelligence.

Biological bases of intelligence

Some theorists have argued that notions of intelligence should be based on biological notions, and usually, on scientific knowledge about the brain. The idea here is that the base of intelligence is in the brain and that behavior is interesting in large part as it elucidates the functioning of the brain.

One of the earlier theories of brain function was proposed by Halstead (1951), who suggested four biologically based abilities: (1) the integrative field factor (C); (2) the abstraction factor (A); (3) the power factor (P); and (4) the directional factor (D). Halstead attributed all four of these abilities primarily to the cortex of the frontal lobes. Halstead's theory became the basis for a test of cognitive functioning, including intellectual aspects (the Halstead–Reitan Neuropsychological Test Battery).

A more influential theory, perhaps, has been that of Donald Hebb (1949). Hebb suggested the necessity of distinguishing among different intelligences. *Intelligence A* is innate potential. It is biologically determined and represents the capacity for development. Hebb described it as "the possession of a good brain and a good neural metabolism" (p. 294). *Intelligence B* is the functioning of the brain in which development has occurred. It represents an average level of performance by a person who is partially grown. Although some inference is necessary in determining either intelligence, Hebb suggested that inferences about intelligence A are far less direct than inference about intelligence B. A further distinction could be made with regard to

Intelligence C, which is the score one obtains on an intelligence test. This intelligence is Boring's intelligence as the tests test it.

A theory with an even greater impact on the field of intelligence research is that of the Russian psychologist, Alexander Luria (1973, 1980). Luria believed that the brain is a highly differentiated system whose parts are responsible for different aspects of a unified whole. In other words, separate cortical regions act together to produce thoughts and actions of various kinds. Luria (1980) suggested that the brain comprises three main units. The first, a unit of arousal, includes the brain stem and midbrain structures. Included within this first unit are the medulla, reticular activating system, pons, thalamus, and hypothalamus. The second unit of the brain is a sensori-input unit, which includes the temporal, parietal, and occipital lobes. The third unit includes the frontal cortex, which is involved in organization and planning. It comprises cortical structures anterior to the central sulcus.

The most active research program based on Luria's theory has been that of J. P. Das and his colleagues (e.g. Das, Kirby, & Jarman, 1979; Das, Naglieri, & Kirby, 1994; Naglieri & Das, 1990, 1997). The theory as they conceive of it is referred to as PASS theory, referring to *planning, attention, simultaneous processing,* and *successive processing.* The idea is that intelligence requires the ability to plan and to pay attention. It also requires the ability to attend to many aspects of a stimulus, such as a picture, simultaneously, or, in some cases, to process stimuli sequentially, as when one memorizes a string of digits to remember a telephone number. Other research and tests have also been based on Luria's theory (e.g. Kaufman & Kaufman, 1983).

An entirely different approach to understanding intellectual abilities has emphasized the analysis of hemispheric specialization in the brain. This work goes back to a finding of an obscure country doctor in France, Marc Dax, who in 1836 presented a little-noticed paper to a medical society meeting in Montpelier. Dax had treated a number of patients suffering from loss of speech as a result of brain damage. The condition, known today as aphasia, had been reported even in ancient Greece. Dax noticed that in more than 40 patients with aphasia, the damage had been to the left hemisphere of the brain and not to the right hemisphere. His results suggested that speech and perhaps verbal intellectual functioning originated in the left hemisphere of the brain.

Perhaps the most well-known figure in the study of hemispheric specialization is Paul Broca. At a meeting of the French Society of Anthropology, Broca claimed that a patient of his who was suffering a loss of speech was shown post-mortem to have a lesion in the left frontal lobe of the brain. At the time no one paid much attention. But Broca soon became associated with a hot controversy over whether functions, particularly speech, are indeed localized in the brain. The area that Broca identified as involved in speech is today referred to as Broca's area. By 1864, Broca was convinced that the left hemisphere was critical for speech. Carl Wernicke, a German neurologist of the late nineteenth century, identified language-deficient patients who could speak, but whose speech made no sense. He also traced language ability to the left hemisphere, although to a different precise location, which now is known as Wernicke's area.

Nobel-prize-winning physiologist and psychologist Roger Sperry (1961) later came to suggest that the two hemispheres behave in many respects like separate brains, with the left hemisphere more localized for analytical and verbal processing and the right hemisphere more localized for holistic and imaginal processing. Today it is known that this view was an oversimplification, and that the two hemispheres of the brain largely work together (Gazzaniga, Ivry, & Mangun, 1998).

When using the biological approach, it is important not to assume that correlation implies causality. Yet, reports based on the biological approach often seem to suggest that the biological response is somehow causal (e.g. Hendrickson & Hendrickson, 1980). Useful though the biological approach may be, it will always need to be supplemented by other approaches. No one approach provides all the answers to understanding intelligence.

Culture and society

A rather different position has been taken by more anthropologically oriented investigators. Modern investigators trace their work back at the very least to the work of Kroeber and Kluckhohn (1952), who studied culture as patterns of behavior acquired and transmitted by symbols. Much of the work in this approach, like that in the cognitive approach, is relatively recent.

The most extreme position is one of radical cultural relativism, proposed by Berry (1974), which rejects assumed psychological universals across cultural systems and requires the generation from within each cultural system of any behavioral concepts to be applied to it (the so-called *emic* approach). According to this viewpoint, therefore, intelligence can be understood only from within a culture, not in terms of views imposed from outside that culture (the so-called *etic* approach). Even in present times, psychologists have argued that the imposition of Western theories or tests on non-Western cultures can result in seriously erroneous conclusions about the capabilities of individuals within those cultures (Greenfield, 1997; Sternberg et al., 2000).

Other theorists have taken a less extreme view. For example, Michael Cole and his colleagues in the Laboratory of Comparative Human Cognition (1982, 1996) argued that the radical position does not take into account the fact that cultures interact. Cole and his colleagues believe that a kind of conditional comparativism is important, so long as one is careful in setting the conditions of the comparison.

Cole and his colleagues gave as an example a study done by Super (1976). Super found evidence that African infants sit and walk earlier than do their counterparts in the USA and Europe. But does such a finding mean that African infants are better walkers, in much the same way that North American psychologists have concluded that American children are better thinkers than African children (e.g. Herrnstein & Murray, 1994)? On the contrary, Super found that mothers in the culture he studied made a self-conscious effort to teach babies to sit and walk as early as possible. He concluded that the African infants are more advanced because they are specifically taught to sit and walk earlier, and are encouraged through the provision of opportunities to practice these behaviors. Other motor behaviors were not more advanced. For example, infants found to sit and walk early were actually found to crawl later than did infants in the USA.

The greatest strength of cultural approaches is their recognition that intelligence cannot be understood fully outside its cultural context. Indeed, however common may be the thought processes that underlie intelligent thinking, the behaviors that are labeled as intelligent by a given culture certainly vary from one place to another, as well as from one epoch to another. The greatest weakness of cultural approaches is their vagueness. They tend to say more about the context of intelligent behavior than they do about the causes of such behavior. Intelligence will probably always have to be understood at many different levels, and any one level in itself will be inadequate. It is for this reason, presumably, that systems models have become particularly popular in recent years. These models attempt to provide an understanding of intelligence at multiple levels.

Systems models

The nature of systems models

In recent times, systems models have been proposed as useful bases for understanding intelligence. These models seek to understand the complexity of intelligence from multiple points of view, and generally combine at least two and often more of the models described above. For example, Gardner (1983, 1993, 1999) has proposed a theory of multiple intelligence, according to which intelligence is not just one thing, but multiple things. According to this theory, there are eight or possibly even ten multiple intelligences— linguistic, logical-mathematical, spatial, musical, bodily-kinesthetic, interpersonal, intrapersonal, naturalist, and possibly existential and spiritual. Sternberg (1985, 1988, 1997, 1999b) has proposed a theory of successful intelligence, according to which intelligence can be seen in terms of various kinds of information-processing components combining in different ways to generate analytical, creative, and practical abilities. Ceci (1996) has proposed a bioecological model of intelligence according to which intelligence is understood in the interaction between the biology of the individual and the ecology in which the individual lives.

The complexity of systems models is both a blessing and a curse. It is a blessing because it enables such models to recognize the multiple complex levels of intelligence. It is a curse because the models become more difficult to test. A theory is not scientific unless it can be adequately tested.

Conclusion: Relations among the various models of the nature of intelligence

In a sense, the history of the field of intelligence bifurcates. Some investigators, perhaps starting with Boring (1923), have suggesting we define intelligence as what intelligence tests measure and get on with testing it, and other investigators, such as Spearman (1904, 1927) and Thurstone (1938) view the battle over what intelligence is as determining what should be tested.

Perhaps the best way to achieve a certain coherence in the field is to recognize that there is no one right "model" or "approach" and that different ones elucidate different aspects of a very complex phenomenon. Models such as the systems models are useful in attempting integrations, but they fall short in integrating all that we know about intelligence. Eventually, the time may come when such large-scale integrations can be achieved in ways that are theoretically meritorious and empirically sound. In the meantime, it is likely that many different conceptions of intelligence will compete for the attention of the scientific as well as the lay public.

Author notes

Preparation of this article was supported by Grant REC-9979843 from the National Science Foundation and by a grant under the Javits Act Program (Grant No. R206R00001) as administered by the Office of Educational Research and Improvement, US Department of Education. Grantees undertaking such projects are encouraged to express freely their professional judgment. This article, therefore, does not necessarily represent the position or policies of the National Science Foundation, Office of Educational Research and Improvement or the US Department of Education, and no official endorsement should be inferred.

References

Anderson, J. R. (1983). *The architecture of cognition*. Cambridge, MA: Harvard University Press.

Au, T. K., Sidle, A. L., & Rollins, K. B. (1993). Developing an intuitive understanding of conservation and contamination: Invisible particles as a plausible mechanism. *Developmental Psychology, 29*, 286–299.

Azuma, H., & Kashiwagi, K. (1987). Descriptions for an intelligent person: A Japanese study. *Japanese Psychological Research, 29*, 17–26.

Baillargeon, R. L. (1987). Young infants' reasoning about the physical and spatial properties of a hidden object. *Cognitive Development, 2(3)*, 179–200.

Belmont, J. M., & Butterfield, E. C. (1971). Learning strategies as determinants of memory deficiencies. *Cognitive Psychology, 2*, 411–420.

Belmont, J. M., Butterfield, E. C., & Ferretti, R. (1982). To secure transfer of training, instruct self-management skills. In D. K. Detterman & R. J. Sternberg (Eds.), *How and how much can intelligence be increased?* (pp. 147–154). Norwood, NJ: Ablex.

Berry, J. W. (1974). Radical cultural relativism and the concept of intelligence. In J. W. Berry & P. R. Dasen (Eds.), *Culture and cognition: Readings in cross-cultural psychology* (pp. 225–229). London: Methuen.

Binet, A., & Simon, T. (1916a). *The development of intelligence in children.* Baltimore, MD: Williams & Wilkins (Original work published 1905).

Binet, A., & Simon, T. (1916b). *The intelligence of the feeble-minded* (E. S. Kite, Trans.). Baltimore, MD: Williams & Wilkins.

Boring, E. G. (1923). Intelligence as the tests test it. *New Republic, June 6*, 35–37.

Borkowski, J. G., & Wanschura, P. B. (1974). Mediational processes in the retarded. In N. R. Ellis (Ed.), *International review of research in mental retardation, 7.* New York: Academic Press.

Bowers, T. G. R. (1967). The development of object-permanence: Some studies of existence constancy. *Perception & Psychophysics, 2*, 411–418.

Bowers, T. G. R. (1974). *Development in infancy.* New York: Freeman.

Brainerd, C. J. (1978). The stage question in cognitive-developmental theory. *Behavioral and Brain Sciences, 1*, 173–182.

Brand, C. (1996). *The g factor: General intelligence and its implications.* Chichester, UK: Wiley.

Brown, A. L., & DeLoache, J. S. (1978). Skills, plans, and self-regulation. In R. Siegler (Ed.), *Children's thinking: What develops?* Hillsdale, NJ: Lawrence Erlbaum Associates Inc.

Brown, A. L., & French, A. L. (1979). The zone of potential development: Implications for intelligence testing in the year 2000. In R. J. Sternberg & D. K. Detterman (Eds.), *Human intelligence: Perspectives on its theory and measurement* (pp. 217–235). Norwood, NJ: Ablex.

Bryant, P. E., & Trabasso, T. (1971). Transitive inferences and memory in young children. *Nature, 232*, 456–458.

Campione, J. C., Brown, A. L., & Ferrara, R. (1982). Mental retardation and intelligence. In R. J. Sternberg (Ed.), *Handbook of human intelligence* (pp. 392–490). New York: Cambridge University Press.

Carey, S. (1985). *Conceptual change in childhood.* Cambridge, MA: MIT Press.

Carroll, J. B. (1981). Ability and task difficulty in cognitive psychology. *Educational Researcher, 10*, 11–21.

Carroll, J. B. (1982). The measurement of intelligence. In R. J. Sternberg (Ed.), *Handbook of human intelligence* (pp. 29–120). New York: Cambridge University Press.

Carroll, J. B. (1993). *Human cognitive abilities: A survey of factor-analytic studies.* New York: Cambridge University Press.

Cattell, J. M. (1890). Mental tests and measurements. *Mind, 15*, 373–380.

Cattell, R. B. (1971). *Abilities: Their structure, growth and action.* Boston, MA: Houghton Mifflin.

Ceci, S. J. (1996). *On intelligence . . . more or less (expanded ed.).* Cambridge, MA: Harvard University Press.

Chase, W. G., & Simon, H. A. (1973). The mind's eye in chess. In W. G. Chase (Ed.), *Visual information processing* (pp. 215–281). New York: Academic Press.

Chen, M. J. (1994). Chinese and Australian concepts of intelligence. *Psychology and Developing Societies, 6,* 101–117.

Chen, M. J., Braithwaite, V., & Huang, J. T. (1982). Attributes of intelligent behaviour: Perceived relevance and difficulty by Australian and Chinese students. *Journal of Cross-Cultural Psychology, 13,* 139–156.

Chen, M. J., & Chen, H. C. (1988). Concepts of intelligence: A comparison of Chinese graduates from Chinese and English schools in Hong Kong. *International Journal of Psychology, 223,* 471–487.

Chi, M. T. H., Feltovich, P. J., & Glaser, R. (1981). Categorization and representation of physics problems by experts and novices. *Cognitive Science, 5,* 121–152.

Chi, M. T. H., Glaser, R., & Rees, E. (1982). Expertise in problem solving. In R. J. Sternberg (Ed.), *Advances in the psychology of human intelligence* (Vol. 1, pp. 7–75). Hillsdale, NJ: Lawrence Erlbaum Associates Inc.

Chiesi, H. L., Spilich, G. J., & Voss, J. F. (1979). Acquisition of domain-related information in relation to high and low domain knowledge. *Journal of Verbal Learning and Verbal Behavior, 18,* 257–273.

Cole, M. (1996). *Cultural psychology: A once and future discipline.* Cambridge, MA: Harvard University Press.

Connolly, H., & Bruner, J. (1974). Competence: Its nature and nurture. In K. Connolly & J. Bruner (Eds.), *The growth of competence* (pp. 3–10). New York: Academic Press.

Cornell, E. H. (1978). Learning to find things: A reinterpretation of object permanence studies. In L. S. Siegel & C. J. Brainerd (Eds.), *Alternatives to Piaget: Critical essays on the theory* (pp. 11–27). New York: Academic Press.

Craik, F. I. M., & Lockhart, R. S. (1972). Levels of processing: A framework for memory research. *Journal of Verbal Learning and Verbal Behavior, 11,* 671–684.

Cronbach, L. J. (1957). The two disciplines of scientific psychology. *American Psychologist, 12,* 671–684.

Darwin, C. (1859). *On the origin of species by means of natural selection.* London: Murray.

Das, J. P. (1994). Eastern views of intelligence. In R. J. Sternberg (Ed.), *Encyclopedia of human intelligence* (Vol. 1, p. 391). New York: Macmillan.

Das, J. P., Kirby, J. R., & Jarman, R. F. (1979). *Simultaneous and successive cognitive processes.* New York: Academic Press.

Das, J. P., Naglieri, J. A., & Kirby, J. R. (1994). *Assessment of cognitive processes: The PASS theory of intelligence.* Needham Heights, MA: Allyn & Bacon.

Dasen, P. (1984). The cross-cultural study of intelligence: Piaget and the Baoule. *International Journal of Psychology, 19,* 407–434.

De Groot, A. D. (1965). *Thought and choice in chess.* The Hague: Mouton.

Demetriou, A. (2002). Tracing psychology's invisible giant and its visible guards. In R. J. Sternberg & E. L. Grigorenko (Eds.), *The general factor of intelligence: How general is it?* (pp. 3–18). Mahwah, NJ: Lawrence Erlbaum Associates Inc.

Detterman, D. K. (2002). General intelligence: Cognitive and biological explanations. In R. J. Sternberg & E. L. Grigorenko (Eds.), *The general factor of intelligence: How general is it?* (pp. 223–243). Mahwah, NJ: Lawrence Erlbaum Associates Inc.

Donders, F. C. (1868/1869). Over de snelheid van psychische processen. Onderzoekingen gedaan in het Physiologisch Laboratorium der Utrechtsche Hoogeschool. *Tweede reeks, II*, 92–120.

Durojaiye, M. O. A. (1993). Indigenous psychology in Africa. In U. Kim & J. W. Berry (Eds.), *Indigenous psychologies: Research and experience in cultural context* (pp. 211–220). Newbury Park, CA: Sage.

Elkind, D. (1961). Children's discovery of the conservation of mass, weight, and volume: Piaget replication study II. *Journal of Genetic Psychology, 98,* 219–227.

Feuerstein, R. (1979). *The dynamic assessment of retarded performers: The learning potential assessment device theory, instruments, and techniques.* Baltimore, MD: University Park Press.

Feuerstein, R. (1980). *Instrumental enrichment: An intervention program for cognitive modifiability.* Baltimore, MD: University Park Press.

Flavell, J. H. (1971). Stage related properties of cognitive development. *Cognitive Psychology, 2,* 421–453.

Flavell, J. H., & Wellman, H. M. (1977). Metamemory. In R. V. Kail, Jr., & J. W. Hagen (Eds.), *Perspectives on the development of memory and cognition* (pp. 3–33). Hillsdale, NJ: Lawrence Erlbaum Associates Inc.

Galton, F. (1869). *Heredity genius: An inquiry into its laws and consequences.* London: Macmillan.

Galton, F. (1883). *Inquiry into human faculty and its development.* London: Macmillan.

Gardner, H. (1983). *Frames of mind: The theory of multiple intelligences.* New York: Basic.

Gardner, H. (1993). *Multiple intelligences: The theory in practice.* New York: Basic Books.

Gardner, H. (1999). Are there additional intelligences? The case for naturalist, spiritual, and existential intelligences. In J. Kane (Ed.), *Education, information, and transformation* (pp. 111–131). Upper Saddle River, NJ: Prentice-Hall.

Gazzaniga, M. S., Ivry, R. B., & Mangun, G. (1998). *Cognitive neuroscience: The biology of the mind.* New York: W. W. Norton & Co.

Gill, R., & Keats, D. M. (1980). Elements of intellectual competence: Judgments by Australian and Malay university students. *Journal of Cross-Cultural Psychology, 11,* 233–243.

Goodnow, J. J. (1976). The nature of intelligent behavior: Questions raised by cross-cultural studies. In L. Resnick (Ed.), *The nature of intelligence* (pp. 169–188). Hillsdale, NJ: Lawrence Erlbaum Associates Inc.

Gottfredson, L. S. (2002). Where and why g matters: Not a mystery. *Human Performance, 15(1–2),* 25–46.

Gould, S. J. (1981). *The mismeasure of man.* New York: Norton.

Greenfield, P. M. (1997). You can't take it with you: Why abilities assessments don't cross cultures. *American Psychologist, 52,* 1115–1124.

Grigorenko, E. L., Geissler, P. W., Prince, R., Okatcha, F., Nokes, C., Kenny, D. A., Bundy, D. A., & Sternberg, R. J. (2001). The organisation of Luo conceptions of intelligence: A study of implicit theories in a Kenyan village. *International Journal of Behavioral Development, 25,* 367–378.

Grigorenko, E. L., & Sternberg, R. J. (1998). Dynamic testing. *Psychological Bulletin, 124*, 75–111.

Grotzer, T. A., & Perkins, D. A. (2000). Teaching of intelligence: A performance conception. In R. J. Sternberg (Ed.), *Handbook of intelligence* (pp. 492–515). New York: Cambridge University Press.

Guilford, J. P. (1967). *The nature of human intelligence.* New York: McGraw-Hill.

Guilford, J. P. (1982). Cognitive psychology's ambiguities: Some suggested remedies. *Psychological Review, 89*, 48–59.

Guilford, J. P., & Hoepfner, R. (1971). *The analysis of intelligence.* New York: McGraw-Hill.

Gustafsson, J. E. (1984). A unifying model for the structure of intellectual abilities. *Intelligence, 8*, 179–203.

Gustafsson, J. E. (1988). Hierarchical models of the structure of cognitive abilities. In R. J. Sternberg (Ed.), *Advances in the psychology of human intelligence* (Vol. 4, pp. 35–71). Hillsdale, NJ: Lawrence Erlbaum Associates Inc.

Guttman, L. (1954). A new approach to factor analysis: The radix. In P. F. Lazarsfeld (Ed.), *Mathematical thinking in the social sciences* (pp. 258–348). New York: Free Press.

Halstead, W. C. (1951). Biological intelligence. *Journal of Personality, 20*, 118–130.

Harkness, S., & Super, C. M. (1983). The cultural construction of child development: A framework for the socialization of affect. *Ethos, 11(4)*, 221–231.

Hebb, D. O. (1949). *The organization of behavior: A neuropsychological theory.* New York: Wiley.

Hendrickson, A. E., & Hendrickson, D. E. (1980). The biological basis for individual differences in intelligence. *Personality and Individual Differences, 1*, 3–33.

Herrnstein, R. J. & Murray, C. (1994). *The bell curve.* New York: Free Press.

Horn, J. L. (1967). On subjectivity in factor analysis. *Educational and Psychological Measurement, 27*, 811–820.

Horn, J. L. (1994). Theory of fluid and crystallized intelligence. In R. J. Sternberg (Ed.), *The encyclopedia of human intelligence* (Vol. 1, pp. 443–451). New York: Macmillan.

Horn, J. L., & Knapp, J. R. (1973). On the subjective character of the empirical base of Guilford's structure-of-intellect model. *Psychological Bulletin, 80*, 33–43.

Humphreys, L. G. (1962). The organization of human abilities. *American Psychologist, 17*, 475–483.

Humphreys, L. G., & Stark, S. (2002). General intelligence: Measurement, correlates, and interpretations of the cultural–genetic construct. In R. J. Sternberg & E. L. Grigorenko (Eds.), *The general factor of intelligence: How general is it?* (pp. 87–115). Mahwah, NJ: Lawrence Erlbaum Associates Inc.

Hunt, E. B. (1978). Mechanics of verbal ability. *Psychological Review, 85*, 109–130.

Hunt, E. B. (1980). Intelligence as an information-processing concept. *British Journal of Psychology, 71*, 449–474.

Hunt, E., Frost, N., & Lunneborg, C. (1973). Individual differences in cognition: A new approach to intelligence. In G. Bower (Ed.), *The psychology of learning and motivation* (Vol. 7, pp. 87–122). New York: Academic Press.

Hunt, E. B., Lunneborg, C., & Lewis, J. (1975). What does it mean to be high verbal? *Cognitive Psychology, 7*, 194–227.

"Intelligence and its measurement": A symposium (1921). *Journal of Educational Psychology, 12*, 123–147, 195–216, 271–275.

Irvine, J. T. (1978). "Wolof magical thinking": Culture and conservation revisited. *Journal of Cross-Cultural Psychology, 9,* 300–310.

Jensen, A. R. (1969). How much can we boost IQ and scholastic achievement? *Harvard Educational Review, 39,* 1–123.

Jensen, A. R. (1979). g: Outmoded theory of unconquered frontier? *Creative Science and Technology, 2,* 16–29.

Jensen, A. R. (1982). Reaction time and psychometric g. In H. J. Eysenck (Ed.), *A model for intelligence* (pp. 93–132). Heidelberg: Springer-Verlag.

Jensen, A. R. (1998). *The g factor: The science of mental ability.* Westport, CT: Praeger/Greenwood.

Jensen, A. R. (2002). Psychometric g: Definition and substantiation. In R. J. Sternberg & E. L. Grigorenko (Eds.), *General factor of intelligence: How general is it?* (pp. 39–53). Mahwah, NJ: Lawrence Erlbaum Associates Inc.

Katz, H., & Beilin, H. (1976). A test of Bryant's claims concerning the young child's understanding of quantitative invariance. *Child Development, 47,* 877–880.

Kaufman, A. S., & Kaufman, N. L. (1983). *Kaufman assessment battery for children: Interpretive manual.* Circle Pines, MN: American Guidance Service.

Keating, D. P., & Bobbitt, B. (1978). Individual and developmental differences in cognitive processing components of mental ability. *Child Development, 49,* 155–169.

Keil, F. C. (1989). *Concepts, kinds, and cognitive development.* Cambridge, MA: MIT Press.

Kroeber, A. L., & Kluckhohn, C. (1952). *Culture: A critical review of concepts and definitions.* Papers in the Peabody Museum of Archaeology & Ethnology, Harvard University. 47, viii, 223.

Kyllonen, P. C. (2002). g: Knowledge, speed, strategies, or working-memory capacity? A systems perspective. In R. J. Sternberg & E. L. Grigorenko (Eds.), *The general factor of intelligence: How general is it?* (pp. 415–445). Mahwah, NJ: Lawrence Erlbaum Associates Inc.

Laboratory of Comparative Human Cognition (1982). Culture and intelligence. In R. J. Sternberg (Ed.), *Handbook of human intelligence* (pp. 642–719). New York: Cambridge University Press.

Larkin, J. H., McDermott, J., Simon, D. P., & Simon, H. A. (1980). Expert and novice performance in solving physics problems. *Science, 208,* 1335–1342.

Luria, A. R. (1973). *The working brain.* New York: Basic Books.

Luria, A. R. (1980). *Higher cortical functions in man.* New York: Basic Books.

Lutz, C. (1985). Ethnopsychology compared to what? Explaining behaviour and consciousness among the Ifaluk. In G. M. White & J. Kirkpatrick (Eds.), *Person, self, and experience: Exploring Pacific ethnopsychologies* (pp. 35–79). Berkeley, CA: University of California Press.

Mackintosh, N. J. (1998). *IQ and human intelligence.* Oxford, UK: Oxford University Press.

Mazzoni, G., & Nelson, T. O. (1998). *Metacognition and cognitive neuropsychology: Monitoring and control processes.* Mahwah, NJ: Lawrence Erlbaum Associates Inc.

McNemar, Q. (1951). The factors in factoring behavior. *Psychometrika, 16,* 353–359.

McNemar, Q. (1964). Lost: Our intelligence? Why? *American Psychologist, 19,* 871–882.

Miles, T. R. (1957). On defining intelligence. *British Journal of Educational Psychology, 27,* 153–165.

Miller, S. A. (1976). Nonverbal assessment of Piagetian concepts. *Psychological Bulletin, 83,* 405–430.

Miller, G. A., Galanter, E. H., & Pribram, K. H. (1960). *Plans and the structure of behavior.* New York: Holt, Rinehart & Winston.

Mundy-Castle, A. C. (1974). Social and technological intelligence in Western or Nonwestern cultures. *Universitas, 4,* 46–52.

Naglieri, J. A., & Das, J. P. (1990). Planning, attention, simultaneous, and successive cognitive processes as a model for intelligence. *Journal of Psychoeducational Assessment, 8,* 303–337.

Naglieri, J. A., & Das, J. P. (1997). *Cognitive Assessment System.* Itasca, IL: Riverside Publishing Company.

Neisser, U. (1976). General, academic, and artificial intelligence. In L. Resnick (Ed.), *Human intelligence: Perspectives on its theory and measurement* (pp. 179–189). Norwood, NJ: Ablex.

Newell, A., & Simon, H. A. (1972). *Human problem solving.* Englewood Cliffs, NJ: Prentice-Hall.

Okagaki, L., & Sternberg, R. J. (1993). Parental beliefs and children's school performance. *Child Development, 64,* 36–56.

Pellegrino, J. W. & Glaser, R. (1979). Cognitive correlates and components in the analysis of individual differences. In R. J. Sternberg & D. K. Detterman (Eds.), *Human intelligence: Perspectives on its theory and measurement* (pp. 61–88). Norwood, NJ: Ablex.

Pellegrino, J. W. & Glaser, R. (1980). Components of inductive reasoning. In R. E. Snow, P.-A. Federico, & W. E. Montague (Eds.), *Aptitude, learning, and instruction: Cognitive process analyses of aptitude* (Vol. 1, pp. 177–217). Hillsdale, NJ: Lawrence Erlbaum Associates Inc.

Pellegrino, J. W. & Glaser, R. (1982). Analyzing aptitudes for learning: Inductive reasoning. In R. Glaser (Ed.), *Advances in instructional psychology* (Vol. 2, pp. 269–345). Hillsdale, NJ: Lawrence Erlbaum Associates Inc.

Piaget, J. (1926). *The language and thought of the child.* New York: Harcourt.

Piaget, J. (1928). *Judgment and reasoning in the child.* London: Routledge & Kegan Paul.

Piaget, J. (1952). *The origins of intelligence in children.* New York: International Universities Press.

Piaget, J. (1972). *The psychology of intelligence.* Totowa, NJ: Littlefield Adams.

Poole, F. J. P. (1985). Coming into social being: Cultural images of infants in Bimin-Kuskusmin folk psychology. In G. M. White & J. Kirkpatrick (Eds.), *Person, self, and experience: Exploring Pacific ethnopsychologies* (pp. 183–244). Berkeley, CA: University of California Press.

Putnam, D. B., & Kilbride, P. L. (1980). *A relativistic understanding of social intelligence among the Songhay of Mali and Smaia of Kenya.* Paper presented at the meeting of the Society for Cross-Cultural Research, Philadelphia, PA.

Posner, M. I., & Mitchell, R. F. (1967). Chronometric analysis of classification. *Psychological Review, 74,* 392–409.

Raven, J. C., Court, J. H., & Raven, J. (1992). *Manual for Raven's Progressive Matrices and Mill Hill Vocabulary Scales.* Oxford: Oxford Psychologists Press.

Reitman, J. (1976). Skilled perception in GO: Deducing memory structures from interresponse times. *Cognitive Psychology, 8*, 336–356.

Royer, F. L. (1971). Information processing of visual figures in the digit symbol substitution task. *Journal of Experimental Psychology, 87*, 335–342.

Rumelhart, D. E., McClelland, J. L., & the PDP Research Group. (1986). *Parallel distributed processing. Explorations in the microstructure of cognition: Vol. 1.* Foundations. Cambridge, MA: MIT Press.

Ruzgis, P. M. & Grigorenko, E. L. (1994). Cultural meaning systems, intelligence and personality. In R. J. Sternberg & P. Ruzgis (Eds.), *Personality and intelligence* (pp. 248–270). New York: Cambridge.

Sacks, P. (1999). *Standardized minds: The high price of America's testing culture and what we can do to change it.* Cambridge, MA: Perseus Books.

Schmidt, F. L., & Hunter, J. E. (1998). The validity and utility of selection methods in personnel psychology: practical and theoretical implications of 85 years of research findings. *Psychological Bulletin, 124*, 262–274.

Serpell, R. (1974). Aspects of intelligence in a developing country. *African Social Research, 17*, 576–596.

Serpell, R. (1982). Measures of perception, skills, and intelligence. In W. W. Hartup (Ed.), *Review of child development research* (Vol. 6, pp. 392–440). Chicago: University of Chicago Press.

Serpell, R. (1996). Cultural models of childhood in indigenous socialization and formal schooling in Zambia. In C. P. Hwang & M. E. Lamb (Eds.), *Images of childhood* (pp. 129–142). Mahwah, NJ: Lawrence Erlbaum Associates Inc.

Sharp, S. E. (1899). Individual psychology: A study in psychological method. *American Journal of Psychology, 10*, 329–391.

Siegler, R. S. (1996). *Emerging minds: The process of change in children's thinking.* New York: Oxford University Press.

Snow, R. E., Kyllonen, P. C., & Marshalek, B. (1984). The topography of ability and learning correlations. In R. J. Sternberg (Ed.), *Advances in the psychology of human intelligence* (Vol. 2, pp. 47–103). Hillsdale, NJ: Lawrence Erlbaum Associates Inc.

Spearman, C. (1904). "General intelligence," objectively determined and measured. *American Journal of Psychology, 15*, 201–293.

Spearman, C. (1923). *The nature of "intelligence" and the principles of cognition.* London: Macmillan.

Spearman, C. (1927). *The abilities of man.* London: Macmillan.

Sperry, R. W. (1961). Cerebral organization and behavior. *Science, 133*, 1749–1757.

Srivastava, A. K., & Misra, G. (1996). Changing perspectives on understanding intelligence: An appraisal. *Indian Psychological Abstracts and Review, 3*, 1–34.

Sternberg, R. J. (1977). *Intelligence, information processing, and analogical reasoning: The componential analysis of human abilities.* Hillsdale, NJ: Lawrence Erlbaum Associates Inc.

Sternberg, R. J. (1980). Factor theories of intelligence are all right almost. *Educational Researcher, 9*, 6–13, 18.

Sternberg, R. J. (1982). Natural, unnatural, and supernatural concepts. *Cognitive Psychology, 14*, 451–488.

Sternberg, R. J. (1983). Components of human intelligence. *Cognition, 15*, 1–48.

Sternberg, R. J. (1985). *Beyond IQ: A triarchic theory of human intelligence.* New York: Cambridge University Press.

Sternberg, R. J. (1988). Mental self-government: A theory of intellectual styles and their development. *Human Development, 31(4)*, 197–224.

Sternberg, R. J. (1990). *Metaphors of mind: Conceptions of the nature of intelligence.* New York: Cambridge University Press.

Sternberg, R. J. (Ed.). (1994). *Encyclopedia of human intelligence.* New York: Macmillan.

Sternberg, R. J. (1997). *Successful intelligence.* New York: Plume.

Sternberg, R. J. (1998). Abilities are forms of developing expertise. *Educational Researcher, 27*, 11–20.

Sternberg, R. J. (1999a). Successful intelligence: Finding a balance. *Trends in Cognitive Sciences, 3*, 436–442.

Sternberg, R. J. (1999b). The theory of successful intelligence. *Review of General Psychology, 3*, 292–316.

Sternberg, R. J. (Ed.). (2000). *Handbook of intelligence.* New York: Cambridge University Press.

Sternberg, R. J., & Berg, C. A. (1986). Quantitative integration: Definitions of intelligence: A comparison of the 1921 and 1986 symposia. In R. J. Sternberg & D. K. Detterman (Eds.), *What is intelligence? Contemporary viewpoints on its nature and definition* (pp. 155–162). Norwood, NJ: Ablex.

Sternberg, R. J., Conway, B. E., Ketron, J. L., & Bernstein, M. (1981). People's conceptions of intelligence. *Journal of Personality and Social Psychology, 41*, 37–55.

Sternberg, R. J., & Detterman, D. K. (1986). *What is intelligence?* Norwood, NJ: Ablex.

Sternberg, R. J., Forsythe, G. B., Hedlund, J., Horvath, J., Snook, S., Williams, W. M., Wagner, R. K., & Grigorenko, E. L. (2000). *Practical intelligence.* New York: Cambridge University Press.

Sternberg, R. J., & Gardner, M. K. (1983). Unities in inductive reasoning. *Journal of Experimental Psychology: General, 112*, 80–116.

Sternberg, S. (1969). Memory-scanning: Mental processes revealed by reaction-time experiments. *American Scientist, 4*, 421–457.

Super, C. M. (1976). Environmental effects on motor development: The case of African infant precocity. *Developmental Medicine and Child Neurology, 18*, 561–567.

Super, C.M, & Harkness, S. (1982). The development of affect in infancy and early childhood. In D. Wagnet & H. Stevenson (Eds.), *Cultural perspectives on child development* (pp. 1–19). San Francisco: W. H. Freeman.

Terman, L. M., & Merrill, M. A. (1937). *Measuring intelligence.* Boston, MA: Houghton Mifflin.

Terman, L. M., & Merrill, M. A. (1973). *Stanford–Binet Intelligence Scale: Manual for the third revision.* Boston, MA: Houghton Mifflin.

Thomson, G. H. (1939). *The factorial analysis of human ability.* London: University of London Press.

Thorndike, E. L., Bregman, E. D., Cobb, M. V., & Woodyard, E. I. (1926). *The measurement of intelligence.* New York: Teachers College.

Thorndike, R. L., Hagen, E. P., & Sattler, J. M. (1986). *Stanford–Binet Intelligence Scale: Guide for administering and scoring the fourth edition.* Chicago, IL: Riverside.

Thurstone, L. L. (1938). *Primary mental abilities*. Chicago, IL: University of Chicago Press.

Thurstone, L. L. (1947). *Multiple factor analysis*. Chicago, IL: University of Chicago Press.

Thurstone, L. L., & Thurstone, T. C. (1941). *Factorial studies of intelligence*. Chicago, IL: University of Chicago Press.

Vernon, P. E. (1971). *The structure of human abilities*. London: Methuen.

Vygotsky, L. S. (1978). *Mind in society: The development of higher psychological processes*. Cambridge, MA: Harvard University Press.

Wechsler, D. (1991). *Manual for the Wechsler Intelligence Scales for Children* (3rd ed.) (WISC-III). San Antonio, TX: Psychological Corporation.

White, G. M. (1985). Premises and purposes in a Solomon Islands ethnopsychology. In G. M. White & J. Kirkpatrick (Eds.), *Person, self, and experience: Exploring Pacific ethnopsychologies* (pp. 328–366). Berkeley, CA: University of California Press.

Wissler, C. (1901). The correlation of mental and physical tests. *Psychological Review, Monograph Supplement 3(6)*.

Yang, S., & Sternberg, R. J. (1997a). Conceptions of intelligence in ancient Chinese philosophy. *Journal of Theoretical and Philosophical Psychology*, *17(2)*, 101–119.

Yang, S., & Sternberg, R. J. (1997b). Taiwanese Chinese people's conceptions of intelligence. *Intelligence*, *25(1)*, 21–36.

9 Language

Michael C. Corballis

Introduction

Everyone knows what language is, but it is not easy to provide a succinct definition. Most obviously, it is a communication system, but it is much more than that. Most animals communicate with one another, but do so in ways that we would not recognize as language. Part of the difference lies in the diversity of information we can communicate. Language allows us to describe places or events, share plans for the future, teach new skills, gossip, make jokes, and generally influence the minds of others. Given this extraordinary versatility, it is not surprising that language is generally regarded as a uniquely human accomplishment, and special even within the compendium of human faculties.

The idea that language defines something special about the human mind goes back at least to Descartes (1647/1985), whose interest in mechanical toys prompted him to raise the question of whether the human mind could be reduced to mechanical principles. He concluded that animals, even apes, were no more than mere mechanisms, but that humans possessed some special quality of mind that must derive from some nonmaterial source. As evidence for this, he noted that the flexibility of language, even among human imbeciles, defies mechanical explanation. This led him to argue that some nonmaterial influence, operating through the pineal gland, gives us humans free will, which is manifest not only in language but also in our choice of action. This influence derives, he thought, from God.

This theme was taken up much more recently by the linguist Noam Chomsky, an avowed neo-Cartesian. Ironically, though, Chomsky has sought to find the basis of language not in God, but in explicit rules, simulable perhaps on a digital computer, which is a modern-day equivalent of the seventeenth-century mechanical toy. Like Descartes, Chomsky also argued that language was uniquely human:

> The unboundedness of human speech, as an expression of limitless thought, is an entirely different matter [from animal communication], because of the freedom from stimulus control; and the appropriateness

to new situations . . . Modern studies of animal communication so far offer no counterevidence to the Cartesian assumption that human language is based on an entirely different principle. Each known animal communication system either consists of a fixed number of signals, each associated with a specific range of eliciting systems or internal states, or a fixed number of "linguistic dimensions", each associated with a non-linguistic dimension

(Chomsky, 1966, pp. 77–78)

Moreover, by referring to "limitless thought", Chomsky seemed to imply that the uniqueness of the human mind goes beyond language itself, although many routine mental abilities, such as memory, perception, attention, even reasoning, can be inferred from the behaviors of other animals, and especially those closest to humans on the evolutionary tree.

Language owes much of its power to two properties. One is its symbolic nature, and the other is what has been termed the *particulate principle*.

Language as symbolic

Language is composed of *symbols*, which bear little or no relation to the objects, actions, or properties they represent. For example, the word *dog* as either heard or seen in print bears no relation to the sight or sound of that faithful animal, the word *run* conveys nothing of the action it refers to, and the word *red* is not—or need not be—actually red. Even the gestures of signed languages, such as American Sign Language (ASL) or British Sign Language (BSL), are for the most part conventionalized to the point that a person unfamiliar with the language in question cannot discern their meanings. Of course there are exceptions: Some spoken words, like the Italian word *zanzara*, meaning mosquito, or onomatopoeic English words like *buzz* or *hum*, do convey something of their meaning in the way they sound. Iconic representation does occur in signed languages, but is generally diminished over time as the signs are simplified with use. Darwin quoted from the second edition of W. R. Scott's 1870 book *The Deaf and the Dumb*:

> [The] contracting of natural gestures into much shorter gestures than the natural gesture requires, is very common amongst the deaf and the dumb. This contracted gesture is frequently so shortened as to lose all resemblance of the natural one, but to the deaf and dumb who still use it, it still has the force of the original expression.
>
> (Darwin, 1904/1965, p. 62)

The primary advantage of conventionalization is that it is much more efficient than any scheme that requires the word or gesture to convey a complete description. To use an analogy, it is like representing a house by the key to the front door, instead of by a description of the house itself. This results in considerable economy of expression, but of course requires the receiver to establish the full meaning—as Burling (1999) put it, "Conventionalization represents, in part, the victory of the producer (signer, writer, speaker) over the receiver (reader, listener)" (p. 335). The decoding of the message depends on the shared knowledge of the sender and receiver, not on the content of the signal itself.

The use of symbols, though, is not unique to human language. For example, vervet monkeys give different warning cries to distinguish between a number of different threats, such as snakes, hawks, eagles, or leopards. When a monkey makes one of these cries, the troop acts appropriately, clambering up trees in response to a leopard call or running into the bushes in response to an eagle call (Cheney & Seyfarth, 1990). These cries bear no obvious relation to the sounds emitted by the predators they stand for, and are in that sense symbolic. Nevertheless they fall well short of having the referential capacity of words. The word *snake*, for example, can be taken to refer to a snake one saw yesterday, or to describe the characteristics of a snake, or to warn a child not to pick up a snake, or to plan a campaign to rid a neighborhood of snakes. The vervet cry for a snake offers nothing like the range of contexts in which the English word *snake* can be used.

Great apes have also been taught to use symbols. The most impressive, perhaps, is a bonobo, known as Kanzi, who has learned to point to symbols on a keyboard. The 256 symbols were deliberately designed to be abstract, and so do not convey iconic information by virtue of their shapes (Savage-Rumbaugh, Shanker, & Taylor, 1998). But it is doubtful whether even Kanzi's performance comes close to the human power of reference.

The particulate principle—and grammar

According to the *particulate principle* (Studdert-Kennedy, 1998), language is made up of particles that can be combined in hierarchical fashion to create meaning. In speech, the smallest elements that make a difference to meaning are *phonemes*, and correspond roughly to the letters of the alphabet—although we shall see below that phonemes are perhaps better understood as gestures rather than sound-based units. Phonemes are combined to form morphemes that convey units of meaning, morphemes are combined to form words, words to form phrases, phrases to form sentences. Similarly, in signed languages, elementary gestures are combined hierarchically to form phrases and sentences.

Some of the advantages of using a combinatorial system over a system in which every possible meaning is conveyed by a single, holistic representation have been discussed by Nowak, Plotkin, and Jansen (2000). In a simple world in which there are relatively few objects and actions, an efficient communication system might involve a separate symbol for each combination. Thus there might be separate animal calls for such combinations as *snake approaches*, *apple falls*, or *hawk hovering*. If each object were associated with a single action or state, only five calls would be necessary. But in a more complex world each object might be associated with more than one action, and it becomes more economical to have separate symbols for each object and each action, and combine them appropriately. This also allows the communicator to signal novel combinations. For example, in a world of 10 objects and 10 actions, one need only learn 20 symbols to convey the 100 possible combinations. As the world grows in complexity, the advantages of such a system becomes more apparent. But there are also costs. Combining symbols puts a strain on short-term memory, as one must process a pair of symbols, and in more complex situations strings of symbols, in order to produce or decode the message. Further, one must code not only the symbol itself but also the category it belongs to—namely, object or action. But at some point in a world of increasing complexity, the benefits of a combinatorial system outweigh the costs. By making certain assumptions, and assuming a world in which there are only pairwise combinations of objects and actions, Nowak et al. (2000) compute that the breakpoint occurs at 18 objects and 18 actions. Clearly, this kind of argument can be extended to cover the emergence of more complex combinatorial systems, and the emergence of strings of symbols, hierarchically organized, such as those that characterize human language.

Yet the advantages of a particulate, combinatorial system cannot lie wholly in the amount of information that can be transmitted. We humans can recognize probably thousands of objects, including faces, in holistic fashion. We can also convey meaning in works of art and sculpture, which are again largely holistic yet capable of infinite variability and creativity. The distinction between language and art is roughly equivalent to that between digital and analogue representation. It is perhaps not an absolute distinction, though, since language also involves prosody, which is analogue rather than digital in form, and some artists do make use of combinatorial principles. As those in the recording industry know, the advantage of a digital system over an analogue one lies in the fidelity with which information can be transmitted. Language is designed for the explicit transfer of information, whereas art leaves much more to the imagination of the viewer. Again, though, the distinction is not an absolute one. Poetry can be relatively free, ambiguous, and subject to different interpretations, whereas some works of art, such as Picasso's *Guernica*, leave little doubt as to their meaning. And even simple sentences can be parsed in different ways to yield quite different meanings; the sentence "Time flies like an arrow", it has been computed, can be parsed in five different ways, which I leave to the reader to discover.

The particulate principle, implying digital representation, is not unique to language, even in the natural world. Genetic information is conveyed in terms of just four bases (adenine, thymine, guanine, and cytosine), which are ordered in specific sequences to form genes, which then determine the growth and shape of the organism. The material world is also composed of particles, in hierarchical arrangements from subatomic particles, to atoms, to molecules. Combinatorial systems allow for the accurate construction of the complex entities that make up the world of material objects, living organisms—and language. Of course, the combinations are not merely random, but must follow rules, and in language those rules are what we call *grammar*.

Apart from human language, however, animal communication systems are at best only weakly combinatorial. For the past half-century or so, there have been strenuous attempts to teach language to the great apes, and especially to our closest relatives the chimpanzee and bonobo. It soon emerged that chimpanzees were essentially unable to speak; in one famous example, a baby chimpanzee reared in a human family proved able to articulate only three or four words, and was soon outstripped by the human children in the family (Hayes, 1952). It was then realized that the failure to speak may have resulted from deficiencies of the vocal apparatus, and perhaps of cortical control of vocal output, and subsequent attempts have been based on manual action and visual representations. For example, the chimpanzee Washoe was taught over 100 manual signs, based loosely on American Sign Language, and was able to combine signs into two- or three- "word" sequences to make simple requests (Gardner & Gardner, 1969). As we have seen, the bonobo Kanzi has an even larger vocabulary, but his ability to construct meaningful sequences appears to be limited to only two or three "words". Nevertheless Kanzi has shown an impressive ability to follow instructions conveyed in spoken sentences, with as many as seven or eight words (Savage-Rumbaugh et al., 1998).

There seems to be a general consensus, though, that these exploits are not *language*—as Pinker (1994, p. 340) put it, the great apes "just don't 'get it'". Kanzi's ability to understand spoken sentences, although seemingly impressive, was shown to be roughly equivalent to that of a two-and-a-half- year-old girl (Savage-Rumbaugh et al., 1998), and is probably based on the extraction of two or three key words rather than a full decoding of the syntax of the sentences. His ability to produce symbol sequences is also at about the level of the average two-year-old human. In human children, grammar typically emerges between the ages of two and four, so that the linguistic capabilities of Kanzi and other great apes is generally taken as equivalent to that of children in whom grammar has not yet emerged. Bickerton (1995, p. 339) wrote that "The chimps' abilities at anything one would want to call grammar were next to nil", and has labeled this pre- grammatical level of linguistic performance "protolanguage".

Bickerton has further suggested, though, that protolanguage may be the precursor of true language, not only in development, but also in evolution, an idea adopted by Jackendoff (2002) in a recent influential book. Yet protolanguage has been taught to such diverse creatures as the great apes, dolphins, a sea lion, and an African gray parrot, implying parallel evolution. Further, it has never been observed in the wild. An alternative view, then, is that it is not a precursor to language, but is rather indicative of a general problem-solving ability. For example, chimpanzees have been observed to solve mechanical problems by combining implements, such as joining two sticks together to rake in food that would not be reachable using either stick alone. The combining of symbols to achieve some end, such as food, may be in principle no different.

In any event, the remarkable advent of grammar, whether in development or in evolution, transformed our ability to communicate. The real question, then, is how our own species acquired grammar, the ability to combine symbols according to rules, and to generate the infinity of meanings that underlies our culture and discourse. That is, how and when did our ancestors progress beyond protolanguage?

Beyond protolanguage to language

The most comprehensive attempt to explain how true grammatical language might have evolved beyond protolanguage is that undertaken by Jackendoff (2002). His general scheme for the evolution of language is shown in Figure 9.1. The assumption is that protolanguage, or something like it, is possible in great apes (as well as in dolphins, sea lions, and African gray parrots), and may reflect general cognitive and conceptual abilities, not necessarily linked to communication. Nevertheless it is perhaps unlikely that any nonhuman species has evolved the step to the top left of protolanguage in Jackendoff's scheme—that is, the development of a system to create an open, unlimited class of symbols. Although great apes may use hundreds of different symbols, there is no evidence that they have the mechanisms required to combine elements such as syllables or phonemes to create new symbols, as we humans do.

Beyond protolanguage, Jackendoff's scheme suggests the emergence of phrase structure, in which words are combined into larger units called phrases. As words themselves are combinations of syllables or phonemes, phrase structure effectively creates a second level in the hierarchy of linguistic structure, resulting in what has been called *duality of structure*. This leads to the establishment of grammar, involving grammatical categories, inflections to signal the grammatical status of individual words, and syntactic categories to govern the role of words in phrases and sentences. Grammar is the scaffold upon which specific meanings can be built.

Hauser, Fitch, and Chomsky (2002) argue similarly that true language evolved from more rudimentary cognitive capacities. They distinguish between what they call the faculty of language in the narrow sense (FLN) and the faculty of language in the broad sense (FLB). The latter, at least, may have its origins in animal behavior, and is presumably what enables protolanguage. Rather than focus on the emergence of grammatical categories, inflection, and hierarchical structure, as Jackendoff does, Hauser et

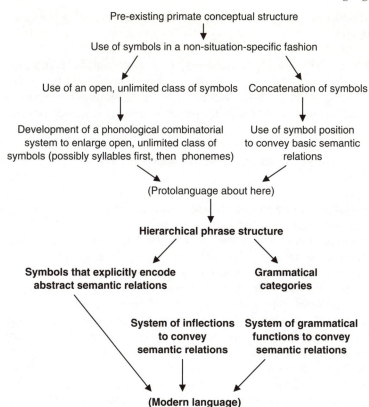

Figure 9.1 Hypothesized evolutionary steps in the evolution of language. Sequential steps are ordered top to bottom; parallel, independent steps are shown side by side. Steps unique to humans are shown in bold type (after Jackendoff, 2002).

al. emphasize *recursion* as the critical ingredient that distinguishes FLN from FLB. Recursion lies at the heart of grammar, and enables us to create a potential infinity of sentences that convey an infinity of meanings.

Recursion: A uniquely human attribute?

Recursion involves the repeated application of a rule, or procedure, to create sequences that can be theoretically without limit. This is well illustrated by the well-known children's story:

This is the house that Jack built.
This is the malt that lay in the house that Jack built.
This is the rat that ate the malt that lay in the house that Jack built.

> This is the cat that killed the rat that ate the malt that lay in the house that Jack built.

As any child will quickly understand, this story can be continued *ad infinitum*. The recursive rules of grammar also allow phrases to be moved around instead of simply being tacked on to the beginning. For example, if one wanted to highlight the *malt* in the story, one could embed phrases as follows:

> The malt that the rat that the cat killed ate lay in the house that Jack built.

Another example came to mind when I recently visited Kyoto, in Japan, and saw a sign on a gate that was translated for me as *Post no bills*. The irony of this sign is that it is itself a bill, and one might imagine that an additional sign might be required that says *Post no "Post no bills" bills*. But, by the same reasoning, this might be supplemented by the sign *Post no "Post no 'Post no bills' bills" bills*. The recursive sequence can continue, of course, *ad infinitum*—and would soon entirely cover the gate.

It is reasonable to suppose that recursive sentences must have evolved to express recursive thought. One sphere of thought that lends itself to recursion is the ability to take the mental perspective of others—or what has been termed *theory of mind*. In our social lives, we may not only know what others are thinking, but we may also know—or guess—that others are thinking what still others are thinking. Recursive beliefs are well conveyed in literature and the theater. In Jane Austen's *Pride and prejudice*, Elizabeth Bennet *thinks* that Darcy *thinks* that she *thinks* he *thinks* too harshly of her family. Or in Shakespeare's *Twelfth night*, Maria *foresees* that Sir Toby will eagerly *anticipate* that Olivia will *judge* Malvolio absurdly impertinent to *suppose* that she *wishes* him to *regard* himself as her preferred suitor. (I am indebted to Brian Boyd for these examples. They are taken from a talk entitled "Evolution, Cognition, Narration, Fiction", which he presented at the Interdisciplinary Symposium on the Nature of Cognition, Tamaki Campus, University of Aukland, on October 13, 2001.) As a count of the italicized words reveals, this last scenario involves sixth-order recursion, and one might add a seventh by preceding it with the phrase "The audience *understands* that . . ."

The question of whether great apes are capable of theory of mind has proven controversial. There is some evidence they are capable of tactical deception, implying some understanding of what another individual can *see*. Whiten and Byrne (1988) collected a database of anecdotal evidence suggesting tactical deception from primate researchers working in field settings. They screened the reports to eliminate cases in which the animals might have learned to deceive through trial and error, and concluded that only the four species of ape occasionally showed evidence of having deceived on the basis of an understanding of what the deceived animal could see or know. Even so, there were relatively few instance—only 12 from common chimpanzees and three each from bonobos, gorillas, and orangutans—that met the authors' rather rigid criteria for *intentional* deception, so there remains some doubt as to whether tactical deception truly shows that great apes can "read the minds" of others.

Experimental studies of the ability of chimpanzees to take the mental perspective have led to conflicting interpretations. Some have taken the view that chimpanzees have little insight into seeming acts of deception or of following the gaze of others (e.g. Povinelli, Bering, & Giambrone, 2000), whereas others have taken the more benign view that chimpanzees can adopt at least the visual perspective of others, if not understand their thoughts (e.g. Hare, Call, Agnetta, & Tomasello, 2000)—although of the 21 cases of intentional deception in great apes identified by Whiten and Byrne (1988), 17 implied *mental* (rather than visual) perspective taking. In any event, these examples imply only second-order recursion at best, and fall far short of the complex recursive patterns of deception and mind reading evident in human social life, and conveyed in literature or the theater. Theory of mind in the great apes may be to theory of mind in humans as protolanguage is to language.

Another example of recursion in a nonlinguistic context is the human ability to count. So long as we have rules that allow us to generate a number from the preceding number in a sequence, there is no limit to the number of objects we can count. The basic rule, of course, is simply to add 1 to the preceding number. This is not an entirely trivial exercise, as there are subrules that tell you how to do this by starting with the rightmost digit, and dealing with the special case where the rightmost digit or digits equal 9. The point is that the procedure is recursive, and the sequence can be continued indefinitely. Thus counting, like language, is an example of what Chomsky (1988) has called "discrete infinity".

Recursion is also apparent in human manufacture. As the modern city illustrates, there seems no limit to human construction, based on recursive principles of combining elements into larger units, then combining those into still larger ones, culminating in the proliferation of buildings, machines, and communication systems that threaten to overwhelm the planet. Whether this extraordinary generativity derives from some common "generative assembling device", or GAD (Corballis, 1991), remains an open question, but there is little question that our species is unique in the ability to create endlessly varied structures from combinatorial principles in recursive fashion.

If recursion is what makes human activity and human thought special, then our specialness is not restricted to language—as indeed Descartes recognized. Recursion may also equip humans with a capacity for multi-level deception, a sense of self, and perhaps even the ability to travel mentally in time (Suddendorf & Corballis, 1997). But the complex rules that enable us to translate recursive thought into recursive sentences are no doubt special to language itself, and presumably evolved in the lineage leading to modern humans during the six million years or so since the split from the great apes.

When did grammar evolve?

There are a number of reasons to believe that the progression from protolanguage to more sophisticated grammatical language may not have begun until the emergence of the genus *Homo* some 2 million years ago, well after the split between the hominid and chimpanzee lineages. Manufactured stone tools, often considered to be a conceptual advance beyond the opportunistic use of sticks or rocks as tools, do not appear in the fossil record until some 2.5 million years ago, perhaps in *Homo rudolfensis*, a precursor to *Homo erectus* (Semaw et al., 1997). From some 1.8 million years, *erectus* began to migrate out of Africa into Asia and later into Europe (Tattersall, 1997), and the Acheulian industry emerged, with large bifacial tools and handaxes that seemed to mark a significant advance over the simple flaked tools of the earlier Oldowan industry (Gowlett, 1992)—although, as we shall see, the advancement manufacturing techniques remained relative slow until the so-called "human revolution" of some 40,000 years ago.

Brain size also began to increase dramatically with the emergence of the genus *Homo* (Deacon, 1997). Indeed, Chomsky has suggested that language may have arisen simply as a consequence of possessing an enlarged brain, without the assistance of natural selection:

> We know very little about what happens when 10^{10} neurons are crammed into something the size of a basketball, with further conditions imposed by the specific manner in which this system developed over time. It would be a serious error to suppose that all properties, or the interesting structures that evolved, can be "explained" in terms of natural selection.
>
> (Chomsky, 1975, p. 59)

Although this seems to ignore the selective processes that must have led to the increase in brain size in the first place, it is plausible to suppose that an enlarged brain provided the extra circuitry required, if not for grammatical language alone, then for recursive thought generally.

Genetic studies have suggested that at least two mutations may have contributed to the increase in brain size from around 2 million years ago. One has to do with a gene on chromosome 7 that encodes the enzyme CMP-N-acetylneuraminic acid (CMP-Neu5Ac) hydroxylase (CMAH). An inactivating mutation of this gene has resulted in the absence in humans of the mammalian sialic acid N-glycolyneuraminic acid (Neu5Gc). This acid appears to be absent in Neanderthal fossils as well as in humans, but is present in present-day primates. It appears to have been down-regulated in the brain in the chimpanzee, and through mammalian evolution, leading to speculation that inactivation of the CMAH gene may have removed a constraint on brain growth in human ancestry (Chou et al., 2002). Chou et al. applied molecular-clock analysis to the CMAH genes in chimpanzees and other great apes, as well as to the pseudogene in humans, which indicated that the mutation occurred some 2.8 million years ago, leading up to the expansion in brain size.

Another inactivating mutation that may also have contributed to the increase in brain size has to do with a gene on chromosome 7 that encodes myosene heavy chain (MYH16), responsible for the heavy masticatory muscles in most primates, including chimpanzees and gorillas, as well as the early hominids. Molecular clock analysis shows that this gene was inactivated an estimated 2.4 million years ago, leading to speculation that the diminution of jaw muscles and their supporting bone structure removed a further constraint on brain growth (Stedman et al., 2004). It is a matter of further speculation as to why this seemingly deleterious mutation became fixed in the ancestral human population. It may have had to do with the change from a predominantly vegetable diet to a meat-eating one, or it may have had to do with the increasing use of the hands rather than the jaws to prepare food (Currie, 2004). Perhaps it was also driven in part by the increasing dependence on social intelligence—and language.

Conclusions about the role of the CMAH and MYH16 genes in shaping the size and shape of the human brain are of course speculative, but it is of interest that both involves *inactivating* mutations, suggesting that human evolution was shaped in part by the *loss* of genetic information. This runs counter to the intuitive idea that the human mind evolved through the accumulation of new genes, such as the "grammar gene" proposed by Pinker (1994).

There are some reasons to suggest that brain size *per se* may not have been the only factor underlying the emergence of grammar and recursion. For example, individuals with Seckel syndrome ("nanocephalic dwarfs") have chimpanzee-sized brains, yet do not show massive deficits in vocabulary size, or in grammatical language (Lenneberg, 1967). Another factor, perhaps an indirect result of the increase in brain size, may have been the prolongation of childhood. To conform to the general primate pattern, human babies should be born at around 18 months, not 9 months (Krogman, 1972), but as any mother will know this would be impossible, given the size of the birth canal. The brain of a newborn chimpanzee is about 60 per cent of its adult weight, that of a newborn human only about 24 per cent. There is evidence that the human developmental pattern was present in *Homo erectus* by 1.6 million years ago (Brown, Harris, Leakey, & Walker, 1985). Surprisingly, however, more recent evidence of the rate of dental growth, inferred from tooth fossils, suggests that prolonged childhood was a feature of Upper Paleolithic humans as well as of modern humans, but not of *Homo antecessor*, *Homo heidelbergensis*, or even of the Neanderthals—all of whom postdate *Homo erectus* (Ramirez-Rossi & Bermudez de Castro, 2004). If the slow rate of growth contributed to, or was a consequence of, the emergence of modern grammar, then these most recent results suggest that modern grammar may have emerged only with *Homo sapiens*. Nevertheless, according to the scheme proposed by Jackendoff (2002) and outlined in Figure 9.1, some degree of grammatical competence may well have preceded the emergence of the slow growth pattern that characterizes modern humans.

In any event, learning during growth may well provide part of the key to recursive grammar. Elman (1993) has devised an artificial network with recurrent loops that can apparently learn something resembling grammar. Given a partial sequence of symbols, analogous to a partial sentence, the network can learn to predict events that would follow according to rules of grammar. In a very limited way, then, the network "learns" the rules of grammar. At first, the network was unable to handle the recursive aspects of grammar, in which phrases are embedded in other phrases, so that words that go together may be separated by several other words. This problem was at least partially surmounted when Elman introduced a "growth" factor, which he simulated by degrading the system early on so that only global aspects of the input were processed, and then gradually decreasing the "noise" in the system so that it was able to process more and more detail. When this was done, the system was able to pick up some of the recursive quality of grammar, and so begin to approximate the processing of true language. This dependence on growth may explain the so-called "critical period" for the development of language, and it is of interest that birds show the same altricial pattern of development (which is to say that they are relatively helpless at birth, and require extensive parental care), and that birdsong also depends on a critical period of exposure (Hauser & Konishi, 1999).

"Big bang" theories of language evolution

According to the scenario suggested above, grammatical language evolved over the last 2 million years, as evidenced by the increase in brain size, the prolongation of childhood, the emergence of tool manufacture, and migrations out of Africa. It may have progressed through the stages proposed by Jackendoff (2002), and shown in Figure 9.1.

This scenario stands in stark contrast to the alternative view that grammatical language evolved in a single step, perhaps with the emergence of our own species, *Homo sapiens*. This so-called "big bang" theory is often attributed to Bickerton (1995), who wrote that ". . . true language, via the emergence of syntax, was a catastrophic event, occurring within the first few generations of *Homo sapiens sapiens*" (p. 69). Even more radically, Crow (2002) has proposed that a genetic mutation gave rise to the speciation of *Homo sapiens*, along with such uniquely human attributes as language, cerebral asymmetry, theory of mind, and a vulnerability to psychosis. There is perhaps an echo of Descartes in these views, and a hint of the miraculous, if not of God.

Part of the argument for a late and sudden emergence of grammatical language is that the development of manufacture in *Homo* was in fact very slow. As Bickerton (2002) roguishly puts it, "for the first 1.95 million years after the emergence of *erectus* almost nothing happened: The clunky stone tools became less clunky and slightly more diversified stone tools, and everything beyond that, from bone tools to supercomputers, happened in the last one-fortieth of the period in question" (p. 104). Although there was something of an advance some 300,000 years ago (Ambrose, 2001), it was not really until the emergence of *Homo sapiens* that manufacture really began to progress, and perhaps it was really only in the last 40,000 years that so-called "modern behavior" became truly evident, in what has been termed the "human revolution" (Mellars & Stringer, 1989). In Bickerton's view, these late developments are evidence of a recent "big bang", not only in language but also in the complexity of human thought and behavior.

Another reason to suppose that language may have emerged only recently in the evolution of *Homo* is that speech appears to have been a recent development. As noted earlier, it has proven virtually impossible to teach chimpanzees to speak, and the fossil evidence suggests that the alterations to the vocal tract necessary for articulate speech were completed late in hominid evolution (e.g. D. Lieberman, 1998; P. Lieberman, Crelin, & Klatt, 1972; MacLarnon & Hewitt, 1999), and perhaps only with the emergence of our own species, *Homo sapiens*, some 170,000 years ago. Thus P. Lieberman's (1998) book *Eve spoke: Human language and human evolution* apparently equates the late emergence of speech with the late emergence of language itself.

However, arguments for the late development of speech need not mean that grammatical language itself developed late, or in a single step. For one thing, language can of course exist without speech. Reading and writing can be accomplished silently, and although they are perhaps parasitic on speech, a skilled reader may have little access to the sounds of the words he or she reads. More compellingly, it is now well documented that signed languages have all of the grammatical sophistication of spoken languages, and in deaf people have no connection with speech (Armstrong, Stokoe, & Wilcox, 1995; Emmorey, 2002; Neidle, Kegl, MacLaughlin, Bahan, & Lee, 2000). Moreover, children exposed only to manual sign language go through the same stages of language development as those exposed to speech, even "babbling" in sign (Pettito & Marentette, 1991), suggesting that manual language is as "natural" as spoken language.

Language as gesture

The independence of language and speech raises the possibility that language emerged in human evolution, not as a vocal system, but as a system of manual gestures. This idea goes back at least to the eighteenth-century philosopher Condillac (1746/1971), but has been advocated many times since, often independently. Wilhelm Wundt, who founded the first laboratory of experimental psychology in 1879, referred to "the assumption, outspokenly held by many anthropologists, that gestural language is the original means of communication" (Wundt, 1916/1921, p. 128). The idea was revived by Hewes (1973), and has since been repeated and elaborated by a number of authors (e.g. Armstrong, 1999; Armstrong et al., 1995; Corballis, 1992, 2002; Givòn, 1995; Rizzolatti & Arbib, 1998). From an evolutionary point of view, the idea makes some sense, as nonhuman primates have little if any cortical control over vocalization (Ploog, 2002), but excellent cortical control over the hands and arms, and we have already seen that there has been much greater success in teaching great apes to communicate through sign or by pointing to visual symbols than in teaching them anything approaching speech. The human equivalents of primate vocalizations are probably emotionally based sounds like laughing, crying, grunting, or shrieking, rather than words.

The transition from manual to vocal language need not have been abrupt. This transition is perhaps best understood if vocal language is also understood as a gestural system, an idea captured by the so-called *motor theory of speech perception* (Liberman, Cooper, Shankweiler, & Studdert-Kennedy, 1967), and in what has more recently become known as *articulatory phonology* (Browman & Goldstein, 1995), in which speech is regarded, not as a system for producing sounds, but rather as a system for producing articulatory gestures, through the independent action of the six articulatory organs—namely, the lips, the velum, the larynx, and the blade, body, and root of the tongue. This conceptualization arose, not from evolutionary considerations, but rather from problems associated with the identification of the acoustic units of speech.

Traditionally, speech has been regarded as made up of discrete elements of sound, called phonemes, but it has been known for some time that phonemes do not exist as discrete units in the acoustic signal (Joos, 1948), and are not discretely discernible in mechanical recordings of sound, such as a sound spectrograph (Liberman et al., 1967). One reason for this is that the acoustic signals corresponding to individual phonemes vary widely, depending on the contexts in which they are embedded. This has led to the view that they exist only in the minds of speakers and hearers, and the acoustic signal must undergo complex transformation for individual phonemes to be perceived as such. Yet we can perceive speech at remarkably high rates, up to at least 10–15 phonemes per second, which seems at odds with the idea that some complex, context-dependent transformation is necessary. The conceptualization of speech as *gesture* overcomes this difficulty, at least to some extent, since the articulatory gestures that give rise to speech partially overlap in time, which makes possible the high rates of production and perception. Unlike phonemes themselves, speech gestures can be discerned by mechanical means, through X-rays, magnetic resonance imaging, and palatography (Studdert-Kennedy, 1998). That is, the "particles" of speech are gestures, not sounds.

From manual to articulatory gesture

If speech itself is a gestural system, then the medium of linguistic transmission can be understood to have evolved from manual to articulatory gestures, although it has perhaps always comprised a mixture of the two. Early language in *Homo erectus* may have consisted primarily of manual gestures punctuated by vocal grunts, whereas modern speech is primarily vocal but embellished by manual gestures, as is well documented by McNeill and his colleagues (e.g. Goldin-Meadow & McNeill, 1999; McNeill, 1985). The transition may well have occurred via the mediation of the face, which plays an important role in modern signed languages (e.g. Neidle et al., 2000), and may well have coopted mechanisms involved in ingestion (MacNeilage, 1998). In the evolution of *Homo*, as the hands were increasingly occupied in the manufacture and use of tools, so the face may have assumed greater importance in communication. Vocalization may have been incorporated initially in order to permit facial gestures that are not visible, including movements of the tongue, so that internal gestures of the mouth would be rendered accessible through audition rather than vision. The addition of voicing would also have added to the repertoire of gestures by creating the contrast between voiced and unvoiced consonants (such as /b/ vs. /p/, or /d/ vs. /t/; Corballis, 2002).

There may have been further advantages to a vocal system, in which the receiver recovers the articulatory gestures emitted by the speaker through acoustic rather than visual information. Although there is no reason to suppose that manual language is in any way inferior to vocal language in purely linguistic terms, there are a number of practical advantages to a vocal system. Speech is less attentionally demanding than signed language; one can attend to speech with one's eyes shut, or when watching something else. Speech also allows communication over longer distances, as well as communication at night or when the speaker is not visible to the listener. The San, a modern hunter-gatherer society, are known to talk late at night, sometimes all through the night, to resolve conflict and share knowledge (Konner, 1982). The switch to predominantly vocal language may also have been partly driven by the more efficient use of bodily resources. Our species had been habitually bipedal from some 6 or 7 million years ago, and from some 2 million years ago was developing systematic procedures for manufacturing tools, which would have increasingly involved the hands. The mouth, in contrast, was relatively under-used, except for the purposes of eating. In other species, such as wild cats, the mouth was adapted for attacking and killing, but in our own forebears it was adapted for an activity that is perhaps equally lethal, albeit indirectly so. That activity is talking.

The mirror system

The notion that speech may have evolved from a system that was initially involved in the production and perception of manual gestures receives support from recent work on the so-called "mirror system" in the primate brain. The initial evidence for such a system came from the recording of single neurons in the region of F5 in the ventral premotor cortex of the monkey. These neurons typically fire when the animal makes grasping movements toward a target with the hand or mouth. A subset of those neurons, dubbed "mirror neurons", also fire when the animal observes another individual making the same movements (Gallese, Fadiga, Fogassi, & Rizzolatti, 1996; Rizzolatti, Fadiga, Fogassi, & Gallese, 1996). This direct mapping of perceived action onto the production of action seems to provide a platform for the evolution of language, and to support, albeit indirectly, the motor theory of speech perception. Furthermore, the area of the human brain that corresponds most closely to area F5 in the monkey includes Broca's area, which is one of the main cortical areas underlying the production of speech. This suggests that speech may have arisen from cortical structures that initially had to do with manual action rather than with vocalization (Rizzolatti & Arbib, 1998).

It has also become apparent that mirror neurons are part of a more general mirror system that involves other regions of the brain as well. The superior temporal sulcus (STS) also contains cells that respond to observed biological actions, including grasping actions (Perrett et al., 1989), although few if any respond when the animal itself performs an action. F5 and STS are connected to area PF in the inferior parietal lobule, where there are also neurons that respond both to the execution and perception of actions. These neurons are now known as "PF mirror neurons" (Rizzolatti, Fogassi, & Gallese, 2001). Other areas, such as amygdala and orbito-frontal cortex, may also be part of the mirror system.

A similar system has been inferred in humans, based on evidence from electroencephalography (Muthukumaraswamy, Johnson, & McNair, 2004), magnetoencephalography (Hari, Forss, Avikainen, Kirveskari, Salenius, & Rizzolatti, 1998), transcranial magnetic stimulation (Fadiga, Fogassi, Pavesi, & Rizzolatti, 1995), and functional magnetic resonance imaging (fMRI; Iacoboni, Woods, Brass, Bekkering, Mazziotta, & Rizzolatti, 1999). Unlike the mirror system in monkeys, the human mirror system appears to be activated by movements that need not be directed toward an object (Rizzolatti et al., 2001), although there is evidence that it is activated more by actions that are object-directed than by those that are not (Muthukumaraswamy et al., 2004). Activation by nonobject-directed action may reflect adaptation of the system for more abstract signaling—as in signed languages. The mirror system in humans appears to involve areas in the frontal, temporal and parietal lobes that are homologous to those in the monkey, although there is some evidence that they tend to be lateralized to the left hemisphere in humans, especially in the frontal lobes (Iacoboni et al., 1999; Nishitani & Hari, 2000). It is well established that manual apraxia, especially for actions involving fine motor control, is associated with left-hemisphere damage (Heilman, Meador, & Loring, 2000). It is possible that the incorporation of vocalization into the mirror system, perhaps unique to *Homo sapiens*, resulted in lateralization of the manual as well as of the vocal system (Corballis, 2003).

The mirror system leads to what has been termed the "direct-matching hypothesis", according to which we understand actions by mapping the visual representations of observed actions onto the motor representations of the same actions (Rizzolatti et al., 2001). This system is tuned to the perception of actions that have a "personal" reference. Evidence from an fMRI study shows, for example, that it is activated when people watch mouth actions, such as biting, lip-smacking, oral movements involved in vocalization (e.g. speech reading, barking), performed by people, but not when they watch such actions performed by a monkey or a dog. Actions belonging to the observer's own motor repertoire are mapped onto the observer's motor system, whereas those that do not belong are not— instead, they are perceived in terms of their visual properties (Buccino et al., 2004). Watching speech movements, and even stills of a mouth making a speech sound, activate the mirror system, including Broca's area (Calvert & Campbell, 2003). This is consistent with the idea that speech may have evolved from visual display that included movements of the face.

Although most of the evidence on the mirror system has to do with visual input, area F5 of the monkey also contains what might be termed "acoustic mirror neurons". These respond to the sounds of actions, such as tearing paper or breaking a peanut, as well as to the performance of those actions. That is, even in the monkey, the direct-matching hypothesis is not restricted to visual input (Kohler, Keysers, Umilta, Fogassi, Gallese, & Rizzolatti, 2002). There is no evidence for mirror neurons in the monkey that fire to both the production and perception of vocalization. It is likely, though, that vocalization was incorporated into the mirror system in humans, and probably only in humans or our hominid forebears (Ploog, 2002), providing the mechanism for the motor theory of speech perception.

The next question is when vocalization was added to the system. A clue to this comes from the *FOXP2* gene

The **FOXP2** *gene*

About half of the members of three generations of an extended family in England, known as the KE family, are affected by a disorder of speech and language. The disorder is evident from the affected child's first attempts to speak and persists into adulthood (Vargha-Khadem, Watkins, Alcock, Fletcher, & Passingham, 1995). The disorder is now known to be due to a point mutation on the *FOXP2* gene (forkhead box P2) on chromosome 7

(Fisher, Vargha-Khadem, Watkins, Monaco, & Pembrey, 1998; Lai, Fisher, Hurst, Vargha-Khadem, & Monaco, 2001). For normal speech to be acquired, two functional copies of this gene seem to be necessary.

The nature of the deficit in the affected members of the KE family, and therefore the role of the *FOXP2* gene, have been debated. Some have argued that *FOXP2* gene is involved in the development of morphosyntax (Gopnik, 1990), and it has even been identified more broadly as the "grammar gene" (Pinker, 1994). Subsequent investigation suggests, however, that the core deficit is one of articulation, with grammatical impairment a secondary outcome (Watkins, Dronkers, & Vargha-Khadem, 2002). It may therefore play a role in the incorporation of vocal articulation into the mirror system.

This is supported by a study in which fMRI was used to record brain activity in both affected and unaffected members of the KE family while they covertly generated verbs in response to nouns (Liégeois, Baldeweg, Connelly, Gadian, Mishkin, & Vargha-Khadem, 2003). Whereas unaffected members showed the expected activity concentrated in Broca's area in the left hemisphere, affected members showed relative *under*activation in both Broca's area and its right-hemisphere homologue, as well as in other cortical language areas. They also showed *over*activation bilaterally in regions not associated with language. However, there was bilateral activation in the posterior superior temporal gyrus; the left side of this area overlaps Wernicke's area, important in the comprehension of language. This suggests that affected members may have generated words in terms of their sounds, rather than in terms of articulatory patterns. Their deficits were not attributable to any difficulty with verb generation itself, as affected and unaffected members did not differ in their ability to generate verbs overtly, and the patterns of brain activity were similar to those recorded during covert verb generation. Another study based on structural MRI showed morphological abnormalities in the same areas (Watkins et al., 2002).

The *FOXP2* gene is highly conserved in mammals, and in humans differs in only three places from that in the mouse. Nevertheless, two of the three changes occurred on the human lineage after the split from the common ancestor we share with the chimpanzee and bonobo. A recent estimate of the date of the more recent of these mutations suggests that it occurred "since the onset of human population growth, some 10,000 to 100,000 years ago" (Enard et al., 2002, p. 871). If this is so, then it might be argued that the final incorporation of vocalization into the mirror system was critical to the emergence of modern human behavior, often dated to the Upper Paleolithic (Corballis, 2004).

It is unlikely, though, that the *FOXP2* mutation was the only event in the transition to speech, which undoubtedly went through several steps and involved other genes (Marcus & Fisher, 2003). Moreover, the *FOXP2* gene is expressed in the embryonic development of structures other than the brain, including the gut, heart, and lung (Shu, Yang, Zhang, Lu, & Morrisey, 2001). It may even have played a role in the modification of breath control for speech (MacLarnon & Hewitt, 1999). A mutation of the *FOXP2* gene may nevertheless have been the most recent event in the incorporation of vocalization into the mirror system, and thus the refinement of vocal control to the point that it could carry the primary burden of language.

The idea that the critical mutation of the *FOXP2* gene occurred less than 100,000 years ago is indirectly supported by recent evidence from African click languages. Two of the many groups that make extensive use of click sounds are the Hadzabe and San, who are separated geographically by some 2000 kilometers, and genetic evidence suggests that the most recent common ancestor of these groups goes back to the root of present-day mitochondrial DNA lineages, perhaps as early as 100,000 years ago (Knight et al., 2003). This could mean that clicks were a prevocal way of adding sound to facial gestures, prior to the *FOXP2* mutation. Evidence from mitochondrial DNA suggests that modern humans outside of Africa date from groups who migrated from Africa from around 52,000 years ago (Ingman, Kaessmann, Pääbo, & Gyllensten, 2000), and these groups may have already developed autonomous speech, leaving behind African speakers who retained click sounds. The only known non-African click language is Damin, an extinct Australian aboriginal language, and migrations to Australia may have been earlier than the presumed migrations of 52,000 years ago. This is not to say that the early Australians and Africans did not have full vocal control of speech; rather, click languages may simply be a vestige of earlier languages in which vocalization was not yet part of the mirror system giving rise to autonomous speech.

The mutation of the *FOXP2* gene some time in the past 100,000 years may therefore have led to the final step in the switch to a form of vocal language that was autonomous to the point that manual gestures were no longer required, and language could be transmitted purely vocally (as on a cell-phone, or via radio). This is not to say that visible gestures have been eradicated—most people still gesture as they speak, and their gestures, both manual and facial, add to meaning. But the emergence of vocal speech may explain why manufacture, art, ornamentation, music, and perhaps the other trappings of modern human behavior, emerged so late in human evolution. As we saw earlier, Bickerton (2002) has argued in favor of the "big bang" theory of language evolution partly on the grounds that manufacture developed only very slowly over the two million or so years prior to the so-called "human revolution" within the past 100,000 years. The alternative scenario, developed above, is that the human revolution was driven, not by the late emergence of language, but by the late emergence of autonomous speech.

Summary and conclusions

The modern understanding of language has become a truly interdisciplinary endeavor, with contributions from linguistics, psychology, genetics, archeology, and neuroscience. The prevailing framework is an evolutionary one, in defiance of the famous ban on discussion of the evolution of language imposed in 1866 by the Linguistic Society of Paris. The emphasis on evolution may also be a reaction against the anthropocentric views of Chomsky, the dominant linguistic theorist of the latter half of the twentieth century, although Chomsky himself seems to have recently accepted that we can learn much about human language from the study of animal communication (Hauser et al., 2002).

In this chapter, I have tried to weave a story as to how language might have evolved, beginning with the Chomskyan notion that true language is uniquely human, and dependent on rules rather than on associative learning. Those rules are embodied in grammar. Although the ability to use symbols to refer to real-world objects and actions may be present in many other species, true language involves *grammar*—the ability to combine symbols according to rules to create an infinity of possible meanings. I have argued that this ability emerged relatively late in hominid evolution, and probably began with the genus *Homo* within the past 2 million years. One of the critical questions is whether it emerged suddenly, as a "big bang", or whether it unfolded in several steps. Another critical question is whether the recursive nature of grammar was specific to language, or whether it represented some more general recursive ability that also underlies such human activities as manufacture, theory of mind, mental time travel, and perhaps music.

Language should not be equated with *speech*. I have taken the provocative step of arguing that language actually evolved from manual gestures rather than from vocal calls. The evidence suggests that the neural and anatomical changes necessary for the production of speech were completed very late in hominid evolution, even later than the emergence of recursive grammar. It may have emerged with, and indeed defined, our own species, *Homo sapiens*, a mere 170,000 or so years ago. I have also provocatively adopted the view that speech itself is fundamentally gestural rather than acoustic, so that the transition from manual to vocal gestures was effectively a continuous process—even today, people ubiquitously gesture with their hands while they speak. Recent work on the mirror system suggests that the perception of gestures, whether manual or articulatory, depends on a direct mapping from perception to production, as long anticipated by the motor theory of speech perception.

Work on the *FOXP2* gene suggests that the final step in the evolution of autonomous speech may have occurred even more recently than the appearance of *Homo sapiens*, perhaps within the past 100,000 years, in Africa. If this is so, then the ability to speak may have finally freed the hands for the advancement of manufacture, and may well explain why the exodus of *Homo sapiens* from Africa around 50,000 years ago eventually led to the extinction of all other extant hominids out of Africa, including the Neanderthals in Europe and Homo erectus in Southeast Asia, and gave rise to the so-called "human revolution" of the past 40,000 or so years.

Language has a lot to answer for.

References

Ambrose, S. H. (2001). Paleolithic technology and human evolution. *Science, 291,* 1748–1753.

Armstrong, D. F. (1999). *Original signs: Gesture, sign, and the source of language.* Washington, DC: Gallaudet University Press.

Armstrong, D. F., Stokoe, W. C., & Wilcox, S. E. (1995). *Gesture and the nature of language.* Cambridge, MA: Cambridge University Press.

Bickerton, D. (1995). *Language and human behavior.* Seattle, WA: University of Washington Press.

Bickerton, D. (2002). From protolanguage to language. In T. J. Crow (Ed.), *The speciation of modern* Homo sapiens (pp. 103–120). Oxford: Oxford University Press.

Browman, C. P., & Goldstein, L. F. (1995). Dynamics and articulatory phonology. In T. van Gelder & R. F. Port (Eds.), *Mind as motion* (pp. 175–193). Cambridge, MA: MIT Press.

Brown, F., Harris, J., Leakey, R., & Walker, A. (1985). Early *Homo erectus* skeleton from west Lake Turkana, Kenya. *Nature, 316,* 788–792.

Buccino, G., Lui, F., Canessa, N., Patteri, I., Lagravinese, G., Benuzzi, F., Porro, C. A., & Rizzolatti, G. (2004). Neural circuits involved in the recognition of actions performed by nonconspecifics: An fMRI study. *Journal of Cognitive Neuroscience, 16,* 114–126.

Burling, R. (1999). Motivation, conventionalization, and arbitrariness in the origin of language. In B. J. King (Ed.), *The origins of language: What nonhuman primates can tell us* (pp. 307–350). Santa Fe, NM: School of America Research Press.

Calvert, G. A., & Campbell, R. (2003). Reading speech from still and moving faces: The neural substrates of visible speech. *Journal of Cognitive Neuroscience, 15,* 57–70.

Cheney, D. L., & Seyfarth, R. S. (1990). *How monkeys see the world.* Chicago, IL: University of Chicago Press.

Chomsky, N. (1966). *Cartesian linguistics: A chapter in the history of rationalist thought.* New York: Harper & Row.

Chomsky, N. (1975). *Reflections on language.* New York: Pantheon.

Chomsky, N. (1988). *Language and problems of knowledge: The Managua lectures.* Cambridge, MA: MIT Press.

Chou, H.-H., Hakayama, T., Diaz, S., Krings, M., Indriati, E., Leakey, M., Pääbo, S., Satta, Y., Takahata, N., & Varki, A. (2002). Inactivation of CMP-*N*-acetylneuraminic acid hydroxylase occurred prior to brain expansion during human evolution. *Proceedings of the National Academy of Sciences, USA, 99,* 11736–11741

Condillac, E. B. de. (1746/1971). *An essay on the origin of human knowledge* (T. Nugent, Trans.). Gainesville, FL: Scholars Facsimiles and Reprints (Original work published in 1746).

Corballis, M. C. (1991). *The lopsided ape.* New York: Oxford University Press.

Corballis, M. C. (1992). On the evolution of language and generativity. *Cognition, 44,* 197–226.

Corballis, M. C. (2002). *From hand to mouth: The origins of language.* Princeton, NJ: Princeton University Press.

Corballis, M. C. (2003). From mouth to hand: Gesture, speech, and the evolution of right-handedness. *Behavioral & Brain Sciences, 26,* 199–260.

Corballis, M. C. (2004). The origins of modernity: Was autonomous speech the critical factor? *Psychological Review, 111,* 543–552.

Crow, T. J. (2002). Sexual selection, timing, and an X-Y homologous gene: Did *Homo sapiens* speciate on the Y chromosome? In T. J. Crow (Ed.), *The speciation of modern* Homo sapiens (pp. 197–216). Oxford, UK: Oxford University Press.

Currie, P. (2004). Muscling in on hominid evolution. *Nature, 428,* 373–374.

Darwin, C. (1904/1965). *The expression of the emotions in man and animals.* Chicago: University of Chicago Press (Original work published by John Murray, London, 1904).

Deacon, T. (1997). *The symbolic species: The co-evolution of language and the brain.* New York: W. W. Norton.

Descartes, R. (1647/1985). *The philosophical writings of Descartes* (J. Cottingham, R. Stoothoff, & D. Murdock, Ed. and Trans.). Cambridge, MA: Cambridge University Press (Original work published 1647).

Elman, J. (1993). Learning and development in neural networks: The importance of starting small. *Cognition, 48,* 71–99.

Emmorey, K. (2002). *Language, cognition, and brain: Insights from sign language research.* Hillsdale, NJ: Lawrence Erlbaum Associates Inc.

Enard, W., Przeworski, M., Fisher, S. E., Lai, C. S. L., Wiebe, V., Kitano, T., Monaco, A. P., & Pääbo, S. (2002). Molecular evolution of FOXP2, a gene involved in speech and language. *Nature, 418,* 869–871.

Fadiga, L., Fogassi, L., Pavesi, G., & Rizzolatti, G. (1995). Motor facilitation during action observation—a magnetic stimulation study. *Journal of Neurophysiology, 73,* 2608–2611.

Fisher, S. E., Vargha-Khadem, F., Watkins, K. E., Monaco, A. P., & Pembrey, M. E. (1998). Localisation of a gene implicated in a severe speech and language disorder. *Nature Genetics, 18,* 168–170.

Gallese, V., Fadiga, L., Fogassi, L., & Rizzolatti, G. (1996). Action recognition in the premotor cortex. *Brain, 119,* 593–609.

Gardner, R. A., & Gardner, B. T. (1969). Teaching sign language to a chimpanzee. *Science, 165,* 664–672.

Givòn, T. (1995). *Functionalism and grammar.* Philadelphia, PA: Benjamins.

Goldin-Meadow, S., & McNeill, D. (1999). The role of gesture and mimetic representation in making language the province of speech. In M. C. Corballis & S. E. G. Lea (Eds.), *The descent of mind* (pp. 155–172). Oxford: Oxford University Press.

Gopnik, M. (1990). Feature-blind grammar and dysphasia. *Nature, 344,* 715.

Gowlett, J. A. J. (1992). Early human mental abilities. In S. Jones, R. Martin, & D. Pilbeam (Eds.), *The Cambridge encyclopedia of human evolution* (pp. 341–345). Cambridge, UK: Cambridge University Press.

Hare, B., Call, J., Agnetta, B., & Tomasello, M. (2000). Chimpanzees know what conspecifics do and do not see. *Animal Behaviour, 59,* 771–785.

Hari, R., Forss, N., Avikainen, S., Kirveskari, E., Salenius, S., & Rizzolatti, G. (1998). Activation of human primary motor cortex during action observation: A neuromagnetic study. *Proceedings of the National Academy of Sciences, USA, 95,* 15061–15065.

Hauser, M. D., Fitch, W. T., & Chomsky, N. (2002). The faculty of language: What is it, who has it, and how did it evolve? *Science, 298*, 1569–1579.

Hauser, M. D., & Konishi, M. (Eds.). (1999). *The design of animal communication.* Cambridge, MA: MIT Press.

Hayes, C. (1952). *The ape in our house.* London: Gollancz.

Heilman, K. M., Meador, K. J., & Loring, D. W. (2000). Hemispheric asymmetries of limb-kinetic apraxia: A loss of deftness. *Neurology, 55*, 523–526.

Hewes, G. W. (1973). Primate communication and the gestural origins of language. *Current Anthropology, 14*, 5–24.

Iacoboni, M., Woods, R. P., Brass, M., Bekkering, H., Mazziotta, J. C., & Rizzolatti, G. (1999). Cortical mechanisms of human imitation. *Science, 286*, 2526–2528.

Ingman, M., Kaessmann, H., Pääbo, S., & Gyllensten, U. (2000). Mitochondrial genome variation and the origin of modern humans. *Nature, 408*, 708–713.

Jackendoff, R. (2002). *Foundations of language: Brain, meaning, grammar, evolution.* Oxford, UK: Oxford University Press.

Joos, M. (1948). *Acoustic phonetics.* Language Monograph No. 23. Baltimore, MD: Linguistic Society of America.

Knight, A., Underhill, P. A., Mortensen, H. M., Zhivotovsky, L. A., Lin, A. A., Henn, B. M., Louis, D., Ruhlen, M., & Mountain, J. L. (2003). African Y chromosome and mtDNA divergence provides insight into the history of click languages *Current Biology, 13*, 464–473.

Kohler, E., Keysers, C., Umilta, M. A., Fogassi, L., Gallese, V., & Rizzolatti, G. (2002). Hearing sounds, understanding actions: Action representation in mirror neurons. *Science, 297*, 846–848.

Konner, M. (1982). *The tangled wing: Biological constraints on the human spirit.* New York: Harper.

Krogman, W. M. (1972). *Child growth.* Ann Arbor, MI: University of Michigan Press.

Lai, C. S., Fisher, S. E., Hurst, J. A., Vargha-Khadem, F., & Monaco, A. P. (2001). A novel forkhead-domain gene is mutated in a severe speech and language disorder. *Nature, 413*, 519–523.

Lenneberg, E. H. (1967). *Biological foundations of language.* New York: Wiley.

Liberman, A. M., Cooper, F. S., Shankweiler, D. P., & Studdert-Kennedy, M. (1967). Perception of the speech code. *Psychological Review, 74*, 431–461.

Lieberman, D. (1998). Sphenoid shortening and the evolution of modern cranial shape. *Nature, 393*, 158–162.

Lieberman, P. (1998). *Eve spoke: Human language and human evolution.* New York: W. W. Norton.

Lieberman, P., Crelin, E. S., & Klatt, D. H. (1972). Phonetic ability and related anatomy of the new-born, adult human, Neanderthal man, and the chimpanzee. *American Anthropologist, 74*, 287–307.

Liégeois, F., Baldeweg, T., Connelly, A., Gadian, D. G., Mishkin, M., & Vargha-Khadem, F. (2003). Language fMRI abnormalities associated with FOXP2 gene mutation. *Nature Neuroscience, 6*, 1230–1237.

MacLarnon, A., & Hewitt, G. (1999). The evolution of human speech: The role of enhanced breathing control. *American Journal of Physical Anthropology, 109*, 341–363.

MacNeilage, P. F. (1998). The frame/content theory of evolution of speech production. *Behavioral and Brain Sciences, 21*, 499–546.

Marcus, G. F., & Fisher, S. E. (2003). FOXP2 in focus: What can genes tell us about speech and language? *Trends in Cognitive Sciences, 7*, 257–262.

McNeill, D. (1985). So you think gestures are nonverbal? *Psychological Review, 92*, 350–371.

Mellars, P. A., & Stringer, C. B. (eds.) (1989). *The human revolution: Behavioral and biological perspectives on the origins of modern humans.* Edinburgh: Edinburgh University Press.

Muthukumaraswamy, S. D., Johnson, B. W., & McNair, N. A. (2004). Mu rhythm modulation during observation of an object-directed grasp. *Cognitive Brain Research, 19*, 195–201.

Neidle, C., Kegl, J., MacLaughlin, D., Bahan, B., & Lee, R. G. (2000). *The syntax of American Sign Language.* Cambridge, MA: MIT Press.

Nishitani, N., & Hari, R. (2000). Temporal dynamics of cortical representation for action. *Proceedings of the National Academy of Sciences, USA, 97*, 913–918.

Nowak, M. A., Plotkin, J. B., & Jansen, V. A. A. (2000). The evolution of syntactic communication. *Nature, 404*, 495–498.

Perrett, D. I., Harries, M. H., Bevan, R., Thomas, S., Benson, P. J., Mistlin, A. J., Chitty, A. J., Hietanen, J. K., & Ortega, J. E. (1989). Frameworks of analysis for the neural representation of animate objects and actions. *Journal of Experimental Biology, 146*, 87–113.

Petitto, L. A., & Marentette, P. (1991). Babbling in the manual mode: Evidence for the ontogeny of language. *Science, 251*, 1483–1496.

Pinker, S. (1994). *The language instinct.* New York: Morrow.

Ploog, D. (2002). Is the neural basis of vocalisation different in non-human primates and *Homo sapiens*? In T. J. Crow (Ed.), *The speciation of modern* Homo sapiens (pp. 121–135). Oxford: Oxford University Press.

Povinelli, D. J., Bering, J. M., & Giambrone, S. (2000). Toward a science of other minds: Escaping the argument by analogy. *Cognitive Science, 24*, 509–541.

Ramirez-Rossi, F. V., & Bermudez de Castro, J. M. (2004). Surprisingly rapid growth in Neanderthals. *Nature, 428*, 936–939.

Rizzolatti, G., & Arbib, M. A. (1998). Language within our grasp. *Trends in Cognitive Science, 21*, 188–194.

Rizzolatti, G., Fadiga, L., Fogassi, L, & Gallese, V. (1996). Premotor cortex and the recognition of motor actions. *Cognitive Brain Research, 3*, 131–141.

Rizzolatti, G., Fogassi, L., & Gallese, V. (2001). Neurophysiological mechanisms underlying the understanding and imitation of action. *Nature Reviews, 2*, 661–670.

Savage-Rumbaugh, S., Shanker, S. G., & Taylor, T. J. (1998). *Apes, language, and the human mind.* New York: Oxford University Press.

Scott, W. R. (1870). *The deaf and dumb* (2nd ed.). Cited by Darwin (1904/1865); publisher unknown).

Semaw, S., Renne, P., Harris, J. W. K., Feibel, C. S., Bernor, R. L., Fesseha, N., & Mowbray, K. (1997). 2.5-million-year-old stone tools from Gona, Ethiopia. *Nature, 385*, 333–336.

Shu, W. G., Yang, H. H., Zhang, L. L., Lu, M. M., & Morrisey, E. E. (2001). Characterization of a new subfamily of winged-helix/forkhead (Fox) genes that are expressed in the lung and act as transcriptional repressors. *Journal of Biological Chemistry, 276*, 27488–27497.

Stedman, H. H., Kozyak, B. W., Nelson, A., Thesier, D. M., Su, L. T., Low, D. W., Bridges, C. R., Shrager, J. B., Minugh-Purvis, N., & Mitchell, M. A. (2004). Myosin gene mutation correlates with anatomical changes in the human lineage. *Nature, 428*, 415–418.

Studdert-Kennedy, M. (1998). The particulate origins of language generativity: From syllable to gesture. In J. R. Hurford, M. Studdert-Kennedy, & C. Knight (Eds), *Approaches to the evolution of language* (pp. 169–176). Cambridge, UK: Cambridge University Press.

Suddendorf, T., & Corballis, M. C. (1997). Mental time travel and the evolution of the human mind. *Genetic, Social, and General Psychology Monographs, 123*, 133–167.

Tattersall, I. (1997). Out of Africa again . . . and again? *Scientific American, 276(4)*, 60–70.

Vargha-Khadem, F., Watkins, K. E., Alcock, K. J., Fletcher, P., & Passingham, R. (1995). Praxic and nonverbal cognitive deficits in a large family with a genetically transmitted speech and language disorder. *Proceedings of the National Academy of Sciences, USA, 92*, 930–933.

Watkins, K. E., Dronkers, N. F., & Vargha-Khadem, F. (2002). Behavioural analysis of an inherited speech and language disorder: Comparison with acquired aphasia. *Brain, 125*, 452–464.

Watkins, K. E., Vargha-Khadem, F., Ashburner, J., Passingham, R. E., Connelly, A., Friston, K. J., Frackowiak, R. S. J., Mishkin, M., & Gadian, D. G. (2002). MRI analysis of an inherited speech and language disorder: structural brain abnormalities. *Brain, 125*, 465–478.

Whiten, A., & Byrne, R. W. (1988). Tactical deception in primates. *Behavioral & Brain Sciences, 11*, 233–244.

Wundt, W. (1916/1921). *Elements of folk psychology*. New York: Macmillan (E. L. Schaub Trans. from the 1916 German version).

10 Learning and memory

Lars-Göran Nilsson and Jerker Rönnberg

Concepts of learning and memory are fragile entities. When memory was in the process of becoming a scientific discipline, Wilhelm Wundt and Hermann Ebbinghaus quarreled about what memory was and what it was not. The basic issue was conceptual in nature, although the real disagreement was about whether memory could be studied by means of experimental methods or not. As described by Danziger (2001), both Wundt and Ebbinghaus distinguished between something they called "memory proper" (*das eigentliche Gedächtnis*) and memory as it was conceived of and used by people outside the laboratory, in the real world.

Both thought that the former was available for scientific investigation, whereas the latter was not. However, Wundt and Ebbinghaus differed in what was to be considered as memory proper. According to Wundt (1887; see Danzinger, 2001), memory proper involved the renewal of conscious contents, in particular self-consciousness, which comes close to what has later been called episodic memory. Ebbinghaus, on the other hand, thought that conscious contents (*Erinnerung* or reminiscence) should be avoided in order to make the scientific task manageable. According to Ebbinghaus, this could be accomplished by studying retention (*das blosse Behalten*), which he argued was another aspect of memory proper that did not involve self-consciousness (Danziger, 2001, p. 49).

Under these premises, Ebbinghaus initiated scientific studies of memory (Ebbinghaus, 1885). He used nonsense syllables as the to-be-remembered materials and so avoided the influence of reminiscence. It was, thus, this conceptualization of memory that started an era of intense scientific study of memory. As will be seen later in this chapter, the conceptualization of memory in present-day research is quite different.

Memory proper according to Wundt was more in line with the conceptualization of memory today. One may wonder what it is that make concepts survive. We will deal with this issue later in this chapter. First, however, we will outline the core space of concepts to be discussed.

Cultural considerations

One obvious distinction to make when taking cultural aspects into account regarding learning and memory is that between societies with an oral culture and societies whose culture is primarily written. In citing Le Geoff (1979), Jedlowski (2001) reasoned that ". . . memory was expressed in prevalently ritualized narrative practices in preliterate societies and that the growth of writing modified the role and functions of memory, enabling on the one hand the birth of commemoration through celebratory monuments and inscriptions and, on the other, the production and collection of documents" (p. 37). Yates (1966) expressed the same line of thinking in saying that the gradual spread of writing made obsolete the techniques that in preliterate societies governed the exercise of memory. In recent years, the means of preserving the past have been more and more sophisticated by the common use of the computer and internet. One can certainly discuss to what extent this development has had and will have an effect on memory *per se*. Will the individual's memory function better or worse when the individual can rely on external memories for remembering the individual or the collective past? Much of the discussion among contemporary sociologists interested in memory and society (e.g. Jedlowski, 2001) seems to be geared towards a consensus that the use of external memories may hamper the function of the individual's memory in general. This view is contrary to the consensus among cognitive psychologists interested in memory training. In these circles the common view is that training of memory techniques has positive effects on what is trained, but has no effect on memory in general. For example, in training how to be able to memorize names of persons, memory will be better on remembering names but will not be better on remembering telephone numbers, capital of countries, or anything else. In contrast to this, recent research (e.g. Klingberg, Forssberg, & Westerberg, 2002) has demonstrated that the training of working memory may not only have positive effects on working memory tasks, but will show transfer effects to other tasks as well. Although this is an interesting topic in itself, it goes beyond the scope of this paper. Moreover, such a discussion requires the definition of certain concepts like working memory. It is to the general space of concepts used in the learning and memory domain we turn next.

Conceptual space

The ability to learn and utilize information that is stored in memory is fundamental for the survival of humans and other animals. The distinction between cognition and behavior is fundamental when trying to outline a landscape of basic concepts in learning and memory.

The conceptual tools used for understanding learning and memory cover a very wide domain, both in terms of theory and method. The specific approaches taken to study a certain phenomenon within the fields of learning and memory vary considerably. The concepts used for describing these various theoretical and empirical endeavours should ideally be clear and unambiguous. Unfortunately, they are not and conceptual confusion is often the case. A single concept is often used to describe different things in the real world, and different concepts are often used for describing the same real-life thing.

In addition to the difficulties implied above with respect to a wide variety of methods, theories and approaches for studying learning and memory, the conceptual subject matter itself, according to Bunge (1998), is not simple. In line with Tulving (2000), we will refer to Bunge when trying to bring some order into the conceptual space regarding learning and memory.

According to Bunge (1998), it is important to distinguish between three levels of analysis: things, concepts, and terms. Things are entities in the real world, whereas concepts are entities that exist as abstract thoughts about real-world entities; concepts are pure abstractions that exist only in the minds of those who use them. Terms designate the concepts that refer to real-world entities. On this basis, it should be acknowledged at the outset that there is great variety in how the terms designate concepts in different persons. Perhaps it should be implied from Bunge's three levels of analysis (linguistic, conceptual, and physical) that it is hardly likely that two scientists would be able to share the exact meaning of a concept, at least not a complex concept (see Tulving, 2000, p. 35). Having said this, we are fully aware that different persons in the scientific community of learning and memory conceptualize the terms that we will discuss differently.

The term "learning" designates the concept of learning, which refers to the process by which humans and other animals acquire knowledge and skills, and form habits. The term "memory" designates many different concepts. The most basic meaning of memory is the ability to encode, store, and retrieve information. Another meaning of memory, and perhaps the most common meaning of the term in everyday language, is that of a receptacle or a storage compartment for information. These latter two views of memory, taken together, are what is conceived of as the basis for what later developed to become the "systems view" of memory (e.g. Tulving 1972, 1983, 1993). Still another meaning of the term is the content itself of what is in the memory store. People talk about "a memory of" certain facts, a person, an event or any kind of happening they have been part of. Yet another conceptualization of memory is that in relation to remembering. In this sense, memory is a process by means which a person manages or fails to retrieve information about a certain event, a person, or the name of that person. Success in retrieving such information is commonly referred to as having a "good memory"; failure to retrieve the information is referred to as having a "poor memory". This "remembering notion" developed into a processing view and typically avoids the storage aspect of memory. In more modern times, it has been conceptualized as "levels of processing" (Craik & Lockhart, 1972) and "transfer appropriate processing" (Bransford, Franks, Morris, & Stein, 1979). These meanings of the term "memory" all refer to some property of the individual. Additionally, however, it can also designate the concept of the research field of memory. Similarly, the term "learning" can designate the concept of the area in which learning is studied.

In addition to the difficulties arising from the many different meanings of the terms learning and memory, there are also conceptual difficulties in the sense that there are many forms of learning and many forms of memory. That is, even if we agree to consider memory as a neurocognitive capacity to encode, store, and retrieve information, there are alternative ways to consider memory this way; the same holds true for learning.

Different forms of learning and memory

With respect to learning, Tolman (1949) claimed in his long-standing debate with Clark Hull that there was more than one kind. The scientific community at the time seemed to agree with Tolman that place learning and response learning are two distinct and different forms of learning. Beyond this, however, there was not any further, or deeper, discussion whether there are still other forms of learning to be classified as separate entities.

With respect to different forms of memory, the discussion was deeper and started much earlier. As described by Schacter (1987) and Schacter and Tulving (1994), the French philosopher Maine de Biran stated with great clarity and emphasis during the nineteenth century that memory is not a single function or entity. Instead, he argued, there are at least three forms of memory, namely representative memory, mechanical memory, and sensitive memory. The content of representative memory was, according to Maine de Biran, conscious recollection of ideas and events. Mechanical memory was the acquisition of motor and verbal habits at a non-conscious level. Sensitive memory was about the acquisition of feelings and affects also at a non-conscious level. Another early conceptualization of memory as consisting of different forms of memory was suggested by William James, who proposed that primary memory and secondary memory served quite different functions. For this reason, he argued, these two terms should be used to enforce conceptual clarity (James, 1890).

These early terms by William James will be discussed in more detail later. At this stage suffice to say that the notion of different forms of learning and memory complicates matters not only because there are more terms to consider. However, a division of learning and memory, respectively, should make the whole enterprise more distinct and clear.

Behavior and cognition

Learning and memory are essential concepts in two different but related domains of the functioning of humans and other animals. One of these domains is expressed in cognition and the other in behavior. The scientific study of learning and memory evolved out of philosophical discussions of how people can know things about the world that they are living in, and how they behave and live in this world. Thus, it is claimed here that the distinction between cognition and behavior, or thought and action, is essential to come to grips with the concepts used in the broad field of learning and memory.

People and other animals can acquire many behaviors through learning that are not knowledge about the world in its cognitive sense. These behaviors may be crucial for the survival of the animal without being a well-defined knowledge about relations and states in the world. The behavior, once it has been acquired, may be triggered by external signs without any reflection or conscious control by the individual. In contrast to this is the domain of knowledge, which is also acquired through learning and held in memory until needed at a later occasion. This knowledge is pure thought that need not be at all expressed in behavior or that behavior is simply a byproduct of a wish to express the acquired knowledge.

A central issue after having made this distinction between behavior and cognition is whether learning that leads to a certain behavior is the same as learning leading to knowledge and whether memory of behavior is the same as memory of knowledge about the world.

The distinction between cognition and behavior is well captured in the distinction between declarative memory and procedural memory. It will be argued here that all central concepts of learning and memory are included in the distinction between these two forms of memory.

Declarative memory provides the basis for conscious recollection of facts and events, including words, scenes, faces, stories, and so on. The term "declarative" has been used to signify that its content can be declared (Cohen, 1984; Cohen & Squire, 1980). By and large it captures what is meant by memory or remembering in everyday language. In scientific contexts declarative memory is assessed by means of recall and recognition.

Although declarative memory is the most common term for this form of memory, several alternative terms are also used to capture a given concept. Alternative terms commonly used to capture the concept of a conscious recollection of facts and events are explicit memory (Schacter, 1987), relational memory (Eichenbaum, 1992, 1997), and configural memory (Rudy & Sutherland, 1989). This multitude of terms is unfortunate because it leads to lack of clarity and to confusion in communication.

Evidence for a separate memory system that can handle conscious recollection of facts and events by means of recall and recognition tests came first from data on amnesic patients with lesions in the medial temporal lobe and diencephalon. These patients typically fail on recall and recognition tests, although they succeed equally well as normal controls on other tests. Such data from neuropsychological studies led researchers to believe that declarative memory depends on the integrity of brain structures and connections between brain structures in the medial temporal lobe and the diencephalon. The observations from clinical studies were later confirmed in studies using brain imaging techniques like positron emission tomography (PET) and functional magnetic resonance imaging (fMRI). As shown in such studies, and summarized by Cabeza and Nyberg (1997), medial–temporal brain regions have been shown to be strongly involved as the neural basis for declarative memory. Divisions between memory systems have been based on whether they are hippocampal dependent or not.

The term originally used as a contrast to describe memory that is not declarative was procedural memory (Cohen & Squire, 1980; Winograd, 1975). The idea was that this term should cover a collection of nonconscious memory abilities that are intact in those amnesic patients failing in tasks assessing declarative memory. At the time—the late 1970s and early 1980s—when the distinction between declarative and procedural memory was made, the tasks known not to fall into the declarative category included a wide variety of skill-based learning tasks. Thus, procedural memory was considered to be an adequate term. Later, however, it was discovered that other tasks that were not declarative in nature could be managed by the patients failing on declarative tasks.

To include these tasks into the same category as the motor-skill tasks, a new term was coined: "non-declarative memory" (Squire & Zola-Morgan, 1988, 1991). This rather imprecise term describes another type of memory that is not as precise as declarative memory. Declarative memory can be seen as relatively precise in terms of underlying biological structures and also in terms of the function of these structures. When the term non-declarative memory was coined, very little was known about its structure and function. Current knowledge about the different terms that are included under the rubric of non-declarative memory with respect to structure and function is certainly better than it used to be. However, much is still waiting to be expressed and, as will be seen, there is considerable confusion as to how the terms used in this domain are conceptualized. The expression "more research is needed" is certainly appropriate here.

In sum, whereas declarative memory has a rather well-defined focus involving recall and recognition of facts and events, non-declarative memory includes a rather large set of fairly divergent forms of learning and memory. Thus, skills and habits constitute major components in non-declarative memory, where motor skills, perceptual skills, and cognitive skills are all included. Formation of habits is typically classified in this same set of non-declarative memory. Classical conditioning, probably also including some forms of emotional learning, constitute another subcategory of non-declarative memory.

Priming is a relatively new concept in memory research. Warrington and Weiskrantz (1974, 1982) and Tulving, Schacter, and Stark (1982) discovered that brain-injured patients who fail completely in recall and recognition of previously acquired information can perform at the same level as normal controls as they are, given the appropriate test conditions that do not require a conscious recollection of this information. Word-fragment completion and word-stem completion constitute adequate test conditions for such unconscious states.

A related term, "implicit memory", was coined in the mid-1980s by Graf and Schacter (1985) to describe tasks that are used for assessing this form of memory. This term, however, has given rise to much confusion. Whereas some researchers use it as intended by Graf and Schacter, others use it to refer to a memory system, still others use it to refer to a process, and still others use it to refer to a certain state of awareness.

Memory systems

The term "memory system" is also rather new in a historical perspective. To the best of our knowledge, this term was coined by Tulving (1972) in a seminal paper on the distinction between episodic and semantic memory within declarative memory. In this early paper, Tulving claimed that these two systems are different, but interacting. The term "episodic memory" was coined by Tulving at the time, but the term "semantic memory" had been used earlier by Quillian (1968). Since 1972, several other memory systems have been proposed. Some of these are taxon and locale memory (O'Keefe & Nadel, 1978), habit memory and cognitive memory (Mishkin & Petri, 1984), working memory and long-term memory (Baddeley, 1986, 1998), implicit and explicit memory (Graf & Schacter, 1985), and fast and slow memory (McClelland, McNaughton, & O'Reilly, 1995; Sherry & Schacter, 1987). This is not the right context to discuss all these. We will focus one conceptualization of memory as consisting of five different systems. It is probably this systems view proposed by Tulving (1983, 1993, 2000) that has been the most influential.

According to Tulving, (1993), memory should be conceived of as consisting of five different but interacting memory systems: procedural memory, perceptual representation system, semantic memory, short-term memory, and episodic memory. Procedural memory is the oldest memory system, phylogenetically and ontogenetically. This memory system exists in all species and is present throughout the life span in humans. Procedural memory is used for learning various kinds of behavioral skills; it operates at an automatic level and its output is non-cognitive. The perceptual representation system is used for identifying objects in the surrounding world; it operates at an automatic, presemantic level. Semantic memory makes it possible to acquire and retain general knowledge about the world at large; its retrieval is implicit. Primary memory makes it possible to hold and process information temporarily; it operates at a conscious level. Episodic memory is used for consciously recollect events and episodes of one's own past; it operates at a conscious level and retrieval is explicit rather than implicit. Episodic memory is the youngest memory system; it is assumed to exist in man and monkey only and it is present at about two years of age in humans, when self-consciousness is acquired.

Dissociations of various sorts have been demonstrated to support this classification of memory into five memory systems. In a review of the memory literature, Nyberg and Tulving (1996) presented an impressive list of such dissociations. Four memory systems were examined—episodic memory, semantic memory, priming, and procedural memory—in relation to four different forms of dissociation: functional, developmental, pharmacological, and brain damage. The review revealed converging dissociations, suggesting that the multiple-systems view provides a more parsimonious account of the empirical facts than the unitary-memory view. It would be relevant to explore whether genetic factors map on to the existing evidence of dissociable memory systems. In the next section we will illustrate the approach advocated here of contrasting the influence of six genetic markers on episodic and semantic memory.

It has been suggested that there are more memory systems than just five as Tulving proposed. People have argued that visual memory, motor memory, auditory memory, verbal memory, memory for names, memory for numbers, and so on, are just other examples of concepts that could be conceived of as memory systems. Although it might be useful to use such terms to describe an empirical finding (e.g. one might see a certain phenomenon in verbal memory but not in olfactory memory), it does not mean that they qualify as memory systems. There are three criteria to identify memory systems, according to Schacter and Tulving (1994): class-inclusion operations, properties and relations, and convergent dissociations.

Schacter and Tulving (1994) argued that as long as a memory system is intact it should operate "class-inclusively, in the sense that it can process any particular input or information of the specified kind" (p. 15). For example, episodic memory can be described as the conscious recollection of personally experienced events. This feature is crucial for episodic memory but not, for example, for short-term memory. Properties and relations as a criterion for a memory system simply means that certain properties of a proposed system should be possible to specify. Given these properties, it should then be possible to relate this particular memory system, holding these properties, to other memory systems that are based on other properties. Finally, empirical data should converge such that certain variables affect one memory system in one way and another memory system in a different way.

Working memory

Earlier in this chapter, we stated that two important terms, primary memory and secondary memory, were introduced by William James in his influential book *Principles of Psychology* in 1890. James did not do any empirical work himself and these two terms were not really incorporated into the scientific community on memory until much later. Independent of each other, Broadbent (1958), Brown (1958), and Peterson and Peterson (1959) started to do experiments over short retention intervals and found empirical regularities that were quite different to those found in studies on longer retention intervals. It was in this context that the two terms by James came into play. However, Broadbent (1958) also had theoretical ambitions in his model of information processing, and primary memory and secondary memory fell into place at a more conceptual level. The terms that became used more and more widely for naming these concepts were "short-term memory" and "long-term memory". At the time, the short-term memory concept stood for holding information in mind over a certain period of time and the concept of long-term memory implied a more permanent storage of information. During the 1960s, researchers debated the duration of short-term memory. To our knowledge, there was no final consensus about its duration and the whole notion of a short-term storage with limited capacity and an important function of transferring information from the perceptual system to permanent storage in long-term memory was abandoned. What remained of the concept of short-term memory was the function of holding information in mind while doing other things at the same time. This ability of human beings is essential in daily life for thought, planning, and language. It makes it possible for us to interact with the world in a flexible and intelligent manner; Miller, Galanter, and Pribram (1960) introduced the term to capture this ability. They postulated an easily accessible brain space where plans can be retained temporarily while they are formed, manipulated, and executed. Thus, in this way the concept of working memory is something like the concept of short-term memory. However, the concepts are not the same. Baddeley (1986) has worked out the characteristics defining working memory and Dudai (2002) formulated the difference between the two concepts in an understandable way:

> Generally speaking, short-term memory is a more comprehensive term, which refers to all internal representations that last for only a short while. It is a universal faculty of nervous systems that can learn. In contrast, working memory combines attention, short- and long-term memory, retrieval, computations over representations, and planning and decision making, to yield goal-directed short-lived internal representations.
>
> (Dudai, 2002, p. 249)

The model of working-memory that Baddeley and Hitch (1974) and Baddeley (1986) developed to capture this includes three basic components: a central executive, a phonological loop, and a visuospatial sketchpad. The central executive is an attentional control system; the phonological loop deals with speech-based information; and the visuospatial sketchpad with visual and spatial information. By means of data from brain-damaged patients and brain-imaging studies it has been demonstrated that multiple distributed systems are involved when working memory is operating. No final consensus about the complete neural substrate of working memory has been reached, but all seem to agree that the frontal lobes play an important role.

Memory trace

In everyday usage of the term "memory", the notion of some kind of a record of an encoded event is common. This view that there are enduring physical changes in the brain has been with us all the way since Plato talked about engraved wax tablets of memory. In modern days this record is usually referred to as a memory trace or an engram. Semon (1904/1921; see Schacter, 1982) formulated the term "engram" and implied the material record engraved by a stimulus in living tissue. More or less entirely, he formulated his two basic laws of memory around the concept of an engram. The first law, the law of engraphy, states that simultaneous excitations within an organism leaves behind a connected engram complex constituting a coherent unity. The second law, the law of ecphory, is about how the engram is awakened out of its latent state to a state of manifest activity. Semon's ideas about memory are still with us in the literature, when researchers talk about cell assemblies, models of neural networks, and about retrieval in general.

Thus, the concept of a memory trace or an engram is still with us and this concept can certainly be said to have survived through many periods of quite different theoretical orientations about memory, despite the fact that not much new is known about the real-world entities that underlie the concept *per se*. Researchers are still searching for the engram, much like Lashley (1950) did in his well-cited paper with title *In search of the engram*. Not only is the pure existence of the engram still on the research agenda, but also the localization of the engram.

Processing view

It was mentioned earlier that one conceptualization of memory in terms of processing and remembering, rather than memory systems, has been very influential since the early 1970s. An influential expression of this view of memory is that of "levels of processing" proposed by Craik and Lockhart (1972). The proposal is that processing of sensory information begins with "shallow" levels and proceeds to "deeper", cognitive ones, and that the deeper the processing is, the more robust is the resulting memory trace. For example, a phonological encoding of some to-be-remembered information is considered to be a shallow processing, whereas a semantic encoding is considered as a deep form of processing. Thus, a semantic encoding would lead to a more robust memory trace than a phonological encoding and therefore to a better memory performance. This is also the result demonstrated in many empirical studies since Craik and Lockhart published their influential paper in the early 1970s. The levels-of-processing concept had a great impact on the scientific community and has continued to influence researchers in the field. In fact, it can be stated that this concept helped change the orientation of memory research in the beginning of the 1970s, and in this sense it has had a very strong communicative impact.

Craik and Lockhart's levels-of-processing view was proposed without any neuroanatomical or physiological connotation. However, as pointed out by Dudai (2002), the same concept also exists in the biological arena and refers to the neuroanatomical and physiological hierarchy of information processing in the nervous system. It is an old concept in this field and its original meaning—of a hierarchy from low to high, where high means a greater distance from sensory receptors—has been replaced by a view that states that processing is assumed to culminate in a more global internal representation (binding).

Survival of concepts

Debate about the memory systems view *per se* and in contrast to the processing view, has been active from time to time and has certainly focused the way various concepts are used in the scientific community. Would it be possible to initiate a similar debate about concepts in general within learning and memory that might produce a result that would lead to a more precise use of any concept of learning and memory?

With this aim in mind, we discussed, when writing this chapter, the three basic conditions that should be in place for any concept of learning and memory to survive as a concept. First, the concept should have a cognitive meaning in the sense that it is possible to collect data in experimental studies and that the cognitive mechanisms that form this concept psychologically should obey to some basic empirical regularities. Second, it should be possible to dissociate the cognitive mechanisms from other mechanisms at the neural network level. And third, the implications of the mechanism should be intimately tied to social interaction and communication with others. The third criterion is based on the emerging bulks of data in the cognitive aging and cognitive disability research, where the social and societal relevance of traditional mainstream cognitive psychology is questioned. That is to say, it is not enough to say, for example, that working memory capacity deteriorates as we grow older, we must find mechanisms that tie working memory capacity to communicative ability and social capacity (e.g. Rönnberg, 2003).

We submit that one future trend for cognitive researchers is to take into account several levels of description and explanation by postulating memory and cognitive mechanisms that clearly fulfill these criteria. The reasoning can be further illustrated by the concept of theory-of-mind (e.g.

Barron-Cohen, 1995). This concept has been possible to dissociate at the neural level (Frith, 2001); it is based on a cognitive mechanism involved in "reading" others' perspective or role taking, and it has definite social land communicative consequences for certain groups of children with disability (Dahlgren, Sandberg, & Hjelmquist, 2003).

In fact, when we study the interactions between language and cognition as an expression of the connection between cognition and communicative form (in this case the comparison between signed and spoken language), language-modality-specific effects occur for traditional concepts such as episodic and semantic memory (Rönnberg, Söderfeldt, & Risberg, 1998), as well as for working memory (Rönnberg, Rudner, & Ingvar, 2004), in ways that could not have been foreseen *a priori*. These data constrain the memory concepts in a communicative direction and show the relativity in assuming memory systems that reflect particular neural networks, without relating the concepts to how they are used for communicative purposes.

The question that we want to leave to the reader to wrestle with is: Which of the memory concepts currently in vogue will in the future survive the three-level criterion posited here?

References

Baddeley, A. D. (1986). *Working memory*. Oxford: Oxford University Press.

Baddeley, A. D. (1998). Recent developments in working memory. *Current Opinion in Neurobiology, 8*, 234–238.

Baddeley, A. D., & Hitch, G. (1974). Working memory. In G. A. Bower (Ed.), *The psychology of learning and motivation* (Vol. 8, pp. 47–89). New York: Academic Press.

Barron-Cohen, S. (1995). *Mindblindness: An essay on autism and theory of mind.* Cambridge, MA: MIT Press.

Bransford, J. D., Franks, J. J., Morris, C. D., & Stein, B. S. (1979). Some general constraints on learning and memory research. In L. S. Cermak & F. I. M. Craik (Eds.), *Levels of processing in human memory* (pp. 331–354). Hillsdale, NJ: Lawrence Erlbaum Associates Inc.

Broadbent, D. E. (1958). *Perception and communication*. New York: Pergamon Press.

Brown, J. (1958). Some tests of the decay theory of immediate memory. *Quarterly Journal of Experimental Psychology, 10*, 12–21.

Bunge, M. (1998). *Philosophy of science* (Vol. 1). New Brunswick, NJ: Transaction Publishers.

Cabeza, R., & Nyberg, L. (1997). Imaging cognition: An empirical review of PET studies with normal subjects. *Journal of Cognitive Neuroscience, 9*, 1–26.

Cohen, N. J. (1984). Preserved learning capacity in amnesia: Evidence for multiple memory systems. In L. R Squire & N. Butters (Eds.), *Neuropsychology of memory* (pp. 83–103). New York: Guilford Press.

Cohen, N. J., & Squire, L. R. (1980). Preserved learning and retention of pattern-analyzing skill in amnesia: Dissociation of knowing how from knowing that. *Science, 210*, 207–210.

Craik, F. I. M., & Lockhart, R. S. (1972). Levels of processing: A framework for memory research. *Journal of Verbal learning and Verbal Behavior, 11*, 671–684.

Dahlgren, S., Sandberg, A. D., & Hjelmquist, E. (2003). The non-specificity of theory of mind deficits: Evidence from children with communicative disabilities. *European Journal of Cognitive Psychology, 15*, 129–155

Danziger, K. (2001). Sealing off the discipline: Wilhelm Wundt and the psychology of memory. In C. D. Green, M. Shore, & T. Teo (Eds.), *The transformation of psychology* (pp. 45–62). Washington, DC: American Psychological Association.

Dudai, Y. (2002). *Memory from A to Z: Keywords, concepts and beyond.* Oxford: Oxford University Press.

Ebbinghaus, H. (1885). *Über das Gedächtnis* [Memory]. Leipzig: Duncker.

Eichenbaum, H. (1992). The hippocampal system and declarative memory in animals. *Journal of Cognitive Neuroscience, 4*, 217–231.

Eichenbaum, H. (1997). Declarative memory: Insights from cognitive psychology. *Annual Review of Psychology, 48*, 547–572.

Frith, U. (2001). Mindblindness and the brain in autism. *Neuron, 32*, 969–979.

Graf, P., & Schacter, D. L. (1985). Implicit and explicit memory for new associations in normal subjects and amnesic patients. *Journal of Experimental Psychology: Learning, Memory, and Cognition, 11*, 501–518.

James, W. (1890). *Principles of psychology.* Cambridge, MA: Harvard University Press.

Jedlowski, P. (2001). Memory and sociology: Themes and issues. *Time & Society, 10*, 29–44.

Klingberg, T., Forssberg, H., & Westerberg, H. (2002). Training of working memory in children with ADHD. *Journal of Clinical and Experimental Neuropsychology, 24*, 781–791.

Lashley, K. S. (1950). In search of the engram. *Symposia of the Society for Experimental Biology, 4*, 454–482.

Le Geoff, J. (1979). Memoria. In *Enciclopedia Einaudi* (Vol. VIII). Torino: Einaudi.

McClelland, J. L., McNaughton, B. L., & O'Reilly, R. C. (1995). Why there are complementary learning systems in the hippocampus and neocortex: Insights from the successes and failures of connectionist models of learning and memory. *Psychological Review, 102*, 419–457.

Miller, G. A., Galanter, E. G., & Pribram, K. H. (1960). *Plans and the structure of behavior.* New York: Holt, Rinehart and Winston.

Mishkin, M., & Petri, H. L. (1984). Memories and habits: Some implications for the analysis of learning and retention. In L. Squire & N. Butters (Eds.), *Neuropsychology of memory* (pp. 287–296). New York: Guilford Press.

Nyberg, L., & Tulving, E. (1996). Classifying human long-term memory: Evidence from converging dissociations. *European Journal of Cognitive Psychology, 8*, 163–183.

O'Keefe, J., & Nadel, L. (1978). *The hippocampus as a cognitive map.* Oxford: Clarendon Press.

Peterson, L. R., & Peterson, M. J. (1959). Short-term retention of individual verbal items. *Journal of Experimental Psychology, 58*, 193–198.

Quillian, M. R. (1968). Semantic memory. In M. Minsky (Ed.), *Semantic information processing* (pp. 216–270). Cambridge, MA: MIT press.

Rönnberg, J. (2003). Cognition in the hearing impaired and deaf as a bridge between signal and dialogue: A framework and a model. *International Journal of Audiology*, *42*, S68–76.

Rönnberg, J., Rudner, M., & Ingvar, M. (2004). Neural correlates of working memory for sign. *Cognitive Brain Research*, *20*, 165–182.

Rönnberg, J., Söderfeldt, B., & Risberg, J. (1998). Regional cerebral blood flow in signed and heard episodic and semantic memory tasks. *Applied Neuropsychology*, *5*, 132–138.

Rudy, J. W., & Sutherland, R. J. (1989). The hippocampus is necessary for rats to learn and remember configural discrimination. *Behavioral Brain Research*, *34*, 97–109.

Schacter, D. L. (1982). *Stranger behind the engram: Theories of memory and the psychology of science*. Hillsdale, NJ: Lawrence Erlbaum Associates Inc.

Schacter, D. L. (1987). Implicit memory: History and current status. *Journal of Experimental Psychology: Learning, Memory, and Cognition*, *13*, 501–518.

Schacter, D. L., & Tulving, E. (1994). What are the memory systems of 1994? In D. L. Schacter & E. Tulving (Eds.), *Memory systems 1994* (pp. 1–38). Cambridge, MA: MIT Press.

Semon, R. (1904/1921). *The mneme*. London: George Allen & Unwin.

Sherry, D. F., & Schacter, D. L. (1987). The evolution of multiple memory systems. *Psychological Review*, *94*, 439–454.

Squire, L. R., & Zola-Morgan, S. (1988). Memory: Brain systems and behavior. *Trends in Neurosciences*, *11*, 170–175.

Squire, L. R., & Zola-Morgan, S. (1991). The medial temporal lobe memory system. *Science*, *253*, 1380–1386.

Tolman, E. C. (1949). Cognitive maps in rats and men. *Psychological Review*, *55*, 189–208.

Tulving, E. (1972). Episodic and semantic memory. In E. Tulving & W. Donaldson (Eds.), *Organization of memory* (pp. 381–403). New York: Academic Press.

Tulving, E. (1983). *Elements of episodic memory*. Oxford: Clarendon Press.

Tulving, E. (1993). Human memory. In P. Andersen, Ö. Hvalby, O. Paulsen, & B. Hökfelt (Eds.), *Memory concepts 1993: Basic and clinical aspects* (pp. 27–45). Amsterdam: Elsevier Science Publications.

Tulving, E. (2000). Concepts of memory. In E. Tulving & F. I. M. Craik (Eds.), *The Oxford handbook of memory* (pp. 33–43). New York: Oxford University Press.

Tulving, E., Schacter, D. L., & Stark, H. A. (1982). Priming effects in word-fragment completion are independent of recognition memory. *Journal of Experimental Psychology: Learning, Memory, and Cognition*, *8*, 336–342.

Warrington, E. K., & Weiskrantz, L. (1974). The effect of prior learning on subsequent retention in amnesic patients. *Neuropsychologia*, *12*, 419–428.

Warrington, E. K., & Weiskrantz, L. (1982). Amnesia: A disconnection syndrome. *Neuropsychologia*, *20*, 233–249.

Winograd, T. (1975). Frame representations and the declarative-procedural controversy. In D. Bobrow & A. Collins (Eds.), *Representation and understanding: Studies in cognitive science* (pp. 185–210). New York: Academic Press.

Wundt, W. (1887). *Grundzüge der physiologischen Psychologie* (3rd ed.) [Principles of physiological psychology]. Leipzig, Germany: Engelmann.

Yates, F. (1966). *The art of memory*. London: Routledge & Kegan Paul.

11 Mind: Ghosts, machines, and concepts

George Mandler

> Cultural influences have set up the assumptions about the mind, the body, and the universe with which we begin; pose the questions we ask; influence the facts we seek; determine the interpretation we give these facts; and direct our reaction to these interpretations and conclusions.
>
> (Gunnar Myrdal, 1944)

"Mind"—at least in one of its versions—is one of those "things" in the world that everybody is willing to talk about but nobody has ever seen or touched. In that respect it is even more intangible than consciousness— about which some remarks later—that at least most people are willing to say that they have in some sense "experienced". In 1949, Gilbert Ryle coined the apposite expression about mind being "the ghost in the machine", which I shall take as my starting point in exploring the concept of mind.

The notion of having a "mind" seems to apply exclusively to humans, as only few would apply it to nonhuman animals, with the possible exception of extending it to other hominids. There exist at least five different meanings that have been used to define the meaning of mind.

I start with these various meanings of mind, followed by a short lexical excursion, and a review of the historical landmarks for the concept. I shall then characterize the contemporary philosophy of mind that often intrudes into psychology, followed by a discussion of how psychologists have used the idea of a mind, and shall end with some thoughts about the mind–body problem. Within the limitations of this chapter it will obviously not be possible to note all the various contributors to our conception of mind. I shall attempt to note the relevant historical and contemporary highlights. I have also used some parts of a previous work on related topics in this current chapter (Mandler, 1998).

The various uses of mind . . .

Much of modern psychology (and some philosophy) has been concerned with the struggle to remove mystical and metaphysical implications from the concept of mind. In the process we have generally banned the ghost from the machine, but are not quite clear what kind of a machine we wish to put in its place. I define various uses of mind, starting with the original postulation of its ghostly characteristic and moving toward functional and even empirical definitions.

Mind as soul. Mind has often been used as a synonym for the ancient sense of spirit or soul. In some versions it harks back to theological origins as a god-given elevation of humans over other animals. The version that became a less mystical mainstay up through the Middle Ages was Aristotle's exposition in *De Anima* (*peri psuché*s). For Aristotle the soul (*psuché*: derived from the original meaning of breath, the vital breath of life) was the organizing principle that realized the body's potential. The meaning of mind as soul still exists in use by everyday speech, by philosophers and even by some psychologists. In this sense, mind still distinguishes humans from other animals, and has many ties to the theological uses of soul.

Mind as faculty. The use of mind without the supernatural sense, but still as some extramaterial manifestation of human thought and action, can be found frequently in contemporary thought. Mind is considered in a sense as a faculty of the body, somehow removed from a basic materialist view.

Mind as a brain function. Under this view, mind is seen as the summary manifestation of human brain functions as in a functionalist description that states that "The mind is what the brain does".

Mind as a summary term for complex human thought and action. Here mind is used as a summary but vaguely defined concept that brings under a single notion human cogitation, cognition, conation, etc. It is similar to the previous definition but without any necessary allusion to brain functions.

Mind as consciousness. The confusion between consciousness and mind, of the equation of mind with human consciousness, creates serious problems for any general concept of mind. As the contents of consciousness are limited in time and restricted to a subset of possible human thoughts and actions, this error makes mind a less powerful concept and by limiting mind to consciousness also confuses our understanding of mind on one hand and of the functions of consciousness on the other (e.g. Mandler, 2002a). There are occasional uses of mind to conform to particular theoretical stances. For example, Baars (1988) equates mind with information and Humphrey (1992) uses its discussion as a vehicle for speculations about human cognitive functions and his interpretation of consciousness.

. . . and its meanings

When we examine the meaning of the word "mind" as put forth in various dictionaries, and also in its translation and use in various Western languages, we find confusions similar to those we came across in the previous section. The following definitions attempt a distillation of definitions found in various dictionaries:

> The origin of the expression "Mind" is partly Germanic, as in *minna* (Old High German: memory, love), but it also has solid Old English ancestry in *gemynd* (Anglo-Saxon: memory); these and most of the other early meanings of mind were tied in part to the notion of memory. When it comes to defining "mind", most dictionaries tend to agree to some version that sees it *as a human faculty, representing understanding and the intellect, but also as the soul in distinction from the body*. However, one also comes across definitions of mind as representing *human consciousness manifested in thought, perception, emotion, will, memory, and imagination*. Here we are faced with a concatenation of mind as consciousness on the one hand and as a summary term on the other. Finally, mind is sometimes seen as the depository and locus of human thought, so that thought may be defined as the content of mind.

I turn briefly to the notion of mind as a repository of functions. The latter are still the classic ones of cognition, conation, and cogitation. Cognition, from the Latin *cognoscere* (to become acquainted with), refers to knowing, knowledge, and perception. Conation, from the Latin *conatio*, refers to mental processes directed toward action or change. And cogitation, from the Latin cogitatio, refers to thinking, thought, and meditation. The currently popular terms "cognitive psychology" and "cognitive science" are sometimes used to refer to thinking organisms, when they actually denote an information-processing psychology.

When we turn to the concept of mind in Western languages in general, the reference is often confusing and confused by different language habits. Although I noted earlier that the English "mind" is derived from Old Germanic and English roots, in fact much of Western usage derives from the Latin *mens*, a less metaphysical reference than the apparently older *anima* (soul)—best known as the Latin translation of Aristotle's Greek psyche/ *psuché*. The Romance languages in general have benefited from this derivation from *mens*, with *mente* (mind) in both Italian and Spanish. Surprisingly there is no equivalent in French, which uses *esprit* for mind in the sense of spirit, but has adopted the adjective *mentale*. German, despite the extensive exploration of the history of mind in German academia, has no true equivalent in modern usage, but relies on *Geist* (spirit: etymologically related to ghost) and *Psyche*, both with metaphysical overtones. Given that there is no objective referent for mind, it is not surprising that different, although intimately related, language cultures fail to agree on terminology. Notwithstanding these ambiguities, the notion of "mind"—however defined or used—is vastly popular. During the past twenty years, the scientific literature has used the term some 500–1000 times per year in its titles (Web of Science).

Landmarks in the history of mind

I have already noted some of the philosophical and theological origins of mind. The major part in Western intellectual history is undoubtedly played by Aristotle. Apart from the notion that the mind/psyche actualizes the body's potential, Aristotle also ascribed to the psyche the potential for rational thought and moral action. These were philosophical/psychological concerns, in contrast to Plato's sometime use of psyche as the vehicle for political thought and structures.

The next major changes in our view of mind came with the Renaissance. It started with a fatal step—René Descartes' bifurcation of body and mind. Some such notions had been implicit before but never before had anybody made the distinction with such force and such success. Descartes made the proposal initially in his *De homine*, which, however, was suppressed and not published until some 12 years after his death; his 1642 *Meditationes* became the banner book for the mind–body distinction (Descartes, 1642, 1662). The so-called "mind–body problem"—how the material body interacts with an "immaterial" mind or how a material body can generate such things as thoughts and consciousness—has been with us ever since. Although we might have given up notions of a rational soul interacting with animal spirits, the distinction still bedevils philosophers today. I will return to this issue later.

Also in the seventeenth century, Thomas Hobbes published his *Leviathan*, which influenced our notions of mind by introducing elaborate categories of thought and by making competition a basic characteristic of the human mind (Hobbes, 1651).

The three major figures in the history of the mind are David Hume, Immanuel Kant, and Franz Brentano. Although Hume's major contributions at the time were his analyses of causal phenomena and his questioning of deistic notions, his philosophizing about mind was more psychological than philosophical because of his insistence that we construct our world from imperfect impressions (Hume, 1739–1740). Kant followed-up Hume's skepticism by developing ideas about the structure of the human mind and its a *priori* dependence on space and time as initially given (Kant, 1781). Then Franz Brentano convinced the philosophical community about the importance of *intentionality*, stressing that human thought is always *about* some object (Brentano, 1874). This idea had been circulating for some time and Aristotle had suggested similar notions about intentionality and the directedness of thought, but it was Brentano who came at the right time and place to make the notion central.

With the end of the nineteenth century came the detachment of psychology from philosophy. The foundations for the separation had been laid earlier in the century (e.g. Herbart, 1816) but a new psychology without the philosophical baggage (and without mind?) was created by the empiricist–experimentalist Wilhelm Wundt and the philosopher–encyclopedist William

James. Contemporary psychology often forgets their breadth of interests in covering all of psychology, but also going beyond it—as in Wundt's interest in purely philosophical issues (see, for example, his autobiography; Wundt, 1920), and his fundamental work in social psychology, linguistics, and anthropological psychology (Wundt, 1912). James' monumental *"Principles"* ranged widely over relevant philosophical speculations but also depended in the last instance on empirical observation (James, 1890). Both of them, in the end, had described the wide-ranging functions and structures of the mind without paying more than lip service to it as a separable function.

Psychology's next step in the functional definition of mind came in its abandonment of consciousness as the be-all and end-all of psychological observation. Although earlier writers had considered problems of unconsciousness (e.g. Hartmann, 1869) and Sigmund Freud made it his foundation stone, as far as the psychologies of cognition were concerned the major insight into the importance of nonconscious processes came early in the twentieth century in the work of the Würzburg School and the discovery of "imageless thought" (properly translated as thought without conscious content; Külpe, 1912). Mandler and Mandler (1964) presented excerpts of this work and a review of the movement.

Internationally, the early twentieth century was a period filled with extensive work on all aspects of empirical and theoretical psychology without much attention to what was taking place, namely the building of the psychological mind as an umbrella notion of a variety of psychological functions. And except for the interlude of behaviorism in the United States and the death of German psychology under National Socialism (Mandler, 2002c), the late twentieth century saw a "mind"less psychology return in full bloom (Mandler, 2002b).

I now turn to conceptual discussions of "mind", starting with philosophy. Given that since the late twentieth century psychologists have been using "mind" only tangentially, the still extensive use of the concept by philosophers is an important influence, and also keeps the concept alive.

Philosophies of mind

With the twentieth century, psychologists had generally given up any systematic investigation of some "mind" entity and primarily used the term as a *façon de parler*. In part, this created a vacuum of interest and it has been in the twentieth century that the philosophy of mind developed as a separate field and took over the topic as its principal domain. That development turned into a storm of contributions in the last quarter of the century as philosophy awakened from a place-holding slumber and abounded with speculations about mind and consciousness. I cannot do justice to the full range of opinions expressed, but I will sketch a few positions relevant to a psychology of consciousness—and mind. Just the sheer number and variety of labels for different and contradictory positions in philosophy are enough to deter one from trying to summarize "contemporary" philosophy. Here is a sample: eliminative materialism, analytic functionalism, analytic behaviorism, homuncular functionalism, direct realism, commonsense relationism.

Two major problems confront an attempt to delimit a philosophy of mind. First, some philosophers are not at all sure that it would be possible to arrive at any understanding of mind, whatever it is. And second, there is no agreement whether "mind" refers to the contents of consciousness or whether something else or more is implied.

Thomas Nagel is an excellent example of a philosopher who, although implicitly claiming otherwise, denies the possibility of understanding the mind, without quite telling us what this "mind" might be. It is described as a "general feature of the world" like matter (Nagel, 1986, p. 19) that cannot be understood by any physical reduction and that is also beyond any evolutionary explanation. Nagel assures us that "something else" must be going on, and he is sure that whatever it may be, it is taking us to a "truer and more detached" understanding of the world (p. 79). Whereas I do not wish to advertise any great advance in contemporary psychology, it is difficult to follow someone who on the one hand refuses to examine current psychological knowledge and on the other hand insists that "the methods needed to understand ourselves do not yet exist" (p. 10). Nagel contends that "the world may be inconceivable to *our* minds". Humans are by no means omniscient, but one cannot truly claim to know or to prejudge what knowledge is or is not attainable. There surely are aspects of the world that are currently inconceivable, and others that were so centuries ago, but many of the latter are not now and the former may not be in the future. It may be characteristic of some basic optimism that psychologists refuse to concede such impossibilities.

As I have shown, there is no public agreement as to the referent for the ubiquitous term "mind". To return briefly to the lexical problem, Webster's dictionaries are quite catholic in admitting "the complex of elements in an individual that feels, perceives, thinks, wills, and esp. reasons" *and* "the conscious mental events and capabilities in an organism" *and* "the organized conscious and unconscious adaptive mental activity of an organism". Philosophers rarely tell us which of these minds they have in mind. Apart from the public display of disunity, it is likely that most philosophers would agree to a use of "mind" as a quasitheoretical entity that is causally involved in mental events, including consciousness. I will return to the conflict between seeing "mind" as representing the contents (and sometimes functions) of consciousness compared with using "mind" as a summary term for the various mechanisms that we assign to conscious and unconscious processes. It is beyond the scope of this chapter to discuss the problems of consciousness which will be explored elsewhere in this volume. Most recently, I discussed my own views of the role of the limited capacity of consciousness and the fact that it is in the unconscious that much of mental processing takes place in Mandler (1998, 2002a).

Philosophical positions

Having happily accepted one or another form of Cartesian dualism for nearly 300 years, anglophone philosophy briefly partook of behaviorist escapades in the first half of the twentieth century while wrestling with the purified attitudes of logical positivism. Things changed radically around 1960 with the advent of the currently favored way of dealing with the mind—functionalism (see Putnam, 1960). At its simplest, philosophical functionalism uses sensory inputs and observable behaviors linked by a set of causal relations to describe (in various ways) the "how" of consciousness and mind. Among the many different uses of the term "functionalism" in science, linguistics and philosophy, the latter has used it rather extensively and sometimes variously.

Partly in reaction against the identity theory of mind and brain (e.g. Smart, 1959), philosophical functionalism was part of the general change in the cognitive and social sciences that took place in the late 1950s and early 1960s. Lycan, in defending a strong version of functionalism as "honest-to-goodness natural teleology", is interested in the various components as they serve (weakly teleologically) the supervening current operation of a system (Lycan, 1987, p. 44). He invokes a hierarchical system for all complex phenomena with any level of the hierarchy being unpacked into many lower levels of lesser complexity, thus avoiding the problem of a simple homuncular regression (see also Dennett, 1978). The general concern—here and elsewhere—is with mechanisms; how does the system/mind/organism manage relations between inputs and outputs, and how does it achieve a particular state? Van Gulick (1980) similarly uses functionalism to define psychological (conscious) states within a network of perceptual conditions and organism behaviors. He concludes that such a functional approach permits us to think about content in a naturalistic way and to discern consistencies that fit the facts about content. I stress this approach because it focuses on the distinction between philosophical and psychological functionalism. Approaching that difference, Sober (1985) made a distinction between the dominant Machine Functionalism and Teleological Functionalism. In contrast to the "how" questions of Machine Functionalism, the Teleological variety asks also what the functions of particular system/organs/processes are. It is this sense of functionalism which asks the kind of questions that psychologists prefer, and which treat various positions as ostensibly fallible theories about the mind.

Psychology—and mind as mechanism

I have already expressed my skepticism about the point of view that mind and consciousness are co-extensive, I now wish to consider another position that sees mind as the sum total of mechanisms that we ascribe to people (or even to nonhuman animals) in order to make their behavior understandable and coherent. Such a position sees mind and consciousness as independent, although related, concepts; it is implicitly present in many psychological discussions of mind and has been at times explicitly defined. For example, some 45 years ago, in the waning years of American behaviorism, Karl Deutsch suggested that *"Mind* might be provisionally defined as any self-sustaining physical process which includes the seven operations of abstracting, communicating, storing, subdividing, recalling, recombining and reapplying items of information" (Deutsch, 1951, p. 216).

Recently, the psychological concept of mind has been used in the "theory of mind" approach, originally introduced by Premack and Woodruff to refer to an ape's ability to understand the goals, thought processes, motives, etc., of another being (Premack & Woodruff, 1978). "Theory of mind" has received wide application in discussions of young children's mental development. Theory of mind clearly uses mind as a collective expression for a variety of mental processes.

Such an approach to mind as a collection of mechanisms is also implied by some philosophers, even though they are preoccupied with the mental functions of consciousness. For example, Searle notes that "most of the mental phenomena in [a] person's existence are not present to consciousness" and "most of our mental life at any given point is unconscious" (Searle, 1992, p. 18). He then, however, maintains that our access to unconscious mental states is derived solely from conscious mental states. Not only does such a view signal a return to an initial *tabula rasa* that only becomes populated by the individual's conscious experiences, but it also denies any kind of acquisition of skills or knowledge without conscious participation or any kind of pre-experientially given structures.

A view of mind as *mere* mechanism may seem like some sort of Rylean behaviorism. Ryle noted, for example, that "[t]o find that most people have minds . . . is simply to find that they are able and prone to do certain sorts of things" (Ryle, 1949, p. 61). Ryle then rejects any "occult" agency behind these acts, but he is unwilling to consider a *theoretical* set of mechanisms (a *mind*?) by which we try to understand the observed working of the individual. One might note that the insistence on going from the observed to the postulated and vice versa is a characteristic of psychological thinking and theorizing; it may sound behavioristic but is in fact no different from what any science does.

Psychologists frequently equate the mind with thought. To the extent that thinking involves the manipulation of conscious symbols it covers only a part of the umbrella notion of mind, since much of human problem solving takes place unconsciously and further some nonmanipulative processes such as sensory perception would probably also fall under a general sense of mind.

And finally, if mind is the repository of perceptual, cognitive, and behavioral mechanisms then it can also be argued to be the function that is performed by the brain. If "mind is what the brain does", then similar relations can be seen in the form and function of other human organs. Before discussing the mind–body problem, I turn to a brief review of non-Western views of mind.

Mind in non-Western psychologies

Scientific psychology—as practised in laboratories and research and theoretical journals—has generally adopted a similar approach and methods regardless of the culture in which it is practised. The shadings are relatively minor. In Western societies mind is frequently seen as spiritual and non-physical. By contrast, in China, for example, psychology has been somewhat under the influence of its recent Marxist history and mind is frequently viewed as having a physical/chemical basis, with praxis as the most important factor in its development. In general, the concept of mind, with its essentially non-scientific origins, has adopted different shadings depending on the culture in which the concept is used. We have already seen some small differences like that in our discussion of different uses of mind in various Western languages, although the influence of the Judeo-Christian tradition can be traced in most Western conceptions. I now take a brief look at the concept of mind in three non-Western cultures. With few exceptions (see, for example, Rosch, 2002) these approaches have had little influence on Western psychologies. However, one of the reasons why the non-Western uses of mind have not influenced Western thought is that the former have used mind often in ways very similar to that practised by the latter.

In *Buddhist* thought the concept of mind is most closely represented by the Pali notion of *citta*. *Citta* is a highly nuanced notion that includes human thinking, knowing and experience. It is primarily concerned with consciousness in both its primitive and advanced functions. Buddhist thought has no equivalent to the Western notion of soul, and thus there is no place to conceive of soul/mind as consciousness (see Kogen, 1996). In *Hindu* psychology the notion of mind is more of a collective concept that includes unconscious, conscious, and superconscious processes (Akhilananda, 1946). The same is true of *Taoist* thinking where the mind concept is much like the Western summary notion (Moore, 1967).

Apart from these general views of mind, specific psychologies in these countries will often incorporate and make use of concepts from their specific religious/secular philosophies—particularly on the mind–body issue. In addition, some specific Western influences may play a part in the use of mental concept, as in the inclusion of some neo-Marxist concepts in Chinese psychology.

Is there a mind–body problem?

There is, strictly speaking, no mind–body *problem*; dealing with so-called minds is not incompatible with a modern materialism. Mind is what the brain does; just as energy conservation is what the liver does. Specific functions are associated with large operational units such as organs, organisms, and machines, and these functions (and their associated concepts) cannot, without loss of meaning, be reduced to the constituent processes of the larger units. The speed of a car, the conserving function of the liver, and the notion of a noun phrase are not reducible to internal combustion engines, liver cells, or neurons (Mandler, 1985). Mind may be viewed as an emergent function. The notion of emergence is a label that has often been applied to these new properties of larger assemblies. A sentiment related to my position is echoed in Lycan's statement that "the mystery of the mental is no more a mystery than the heart, the kidney, the carburattor or the pocket calculator" (Lycan, 1987, p. 44).

Just as philosophers have advanced a multitude of interpretations of mind, so have neurophysiologists and neuropsychologists proposed many different suggestions for the physical location or realization of consciousness—and by implication of mind. Kinsbourne (1996) has summarized some of the various localizations of consciousness that have been proposed. This discussion is beyond the scope of this chapter because as far as I know nobody has proposed any localization of mind—other than the whole brain—or organism.

The argument about mind as an emergent function of brains also needs to be placed in the context of reductionist arguments. Most current commentators are materialists and, as such, they subscribe to the first part of what Weinberg has called *grand reductionism*, i.e. "the view that all of nature is the way it is . . . because of simple universal laws, to which in some sense all other scientific laws may in some sense be reduced" (Weinberg, 1995, p. 39). The claim of reduction contained in the second half does not follow, and it actually only refers to a subset of materialist dogma, i.e. physicalism. In any case, complex emergent functions need their own laws and principles which cannot without loss of meaning be reduced to the "universal laws" (see, for example, Putnam, 1980).

Coda

I have tried to show the multifaceted aspects of the concept of mind. It varies with cultures, with disciplines, with ontological presuppositions. Today, psychologists use it primarily as a summary term to bundle all the various characteristics, abilities, and functions that we use to understand and describe complex human thought and action. Attempts to understand what mind may "really" be are mainly confined to philosophical speculations. Psychologists have also generally accepted the notion that the mind is what the brain does, and thus have adopted a basic materialist stance. Having exorcised the ghost in the machine we still are willing to think about the machine and its function.

References

Akhilananda, S. (1946). *Hindu psychology: Its meaning for the West*. New York: Harper.

Baars, B. J. (1988). *A cognitive theory of consciousness*. New York: Cambridge University Press.

Brentano, F. C. (1874). *Psychologie vom empirischen Standpunkt* (Vol. 1). Leipzig: Duncker & Humblot.

Dennett, D. C. (1978). *Brainstorms*. Montgomery, VT: Bradford Books.

Descartes, R. (1642). *Meditationes de prima philosophia, in qua Dei existentia et animae immortalitas demonstratur*. Paris: Michaelem Soly.

Descartes, R. (1662). *De homine, figuris et latinitate donatus a Florentio Schuyl*. Lugduni Batavorum, Leiden: Petrum Leffen & Franciscum Moyardum.

Deutsch, K. W. (1951). Mechanism, teleology, and mind. *Philosophy and Phenomenological Research, 12*, 185–223.

Hartmann, E. V. (1869). *Philosophie des Unbewussten*. Berlin: Duncker.

Herbart, J. F. (1816). *Lehrbuch zur Psychologie*. Königsberg und Leipzig: A. W. Unzer.

Hobbes, T. (1651). *Leviathan; or, The matter, form, and power of a common-wealth ecclesiastical and civil*. London: Andrew Crooke.

Hume, D. (1739–1740). *A treatise of human nature: Being an attempt to introduce the experimental method of reasoning into moral subjects*. London: J. Noon.

Humphrey, N. (1992). *A history of the mind*. London: Chatto & Windus.

James, W. (1890). *The principles of psychology*. New York: Holt.

Kant, I. (1781). *Kritik der reinen Vernunft*. Riga: Johann Friedrich Hartknoch.

Kinsbourne, M. (1996). What qualifies a representation for a role in consciousness? In J. D. Cohen & J. W. Schooler (Eds.), *Scientific approaches to consciousness. The Twenty-fifth Annual Carnegie Symposium on Cognition*. Hillsdale, NJ: Lawrence Erlbaum Associates Inc.

Kogen, M. (1996). *Essentials of Buddhism: Basic terminology and concepts of Buddhist philosophy and practice* (Gaynor Sekimori, Trans.). Tokyo: Kosei.

Külpe, O. (1912). Über die moderne Psychologie des Denkens. *Internationale Monatsschrift für Wissenschaft, Kunst und Technik June*, 1070 ff.

Lycan, W. G. (1987). *Consciousness*. Cambridge, MA: MIT Press.

Mandler, G. (1985). *Cognitive psychology: An essay in cognitive science*. Hillsdale, NJ: Lawrence Erlbaum Associates Inc.

Mandler, G. (1998). Consciousness and mind as philosophical problems and psychological issues. In J. Hochberg (Ed.), *Perception and cognition at century's end: History, philosophy, theory*. San Diego: Academic Press.

Mandler, G. (2002a). *Consciousness recovered: Psychological functions and origins of conscious thought*. Amsterdam/Philadelphia: John Benjamins.

Mandler, G. (2002b). Origins of the cognitive (r)evolution. *Journal of the History of the Behavioral Sciences, 38*, 339–353.

Mandler, G. (2002c). Psychologists and the national socialist access to power. *History of Psychology, 5*, 190–200.

Mandler, J. M., & Mandler, G. (1964). *Thinking: From association to Gestalt*. New York: Wiley (Reprint edition: Westport, CT: Greenwood Press, 1981).

Moore, C. A. (Ed.). (1967). *The Chinese mind: Essentials of Chinese philosophy and culture*. Honolulu: East–West Center Press.

Myrdal, G. (1944). *An American dilemma*. New York: Harper & Brothers.

Nagel, T. (1986). *The view from nowhere*. New York: Oxford University Press.

Premack, D., & Woodruff, G. (1978). Does the chimpanzee have a theory of mind? *Behavioral & Brain Sciences, 1*, 515–526.

Putnam, H. (1960). Minds and machines. In S. Hook (Ed.), *Dimensions of mind*. New York: Collier Books.

Putnam, H. (1980). Philosophy and our mental life. In N. Block (Ed.), *Readings in the philosophy of psychology* (Vol. 1). Cambridge, MA: Harvard University Press.

Rosch, E. (2002). How to catch James's mystic germ: Religious experience, Buddhist meditation and psychology. *Journal of Consciousness Studies, 9*, 37–56.

Ryle, G. (1949). *The concept of mind*. London: Hutchinson's University Library.

Searle, J. R. (1992). *The rediscovery of the mind*. Cambridge, MA: MIT Press.

Smart, J. J. C. (1959). Sensations and brain processes. *Philosophical Review, 68*, 141–156.

Sober, E. (1985). Panglossian functionalism and the philosophy of mind. *Synthese, 64*, 165–193.

Van Gulick, R. (1980). Functionalism, information and content. *Nature and System, 2*, 139–162.

Weinberg, S. (1995). Reductionism redux. *The New York Review of Books, 62*(15), 39–42.

Wundt, W. (1912). *Elemente der Völkerpsychologie: Grundlinien einer psychologischen Entwicklungsgeschichte der Menschheit*. Leipzig: A. Kröner Verlag.

Wundt, W. (1920). *Erlebtes und Erkanntes*. Stuttgart: Alfred Kröner Verlag.

12 Motivation: About the "why" and "what for" of human behavior

Willy Lens and Maarten Vansteenkiste

Introduction

The word "motivation" is derived from the Latin *"movere"*, which means "to move". Motivation refers to psychological forces that move psychological beings (animals and humans) or bring them into action. Motivational psychology is about covert psychological processes that are assumed to explain particular behavioral characteristics. The basic motivational question is to explain which behavior or action an individual performs at each moment in time: the *initiation* and *persistence* of an intentional, *goal-directed* activity. Motivation also explains the degree of *effort* that is spent while performing an activity and the *satisfaction* that is derived from an activity and/or its outcome(s). For example, the type (content) and strength of individuals' work motivation is related to how much time they spend working, how much they like it, but also to the *efficiency* of the performance, to the level of performance. In general, the more students, employees, and so on, are motivated, the better their results will be and the more they will like to study.

Intentionality

Many of our behaviors are not re-actions to internal or external stimuli, but action intended to reach or achieve a goal. As explicitly suggested by Tolman in the 1920s, and by Lewin in the 1930s, actions are intentional and goal directed. People (but also animals) actively try to reach some result (e.g. to earn a promotion, to succeed in the entrance exam, to become a psychologist, to make a lot of money, to avoid failure). Motivational processes are not only instigating and maintaining goal-directed actions, they are in the first place responsible for formulating or setting goals. Due to our higher cognitive functioning, humans can translate or concretize general needs or motives (e.g. need for achievement, curiosity, power) into more specific goals (e.g. to win the gold medal, to learn more about motivational processes in humans, to become a senator). Goal setting is an important step in need satisfaction. Having a strong need for self-realization, for example, but not knowing (yet) how to do that, creates frustration. Motivational goals can be situated in the immediate future (e.g. to go for a coffee) but also in a very distant future (e.g. to move to Portugal after retirement). Motivational goal setting creates a longer or shorter future time perspective (Lens, 1986; Nuttin, 1984; Nuttin & Lens, 1985).

Initiation and persistence

Motivational psychology was traditionally concerned about the initiation and the persistence of a particular goal-oriented activity. The goal of an activity defines its nature: learning, performing, playing, eating. The amount of time spent studying was assumed to be a positive linear function of the strength of the motivation for that activity: the more motivated students are, the more time they will spend studying. Atkinson and Birch (1970, 1978) argued, however, that the basic phenomenon to be explained by motivational psychology is not a series of isolated, episodic actions but a continuous stream of activities and changes in activities. The initiation of an activity (e.g. reading a newspaper) defines at the same time the end or persistence of the foregoing activity (e.g. writing a term paper). That means that the initiation at a certain moment in time and the duration or persistence of an action depends not only on the strength of the motivation for that action but also on the number and the strength of competing action tendencies. To increase, for example, the time spent studying one can increase the student's motivation to study and decrease the number and the strength of competing action alternatives (e.g. playing, sport, going to the movies, watching TV).

Level of performance

Motivation is an important determinant of the level of performance in sport, work, study, and so on. In general, the level of performance is considered to be a multiplicative function of abilities and motivation, hence the well-known saying by Edison "Genius is 1% inspiration and 99% transpiration". But we would argue that Edison's percentages are wrong. In the educational domain, about 66 per cent of individual differences in school results can be accounted for by individual differences in ability and about 33 per cent by motivational differences (Atkinson, 1974a).

This formula also implies that low levels of performance are not always an indication of underachievement due to lack of motivation. They may be the result of low ability.

In many tasks, motivation affects performance levels via the amount of time spent at the task (see above) and via the efficiency with which abilities are used. But the relationship between strength of motivation and efficiency is not always positive and linear, it can be curvilinear or inverted U-shaped (Atkinson, 1974b; Yerkes & Dodson, 1908). When the strength of motivation increases from low to medium or medium high, the efficiency of the performance will also increase. At the optimal level of motivation, the efficiency is 100% and the level of performance maximal. If the strength of the motivation increases beyond the optimum, the efficiency and the level of performance will decrease. A second component of the Yerkes–Dodson law says that the more difficult the task, the lower the optimal level of motivation. Such a curvilinear relationship implies that the correlation between the strength of motivation and the level of performance can be positive, zero or even negative and that blindly calculating linear correlations may be misleading, hiding existing meaningful but non-linear relationships.

Motivation and volition

Heckhausen (1991) and his former collaborators (Gollwitzer, 1999; Gollwitzer & Bargh, 1996; Kuhl & Beckman, 1994) distinguish motivational and volitional processes. For them, motivational processes lead to goal setting. Goal attainment, however, requires additional motivational and volitional processes. Quite often, one does not only formulate a goal but also action plans or behavioral means–end structures regarding how to achieve the goal (Nuttin, 1984). These action intentions must be implemented in order to achieve the goal. Volitional processes and action-control mechanisms protect the intentions and facilitate their enactment. Very often there is a big gap between action intentions and actions. We forget to implement an intention, we may postpone it (procrastination), give priority to another intention or replace it by a new goal and action plan. Volitional processes are also active when we would prefer to stop what we are doing (but should finish first) and do something else that is more attractive at that moment (e.g. to continue preparing tomorrow's exam rather than watch a movie on TV). We also need will or volitional control to stop an interesting activity and start doing something that we have to do and that is less pleasant at the moment (e.g. to stop playing soccer in order to study for tomorrow's exam) (Dewitte & Lens, 2000).

From content theories to process theories of motivation

Needs and motives

The basic concepts in motivational psychology are instincts, drives, needs, and motives. These refer to innate or acquired and more or less stable personality dispositions, which must be satisfied by contacting appropriate goal objects towards which they direct behavior. The innate biological need for food (hunger) directs behavior to food objects that have a positive value because they can reduce and satisfy the hunger. Which particular food is searched for (rice, bread, manioc or corn) results from rewarding experiences or learning processes. Success in an achievement task satisfies the acquired need for success and failure experiences frustrate this need. From the very beginning of scientific psychology, exhaustive lists of instincts and needs or motives were formulated. Some resulted from armchair psychology, others were based on empirical research (Bernard, 1924; Freud, 1915/1949; Maslow, 1954; McClelland, 1987; Murray, 1938; Nuttin, 1984). Most people probably experience the many different types of human needs. There are, however, large inter- and intra-individual differences in the strength of needs or motives. Some people are characterized by a strong need for achievement and a low fear of failure, whereas others have a strong fear of failure but no need for success. Questionnaires and indirect or projective techniques (e.g. Thematic Apperception Test; TAT) have been developed to measure these differences. Correlations between direct and indirect or projective measures of the same motives (e.g. the need for achievement, the need for power) do not usually correlate very highly, suggesting that they do not measure the same latent motivational variable (McClelland, 1980).

In motivational psychology an important distinction is made between physiological needs (e.g. homeostasis, pain, thirst, hunger, sex) and psychological needs (e.g. curiosity, achievement, power, affiliation, aggression). These two categories of motivation are studied in separate lines of research without much interaction. We will not discuss the biological needs, nor do we give any attention to unconscious motives. In his psychodynamic theory, Freud (1915/1949) stressed the importance of unconscious desires or wishes and their indirect expression in fantasy and in behavior; this subsection of motivational psychology is not addressed in this chapter.

Based on biological models, for a long time motivational psychologists assumed that frustrating a need increases its intensity and that satisfying a need decreases its intensity. The second part of this assumption cannot, however, be generalized to all kinds of needs (White, 1959). Need satisfaction can increase the importance or intensity of a need. Curiosity, for example, can indeed be satisfied by new information, but that need for knowledge can grow by satisfying it: The more people know, the more they want to learn (Deci & Ryan, 1985). Success satisfies the need for achievement but, at the same time, it may stimulate that need. Failure in an achievement task frustrates both the need for achievement and the fear of failure. After failure, both motivational tendencies will persist as inertial tendencies to strive for success and to avoid failure (Atkinson & Feather, 1966). But even a highly success-oriented individual who repeatedly experiences failure after failure will lose all interest in achievement tasks. The need for achievement and the fear of failure will disappear.

Maslow (1954) made a distinction between deficiency needs and growth needs. Deficiency needs motivate behavior because a deficiency or shortage is experienced (lack of sugar or affection, for example). Growth needs motivate behavior even when the present situation is not experienced as deficient. People can be motivated to experience more affection or love, even when they do not experience their present life situation as insufficient in that regard.

Ryan and Deci (2000) distinguish three intrinsic or what they call "organismic" needs (the need for competence, the need for autonomy and the need for relatedness or belongingness). They argue that these needs are innate and hence characteristic for all human beings. Their research shows that the more these needs can be satisfied, the more motivated and happy people are. Contrary to most content theories, Deci and Ryan do not consider individual differences in the importance or strength of these organismic needs.

Not all motivational theories make use of concepts such as needs. The best example is probably Vroom's cognitive theory of work motivation and the valence–instrumentality–expectancy (VIE) models that are based on that theory (Pinder, 1998). In general, these models consider the strength of the motivation for an action alternative to be a multiplicative function of the expectancy that the action will lead to the desired and anticipated outcome and the anticipated value of that outcome (see the expectancy × value models in cognitive theories of motivation; Feather, 1982). However, one must also be able to explain why action outcomes have an incentive value, why we prefer some outcomes more than others. The more we (think we) need them, the more value we attach to an outcome.

Incentive motivation

Motivational tendencies are very often conceptualized as psychological forces that energize and direct actions towards a positively valued goal (approach tendencies) or away from a negatively valued situation or outcome (avoidance tendencies). Animals and people are "pushed" by their instincts, drives and needs. But, as said above for the expectancy × value theories, people are also "attracted" by incentives. The anticipated value of a goal or action outcome (e.g. success in a competition) can also function as a pulling force. As shown by Tolman, Spence, and since then by many others, the quality and quantity of rewards and goals affect the strength of the motivation to strive for those goals.

The distinction between these two types of motivational forces is, however, not very fundamental. Indeed, needs and motives have objects, when we are "in need" we need something, and action outcomes or goals have only incentive value if there is a need for them.

Process theories

Content theories of motivation reduce motivation to needs and motives as innate or acquired personality dispositions. In 1935, Lewin stressed the fact that motivation is not so much a disposition but a psychological process in his general behavioral formula:

$$B = f(P,E)$$

He also applied this formula to motivational processes. Not only overt behavior (B), but also covert psychological processes such as motivation result from the interaction of personality characteristics (P) and characteristics of the psychological or perceived environment (E). This approach to motivation as a psychological process—and not as a personality trait— will now be illustrated first with Lewin's formula for psychological force and then with Atkinson's theory of achievement motivation.

For Lewin, motivation is a psychological force, represented as a vector. The strength of the motivation or the psychological force (F) to strive for a goal (g) by individual (p), or $F(p,g)$, is a direct positive function of the valence of the goal $Va(G)$ and a direct negative function of the psychological distance between the person and the goal ($e_{p,g}$) or:

$$F(p,g) = f[Va(G)]/e_{p,g}$$

The anticipated value or the valence of a goal depends on the need or tension of the person (t) and on the perceived nature or quality of the object G. So the formula can be rewritten as follows:

$$F(p,g) = f[Va(G)]/e_{p,g} = f(t,G)/e_{p,g}$$

The force that acts on an individual to strive for a goal can be increased by increasing the need for that goal object and/or the quality and/or quantity of the goal, and by decreasing the psychological distance between the individual and the goal object.

The theory of achievement motivation is a good example of a cognitive process theory of human motivation. McClelland, Atkinson, Clark, and Lowell (1953; Atkinson, 1958) developed a measure of individual differences in the strength of the need for achievement (as well as for need for affiliation and the need for power). McClelland studied behavioral correlates of individual differences in the need for achievement (McClelland, 1961, 1975; McClelland & Winter, 1969).

More in line with Lewin's approach to motivation, Atkinson (1964; Atkinson & Feather, 1966) made a distinction between motives as personality dispositions and motivational processes. Not the latent achievement motive as such, but the aroused motive or motivation that affects behavior in an achievement task. The strength of the motivation to strive for success in an achievement task (Ts) is considered to be a multiplicative function of the need for achievement or the motive to succeed (Ms), the difficulty of the task or the probability of success (Ps) and the anticipated incentive value or rewarding value of success (Is) or:

$$Ts = Ms \times Ps \times Is$$

The probability of success depends on the difficulty of the task. The strength of the achievement motivation is hence a function of a person characteristic (Ms) and a situational characteristic (Ps). So we can recognize Lewin's formula $B = f(P,E)$ in Atkinson's theory of achievement motivation.

The problem remains, however, how to measure individual differences in motives. We can distinguish direct, explicit self-report measures or questionnaires and indirect, implicit measures such as content analysis of TAT stories (McClelland, 1980; Smith, 1992). They certainly do not measure the same underlying dispositions and hence they do not usually correlate highly. As a consequence, research using such different measures can hardly be cumulative.

From general to mini-theories

Motivational psychology started by developing all encompassing theories answering to the "why" question of behavior. The philosophical precursors referred to the will (see, for example, Descartes). In line with Darwin's theory of biological evolution came first the instinct theories (James, McDougall, Bernard) and then the drive theories (Woodworth, Freud, Hull). But starting in the 1950s, biological models of motivation were more and more replaced by cognitive models, taking into account the complexity and diversity of human behavior as well as the impact of higher cognitive functioning. As a consequence, more partial theories of motivation were developed. Whereas the original general theories tried "to explain the full range of motivation, mini-theories limit their attention to specific motivational phenomenon. Mini-theories seek to understand or investigate one particular behavioral phenomenon" (Reeve, 2005, p. 33). A few examples are the theory of achievement motivation, attribution theory, goal-setting theory in work motivation and achievement goal-orientation theories in educational psychology. The Self-determination theory (Deci & Ryan, 2002) is probably the only example of a more recent motivational theory that intends to cover a broad scope—if not the total field—of human goal striving and behavior. It grew out of Deci's Cognitive Evaluation Theory and his research on the interaction of intrinsic and extrinsic motivation (Deci, 1975; Deci & Ryan, 1985).

Intrinsic versus extrinsic motivation

A good example of a motivational theory that is neither a really global or holistic approach to motivation, nor a very limited theory such as the theory of achievement motivation, is the distinction made between intrinsic and extrinsic motivation. Since the 1970s, and until quite recently, much research was devoted to these two distinct categories or types of motivation. An action is intrinsically motivated when it is autotelic, the goal is the action itself. Good examples are curiosity or the need for knowledge, the need for competence and the need for autonomy. People can be intrinsically interested in gaining knowledge, in feeling competent, and in being autonomous or self-regulating. Intrinsically motivated activities are not instrumental, the satisfaction is inherently associated with the activity as such (e.g. to learn about or get more insight into something; to play tennis for the fun of it). An activity is extrinsically motivated when it is instrumental for reaching a goal that is not inherently related to that action (e.g. to study in order to get a reward; to play tennis to become a pro and make a lot of money).

Motivational research in educational psychology is mostly limited to intrinsic motivation (Pintrich & Schunk, 2002), whereas theories about work motivation are more often about extrinsic motivation (Pinder, 1998). It is, however, quite evident that many activities are both intrinsically and extrinsically motivated. Students study hard because they are thrilled by insight into and understanding of a particular phenomenon (e.g. human motivation) but also because they are motivated to succeed in the exams following the course on motivation. Employees, as well as their employers, are motivated for their job by financial incentives in order to make a living for themselves and their families, but very often also because they like to feel competent and be efficient at their job. This implies that the total motivation for many of our daily activities must be conceived of as the sum of an intrinsic and an extrinsic component. The strength of the total motivation to study, to work, and so on can hence be increased by intensifying the intrinsic or the extrinsic component, or both. This does not, however, imply that the two types of motivation are always additive. The title of Lepper and Greene's 1978 book *The hidden costs of reward* refers to a phenomenon much under study since the 1970s: that offering extrinsic rewards (to induce extrinsic motivation) for already intrinsically motivated activities may undermine the intrinsic motivation. Much experimental research was devoted to how general the phenomenon is and under which conditions it is found (see Cameron, 2001; Deci, Koestner, & Ryan, 2001). Extrinsic rewards and other external events that are perceived by individuals as controlling their behavior will undermine the intrinsic motivation. When they are informative and positive, they will satisfy the need for competence and efficacy, and hence increase the intrinsic motivation.

When there is no intrinsic motivation or interest at all for a given activity (e.g. studying a foreign language), teachers, employers, and so on have no other choice than to use extrinsic rewards and other external means to motivate and instigate action. The individual may engage in the activity. If he or she can then experience feelings of competence or efficacy, an intrinsic motivation or interest may arise and grow. This is what Allport (1961) referred to in his concept of "functional autonomy of needs" and

Woodworth (1918) in his expression "mechanisms become drives". What was originally an instrumental activity may become a final goal or a goal on its own (e.g. from "writing books to make a living" to "writing books for the fun of it").

Motivation: Quantity and quality

Inter- and intra-individual differences in motivation usually refer to differences in strength or intensity. People are more or less motivated for something (e.g. students and study motivation; employees and work motivation; friends or partners and social motivation for affiliation). There are also differences in the content or direction of the motivation. People have different interests, different goals to which they attach importance. Some people are strongly motivated for success in difficult achievement tasks, others are much more interested in positive social contacts (need for affiliation) or in interpersonal power (need for power). In a certain sense, this second type of difference refers to qualitative differences. A distinction is made between intrinsic and extrinsic motivation (see above) and, in the Self-determination Theory (Deci & Ryan, 1985, 2002) in particular, some types of motivation are considered to be qualitatively better than others. In educational research, intrinsic motivation is considered (and found) to be "a better quality" of motivation than extrinsic motivation. It leads to interest, enjoyment, inherent satisfaction, challenge seeking, deep-level learning, and persistent learning (Stipek, 2002). But, as we will discuss in the next section, not all types of extrinsic motivation are of a low "quality".

In the Self-determination Theory, an important distinction is made between two different motivational questions, "why" versus "what for". What do you want to reach? What is the goal of your activity and why do you want to achieve that goal? What are the reasons for your goal striving?

When an activity is intrinsically motivated one can hardly make a distinction between what its intentionality or goal is and for what reason it is performed. The activity is intrinsically satisfying, its goal and the reason for doing it are the same (e.g. developing competencies, gaining knowledge, being successful in competition with a task-inherent criterion of success or excellence). For extrinsically motivated activities it seems, however, to be useful to make a distinction between the goal(s) one tries to achieve and the reason for such goal striving or for doing the activity. One can try to reach a multitude of extrinsic goals by studying, working, sport, and so on. Self-determination Theory (Ryan & Deci, 2000) distinguishes five types of behavioral regulation of the reasons for an activity, one for intrinsically motivated and four for extrinsically motivated actions:

When an action is *intrinsically motivated*, it is also *intrinsically regulated*, its locus of causality is internal (within the actor). Intrinsic interest, enjoyment, and inherent satisfaction regulate or control the activity.

For *extrinsically motivated* actions, Ryan and Deci (2002) distinguish four different types of reason or behavioral regulation. They also argue that these four types of behavioral regulation or control differ in quality. A number of empirical studies could validate this last hypothesis.

External regulation is worst because it correlates more strongly with lower well-being, depressive feelings, less persistence and less behavioral effectiveness (Vansteenkiste, 2005; Vansteenkiste, Lens, De Witte, & Feather, 2005). The locus of control or the reason for the action is external or totally outside the individual (e.g. a promised extrinsic reward, a threatening punishment, an order, a supervision). For example, a student is (perhaps even highly) motivated to study on Friday evening because he will then be allowed by his mother to go to a party on Saturday evening (extrinsic motivation and external regulation).

Introjected regulation is somewhat better. The individual introjected the external reason for the activity without accepting it as a personal reason or without really internalizing it. For example, a student may do her best for school because her parents require her to do so and she does not want to disobey them, because that would create guilt feelings. So she studies because she does not want to feel guilty.

Identified regulation means that the reason for doing something is external but, to some degree, also internal because the individual perceives the reason as personally important. A student may do her best at school because she wants to go to college and become an architect. She perceives herself as a future architect. This student's motivation is instrumental, hence extrinsic (see further), but she identifies with the reason for studying. Also the goal has personal value, relevance, and importance.

Finally, the qualitatively best type of extrinsic motivation is characterized by *integrated regulation*. The external reason for the activity is perceived as totally congruent with the self-concept. It is the most self-determined type of extrinsically motivated behavior. The locus of control is internal, as it is with intrinsic motivation.

It follows from the foregoing that the distinction between intrinsic and extrinsic motivation becomes less relevant when we consider the different types of behavioral regulation. What matters more is what regulates my action. Is the cause or reason an integrated part of myself or is it something that I experience as external to me? Do I control my behavior or is it externally controlled? See deCharms' distinction between "origins" versus "pawns" or people with respectively an internal and an external locus of control (deCharms, 1968).

Goal theories

Due to the cognitive (r)evolution in psychology, the psychology of motivation has become more cognitive. Cognitions such as thoughts, future anticipations, expectancies, perceived instrumentality, and causal attributions were perceived as motivational sources or causes of action. Actions were no longer solely modeled on neurological reflexes but, more and more, on information-processing processes such as computer programs, which have an inbuilt end or exit term. When this criterion is reached, the information processing stops. Analogously, motivated behavior is goal directed. When the goal is reached, the activity comes to a halt. In terms of the Test–Operate–Test–Exit, or TOTE, Model (Miller, Galanter, & Pribram, 1960; Nuttin, 1984), the action continues as long as a discrepancy or incongruity is detected in the test phase between the present state of affairs (the input) and what is desired (the goal, the end term or the standard with which the input is compared). When congruity is detected, the goal is reached and the individual exits. This implies that motivation results from perceived or experienced incongruity or discrepancy and that motivated action is intended to reduce and do away with this discrepancy. We should, however, not forget that in an earlier phase the discrepancy itself is first created by formulating goals or desired end states (the Standard or S in Nuttin's (1984) STOTE-model as an elaboration of the TOTE-model). Motivation is at the same time the origin and a consequence of discrepancy (Bandura, 1991; Nuttin, 1984).

Motivated behavior that is directed towards a goal that is discrepant from what is already achieved expresses what Raynor (1981) called the "attaining type of striving". A positive goal discrepancy is experienced or created and the individual is motivated to eliminate that discrepancy by attaining the goal (e.g. a high-school graduate who is highly motivated to graduate from college wants to attain that goal). Most theories and research on motivation implicitly or explicitly refer to this type of striving. There is, however, a second type of motivational striving, called by Raynor (1981) the "maintaining type of striving", which is much less studied. Even when there is no discrepancy between what is already achieved and what one wants to realize in the near future, one can be highly motivated and put in a lot of effort to keep things the way they are now. One is motivated to maintain a satisfying state of affairs and to do so may require much effort and hard work. For example, an employee is very happy with his job and his employer is very satisfied with the man and his work. The employee is not at all motivated to obtain a promotion but he is highly motivated to keep his present job. There is no discrepancy between what is and what is hoped for in the future, but nevertheless, the employee is highly motivated and works hard. If he did not, he might indeed lose his job.

We will now discuss two types of goal theory: first the Locke–Latham goal-setting theory from organizational psychology and work motivation, and then the achievement goal-orientation theory from educational psychology.

Goal-setting theory

In the field of organizational and industrial psychology, Locke and Latham (1990, 2002) relate motivation and task performance via the goal concept.

For them, actions are goal directed. They define goals as action outcomes an individual tries to achieve or to avoid. Their goal-setting theory is strongly related to management-by-objectives techniques.

Goal characteristics affect the strength of motivation to strive for that goal and hence also the level of task performance. However, it is not the future goal, as such, that has causal effects in the present. That would be an unscientific teleological explanation. It is the actual anticipation of the goal and its characteristics that motivates present task performance.

Locke and Latham stress that in order to be motivating, task goals must be accepted as such by the individual. We would say that an "unaccepted motivational goal" is a contradiction. From a motivational point of view, an action purpose such as a certain level of performance (e.g. cutting 25 trees today; scoring three goals in one game) must be *accepted* by an individual as a valuable action outcome if it is to be a motivational goal. If I accept "an imposed goal" (e.g. my parents want me to score an AA in a given course) then it becomes a motivational goal for me. If I do *not* accept it as a goal, it will not motivate me. I may do my best because I do not want disappoint my parents, but I am not motivated by the AA, rather by that social motive. This means that, in an organizational context but also in many other circumstances, it is very important for employees, students, parents, and so on to be able to participate in setting the goals they have to achieve. This would indeed enhance goal acceptance and turn a perform-ance outcome or level of performance (e.g. selling 30 cars a month) into a motivational goal.

Locke and his colleagues showed in numerous empirical studies that, to be motivating, goals should be perceived as *difficult* (but not *too* difficult) and that they should also be *specific*. Imposed goals that are too difficult will not be accepted because they are experienced as unreachable. Research on the theory of (intrinsic) achievement motivation has shown that success-oriented individuals prefer and are most strongly motivated by achievement goals with a medium to medium-high level of difficulty (probability of success being .50 to .40). Goals will also be more motivating when they allow for informative feedback about the progress already made towards goal achievement (Erez, 1977). Such feedback is more feasible when the goal is specific (e.g. writing two pages) than when it is unspecific (e.g. writing a few pages).

Goal theory and motivation in education

The original cognitive theory of achievement motivation (Atkinson & Feather, 1966) distinguished two uncorrelated goals in achievement situ-ations and achievement tasks: the goal to be successful and the goal not to fail. The first goal satisfies the need for achievement, the second one the need to avoid failure (see above). In educational psychology, the theory of achievement motivation was replaced by achievement goal-orientation theories (Pintrich & Schunk, 2002). In an achievement task, individuals may be oriented towards different types of goal and they may have different reasons for engaging in such tasks. Although one can have a broad variety of goals or reasons in an achievement task, almost all theories only consider learning goals versus performance goals (Dweck, 1986) or, in other words, mastery goals versus performance goals (Ames, 1992). Maehr and Midgley (1991) refer to this distinction as being "task focused versus ability-focused". Nicholls (1984)—who started this new approach to motivation—distinguished between being task oriented and ego oriented.

To be mastery oriented, task focused or having learning goals means to be intrinsically motivated to understand, to master the achievement task, to learn, and to develop abilities and competencies. With such a goal orientation, challenging tasks are attractive, and mistakes and errors are possible but not perceived as failures. People don't mind working hard because high investment is not perceived as a compensation for low ability.

To be performance-oriented can mean two things: performance-approach oriented or performance-avoidance oriented. A performance orientation means that one is not focused on the task that must be learned or mastered but more on how one will do at the task (good or bad) and on how one will be perceived by others. An achievement task is understood as a competition with others, one wants to perform better than the other, to show high ability in comparison with others. Success means doing better than someone else. This is the performance-approach orientation.

Performance avoidance means that one does not want to show lack of ability or low ability (in comparison with others). Such individuals avoid challenging tasks because mistakes are understood as failures, undermining the self-esteem, which is mostly based on social comparisons. Performance-oriented students—certainly the avoidance-oriented ones—perceive high effort and persistence as a compensation for a lack of ability. That is why they do not invest much; they do not want to look less able. Skaalvik (1997) refers to the distinction between a self-enhancing ego orientation (e.g. outperforming others; looking smart) and a self-defeating ego orientation (e.g. not looking dumb). More recently, Elliot and McGregor (2001) developed a 2×2 achievement goal framework. In addition to the performance-approach and performance-avoidance goals, they also distinguish mastery-approach and mastery-avoidance goals. Mastery-approach refers to what used (until 2001) to be referred to as mastery goals. Examples of mastery-avoidance goals are "striving to avoid misunderstanding or failing to learn course material, striving not to make an error . . . focusing on not performing worse than before . . ." (Elliot & McGregor, 2001, p. 502). They report data showing that mastery-avoidance goals are more negative and have more debilitating effects than mastery-approach goals, but are more positive than performance-avoidance goals.

Children can, of course, have many more goals for which they study and work hard for school. Students may have social goals when they do an achievement task (Urdan & Maehr, 1995). Many students are largely extrinsically motivated, they have extrinsic goals (Lens & Decruyenaere, 1991; Pintrich & Schunk, 2002).

Achievement Goal-orientation Theory is mostly concerned about the task and performance goals students are oriented towards when studying, doing homework, or taking a test. Those are rather immediate goals, situated in the present or the very near future. It cannot, however, be denied that for may students schooling is future oriented: What they do at school (learning and performing) can also be directed towards (different types of) goals in the more distant future (e.g. to becoming a plumber). The present goals are instrumental goals or means towards more final goals in the future. In the following section we will discuss the motivational implications of different types of future time perspective that can be distinguished in motivational goal setting.

A motivating future

People formulate motivational goals they want to achieve because they will satisfy biological or psychological needs: Based on her need for achievement a student aspires to score an A in a certain course; she also plans to become a medical doctor in a developing country because she expects this to be, for her, an optimal way of self-realization. This example shows how different goals can be situated at different moments in the future (e.g. at the end of the semester; after finishing medical school; in adult life). Goal setting creates a future time perspective and the anticipation of future goals can motivate present goal-oriented actions. Many of the goals we strive for are means towards other goals in the future (e.g. to pass the entrance examination for medical school, to become a medical doctor first and then a practitioner in a developing country). This type of future goals and future-oriented motivational means–end structures (achieving more immediate subgoals as means for achieving more final goals in the more distant future) gives utility value (Wigfield & Eccles, 2002) to present actions and subgoals and it creates instrumental motivation. The individual is then also motivated to achieve the immediate goal as a means towards one or more future goals.

To the extent that an activity is motivated by future goals, it is not in itself rewarding. Instrumental motivation is—by definition—a type of extrinsic motivation. Also, Eccles (1984) characterized "utility value" as a form of extrinsic motivation and "interest value" as a form of intrinsic motivation. Raynor (1981), however, elaborated Atkinson's theory of achievement motivation by incorporating the motivational effects of future successes that are contingent on present success. The present and the future goals are intrinsic achievement-related goals: achieving success and avoiding failure in an achievement task. The present and the future goal belong to the same motivational category: success in an achievement task. Hence, the present motivation that originates in the future goals is of the same type as the motivation that finds its origin in the present task: intrinsic achievement motivation (to strive for success and to avoid failure, as such). For Husman and Lens (1999), this is endogenous instrumentality. When the present and future goals do not belong to the same motivational category they call it exogenous instrumentality (e.g. an intrinsically motivated action here and now to achieve an extrinsic goal in the future). Lens and Rand (1997) argued that instrumental motivation does not necessarily undermine present intrinsic motivation. It depends on the type of relationship between present and future goals. In more recent research we have repeatedly shown that the present intrinsic motivation and task orientation will be facilitated when the task is instrumental for achieving the opportunity to strive for the same type of goal(s) in the future, certainly when this goal striving can happen in an autonomy-supportive context (Lens, Simons, & Dewitte, 2002; Simons, Dewitte, & Lens, 2000, 2003, in press). Research on the motivational effects of different types of being future oriented is mostly limited to the learning and performance goals. It needs to be extended to other motivational domains such as affiliation, prosocial behavior, religion, and/or spirituality.

A cross-cultural approach

As for most, if not all, theories in psychology, theories of motivation were and still are mostly based on empirical research in Western cultures, more specifically in North America and Western Europe. For example, the theory of achievement motivation (Atkinson & Feather, 1966; McClelland et al., 1953) defines success, failure, and competition in a typical male-dominated, individualistic Western society. Cross-cultural research was limited to comparing employees' (e.g. entrepreneurs) scores for the need for achievement and work attitudes (McClelland, 1961). The same is true for the work on power motivation (McClelland, 1975) and the need for affiliation (Mehrabian & Ksionzky, 1974). This raises the question of the generality of these theories for other ethnic groups and cultures around the world (Berry, Poortinga, Segall, & Dasen, 2002). Do hypotheses based on Western theories of motivation hold true in other cultures? Do typical Western definitions of psychosocial needs such as achievement, power, affiliation, and curiosity, apply in other cultures or ethnic groups? Do they have the same meaning in different cultures? Are there cultural differences in motivational processes or motivational functioning (e.g. their components, individual and situational determinants, behavioral and emotional consequences)?

Even if there are motivational universals, these may vary across cultures in the way they develop, are expressed or should be measured (Berry et al., 2002, p. 4). Until fairly recently, such a cross-cultural approach was lacking in motivational psychology, certainly in more basic research (Heckhausen, 1991; Reeve, 2005). But the picture is changing, perhaps more so in more applied motivational research in organizational and educational psychology. Research on work motivation and student motivation refers to the importance of taking into account the important role of ethnic and cross-cultural differences (Latham & Pinder, 2005; McInerney & Van Etten, 2001; Pintrich & Schunk, 2002).

Motivational psychology has become very cognitive: Goal setting, planning, anticipating future outcomes of present behavior and persistent goal striving are much studied motivational phenomena. One might wonder if such a rational approach to motivation and goal-oriented actions has the same validity for different ethnic subgroups in, for example, the USA or Australia, or for minority students in Western Europe (Phalet, Andriessen, & Lens, 2004; Phalet & Lens, 1995).

Achievement Goal Theory was originally developed and validated in research with mostly white North American students, but was very soon cross-validated in many other Western and non-Western cultures (Kaplan & Maehr, 2002). It is indeed important to know if: (1) the definition of and the distinction between task goals and (competitive) performance goals; (2) the structure of the (adapted; translated) questionnaires measuring those goal-orientations; and (3) the behavioral and well-being correlates of the different goal orientations are the same in different cultures and ethnic groups (Bempechat & Boulay, 2001; Matos, Vansteenkiste, & Lens, unpublished data; McInerney & Van Etten, 2002).

The same types of question must be raised regarding the Self-determination Theory (SDT) and its distinction between three basic human needs and two types of behavioral regulation (autonomous vs. controlled). SDT maintains that autonomously regulating one's behavior should yield beneficial effects for individuals in all cultures (Ryan & Deci, 2003), even collectivistic cultures that more strongly emphasize the development and maintenance of social bonds. This universalistic claim was doubted by some cross-cultural researchers (e.g. Cross & Goore, 2003; Markus & Kitayama, 1991, 2003) who argued that the pursuit of autonomy, when defined as the striving for independence, individualism, and uniqueness, represents a typical Western phenomenon. Therefore, individuals living in collectivistic (instead of individualistic) societies or holding an interdependent (instead of independent) self-concept would not benefit from autonomously regulating their behavior. Unfortunately, in criticizing SDT, cross-cultural researchers misinterpret SDT's conceptualization of autonomy. Specifically, whereas cross-cultural researchers' concept of independence refers to the *inter*personal issue of not relying on others, autonomy, as defined within SDT, reflects the *intra*personal and phenomenological experience of volition and choicefulness. Within SDT, the opposite of autonomy is not dependence, that is, relying on others for support or guidance, but "heteronomy", that is, the experience of feeling controlled and manipulated (Ryan & Deci, 2003). As a consequence, the constructs of autonomy and independence are largely orthogonal. One can willingly accept guidance or support from without, but one can also feel coerced to submit to the advice or the instruction. To put it differently, autonomy does not necessarily imply the denial of reliance on others and does not require the separation from relations (Ryan & Deci, 2003), as (implicitly) suggested by some cross-cultural perspectives (e.g. Iyengar & DeVoe, 2003; Markus & Kitayama, 2003). In contrast, feelings of autonomy and relatedness are compatible with SDT (Koestner & Losier, 1996). Consistent with SDT, studies have found that an autonomous regulation of one's behavior also positively predicts the well-being of individuals who live or have grown up in a collectivistic society, such as Russia (Chirkov & Ryan, 2001) or China (Vansteenkiste, Zhou, Lens, & Soenens, in press).

Conclusion

It was not our goal to give an exhaustive review of the field of motivational psychology. The field became too fragmentated to do so in a book chapter. We did, however, try to describe a few important developments in theory and research. It is quite evident that the cognitive (r)evolution in psychology in general had a strong impact on motivational psychology in particular. As a consequence, a Hullian kind of general motivational theory (Hull, 1943, 1952) was no longer searched for and was replaced by more limited or partial theories about more specific types of human concerns, goals, and motivations (Reeve, 2005). These acknowledge the richness and complexity of human psychological processes (such as motivation) that result from the higher cognitive functioning of human beings. Motivational research with human participants and animal research on motivation became two independent streams.

However, one can wonder if this divorce will last very long. We expect that it will develop soon into a LAT-relation (living-apart-together). Although the heyday of the cognitive approach in psychology are certainly not (yet) over, the biological approach to behavior and its underlying psychological processes is gaining in strength and scope. Given, on the one hand, the close and reciprocal interconnections between motivational and emotional processes and, on the other hand, the growing research on the biological underpinnings of emotions and their expressions, it is, at least for us, highly likely that the biological approach will become more important in the study of different (although perhaps not all) types of human motivation. But cross-cultural perspectives also need to receive more attention in motivational research (different ethnic groups living in the same country and culturally very different societies, e.g. Western, Eastern and African cultures). The broader validity of motivational theories, the (functional) meaning of the concepts involved, and the validity/reliability of the measures also need much more research attention.

It is true that the field of motivational psychology suffered a lot from the cognitive revolution in psychology in the 1970s and 1980s, but since then a lot has changed. Basic and more applied research on motivation and emotion (in education, organizations, sports, health, etc.) is thriving again.

References

Allport, G. W. (1961). *Patterns and growth in personality*. New York: Holt, Rinehart & Winston.

Ames, C. (1992). Classrooms: Goals, structures, and student motivation. *Journal of Educational Psychology, 84*, 261–271.

Atkinson, J. W. (Ed.). (1958). *Motives in fantasy, action, and society*. Princeton, NJ: Van Nostrand.

Atkinson, J. W. (1964). *An introduction to motivation*. New York: Van Nostrand.

Atkinson, J. W. (1974a). Motivational determinants of intellective performance and cumulative achievement. In J. W. Atkinson & J. O. Raynor (Eds.), *Motivation, and achievement* (pp. 389–410). Washington, DC: Hemisphere.

Atkinson, J. W. (1974b). Strength of motivation and efficiency of performance. In J. W. Atkinson & J. O. Raynor (Eds.), *Motivation, and achievement* (pp. 193–218). Washington, DC: Hemisphere.

Atkinson, J. W., & Birch, D. (1970). *The dynamics of action*. New York: Wiley.

Atkinson, J. W., & Birch, D. (1978). *Introduction to motivation*. New York: Van Nostrand.

Atkinson, J. W., & Feather, N. T. (1966). (Eds.), *A theory of achievement motivation*. New York: Wiley.

Bandura, A. (1991). Self-regulation of motivation through anticipatory and self-regulatory mechanisms. *Nebraska Symposium on Motivation, 38*, 69–104.

Bempechat, J., & Boulay, B. A. (2001). Beyond dichotomous characterizations of student learning: New directions in achievement motivation research. In D. M. McInerney & S. Van Etten (Eds.), *Research on sociocultural influences on motivation and learning* (Vol. 1, pp. 15–36). Greenwich, CT: Informagion Age.

Bernard, L. L. (1924). *Instinct: A study of social psychology*. New York: Holt.

Berry, J. W., Poortinga, Y. H., Segall, M. H., & Dasen, P. R. (2002). *Cross-cultural psychology: Research and applications*. Cambridge, MA: Cambridge University Press.

Cameron, J. (2001). Negative effects of reward on intrinsic motivation – A limited phenomenon: Comment on Deci, Koestner, and Ryan (2001). *Review of Educational Research, 71*, 29–42.

Chirkov, V. I., & Ryan, R. M. (2001). Parent and teacher autonomy support in Russian and U.S. Adolescents: Common effects on well-being and academic motivation. *Journal of Cross Cultural Psychology, 32*, 618–635.

Cross, S. E., & Gore, J. S. (2003). Cultural models of the self. In M. R. Leary & J. P. Tangney (Eds.), *Handbook of self and identity* (pp. 536–566). New York: Guilford Press.

deCharms, R. (1968). *Personal causation: The internal affective determinants of behavior*. New York: Academic Press.

Deci, E. L. (1975). *Intrinsic motivation*. New York: Plenum Press.

Deci, E. L., Koestner, R., & Ryan, R. M. (2001). Extrinsic rewards and intrinsic motivation in education: Reconsidered once again. *Review of Educational Research, 71*, 1–27.

Deci, E. L., & Ryan, R. M. (1985). *Intrinsic motivation and self-determination in human behavior*. New York: Plenum.

Deci, E. L., & Ryan, R. M. (Eds.). (2002). *Handbook of self-determination theory*. Rochester, NY: The University of Rochester Press.

Dewitte, S., & Lens, W. (2000). Exploring volitional problems in academic procrastinators. *International Journal of Educational Research, 33,* 733–750.

Dweck, C. S. (1986). Motivational processes affecting learning. *American Psychologist, 41,* 1040–1048.

Eccles, J. (1984). Sex differences in achievement patterns. *Nebraska Symposium on Motivation, 32,* 97–132.

Elliot, A. J., & McGregor, H. A. (2001). A 2 × 2 achievement goal framework. *Journal of Personality and Social Psychology, 80,* 501–559.

Erez, M. (1977). Feedback: A necessary condition for the goal setting performance relationship. *Journal of Applied Psychology, 62,* 624–627.

Feather, N. T. (1982). (Ed.). *Expectations and actions: Expectancy-value models in psychology*. Hillsdale, NJ: Lawrence Erlbaum Associates Inc.

Freud, S. (1915/1949). Instincts and their vicissitudes. In *Collected papers of Sigmund Freud* (Vol. 4, pp. 60–83). London: Hogarth.

Gollwitzer, P. M. (1999). Implementation intentions: Strong effects of simple plans. *American Psychologist, 54,* 493–503.

Gollwitzer, P. M., & Bargh, J. A. (1996). *The psychology of action: Linking cognition and motivation*. New York: Guilford Press.

Heckhausen, H. (1991). *Motivation and action*. Berlin: Springer-Verlag.

Hull, C. L. (1943). *Principles of behavior*. New York: Appleton-Century Crofts.

Hull, C. L. (1952). *A behavior system: An introduction to behavior theory concerning the individual organism*. New Haven, CT: Yale University Press.

Husman, J., & Lens, W. (1999). The role of the future in student motivation. *Educational Psychologist, 34,* 113–125.

Iyengar, S. I., & DeVoe, S. E. (2003). Rethinking the value of choice: Considering cultural mediators of intrinsic motivation. In V. Murphy-Berman & J. J. Berman (Eds.), *Nebraska symposium on motivation: Vol. 49. Cross-cultural differences in perspectives on the self* (pp. 129–176). Lincoln, NE: University of Nebraska Press.

Kaplan, A., & Maehr, M. (2002). Adolescents' achievement goals: Situating motivation in sociocultural contexts. In F. Pajares & T. Urdan (Eds.), *Academic motivation of adolescents* (pp. 125–167). Greenwich, CT: Information Age.

Koestner, R., & Loiser, G. E. (1996). Distinguishing reactive and reflective forms of autonomy. *Journal of Personality, 64,* 465–494.

Kuhl, J., & Beckman, J. (Eds.). (1994). *Volition and personality: Action versus state orientation*. Seattle, WA: Hogrefe & Huber.

Latham, G. P., & Pinder, C. C. (2005). Work motivation theory and research at the dawn of the twenty-first century. *Annual Review of Psychology, 56,* 485–516.

Lens, W. (1986). Future time perspective: A cognitive–motivational concept. In D. R. Brown & J. Veroff (Eds.), *Frontiers of motivational psychology* (pp. 173–190). New York: Springer-Verlag.

Lens, W., & Decruyenaere, M. (1991). Motivation and demotivation in secondary education: Student characteristics. *Learning and Instruction, 1,* 145–159.

Lens, W., & Rand, P. (1997). Combining intrinsic goal orientations with professional instrumentality/utility in student motivation. *Polish Psychological Bulletin, 28,* 103–123.

Lens, W., Simons, J., & Dewitte, S. (2002). From duty to desire: The role of students' future time perspective and instrumentality perceptions for study motivation and self-regulation. In F. Pajares & T. Urdan (Eds.), *Academic motivation of adolescents* (pp. 221–245). Greenwich, CT: Information Age Publishing.

Lepper, M. R., & Greene, D. (1978). *The hidden costs of reward: New perspectives on the psychology of human motivation.* Hillsdale, NJ: Lawrence Erlbaum Associates Inc.

Lewin, K. (1935). *A dynamic theory of personality.* New York: McGraw-Hill.

Locke, E. A., & Latham, G. P. (1990). *A theory of goal setting and task performance.* Englewood Cliffs, NJ: Prentice Hall.

Locke, E. A., & Latham, G. P. (2002). Building a practically useful theory of goal setting and task motivation: A 35-year odyssey. *American Psychologist, 57,* 705–717.

Maehr, M. L., & Midgley, C. (1991). Enhancing student motivation: A schoolwide approach. *Educational Psychologist, 26,* 399–427.

Markus, H. R., & Kitayama, S. K. (1991). Culture and the self: Implications for cognition, emotion, and motivation. *Psychological Review, 98,* 224–253.

Markus, H. R., & Kitayama, S. K. (2003). Models of agency: Sociocultural diversity in the construction of action. In V. Murphy-Berman & J. J. Berman (Ed.), *Nebraska symposium on motivation: Vol. 49. Cross-cultural differences in perspectives on the self* (pp. 1–57). Lincoln: University of Nebraska Press.

Maslow, A. H. (1954). *Motivation and personality.* New York: Harper.

McClelland, D. C. (1961). *The achieving society.* Princeton, NJ: Van Nostrand.

McClelland, D. C. (1975). *Power: The inner experience.* New York: Irvington.

McClelland, D. C. (1980). Motive dispositions: The merits of operant and respondent measures. In L. Wheeler (Ed.), *Review of personality and social psychology: I* (pp. 10–41). Beverley Hills, CA: Sage.

McClelland, D. C. (1987). *Human motivation.* New York: Cambridge University Press.

McClelland, D. C., Atkinson, J. W., Clark, R. A., & Lowell, E. L. (1953). *The achievement motive.* New York: Appleton Century Crofts.

McClelland, D. C., & Winter, D. G. (1969). *Motivating economic achievement.* New York: Free Press.

McInerney, D. M., & Van Etten, S. (Eds.). (2001). *Sociocultural influences on motivation and learning (Vol. 1).* Greenwich, CT: Information Publishing.

Mehrabian, A., & Ksionzky, S. (1974). *A theory of affiliation.* London: Lexington Books.

Miller, G. A., Galanter, E. H., & Pribram, K. H. (1960). *Plans and the structure of behavior.* New Holt: Holt, Rinehart, & Winston.

Murray, H. A. (1938). *Explorations in personality.* New York: Oxford University Press.

Nicholls, J. (1984). Achievement motivation: Conceptions of ability, subjective experience, task choice, and performance. *Psychological Review, 91,* 328–346.

Nuttin, J. (1984). *Motivation, planning, and action: A relational theory of behavior dynamics.* Leuven & Hillsdale, NJ: Leuven University Press & Lawrence Erlbaum Associates Inc.

Nuttin, J., & Lens, W. (1985). *Future time perspective and motivation: Theory and research method.* Leuven & Hillsdale, NJ: Leuven University Press & Lawrence Erlbaum Associates Inc.

Phalet, K., Andriessen, I., & Lens, W. (2004). How future goals enhance motivation and learning in multicultural classrooms. *Educational Psychology Review, 16,* 59–89.

Phalet, K., & Lens, W. (1995). Achievement motivation and group loyalty among Turkish and Belgian youngsters. In M. L. Maehr & P. R. Pintrich (Eds.), *Advances in motivation and achievement. Volume 9. Culture, motivation and achievement* (pp. 32–72). Greenwich, CT: Jai Press Inc.

Pinder, C. C. (1998). *Work motivation in organizational behavior.* Upper Saddle River, NJ: Prentice Hall.

Pintrich, P. R., & Schunk, D. H. (2002). *Motivation in education: Theory, research, and applications.* Upper Saddle River, NJ: Merrill/Prentice Hall.

Raynor, J. O. (1981). Future orientation and achievement motivation: Toward a theory of personality functioning and change. In G. d'Ydewalle & W. Lens (Eds.), *Cognition in human motivation and learning* (pp. 199–231). Leuven & Hillsdale, NJ: Leuven University Press & Lawrence Erlbaum Associates Inc.

Reeve, J. (2005). *Understanding motivation and emotion.* New York: Harcourt College Publishers.

Ryan, R. M., & Deci, E. L. (2000). Self-determination theory and the facilitation of intrinsic motivation, social development, and well-being. *American Psychologist, 55,* 68–78.

Ryan, R. M., & Deci, E. L. (2003). On assimilating identities to the self: A self-determination theory perspective on internalization and integration within cultures. In M. R. Leary & J. P. Tangney (Ed.), *Handbook of self and identity* (pp. 253–274). New York: Guilford Press.

Simons, J., Dewitte, S., & Lens, W. (2000). Wanting to have versus wanting to be: The effect of perceived instrumentality on goal orientation. *British Journal of Psychology, 91,* 335–351.

Simons, J., Dewitte, S., & Lens, W. (2003). "Don't do it for me, do it for yourself". Stressing the personal relevance enhances motivation in physical education. *Journal of Sport and Exercise Psychology, 25,* 145–160.

Simons, J., Dewitte, S., & Lens, W. (in press). The role of different types of instrumentality in motivation, study strategies, and performance: Know what you learn, so you'll know what you learn. *British Journal of Educational Psychology.*

Skaalvik, E. ((1997). Self-enhancing and self-defeating ego orientation: Relations with task avoidance orientation, achievement, self-perceptions, and anxiety. *Journal of Educational Psychology, 89,* 71–81.

Smith, Ch. (Ed.). (1992). *Motivation and personality: Handbook of thematic content analysis.* New York: Cambridge University Press.

Stipek, D. J. (2002). *Motivation to learn: Integrating theory and practice.* Boston, MA: Allyn and Bacon.

Urdan, T., & Maehr, M. (1995). Beyond a two-goal theory of motivation: A case for social goals. *Review of Educational Research, 65,* 213–244.

Vansteenkiste, M. (2005). *Intrinsic versus extrinsic goal promotion and autonomy support versus control: Facilitating performance, persistence, socially adaptive functioning, and well-being.* Unpublished doctoral dissertation. Leuven (Belgium): University of Leuven.

Vansteenkiste, M., Lens, W., De Witte, H., & Feather, N. (2005). Understanding unemployed people's job-search behaviour, unemployment experience and well-being: A comparison of expectancy-value theory and self-determination theory. *British Journal of Social Psychology*, *44*, 268–286.

Vansteenkiste, M., Zhou, M., Lens, W., & Soenens, B. (in press). Experiences of autonomy and control among Chinese learners. Vitalizing or immobilizing? *Journal of Educational Psychology*.

White, R. (1959). Motivation reconsidered: The concept of competence. *Psychological Review*, *66*, 297–333.

Wigfield, A., & Eccles, J. S. (2002). The development of competence beliefs, expectancies for success, and achievement values from childhood through adolescence. In A. Wigfield & J. S. Eccles (Eds.), *Development of achievement motivation* (pp. 91–120). San Diego: Academic Press.

Woodworth, R. S. (1918). *Dynamic psychology*. New York: Columbia University Press.

Yerkes, R. M., & Dodson, J. D. (1908). The relation of strength of stimulus to rapidity of habit formation. *Journal of Comparative and Neurological Psychology*, *18*, 459–482.

13 Perception: The pursuit of illusion

Nicholas J. Wade

Recording perception

Perception is an experience that results from stimulation of the senses. It can be examined in its own right, by psychophysical experiment, or it can be related to the processes in the nervous system that accompany the experience. The electrochemical activities initiated in the sensory receptors trigger nerve impulses in the sensory nerves, and these impulses are relayed to the brain. Behavior can, and usually does, result from this sequence of events. Thus, these behaviors provide records of action of the senses. In humans the range of behaviors is broad and includes describing the experiences initiated by sensory stimulation and the links it might have with previous stimulations. We refer to these as observations and we associate them with verbal descriptions. Observations provide the bedrock of perception and of other actions of the brain. Records of observation precede records of their verbal descriptions; that is, the products of art precede those of writing. Verbal descriptions of observations were refined by Greek philosophers, who also introduced theories to account for the characteristics of perception. Relatively little is known about the origins of visual art. Examples of marks made on tools and cave walls have been dated to many thousands of years ago, but we do not know when such activities began. Writing had its origins around 5000 years ago. The adoption of experimental methods to record observations is a much more recent development. An early example can be found in the work of Claudius Ptolemy (see Smith, 1996) on optics, but it was more widely adopted after the investigations of Isaac Newton (1704) on color phenomena.

The senses have evolved to make and maintain adaptive contact with the environment. Receptors for sources of environmental energy that have proved beneficial for survival have emerged and become more specialized for the needs of each species. Through the action of the senses an organism seeks sustenance, shelter, and sex to survive and reproduce. The process was described more poetically by that giant of evolution, Erasmus Darwin (1794), who wrote, in the first volume of *Zoonomia*: "The three great objects of desire, which changed the forms of many animals by their exertions to gratify them, are those of lust, hunger, and security" (p. 506). Thus, there is sensitivity to the visual, auditory, aromatic, and tactile characteristics of a mate; the smell, taste, texture, and appearance of food would be sought; and the environmental features that afford protection from the elements will be selected and fought over. As Erasmus Darwin hinted at, and his grandson Charles Darwin clarified and amplified, individual members of species compete for these resources and adapt to changes in the environment. Charles Darwin also indicated that communication via the senses provides social intercourse, which assists survival and accelerates the transmission of useful information. This occurred in species before humankind, but it is with human perception that we are principally concerned.

The senses of all species have become adapted to the demands of their survival and reproduction, and there is a great variety in the ways in which senses have evolved. In addition, the senses are linked to an intricately organized brain, which has evolved to extract more than the elements of material sustenance. It furnishes us with intellectual sustenance, too, and extracts from the patterns of sensory stimulation links to language and thought. Humans not only use their senses, they also muse about them. Paradoxically, much of this musing has concerned minor errors of perception (often called illusions) rather than the constancies of what we perceive. Experience of the world is generally stable, and the ability to perceive it is easily taken for granted. Objects have positions, shapes, and colors that seem to be perceived instantly, and we can reach for them or move to where they are, without any apparent effort. We can recognize small differences between objects and yet we can categorize them despite small differences. Clearly, there must be some process that gives rise to visual experience, and it is not surprising that throughout history students of the senses have found it fascinating. A variety of questions arises from such considerations; the questions have been asked since antiquity. If what we perceive is what we take to be true or factual about the world, are everyone's experiences the same? What is the perceptual world of infants like? What sorts of errors do we make in perceiving? Can perceptual experience be communicated to others? Artists, philosophers, physicians, and, more recently, psychologists, have tried to find answers to such questions, which can be considered among the most fundamental that can be posed about the human mind.

Although we perceive the world around us with alacrity and ease, we have no direct knowledge of how this experience comes about. In fact, it can often be hard to believe that there is any mechanism involved in perception at all; for most people, most of the time, perceptions are simply "given" as facts about the world that are obviously correct. Perception is not only a basic psychological process, but also a very remarkable one. Its success in providing us with accurate information about the characteristics of the world around us is an index of its power, because there are relatively few situations in which it is seriously in error. A perceptual process that gave rise to subjective experiences grossly different from physical reality would make survival virtually impossible. The function of perception is not to furnish us with subjective impressions of our surroundings and the significant objects in the environment. Rather, it is to provide an effective platform for action.

Perception engages all the senses but the language in which our experiences are expressed tends to reflect the operation of particular senses. It might seem as though the senses worked in isolation rather than in concert. The vocabulary of the senses is not evenly distributed either. Vision has the lion's share of words as well as work associated with our perceptual experiences. Moreover, within vision finer distinctions are made. Contour and color are considered as separate mechanisms. This results in space and color being treated as independent aspects of vision, and students tend to pursue one or the other. This was not the case when the initial steps were made at recording perception. The early artists used their skills to decorate and depict with whatever means were at their disposal.

Humans enjoy contemplating the experiences provided by the senses, and much of our language is associated with describing them. In human cultures considerable effort is devoted to enhancing perceptual experiences by decorating our bodies and our surroundings and by producing artifacts (like pictures) to stimulate the senses and to channel our contemplations. With so much emphasis on extending our perceptual experiences it is tempting to think of their function as enabling us to enjoy and describe them. Paradoxically, it is in the area of representation that we have the earliest records of human perceptual experience. We have evidence of perception from the past because records have been kept. We associate these records with written texts, but earlier marks of human perception have been left in the art that was produced before writing was invented.

Perception and error

Despite the long history of recording perceptions, attention continues to be directed to the minor deviations from constancy that we call errors of perception or illusions. The term "perceptual error" is a very strange one. There can only be perceptions. Errors are associated with some deviation from a reference or standard. Thus, an error of measurement refers to some deviation from a reading that can be shown (either by another instrument or by other observers) to be discrepant. By the same token, the term "misperception" is a misnomer. However, there is some utility in the term if the dimensions of time and space are incorporated. A discrepancy in the perception of the same object can occur over time, as Aristotle noted in the context of the motion aftereffect. In like manner, the color of a surface can be modified by surrounding it by one of a different color. In these cases, perceived object properties are variable. It is in this sense that perceptual errors were initially described (see Wade, 1998, 2005).

Errors in perception were remarked on before the basic perceptual processes were either described or appreciated. This was so because it was possible to compare observations of the same objects over time and to note any discrepancies between them. The modern definition of illusions applies to differences between the perception of figures and their physical characteristics. Consensus concerning an external reality did not exist in antiquity, and so attention was directed to those instances in which changes in perception occurred. That is, when the same object appeared to have different properties under different conditions. According to this observational definition of illusions, all that is required is an assumption of object permanence; thereafter, any changes in the appearance of the same object will be classified as illusions.

An abiding example of this is the variations in apparent sizes of celestial bodies. The moon illusion—its larger appearance near the horizon than high in the sky—is, of course, a size illusion, but it has also be interpreted as a distance illusion. The moon illusion presented an enigma in the past and it is one that still persists. Modern attempts at explaining it remain problematical (see Ross & Plug, 2002). It provides a quintessential example of illusion because the observations have been consistent but the interpretations have shown a progressive change: It was analyzed initially as a problem of physics, then physiology, and finally psychology.

Ptolemy and Ibn al-Haytham (also known as Alhazen; see Sabra, 1989) presented their interpretations of celestial illusions, but they were concerned with more general features of perception. Alhazen was more explicit in categorizing the three modes of vision in which illusions can occur. Illusions were to be understood in terms of the breakdown of the process of inference. Nonetheless, the categories he gave for the errors of sight were fewer than the visible properties he listed. Errors of inference were confined to distance, position, illumination, size, opacity, transparency, duration, and condition of the eye. After the Renaissance, linear perspective was one of the techniques of visual illusion that could be manipulated, as is evident from the remarks of Francis Bacon (1625/1857). The mythical House of Salomon, described by Bacon in his *New Atlantis*, displayed "all delusions and deceipts of sight" as evidence of the advancement of science. Size and distance played a prominent role in such deceipts.

Illusions as comparisons of percepts

Although emphasizing the veridicality of sensing in general, Aristotle did entertain the possibility of errors (illusions) entering into a particular sense. The examples he mentioned were those of color or sound confusion and errors in spatial localization of colors or sounds. Assuming that the physical world is stable, then an illusion occurs when the same object appears to have different properties (of color, position, size, shape, motion, etc.) under different circumstances. Aristotle's description of the motion aftereffect was based on a comparison of percepts: "When persons turn away from looking at objects in motion, e.g., rivers, and especially those which flow very rapidly, they find that the visual stimulations still present themselves, for the things really at rest are then seen moving" (Ross, 1931, p. 459b). The phenomenon was presumably considered worthy of note because the stones at the side of the river appeared stationary before peering at the flowing water but not afterwards (see Wade & Verstraten, 1998). The changing perception of objects was the source of Aristotle's interest in phenomena like afterimages, aftereffects, color contrasts, and diplopia. It was precisely such variation in perception that led to the Platonic distrust of the senses.

Ptolemy drew a distinction between subjective and objective aspects of visual phenomena, and devoted considerable space to errors of perception. Indeed, he was one of the first writers to provide a detailed account of illusions; they are classified, and then considered under the headings of color, position, size, shape, and movement. Alhazen adopted a similar analysis of the errors of direct vision although he extended the range of phenomena for which they occur.

Many commentators have argued that illusions are a modern preoccupation in the study of perception. This statement, when restricted to geometrical optical illusions, is certainly correct because they only received this name in the mid-nineteenth century. Moreover, the phenomena so called are often associated with a particular theoretical outlook. Empiricist philosophers, and those students of perception who followed them, set out from an ambiguous starting point. They assumed that the retinal image was static and impoverished, and that something had to be added from past experience to remove the equivocality. Illusions could intrude during this amplification of the retinal information (see Gregory, 2003). However, the studies of illusions (as errors of perception) have a much longer history, and it is one that is not tied to particular theoretical approaches. If perception of the same object properties undergoes change without any obvious external intervention, then an illusion can be said to have occurred. The benchmark applied is perception itself, bound with an assumption of object permanence.

Illusions as comparisons with physics

An illusion requires a yardstick or reference relative to which it can be assessed. In fact, underlying virtually all illusions are the mismatches of observation described above. However, in terms of interpretations the interest is applied to the source of the mismatch. A classic example is the apparent bending of a stick when immersed in water. There is a compelling contrast between the appearance of the stick in air and partially immersed, but does the stick change its characteristics? The investigation of aspects of optics derived from precisely such observations. Ptolemy examined such instances of refraction, and formulated some general properties of it.

However, it was the appreciation that the retinal image could be described in geometrical terms that provided the physical yardstick. In 1604, Kepler wrote: "Thus vision is brought about by a picture of the thing seen being formed on the concave surface of the retina. That which is to the right outside is depicted on the left on the retina, that to the left on the right, that above below, and that below above. Green is depicted green, and in general things are depicted by whatever colour they have . . . the greater the acuity of vision of a given person, the finer will be the picture formed in his eye" (Crombie, 1964, p. 150). Kepler formulated the problem that generations of students of vision have since attempted to resolve: How do we perceive the world as three-dimensional on the basis of a two-dimensional retinal image? Indeed, this "legacy of Kepler" can be considered as having defined the problem in terms of single, static retinal images rather than considering the starting point as binocular and dynamic (Wade, 1990). Kepler himself was cautious regarding the conclusions that could be deduced from the inverted and reversed retinal image: "I leave it to the natural philosophers to discuss the way in which this image or picture is put together by the spiritual principles of vision" (Crombie, 1964, p. 147). Philosophers have not been united in their opinions, but they have appreciated that physical optics was not the solution to vision.

Illusions as comparisons with physiology

The situation regarding the senses was radically revised in the nineteenth century, with developments in physics, anatomy, and physiology. Sources of stimulation could be specified and controlled more precisely. This had already occurred in the context of color, with Newton's methods of spectral separation of white light and mixing components of it (Newton, 1704). Thomas Young (1802) proposed that all colors could be produced by appropriately compounding three primaries; he suggested that the eye was selectively sensitive to each. Young (1807/2002) also introduced the term "energy" in the context of weight, and this concept was related by others to different dimensions of sensitivity, like light and sound.

The link between energy and sense organs was forged soon thereafter. Charles Bell (1811/2000) is noted for discovering that the anterior spinal nerve roots are motor (see Cranefield, 1974). His principal concern, however, was in specifying the senses and their nerve pathways to the brain. In the context of vision, the demonstration of variation in the pattern of stimulation resulting in the same experience had been known to Alcmaeon (fl. 500 BC): Pressure to the eye, even in darkness, produced the experience of light (see Grüsser & Hagner, 1990). Bell was able to bolster this observation with the application of electricity to the eye: "If light, pressure, galvanism, or electricity produce vision, we must conclude that the idea in the mind is the result of an action excited in the eye or in the brain, not any thing received, though caused by an impression from without. The operations of the mind are confined not by the limited nature of things created, but by the limited number of our organs of sense" (Bell, 1811/2000, p. 12). Bell's attempts to link perception with physiological processes in the visual system reflected the growing body of physiological evidence that was accruing in the nineteenth century. The pace quickened with developments in anatomy and physiology. Achromatic microscopes enabled cells to be seen, and electrical stimulation of nerve fibers led to the neuron doctrine.

The microscopic world was transformed by the introduction of powerful achromatic instruments in the 1820s, and rapid advances were made thereafter. The cell doctrine was most clearly articulated at the end of the next decade. Nerves were thought to consist of bundles of fibrils, filaments, capillaments, threads, or villi (as they were variously called), the dimensions of which were exceedingly small, but beyond the resolution of the early microscopes. Nonetheless, estimates of their dimensions were made on the basis of the limits of vision rather than those of microscopes. Moreover, it was a growing concern with vision and its functions that led to the estimates of nerve fibre diameters. What is, perhaps, more remarkable is that the speculations were made before the cell doctrine had been proposed and before the structure of nerve cells was established (Wade, 2004b).

With the growth of knowledge about cells and neurons they were used increasingly to interpret perceptual phenomena. That is, structure was used to define function. This was epitomized in the writing of Helmholtz (1867/2000). He gave an account of the structure of the retina in his *Handbüch der physiologischen Optik*, and he applied it to the interpretation of visual resolution in terms of the size of retinal elements. The views he expressed were bolstered by the recent microscopic revelations.

Visual resolution provides a good example of the manner in which structure and function have been related. In the eighteenth century, when little about detailed anatomical structure was known, function (in terms of measures of visual resolution) determined structure (the dimensions of retinal elements). With increasing microscopic knowledge about sense organs, structure was used to define function.

The nineteenth-century instrumental and response revolutions

The nineteenth century witnessed an explosion of experimental ingenuity in all areas of science. Natural philosophers devised the principles on which the perception of color, motion, and depth could be rendered experimentally tractable. Young (1802) speculated that color perception could be based upon the detection of three primaries and Maxwell (1855) provided experimental support for this trichromatic theory. Faraday (1831) suggested how successive images presented in close temporal sequence could result in the perception of movement, setting in train the long line of research on stroboscopic motion (see Wade, 2004a). Talbot (1834), before he turned to photography, established a lawful relationship between apparent brightness and intermittent light stimulation. Wheatstone (1838, 1852) demonstrated that depth could be synthesized from two slightly disparate images presented to separate eyes, dissociating depth perception from its object base. William James (1890) noted that Wheatstone's first paper: "contains the germ of almost all the methods applied since the study of optical perception. It seems a pity that England, leading off so brilliantly the modern epoch of this study, should so quickly have dropped out of the field. Almost all subsequent progress has been made in Germany, Holland, and, *longo intervallo*, America" (pp. 226–227). Wheatstone also developed the electromagnetic chronoscope that was subsequently used for reaction time measurements (see Edgell & Symes, 1906).

Helmholtz (1867/2000) was particularly attracted to the experimental approach and his students developed methods further (see Cahan, 1993). Boring (1942) remarked that Helmholtz carried the torch for philosophical empiricism in a hostile Kantian climate, as did his erstwhile assistant Wundt. However, their brands of empiricism were quite different. Helmholtz borrowed the notion of unconscious inference from Berkeley (1709) to account for characteristics of color and space perception, and the concept is still active in some theories. Wundt (1874) was more ambitious and applied empiricist and associationist ideas to account for consciousness itself. His ideas were carried to America by the likes of Titchener, whose structuralist theory was not widely followed and in fact opposed by the theories of both Gestalt and behaviorism.

Thus, the senses were at the center of many of the dramatic departures in the nineteenth century, and the experimental advances in turn influenced theories of perception. In the 1830s, Weber (1834) demonstrated that the nuances of visual discrimination could be measured, by applying what became called psychophysical methods; Plateau (1833) devised a contrivance for synthezising visual motion from a series of static pictures; Wheatstone (1838) demonstrated that depth perception was influenced by retinal disparity; Treviranus (1837) described the cellular structure of the retina, heralding a new era for visual science, in which function could be related to microscopic structure. These instruments, and many others that were invented in the latter half of the nineteenth century, greatly expanded the range of visual phenomena, and the ways in which they could be investigated.

The strides made up to the middle of the nineteenth century at stimulus control, via novel instruments, were not matched by attempts to measure the characteristics of the ensuing percepts. The response was not accorded the attention that was lavished on the stimulus. This was about to change, and the measurement of responses became a prominent component in establishing psychology as a discipline independent of philosophy or physiology. In fact, the changes had been quietly afoot for some time. Weber reported his experiments on sensory discriminations of touch and temperature in 1834 and 1845 (see Ross & Murray, 1978). This was followed by the synthesizing studies of Fechner (1860), who integrated Weber's fraction to provide the basis for the new discipline of psychophysics—the investigation of the links between psychological dimensions of perception and their physical correlates. From the mid-nineteenth century, new methods were developed for studying perception and performance that distinguished psychology from both philosophy and physiology, and the arbitrary birth of the independent discipline is often taken as the founding by Wundt of the Institute of Experimental Psychology at Leipzig in 1879. The founding fathers of psychology—Weber, Fechner, and Helmholtz—who influenced Wundt were all students of perception, and their more general contributions were based firmly on their perceptual research. Responses were measured in a variety of ways at Wundt's Institute. Foremost was the application of the new psychophysics, but this was followed by measurement of reaction times. Wundt, like Helmholtz, was an empiricist and an associationist, and the motor components of perception and learning were of central importance.

Distal and proximal comparisons

The importance of function over structure was re-emphasized by the Gestalt psychologists in the early twentieth century. They drew a distinction between the distal and the proximal stimulus, and this was used to assess perception and its veridicality. If we understand something about the transmission of light through different media, then we should incorporate it in our definition of perception and of illusions. If the light striking the retina (the proximal stimulus) has been transformed in some way, it would be remiss not to incorporate that knowledge in the analysis of its perception. Therefore, Gestalt psychologists would say that an illusion occurs when there is a mismatch between the proximal stimulus and perception.

The Gestalt movement had its origins (as did behaviorism) in the rejection of the "New Psychology" of Wundt. The reasons, however, were quite different. Behaviorists rejected Wundt's methods whereas Gestaltists rejected Wundt's atomism. In redefining psychology as the study of behavior, Watson (1913) turned his back on its short history as the study of conscious experience. He avoided working with human subjects because he considered that introspection was unreliable and an unsuitable method on which to base any science, and so established the rat and the maze as the subjects for psychology. His views were both radical and initially unpopular, but they were propagated with a religious fervor. His dissatisfaction was with the method rather than the theory; in fact behaviorist theory was also empiricist and associationist.

The Gestalt psychologists opposed Wundt's atomism, considering that complex percepts could not be reduced to simple sensory elements. Wertheimer redefined psychology as the study of configurations or *Gestalten*. Gestalt psychology had its origins in perception but its ambition extended throughout the whole of psychology (see Ash, 1995). Its precursors were to be found in Kant's innate categories of space and time, and in Goethe's phenomenology. Wertheimer (1912) conducted a series of experiments on apparent movement—motion seen between two stationary and separated stimuli when presented in rapid succession. The inability to distinguish between real and apparent motion was taken as damning any approach that explained perception in terms of its sensations. Perception was considered to be holistic rather than atomistic: "There are wholes, the behaviour of which is not determined by that of their individual elements, but where the part-processes are themselves determined by the intrinsic nature of the whole. It is the hope of Gestalt theory to determine the nature of such wholes" (Wertheimer, 1938, p. 2). Not only was it said that the whole is more than the sum of its parts, but the perception of the whole is prior to that of its parts. Publication of Wertheimer's thesis on the phi phenomenon, in 1912, is taken as the origin of Gestalt psychology; it was principally concerned with perception, and a range of robust demonstrations was devised to support its holistic nature. Much of its attraction lay in the power of the perceptual demonstrations (see Wertheimer, 1922, 1923).

Koffka was the second member of the Gestalt triumvirate. He served as a subject in Wertheimer's experiments on the phi phenomenon, which were conducted in Frankfurt in 1910. After being apprised of their significance Koffka (1922) became the leading advocate of the Gestalt approach. He used Gestalt concepts in studies of development and thinking, and he made American psychologists aware of the new movement in his writings and lectures on Gestalt psychology in the United States. Koffka posed the fundamental question of "Why do things look as they do?" He also emphasized that visual perception is three-dimensional and that our perception is in terms of the object properties (the distal stimulus) rather than those at the receptor surface (the proximal stimulus).

Köhler introduced the concept of field forces operating in both perception and in its underlying neurophysiology. Moreover, the brain processes were considered to be isomorphic (having the same form) with the percept, so that principles of brain function could be inferred from perceptual phenomena. He went on to develop a speculative neurophysiology based mainly on the principles of perceptual grouping and on his experiments with figural aftereffects. It could be said that these speculations did more to hasten the demise of Gestalt theory than any other factor: neurophysiologists failed to find any evidence for such fields of electrical activity in the brain, and so tended to dismiss Gestalt theory in general rather than Köhler's (1930, 1940) unsuccessful attempt at neuroreductionism in particular. The robust visual phenomena at the heart of Gestalt psychology remained an enigma.

Wertheimer formulated some descriptive rules for perceptual organization and produced a wide range of demonstrations that could be used to support them. The principles were described by Wertheimer in two papers published in 1922 and 1923; they appeared in the journal *Psychologische*

Forschung (now *Psychological Research*), which the Gestalt psychologists founded to propagate their theory. The figures used by Wertheimer consisted mainly of open and closed circles. The initial and fundamental perceptual process is the separation of a figure from its background, because all the other grouping principles can only operate with segregated figures. Normally, a figure is defined by contours that surround it completely, whereas the ground is larger or lacking a defined boundary. Under certain circumstances neither of these conditions are met, and perceptual instability ensues—first one part and then the other is seen as figure, and this perceptual alternation continues.

Most of the remaining demonstrations of Gestalt grouping principles have clearly segregated figures; they are usually outline drawings, and these are shown to observers who are asked to describe what they see. The main grouping principles were said to be proximity, similarity, symmetry, good continuation, goodness of figure, and closure. Many more organizing principles have been described by Gestalt psychologists, although these are the main ones. Their intention initially was to provide an alternative theory of active, innately organized perception to counter the passive, structuralist views of Wundt and his adherents. The theory was supported by these demonstrations, which drew on phenomenology. However, it should be noted that the demonstrations themselves were not representative of normal object perception because they were based upon line drawings. That is, the evidence for the principles of organization is based upon the manner in which two-dimensional pictures are perceived rather than three-dimensional objects.

Twentieth-century illusions

The pursuit of perception in the twentieth century has followed many paths: It became even more interdisciplinary than it was in the nineteenth century. The strides made in physiology and computer science impacted critically on observation, experiment, and theory. The discovery by Hubel and Wiesel (1962) of single cells in the visual cortex that respond to oriented edges fuelled a fury of research. Similarly, the development of high-speed digital computing changed the ways in which human information processing was conceived. Thus, many of the paths have been determined by advances in technology, which have rendered aspects of perception experimentally tractable. Others have explored aspects of perception that were neglected in the nineteenth century.

One of these is the developmental dimension. Charles Darwin (1877) had earlier made a detailed record of his firstborn's development from a few days to over two years of age, and these were published in the journal *Mind*; they implicitly suggest that the development of the individual mirrors the evolution of species. Evolutionary theory transformed biology and it was the motive force in defining a distinct brand of American psychology.

Uncovering the details of infant perception has been one of the achievements of twentieth-century psychology.

The developmental dimension

William James remarked, from his armchair, that "The baby, assailed by eyes, ears, nose, skin, and entrails at once feels it all as one great blooming, buzzing confusion" (1890, p. 488). The conclusion concerning infantile confusion was based on the observation of their seemingly random and chaotic movements. More detailed scrutiny indicated that some aspects of behavior were systematic and could be used to determine what interests infants. Many novel methods were devised to study infant vision in the 1960s. For example, it was noted that infants spent different amounts of time fixating on visual patterns and so infant perceptual discrimination was inferred from the patterns of preferential fixation. Recordings of eye movements in infants only a few days old showed that they were concentrated on contours or corners of simple patterns. When a stimulus is presented many times the response to it typically declines or habituates. Habituation to repeated presentations of patterns provided another source of inference regarding discrimination, particularly when novel patterns were presented; if the infants dishabituated, then it was assumed that the novel pattern was discriminated from the habituated pattern. Operant conditioning techniques were applied to demonstrate the emergence of perceptual constancies. These methods were refined and the course of perceptual development began to be charted.

To extract the spatial detail from an object it needs to be focused on the retina, and the state of focus will need to change for objects at different distances. This process of accommodation is poorly developed at birth and newborns can only focus on objects within their reach. Indeed, the receptors in the retina are not fully developed at birth nor are the nerve cells in the visual cortex, and so their development is likely to have a profound effect on what can be seen. It is not surprising, therefore, that the visual acuity of the newborn is more than ten times poorer than that of adults, but it improves rapidly in the first months of life until it reaches almost adult level at age six months. Similarly, infants in the first few months of life are not able to detect low contrast patterns (where the differences between the lightest and darkest parts are small) that are readily detectable by adults.

The cortical mapping of visual receptive fields had an unexpected influence on the age-old nativist/empiricist debate, providing fuel for both sides. Hubel and Wiesel (1963) demonstrated that receptive fields were present prior to visual experience but that they could be modified by it. This applied to both binocularity and orientation selectivity. For example, the responsiveness of cortical cells to stimulation by either eye, present at birth, could be modified by monocular deprivation from birth. The timing of such modification was critical.

The new physiology

Wundt's "New Psychology" was accompanied by a "New Physiology", which was actively pursued by Ferrier, Hughlings Jackson, Sherrington and others. The continuing research on color vision was driven by the physical control of the stimulus, and by increasing understanding of receptor function and color anomalies. Indeed, it was the concept of "schema", developed within this new physiology by Head (1920), that was applied by Bartlett (1932) to skilled tasks of memory and perception. According to Bartlett "'Schema' refers to an active organization of past reactions, or of past experiences, which must always be supposed to be operating in the well-adapted organic response" (1932, p. 201). The constructive aspects of both memory and perception were emphasized at the expense of their holistic or sequential features. Perception was attached to a new type of theory linking perception to prediction and action.

Emphasis on the constructive and individual aspects of perception contradicted approaches that stressed perceptual constancy, and equations for quantifying this had been proposed by Brunswik (1928) and Thouless (1931). Both proposed ratios involving differences between perceived and projected values on the one hand and physical and projected on the other, although Thouless used logarithmic transformations in order to avoid anomalies that arose with the direct ratios. Thouless referred to perceptual constancy as "phenomenal regression to the real object", and provided plentiful evidence to support its operation for shape, size, orientation, brightness, and color perception.

The approach to perception adopted by Bartlett was applied to human operators of complex systems. The experimental research on perception in the 1940s harmonized with developments in cybernetics (Wiener, 1948), and Craik (1943) conflated the two by considering the human operator as a complex, self-organizing system. His studies of visual adaptation had indicated that there was constant feedback from previous and concurrent stimulation, and that it could be modeled by physical processes. He wrote: "Some of the flexibility of the perceptual process—for instance, the recognition of relational rather than absolute properties and of changes rather than constant stimulation, and a primitive type of abstraction— follows from the known properties of the physiological structure and can be imitated by physical mechanisms" (Craik, 1966, p. 6).

Feature detectors

Research on patterned stimulation at the receptor level had proceeded throughout the first half of the twentieth century, but its pace quickened thereafter. The glimmerings of pattern processing beyond the receptors emerged in the 1950s, and were amplified in the 1960s. When recordings of nerve impulses could be made from individual cells in the visual pathway, their adequate stimuli could be determined. Adrian (1928) coined the term "receptive field" and Hartline (1938) applied it to describe the region of the receptor surface over which the action of light modified the activity of a neuron. It came as something of a surprise that retinal ganglion cells of frog responded to quite complex features of stimulation (like moving dark regions of a specific visual angle, resembling a bug), and stimulus properties that excited or inhibited neurons were generally called "trigger features" (Barlow, 1953). Retinal ganglion cells of cat, on the other hand, were excited by rather simpler stimulus arrangements. Kuffler (1953) found that they were concentrically and antagonistically organized; if the center was excited by light, the surround was inhibited, and vice versa. Such an arrangement served the detection of differences in luminance well, but steady states would have little effect, since excitation nullified inhibition. This pattern of neural activity was retained in the lateral geniculate body, but it underwent a radical change at the level of the visual cortex. Hubel and Wiesel (1962, 1968) found that single cells in primary visual cortex (V1), first of cat then of monkey, responded to specifically oriented edges; they had different receptive field properties which were called simple, complex, and hypercomplex.

Physiologists refined the stimulus characteristics of trigger features throughout the 1960s, while psychologists sought their phenomenal counterparts. Almost any experiment involving contours paid lip service to Hubel and Wiesel, despite the tenuousness of the links between particular phenomena and their underlying physiology. At least an appeal to trigger features was considered preferable to reliance on the speculative neurophysiology advanced by Köhler (1940). Spatial illusions, for example, attempted to rise above their enigmatic status by adopting this reductionist path; despite its attractions the greatest success was found for contour repulsion (Blakemore, Carpenter, & Georgeson, 1970). The alternative lure of illusions was to relate them to the traditional empiricist concept of constancy (Gregory, 1963). The links between perception and physiology were made explicit for the motion aftereffect by Barlow and Hill (1963) resulting in an explosion of empirical studies examining their consequences. Barlow (1963) also investigated the link between visibility and retinal image motion using afterimages and optically stabilized retinal images.

The concept of channels or spatial filters emerged during the decade, and it was applied with particular rigor by Campbell and his colleagues to the detection of and adaptation to sine-wave gratings (see Campbell & Robson, 1968). The attraction of gratings was that they provided at one and the same time a definition of the stimulus and theory of the response to it. Craik characteristically foresaw the principle behind these developments: "the action of various physical devices which 'recognize' or respond identically to certain simple objects can be treated in terms of such [mathematical] transformations. Thus the essential part of physical 'recognizing' instruments is usually a filter—whether it be a mechanical sieve, an optical filter, or a tuned electrical circuit—which 'passes' only quantities of the kind it is required to identify and rejects all others" (1966, pp. 44–45).

Two visual pathways

As the functional specialization of visual areas of the cortex became better understood, so there have also been suggestions that different regions of the visual brain are organized into two rather different kinds of processing pathway or stream. An early idea was that of "two visual systems" (Ungerleider & Mishkin, 1982), which developed the distinction drawn in the 1960s between the "what" and "where" systems of the cortex and superior colliculi, respectively. Their proposal was that there were two distinct cortical streams of processing, the inferotemporal pathway or "ventral" route allowing the detailed perception and recognition of an object (its size, shape, orientation, and color) with the posterior parietal or "dorsal" route allowing the perception of an object's location. Milner and Goodale (1995) produced an important development of this theory by suggesting that these two parallel streams of visual processing are actually separately specialized for action (dorsal stream) and for visual experience of the world (ventral stream). The dorsal route is said to be the evolutionarily older visual system, which enables a creature to navigate through the world and catch prey. The ventral route is developed particularly in primates to allow the detailed perception and interpretation of objects and, it seems, a conscious awareness of these.

The distinction between conscious form perception and perception for action assists the interpretation of the puzzling phenomena of "blindsight". Human patients who had damage to the visual cortex that left them apparently blind could nevertheless respond much better than chance when asked to make certain kinds of visual judgment—particularly about the locations of lights that moved or had abrupt onsets (Weiskrantz, 1986). It seemed that not only was there residual visual capacity in areas of the visual system outside visual cortex, but that this activity apparently did not reach consciousness. The blindsight patients were not aware of the lights they pointed to, but felt as though they were guessing, or using some "feeling" about the target.

The information revolution

Information theory was developed in the context of telecommunications, and the mathematical measurement of information was formalized by Shannon and Weaver (1949); its powerful impact on perception was felt in the 1950s. Miller (1957) linked the concept of limited information capacity to absolute perceptual judgments. Attneave (1954) devised procedures to determine the locations of highest information in simple patterns. These corresponded to boundaries of brightness (contours) and particularly to abrupt changes in contour direction (corners). Support for the significance of contours in perception derived from two other sources—single-unit recordings from various levels in the visual pathway, and scanning eye movements. Indeed, early attempts to stabilize the retinal image by compensating for any involuntary eye movements resulted in disappearance of the target (Ditchburn & Ginsborg, 1952; Riggs & Ratliff, 1952). However, it was the qualitative concept of information processing rather than quantitative information measures that was to have lasting appeal. The perceiver was conceived of as a limited capacity information processor, and the information could be filtered, filed, or reformulated on the basis of stored events. Broadbent's (1958) model was amongst the first to formalize and represent pictorially the putative processing stages. He stated that the "advantage of information theory terms is . . . that they emphasize the relationship between the stimulus now present and the others that might have been present but are not" (1958, pp. 306–307). Thus, Broadbent combined Bartlett's approach of examining skilled tasks with Craik's modeling metaphor.

Theoretical attention shifted towards pattern recognition by both humans and computers because they were both thought of as information processors or manipulators of symbolic information. The patterns were typically outline figures or alphanumeric symbols and rival theories, based on template matching and feature analysis (Uhr, 1966), vied for simulated supremacy at recognition and one result was pandemonium (Selfridge, 1959)! Sutherland sounded a cautionary note on this endeavor; this was not generally heeded then nor has been subsequently: "Patterns are of importance to animals and man only in so far as they signify objects. It is the recognition of objects that is vital for survival and as a guide to action, and the patterned stimulation of our receptors is of use only because it is possible to construct from it the nature of the object from which it emanated" (1973, p. 157).

Although there were dangers in the oversimplification of the stimulus, the approach also allowed important tools to be developed to probe discrete visual achievements. One example was the random-dot stereogram developed by Julesz (1960). Wheatstone (1838) had employed outline figures for his stereoscope in order to reduce any monocular cues to depth, but he was acutely aware that some remained. Julesz employed the dawning power of the computer to produce pairs of matrices of black and white dots, the central areas of which were displaced with respect to the common backgrounds, and hence disparate. The displays looked amorphous when viewed by each eye alone, but when viewed binocularly patterns gradually arose or descended from the background. This not only spawned a new area called cyclopean perception (Julesz, 1971), but the technique was adopted in the clinic as a test for stereoscopic depth perception. Analogous developments in the temporal domain produced random-dot kinematograms, which were used by Braddick (1974) and others to make important discoveries about different types of motion processing.

The machine metaphor

The machine metaphor was to prove particularly attractive to experimental psychologists, although only relatively simple machines were enlisted initially. For example, Craik (1966) worked with analogue devices as the digital computer was still embryonic. Nonetheless, he did formalize the input, processing, and output components of servo-systems in a manner that could be applied to digital computers. When computing machines increased in speed and complexity, the tasks that they could simulate became more complex. Concepts from engineering, like information and self-organization, were also integrated with a growing knowledge of neurophysiology resulting in the computer becoming a metaphor for the brain.

The computers mounted for this metaphorical odyssey were digital and serial, but at around the same time the ground was being laid for principles of parallel processing. McCulloch and Pitts' (1943) model of the neuron provided the foundation for later connectionist models of pattern recognition, and the networks connecting perception to its underlying physiology were further woven by Hebb (1949) in his speculative synthesis of perception and learning. Hebb proposed that perceptual learning takes place when assemblies of cells fire together; their reverberating activity resulted in synaptic changes which further increased the probability of the nerves firing together. The functions of cell-assemblies and phase sequences were based on his neurophysiological postulate: "When an axon of cell A is near enough to excite cell B and repeatedly or persistently takes part in firing it, some growth process or metabolic change takes place in one or both cells such that A's efficiency, as one of the cells firing B, is increased" (Hebb, 1949, p. 62). Hebb's postulate is taken as providing the foundation for current connectionist models of recognition and learning despite the fact that the principle had been enunciated over 70 years earlier by Bain (see Wilkes & Wade, 1997). Hebb later applied the concepts to account for a wide range of phenomena, from stabilized retinal images to sensory deprivation.

Bartlett's emphasis on the constructive nature of perception found an echo in America in the "New Look" experiments, like those reported by Bruner and Postman (1947), where motivation was considered to interact with perception. Similar experimental investigations had been undertaken earlier by Brunswik (1934, 1935) who examined the perceived sizes of postage stamps of different value. Ames' many demonstrations of the ambiguities of stimulation and their perceptual resolutions (see Ittelson, 1952) were also accorded renewed attention in this cognitive climate. In these heady postwar years personality flirted with perception, but their liaison was not lasting. Certain subthreshold recognition phenomena were brought to their perceptual defence (McGinnies, 1949), but the sober verdict was not in their favour: "It would seem wise to regard with great caution the existence of limitations on speed and accuracy of perception imposed by personality factors, at least in normal observers" (Vernon, 1970, p. 237).

Computers and vision

Craik, as well as Turing (see Millican & Clark, 1996), anticipated that the computer would be a powerful tool to simulate theories of perception, as well as providing a metaphor for the processes of perception and cognition themselves. Since the late 1960s, the study of visual perception had been profoundly influenced by computers. As well as allowing scientists to collect or to analyze data more quickly, the digital computer provided a tool for the laboratory scientist to develop new ways of testing the visual system with novel kinds of visual displays. The move away from reliance on oscilloscopes to present sine wave and other simple patterns facilitated the increasing use of more naturalistic patterns, as well as those that can be constructed and manipulated in controlled ways. Computer developments also enabled the better recording of eye movements and the linkage of eye movements to changes in display features, allowing a number of groups to conduct ingenious experiments into the control of eye movements in reading (see Findlay & Gilchrist, 2003; Wade & Tatler, 2005). Computer developments also created new problems. Unknown non-linearities in screen display properties or their temporal characteristics present problems that were not initially foreseen, in addition to a variety of problems that have been termed visual stress.

During the 1970s, Marr (1976, 1982) set out to develop a complete framework for vision, spanning the very lowest level processes within the retina up to the process of visual object recognition. The key feature of Marr's theory was that vision can be understood at different levels. The first "computational" level is a theory of the task that the visual system is to solve, and an understanding of the constraints that can enable solution of that task. The second level, of "representation and algorithm", is a means of achieving the task, and the final "hardware implementation" level describes how the brain, or a computer, actually implements these algorithms in neural tissue or silicon. Marr argued that: "For the subject of vision, there is no single equation or view that explains everything. Each problem has to be addressed from several points of view—as a problem in representing information, as a computation capable of deriving that representation, and as a problem in the architecture of a computer capable of carrying out both things quickly and reliably" (1982, p. 5).

In addition to presenting a unified approach to different topics within vision, Marr and his colleagues presented a theory of the different stages of representation (called primal sketch, 2.5D sketch, three-dimensional models) involved in the interpretation of a retinal image. In so doing, Marr distinguished a stage that made explicit the three-dimensional layout of the world with respect to the viewer (the 2.5D sketch), and potentially more useful for action in the world than the more abstract three-dimensional models, which allowed object recognition. Despite this distinction, however, his framework fails to anticipate the more recent idea of a separation of visual pathways for action and for object categorization.

Marr's framework for visual object recognition was developed and extended by many others. Subsequent theories about object recognition, however, departed from Marr's economical object-centered representations to develop representational ideas based around the representation of multiple viewpoints. Thus, it is not the details of Marr's theory that have so far stood the test of time, but the approach itself.

Another key feature of Marr's theory was the principle of modularity: "Computer scientists call the separate pieces of a process its modules, and the idea that a large computation can be split up and implemented as a collection of parts that are as nearly independent of one another as the overall task allows, is so important that I was moved to elevate it to a principle: the principle of modular design" (1982, p. 102).

The new image

The activity of the human brain has been studied using external measurements of electrical and/or magnetic activity for some 80 years. Berger (1930) discovered that electrical activity could be measured by placing electrical conductors on the human scalp and amplifying and transcribing the resulting signals. This electroencephalogram (EEG) was an early and important tool for diagnosing brain damage, but also provided a research tool for examining electrical responses to events (event-related potentials, or ERPs). Productive research using ERPs to map cognitive activity in the brain was conducted in the last decades of the twentieth century, but there have always been problems of interpretation due to limited information about the spatial origins of ERP components. Subsequent developments of dense-mapped ERP and the related technique of using a magnetometer to record the magnetoencephalogram (MEG) and detect magnetic event-related fields (ERFs) attracted much more attention. In part, this was because the precise temporal information gained by these techniques could complement the spatial precision achieved with newer techniques of brain imaging.

Another technique based on magnetic fields generated in the cortex is called transcranial magnetic stimulation (TMS). Following the lead of Thompson (1910), alternating magnetic fields can be applied to restricted regions of the head to stimulate or to disrupt neural activity in some way. In TMS, a magnetic coil is positioned over a particular area of a subject's head and a current is briefly passed through the coil. The magnetic field so produced induces an electrical current in a specific part of the subject's brain (see Walsh & Cowey, 1998). The timing of such TMS is very precise and so it can be applied at known intervals after some visual stimulation has taken place. It is as if the technique produced virtual patients because the disruption is temporary.

Neuroimaging of visual function in normal human brains proceeded apace in the last decade of the twentieth century. Initially, positron emission tomography (PET) scans were used to examine the regional cerebral blood flow when volunteers looked at different kinds of visual patterns. A colored pattern produced activation in regions corresponding to monkey V1, V2 and V4. When the same pattern was shown in shades of gray, the activation in V4 was much reduced, suggesting that V4 was an area for the analysis of color in humans. Similarly, a moving compared with a static pattern produced specific activation of "human V5", and illusory motion seen in static patterns has also been attributed to this area (see Zeki, 1999).

These are sophisticated ways of examining human brain activity during perceptual processing but all techniques have drawbacks, and experiments must be designed with great care if they are to be clearly interpretable. In comparison to PET scans, magnetic resonance imaging (MRI) yields more precise spatial resolution. Developments in functional MRI (fMRI) allow activity to be temporally as well as spatially mapped, and it will be work using fMRI combined with developments in other technologies with more temporal precision such as TMS and MEG, which is likely to hold the key to understanding the neural processing of visual information by people.

The growth in visual neuroscience has revealed an increasingly complex, but elegant, picture and diagrams of visual areas, their interconnections, and their microstructure are likely to get increasingly complicated. For example, the route map of primate visual systems charted by Van Essen, Anderson, and Felleman (1992) would place great demands on a navigator. Evidence for the analytic separation of different aspects of the visual scene—motions, forms, colors, etc.—raises the question of how these elements become associated, or "bound". In addition to the problem of binding within the visual domain, however, there is the problem of how and when different modalities (vision, touch, hearing) become integrated or otherwise influence each other.

The new veridicality

Gibson (1966) sought to stem the cognitive current and developed a novel theory that owed more to Reid (1764) than to his own contemporaries: "When the senses are considered as perceptual systems, all theories of perception become at one stroke unnecessary. It is no longer a question of how the mind operates on the deliverances of sense, or how past experience can organize the data, or even how the brain can process the inputs of the nerves, but simply how information is picked up" (Gibson, 1966, p. 319). Gibson abolished the senses when he replaced them by perceptual systems. That is, the distinction between sensation and perception was abandoned, and perceptual systems afforded useful information for interaction with the external world: "We shall have to conceive the external senses in a new way, as active rather than passive, as systems rather than channels, and as interrelated rather than mutually exclusive. If they function to pick up information, not simply to arouse sensations, this function should be denoted by a different term. They will be called here *perceptual systems*" (Gibson, 1966, p. 47). Moreover, there was considered to be a perfect correlation between the stimulus and its perception; no stages of representation were involved in perception. The doctrine of specific nerve energies, that had informed almost all studies of the senses since the time of Müller (1843/2003), emphasized the indirectness of perception. The brain had access only to the nerve signals initiated by external objects, not to the objects themselves. Gibson cast aside this tradition in favor of direct perception. However, Gibson retained separate perceptual systems, which he called orienting, auditory, haptic–somatic, tasting and smelling, and visual. Despite Gibson's pejorative purview of conventional perceptual experiments, the strongest support for his position derived therefrom: Simplified dynamic dot patterns could be recognized far more easily than static ones (Johannson, 1964). Gibson's ideas established a new field of "ecological" optics, which has been tilled by many.

The 1960s saw the beginnings of a split between a "cognitive" approach, where the goal of vision could be seen as an abstract categorization of the objects of vision, and an "action" approach, where vision was part of an integrated system allowing manipulation of and navigation through the world. This distinction has matured in contemporary approaches to vision, both through the influence of Marr and through further developments in neuroscience and neuropsychology.

Illusions and veridicality

As mentioned at the beginning of the chapter, for an illusion to be so considered two measurements of the stimulus are required. The most common are the physical characteristics of the stimulus and some suitable index of its perception. Illusions were studied in the late nineteenth century because they were not amenable to the extant physiology—hence their place in psychology. They also fostered the use of two-dimensional stimuli in perceptual experiments, giving vision the aura of scientific respectability. Such stimulus manipulation is grist to the modern neuroscientist's mill, and so that a common stimulus language binds vision and neuroscience—the language of single stimulus dimensions. However, this degree of common stimulus control has nurtured a new neuroreductionism, and illusions are often interpreted in terms of underlying signs of neural activity. The giant step to solid objects remains elusive both for illusions and for neuroscience.

Illusions can provide signs for the neuroscientists to pursue. It is doubtful whether neuroscientists can provide signs to direct research on illusions until there is an adequate neurophysiological theory of visual processing. At present, there are sets of subtheories, which are overinterpreted in terms of visual psychophysics. It might seem unreasonable to demand a theory of neuroscience before applying it to visual perception, but I think it is realistic. It will take a long time, but that might be shorter than making many false starts, as has happened in the last decades of the twentieth century. It would also have the positive effect of making us concentrate on perception rather than its putative underpinnings. The conundrum is that there is a demand to conduct theory-driven experiments, and most of the theories are based on inadequate neuroscience. The need for a good perceptual taxonomy becomes pressing under such circumstances.

Many attempts were made throughout the twentieth century to classify illusions in a manner that facilitates interpreting them. For example, Gregory (1966, 2003) has presented a fascinating classification of illusions, in terms of ambiguities, distortions, paradoxes, and fictions. He has also pointed to the difficulty of defining what an illusion is. The interest in the physiological and cognitive categories of illusions is that interpretations at this level are no longer feasible. What is sought for these is an internal correlation with perception—either in terms of neurophysiological signals for the physiological or inferential processes for the cognitive. The point worth making again here is that we are only dealing with correlations, and the tenuous link between correlation and causation is well known.

Illusions freed psychology from physiology at its birth, now it is in danger of being strangled by it. The virtue of Gregory's classification is that it is tied to perception rather than to neuroscience: It emphasizes the primacy of measurements of vision over measurements of intervening processes.

Summary

Perception has been a continuing concern of philosophers for many centuries. A common thread that has linked the approaches to perception over this time-span has been a concern with the unusual and atypical; that is with illusions. Illusions have been defined in many different ways, but all have involved comparison with some reference. The constancies of perception have not received the same concerted attention.

The twentieth century can be thought of as the age of illusion, *par excellence*. The technological advances that were introduced expanded the ways in which stimuli could be presented so that novel phenomena were discovered and old ones were given new twists. Moreover, the responses elicited by the stimuli could be analyzed with far greater sophistication: Dynamic processes like eye movements could be fractionated and neural activity could be sampled in alert observers. Some phenomena weathered this technological storm and fitted to each passing fashion. For example, Addams (1834) observed the descending waters in the Falls of Foyers, in northern Scotland, and described the waterfall illusion. This was investigated sporadically throughout the nineteenth century but the vast majority of studies were conducted in the second half of the twentieth century (see Wade, 1994); whereas around two-dozen reports fell into the first period, well over 400 could be found in the second! A similar pattern applies to optical illusions generally (Zusne, 1967).

However, the illusion of the century was not a specific phenomenon but a preoccupation with a particular type of stimulus—the two-dimensional display. Drawings can easily be made and manipulated to produce stimuli for experiments. The task becomes easier when computer graphics are enlisted. Visual science has been seduced by such stimulus simplicity; it is evident in the topics that have been described in this chapter. Infant vision has been investigated predominantly with the stimuli that infants would never naturally encounter—two-dimensional displays rather than three-dimensional objects. A great deal has been discovered about the limits of vision in infants using such procedures—what they can discriminate at different developmental stages. However, we know little about the objects that they can discriminate because equivalent experiments have not been conducted. Indeed, the same applies to all aspects of object recognition. We know a lot about recognizing pictures of objects but not very much about object recognition.

The seductive allure of the pictorial image has amplified the legacy of Kepler—the belief that the first stage of vision is a two-dimensional image in the eye. The task of the theorist is then seen as restoring the third dimension. An impressive array of neurophysiological results can be brought to bear on this problem: Single cells in the visual cortex are excited by particular stimulus features and different visual modules process those features further. Most of the information is derived from the ideal assay for Kepler's legacy—an anaesthetized animal with a nonmoving eye. Neuroimaging techniques for studying human perception have generally supported these conclusions. Of course, the stimuli used in the constrained confines of the devices are pictorial. Much has been learned from the use of two-dimensional stimuli but sight must not be lost of the goal of perceptual research—understanding our interactions with a world of solid structures.

The history of studies of the perceptual process is essentially a history of art and illusion. Art has been produced by humans for thousands of years and it involves distilling aspects of perception and re-presenting them in a way that can be recognized by others. Paintings on cave walls are highly sophisticated because they can be recognized by observers who have had no contact with the civilizations that produced them. Perhaps it is this universality of the pictorial image that has proved so attractive to both observers and theorists of vision. When it was combined by Kepler with the principles of image formation in the eye its appeal was overwhelming. The metaphor of the picture-in-the-eye drives contemporary visual science in much they same way it did students in the seventeenth century. We now know much more about the optics of the eye and the physiology of vision, but the conceptual problems posed remain essentially unchanged.

References

Addams, R. (1834). An account of a peculiar optical phænomenon seen after having looked at a moving body. *London and Edinburgh Philosophical Magazine and Journal of Science, 5*, 373–374.

Adrian, E. D. (1928). *The basis of sensation*. London: Christophers.

Ash, M. G. (1995). *Gestalt psychology in German culture, 1890–1967: Holism and the quest for objectivity*. Cambridge, MA: Cambridge University Press.

Attneave, F. (1954). Some informational aspects of visual perception. *Psychological Review, 61*, 183–193.

Bacon, F. (1625/1857). *Sylva sylvarum: Or a natural history*. In J. Spedding, R. L. Ellis, & D. D. Heath (Eds.), *The works of Francis Bacon* (Vol. 2). London: Longman.

Barlow, H. B. (1953). Summation and inhibition in the frog's retina. *Journal of Physiology, 119*, 69–88.

Barlow, H. B. (1963). Slippage of contact lenses and other artifacts in relation to fading and regeneration of supposedly stable retinal images. *Quarterly Journal of Experimental Psychology, 15*, 36–51.

Barlow, H. B., & Hill, R. M. (1963). Evidence for a physiological explanation of the waterfall illusion and figural aftereffects. *Nature (London), 200*, 1345–1347.

Bartlett, F. C. (1932). *Remembering: A study in experimental and social psychology*. Cambridge, UK: University Press.

Bell, C. (1811). *Idea of a new anatomy of the brain: Submitted for the observations of his friends*, London: Published by the author; printed by Strahan and Preston. (Reprinted in N. J. Wade (2000). (Ed.), *The emergence of neuroscience in the nineteenth century* (Vol. 1). London: Routledge/Thoemmes Press.)

Berger, H. (1930). Über das Elektrenkephalogramm des Menschen. Zweite Mitteilung. *Journal für Psychologie und Neurologie, 40*, 160–179.

Berkeley, G. (1709). *An essay towards a new theory of vision*. Dublin: Pepyat.

Blakemore, C., Carpenter, R. H. S., & Georgeson, M. A. (1970). Lateral inhibition between orientation detectors in the human visual system. *Nature (London), 228*, 37–39.

Boring, E. G. (1942). *Sensation and perception in the history of experimental psychology*. New York: Appleton-Century.

Braddick, O. J. (1974). A short-range process in apparent motion. *Vision Research, 14*, 519–527.

Broadbent, D. E. (1958). *Perception and communication*. London: Pergamon Press.

Bruner, J. S., & Postman, L. (1947). Emotional selectivity in perception and reaction. *Journal of Personality, 16*, 69–77.

Brunswik, E. (1928). Zur Entwicklung der Albedowahrnehmung. *Zeitschrift für Psychologie, 109*, 40–115.

Brunswik, E. (1934). *Wahrnehmumg und Gegenstandwelt: Grundlegung einer Psychologie vom Gegenstand her*. Leipzig: Deuticke.

Brunswik, E. (1935). *Experimentelle Psychologie in Demonstrationen*. Vienna: Springer.

Cahan, D. (Ed.). (1993). *Hermann von Helmholtz and the foundations of nineteenth-century science*. Berkeley, CA: University of California Press.

Campbell, F. C., & Robson, J. G. (1968). Application of Fourier analysis to the visibility of gratings. *Journal of Physiology, 197*, 551–566.

Craik, K. J. W. (1943). *The nature of explanation*. Cambridge, UK: Cambridge University Press.

Craik, K. J. W. (1966). The nature of psychology. In S. L. Sherwood (Ed.), *A selection of papers, essays and other writings by the late Kenneth J. W. Craik*. Cambridge, UK: Cambridge University Press.

Cranefield, P. F. (1974). *The way in and the way out: François Magendie, Charles Bell and the roots of the spinal nerves*. Mount Kisco, NY: Futura.

Crombie, A. C. (1964). Kepler: De modo visionis. In *Mélange Alexandre Koyré I. L'Aventure de la science* (pp. 135–172). Paris: Hermann.

Darwin, C. (1877). A biographical sketch of an infant. *Mind, 2*, 285–294.

Darwin, E. (1794). *Zoonomia; or, the laws of organic life* (Vol. 1). London: Johnson.

Ditchburn, R. W., & Ginsborg, B. L. (1952). Vision with a stabilized retinal image. *Nature (London), 170*, 36–37.

Edgell, B., & Symes, W. L. (1906). The Wheatstone–Hipp chronoscope: Its adjustments, accuracy, and control. *British Journal of Psychology, 2*, 58–87.

Faraday, M. (1831). On a peculiar class of optical deception. *Journal of the Royal Institution of Great Britain, 1*, 205–223.

Fechner, G. T. (1860). *Elemente der Psychophysik*. Leipzig: Breitkopf and Härtel.

Findlay, J. M., & Gilchrist, I. D. (2003). *Active vision: The psychology of looking and seeing*. Oxford, UK: Oxford University Press.

Gibson, J. J. (1966). *The senses considered as perceptual systems*. Boston, MA: Houghton Mifflin.

Gregory, R. L. (1963). Distortion of space as inappropriate constancy scaling. *Nature (London), 199*, 678–680.

Gregory, R. L. (1966). *Eye and brain: The psychology of seeing*. London: Weidenfeld and Nicolson.

Gregory, R. L. (2003). Delusions. *Perception, 32*, 257–261.

Grüsser, O.-J., & Hagner, M. (1990). On the history of deformation phosphenes and the idea of internal light generated in the eye for the purpose of vision. *Documenta Ophthalmologica, 74*, 57–85.

Hartline, H. K. (1938). The response of single optic nerve fibres of the vertebrate eye to illumination of the retina. *American Journal of Physiology, 121*, 400–415.

Head, H. (1920). *Studies in neurology*. London: Oxford University Press.

Hebb, D. O. (1949). *Organization of behavior: A neuropsychological theory*. New York: Wiley.

Helmholtz, H. (1867). *Handbuch der physiologischen Optik*. In G. Karsten (Ed.), *Allgemeine Encyklopädie der Physik* (Vol. 9). Leipzig: Voss. (Reprinted in Helmholtz, H. (2000). *Helmholtz's Treatise on physiological optics* (3 Volumes). (J. P. C. Southall Trans.). Bristol: Thoemmes.

Hubel, D. H., & Wiesel, T. N. (1962). Receptive fields, binocular interaction and functional architecture in the cat's visual cortex. *Journal of Physiology, 166*, 106–154.

Hubel, D. H., & Wiesel, T. N. (1963). Receptive fields of cells in striate cortex of very young, visually inexperienced kittens. *Journal of Neurophysiology, 26*, 994–1002.

Hubel, D. H., & Wiesel, T. N. (1968). Receptive fields and functional architecture of the monkey visual cortex. *Journal of Physiology, 195*, 215–243.

Ittelson, W. H. (1952). *The Ames demonstrations in perception: A guide to their construction and use*. Princeton, NJ: Princeton University Press.

James, W. (1890). *Principles of psychology* (Vol. 2). London: Macmillan.

Johannson, G. (1964). Perception of motion and changing form. *Scandinavian Journal of Psychology, 5,* 181–208.

Julesz, B. (1960). Binocular depth perception of computer-generated patterns. *Bell System Technical Journal, 39,* 1125–1162.

Julesz, B. (1971). *Foundations of cyclopean perception.* Chicago, IL: Chicago University Press.

Koffka, K. 1922. Perception: An introduction to Gestalt-theorie. *Psychological Bulletin, 19,* 531–585.

Köhler, W. (1930). *Gestalt psychology.* London: Bell.

Köhler, W. (1940). *Dynamics in psychology.* New York: Liveright.

Kuffler, S. W. (1953). Discharge pattern and functional organisation of mammalian retina. *Journal of Neurophysiology, 16,* 37–68.

Marr, D. (1976). Early processing of visual information. *Proceedings of the Royal Society of London, B176,* 161–234.

Marr, D. (1982). *Vision: A computational investigation into the human representation and processing of visual information.* New York: Freeman.

Maxwell, J. C. (1855). Experiments on colour as perceived by the eye. *Transactions of the Royal Society of Edinburgh, 21,* 275–298.

McCulloch, W. S., & Pitts, W. H. (1943). A logical calculus of the ideas immanent in nervous activity. *Bulletin of Mathematical Biophysics, 5,* 115–133.

McGinnies, E. (1949). Emotionality and perceptual defence. *Psychological Review, 56,* 244–251.

Miller, G. A. (1957). The magical number seven, plus or minus two: Some limits on our capacity for processing information. *Psychological Review, 63,* 81–97.

Millican, P. J. R., & Clark, A. (Eds.). (1996). *Machines and thought: The legacy of Alan Turing* (Vol. 1). Oxford, UK: Clarendon Press.

Milner, A. D., & Goodale, M. A. (1995). *The visual brain in action.* Oxford, UK: Oxford University Press.

Müller, J. (1843/2003). *Müller's Elements of physiology* (Vol. 2). (W. Baly Trans.) London: Taylor and Walton (Reprinted, Bristol: Thoemmes).

Newton, I. (1704). *Opticks: Or, a treatise of the reflections, refractions, inflections and colours of light.* London: Smith and Walford.

Plateau, J. (1833). Des illusions sur lesquelles se fonde le petit appareil appelé récemment Phénakisticope. *Annales de Chimie et de Physique de Paris, 53,* 304–308.

Reid, T. (1764). *An inquiry into the human mind: On the principles of common sense.* Edinburgh: Millar, Kincaid & Bell.

Riggs, L. A., & Ratliff, F. (1952). The effects of counteracting the normal movements of the eye. *Journal of the Optical Society of America, 42,* 872–873.

Ross, H. E., & Murray, D. J. (1978). *E. H. Weber: The sense of touch.* London: Academic Press.

Ross, H. E., & Plug, C. (2002). *The mystery of the moon illusion: Exploring size perception.* Oxford, UK: Oxford University Press.

Ross, W. D. (Ed.), (1931). *The works of Aristotle* (Vol. 3). Oxford, UK: Clarendon Press.

Sabra, A. I. (Trans. and Ed.), (1989). *The optics of Ibn Al-Haytham. Books I–III. On direct vision.* London: Warburg Institute.

Selfridge, O. G. (1959). Pandemonium: A paradigm for learning. In *The mechanisation of thought processes*. London: HMSO.

Shannon, C. E., & Weaver, W. (1949). *The mathematical theory of communication*. Urbana, IL: University of Illinois Press.

Smith, A. M. (1996). *Ptolemy's theory of visual perception: An English translation of the* Optics *with introduction and commentary*. Philadelphia, PA: The American Philosophical Society.

Sutherland, N. S. (1973). Object recognition. In E. C. Carterette & M. P. Friedman (Eds.), *Handbook of perception. Vol. 3, Biology of perceptual systems* (pp. 157–185). New York: Academic Press.

Talbot, H. F. (1834). Experiments on light. *London and Edinburgh Philosophical Magazine and Journal of Science*, *15*, 321–334.

Thompson, S. P. (1910). A physiological effect of alternating magnetic field. *Proceedings of the Royal Society of London. Series B*, *82*, 396–398.

Thouless, R. H. (1931). Phenomenal regression to the real object: I. *British Journal of Psychology*, *21*, 339–359.

Treviranus, G. R. (1837). *Beiträge zur Aufklärung der Erscheinungen und Gesetze des organischen Lebens. Volume 1, Issue 3: Resultate neuer Untersuchungen über die Theorie des Sehens und über den innern Bau der Netzhaut des Auges*. Bremen: Heyse.

Uhr, L. (Ed.), (1966). *Pattern recognition: Theory, experiment, computer simulations, and dynamic models of form perception and discovery*. New York: Wiley.

Ungerleider, L. G., & Mishkin, M. (1982). Two cortical visual systems. In D. J. Ingle, M. A. Goodale, & R. J. W. Mansfield (Eds.), *Analysis of visual behavior* (pp. 549–586). Cambridge, MA: MIT Press.

Van Essen, D. C., Anderson, C. H., & Felleman, D. J. (1992). Information processing in the primate visual system: An integrated systems perspective. *Science*, *255*, 419–423.

Vernon, M. D. (1970). *Perception through experience*. London: Methuen.

Wade, N. J. (1990). *Visual allusions: Pictures of perception*. Hove, UK: Lawrence Erlbaum Associates Inc.

Wade, N. J. (1994). A selective history of the study of visual motion aftereffects. *Perception*, *23*, 1111–1134.

Wade, N. J. (1998). *A natural history of vision*. Cambridge, MA: MIT Press.

Wade, N. J. (2004a). Philosophical instruments and toys: Optical devices extending the art of seeing. *Journal of the History of the Neurosciences*, *13*, 102–124.

Wade, N. J. (2004b). Visual neuroscience before the neuron. *Perception*, *33*, 869–889.

Wade, N. J. (2005). *Perception and illusion: Historical perspectives*. New York: Springer.

Wade, N. J., & Tatler, B. W. (2005). *The moving tablet of the eye: The origins of modern eye movement research*. Oxford, UK: Oxford University Press.

Wade, N. J., & Verstraten, F. A. J. (1998). Introduction and historical overview. In G. Mather, F. Verstraten, & S. Anstis (Eds.), *The motion after-effect: A modern perspective* (pp 1–23). Cambridge, MA: MIT Press.

Walsh, V., & Cowey, A. (1998). Magnetic stimulation studies of visual cognition. *Trends in Cognitive Sciences*, *2*, 103–110.

Watson, J. B. (1913). Psychology as the behaviorist views it. *Psychological Review*, *20*, 158–177.

Weber, E. H. (1834). *De pulsu, resorptione, auditu et tactu.* Leipzig: Koehler.

Weiskrantz, L. (1986). *Blindsight: A case study and its implications.* Oxford, UK: Oxford University Press.

Wertheimer, M. (1912). Experimentelle Studien über das Sehen von Bewegung. *Zeitschrift für Psychologie, 60,* 321–378.

Wertheimer, M. (1922). Untersuchungen zur Lehre von der Gestalt: I. Prinzipielle Bemerkungen. *Psychologische Forschung, 1,* 47–58.

Wertheimer, M. (1923). Untersuchungen zur Lehre von der Gestalt: II. *Psychologische Forschung, 4,* 301–305.

Wertheimer, M. (1938). Gestalt theory. In W. D. Ellis (Ed.), *A source book of Gestalt psychology* (pp. 1–11). New York: Humanities Press.

Wheatstone, C. (1838). Contributions to the physiology of vision – Part the first. On some remarkable, and hitherto unobserved, phenomena of binocular vision. *Philosophical Transactions of the Royal Society, 128,* 371–394.

Wheatstone, C. (1852). Contributions to the physiology of vision – Part the second. On some remarkable, and hitherto unobserved, phenomena of binocular vision. *Philosophical Transactions of the Royal Society, 142,* 1–17.

Wiener, N. (1948). *Cybernetics: Control and communication in the animal and machine.* Cambridge, MA: MIT Press.

Wilkes, A. L., & Wade, N. J. (1997). Brain on neural networks. *Brain and Cognition, 33,* 295–305.

Wundt, W. (1874). *Grundzüge der physiologischen Psychologie.* Leipzig: Engelmann.

Young, T. (1802). On the theory of lights and colours. *Philosophical Transactions of the Royal Society, 92,* 12–48.

Young, T. (1807/2002). *A course of lectures on natural philosophy and the mechanical arts.* London: Johnson (Reprinted, Bristol: Thoemmes).

Zeki, S. (1999). *Inner vision.* Oxford, UK: Oxford University Press.

Zusne, L. (1967). Optical illusions: Output of publications. *Perceptual and Motor Skills, 27,* 175–177.

14 Individuality and personality

Boele de Raad

This chapter traces the concepts of personality and individuality back to their historical roots. Both etymological and historical interpretations of the related concepts of character, temperament and personality are given, emphasizing morality, equilibrium, and reputation as important characteristics. The historical description is supplemented with the history of about the last hundred years, in which personality and temperament had their own separate developments; character almost disappearing from the stage. In this description, intelligence is also recognized as a concept by which humans are distinguished. The main theoretical orientations in personality are briefly sketched, with particular emphasis on their modest role in personality research. The main part of this chapter is about the language of individual differences, including a brief review of the psycholexical approach that has led to the Big Five model of traits. The chapter opens and closes with observations concerning the impact of personality in everyday and professional life, as well as in research.

Throughout its history, the main appeal of the study of personality, particularly in Western society, has been in the *individual* person, rather than in parts or slices of the person such as in the study of the perceptual system, the nervous system, or unconscious processes. This interest in the whole, undivided person was accompanied by comprehensive views that indeed aimed to provide integrated perspectives on the whole person, for example Freud's Psychoanalytic Theory and Murray's Personology (e.g. Hall, Lindzey, & Campbell, 1998; Schultz & Schultz, 2005). Those comprehensive systems dominated the field at least during the first half of personality's scientific century. There is no overarching theory of personality that unifies the various general theoretical perspectives; on the contrary, the grand theories of personality often evolved from specific or personal experiences, and tended to criticize each other or even challenged the usefulness of each other's viewpoints. Freud's theory was largely based on neurotic moaning and lamentation by white, upper-class, European females during the nineteenth century. Maslow, the founder of the humanistic movement in psychology, reported that his theory had its roots in a hatred for and revulsion against everything his mother stood for (Hoffman,

1988). He was strongly critical of Freud's approach because of its ignorance of positive qualities in persons.

In his fascinating book on personality, Kouwer (1963) argued that personality theorists and related schools of thought have often excelled in entertaining rather primitive, amateurish and unscientific contacts with colleagues of different schools, at the same time presenting their own views as inevitable and universal, and those of others as untargeted, unfruitful, and based on false premises. Larsen and Buss (2005) similarly observed that "statements about the universal core of human nature typically lie at the center of all such grand theories of personality" (p. 13), and that taking one perspective on human nature usually means that other points of view are closed. Both Kouwer (1963) and Larsen and Buss (2005) have pointed out that the different views on personality may be possible at the same time because they address different domains of knowledge.

Significance of personality

The concepts of individuality and personality have permeated everyday and professional life. In Western civilization, where personal initiative, autonomy, and individual responsibility seem to be relatively important values, "personality" is almost unavoidable: the internet offers a large array of so-called personality "tests", personality is a sought-after commodity in career planning and popular magazines, in partner selection and education, and especially in commerce: emotional individualization of products has become a distinct work area (see, e.g., Govers, 2004). About personality, Schultz and Schultz (2005) write: "Everybody has one, and yours will help determine the limits of success, happiness, and fulfillment in your life" (p. 4). Similarly then, with respect to the personality of products, one might say that everything has one, and theirs will help determine "the likelihood of purchase" (Govers, 2004, p. 11).

In non-Western civilization, however, the concepts of individuality and personality may be much less central for the understanding of behavior. Hsu (1985), for example, considers the concept of personality as a typical expression of the Western emphasis on individualism. According to Triandis (1995), in collectivistic cultures personality is not as evident as in individualistic cultures. Eastern philosophies (e.g. Confucianism and Buddhism) consider relational characteristics to be constitutional of the core of personality (e.g. Church, 2001).

In psychology, personality and individual differences have become issues, themes, or centers of attention in almost all of its subdisciplines. Sechrest (1976) concluded that personality was in a bad shape, in terms of research, in terms of theory, and in terms of consequences. Personality had no identity, except a "social" or a "clinical" (p. 4) one. Following Revelle (1995), the conclusion by Sechrest was drawn in a period of "bleak pessimism", which was part of a cycle that has since turned into enthusiasm. The field of personality is now characterized by exciting developments in such areas as behavior genetics, evolutionary theory, longitudinal studies, and personality structure. In addition, the two spellings of personality observed by Sechrest have now been supplemented with spellings from most of the subdisciplines of psychology. According to Funder, Parke, Tomlinson-Keasey, and Widaman (1993), for example, personality psychology and *developmental* psychology should be "natural partners", with developmental psychology being "concerned with the factors that created the personality and continue to shape it over a lifetime" (p. xiii). The majority of studies at the crossing of personality and *education* report on temperamental and personality influences in the learning process and on their effects on educational achievement (cf. De Raad & Schouwenburg, 1996). Krahé (1992) attempted to synthesize personality and *social* psychology where the study of "personality takes place within the confines of a social world that poses its own constraints on the manifestation of unique and enduring personal characteristics" (p. 2). The past few decades have witnessed an increasing amount of activity in the study of personality and *health*. Personality variables have been shown to play an important role in the onset and course of chronic disease (cf. Hampson & De Raad, 1997; see also Smith & Williams, 1992). De Fruyt and Salgado (2003) summarized the role of personality in *organizational* psychology by conveying that personality has "successfully exported its insights and developments over the past 15 years to a wide variety of applied areas, including industrial, work, and organizational psychology" (p. S1).

The main focus of the field of personality is *dispositional* in orientation, which defines the field essentially as a research domain with a "psychometric" connotation (cf. Hofstee, 1984) that "cuts across all the other domains" (Larsen & Buss, 2005, p. 15). Personality psychology is about traits or individual differences, argued Hofstee (1984) convincingly. Traits are here defined broadly, in terms of generalized determining tendencies of a personalized character; they may include interests, values, philosophies of life, habits, and characteristic ways of reacting to situations (De Raad, 2000, p. 26; cf. Guilford, 1959). The main gist of the "psychometric" orientation is in finding relevant trait concepts that ultimately lead to an enhanced predictive validity of statements about personality (Wiggins, 1973). People differ from each other in an almost infinite number of ways. A fundamental question for personality psychology is thus to develop an adequate descriptive taxonomy of how people differ (cf. Revelle, 2000).

The concept of individuality (or individual differences) and its romantic counter-concept, uniqueness, refer to anything that marks a person as a distinct human being. This may run from superficial "stage-properties" such as a flattering hat or one's bodily characteristics to basic qualities such as instincts, motives, and dispositions. The set of individual differences comprises more than a set of personality traits. Besides attitudes, values, ideologies, interests, and emotions, the set of individual differences may include capacities, skills, socioeconomic status, gender, and height. So, differential psychology is concerned with individual differences in the broadest sense of the word.

History of individual differences

Personality and individuality have alternatively been referred to by "temperament" and "character". The different concepts have etymological and historical connotations that are important both for the understanding of the differences of those concepts and of the differences between the related contemporary research traditions.

In the history of scientific psychology, the onset of personality is often related to Wundt's student, James McKean Cattell, who is credited with the individual differences movement in psychology: In his experiments, he observed noticeable individual differences among subjects in reaction time (to light). Wundt tended to view those differences as "error", whereas Cattell thought that the differences might express more systematic differences in reaction to all kinds of stimulation. This was in the second half of the nineteenth century. In the first half of the same century, Gall (1819) had consistently aimed at finding the various sources of individual differences. In the same period, Fourier (1808) systematically worked out the idea of a utopian community on the basis of natural inclinations ("passions") through which people could be distinguished.

History has provided a storehouse of systems of presumably basic psychological forces, variably called temperaments, faculties, instincts, and propensities, in which certain characteristics are emphasized, largely depending on philosophies and ideologies operative in the different epochs of human history. Individual differences may not have been a systematic focus of attention throughout history, but differentiating between people in terms of their psychological traits certainly has been: Plato's categorization into those who are developed well intellectually, those in whom passion and competition plays an important role, and those who are mainly led by lust and desire, is an early example.

For the emergence of the study of individual differences, modern trait psychologists refer to ancient Greece: to the characters of Theophrastus for the *descriptive* aspect, and to the "humores" of Galen for the *causative* aspect (cf. Roback, 1952). Usually, such a reference goes without much argument, and is put to set the stage for the presentation of contemporary research findings.

There is an interesting commonality between these two ancient conceptualizations. Both seem to emphasize the notion of an *optimal balance*, an equilibrium. Galen (Galenus, ca. AD 170/1938) described optimal temperament as one with qualities in balance: "The best temperate man is he who in the body seems to be in the mean of all extremities, that is skinniness and fatness, heat and coldness. . . Similarly in his soul he is in the middle of boldness and timidity, of negligence and impertinence, of compassion and envy" (p. 86). To Aristotle (trans., 1988) character was found in (moral) virtue, and moral virtue is a disposition to choose the mean. For example (p. 40): "With regard to giving and taking money the mean is liberality, the excess and the defect prodigality and meanness" and "With regard to feelings of fear and confidence courage is the mean; of the people who exceed, he who exceeds in fearlessness has no name . . . while the man who exceeds in confidence is rash, and he who exceeds in fear and falls short in confidence is a coward".

Most of the attributes that have been considered important since ancient history were directly or indirectly linked to societal values; they are moral attributes, which are characterized by having two faces: that of personality trait and that of virtue. Politeness, for example, is both a trait and a virtue, and so are courage, tolerance, and loyalty (see, e.g., Comte-Sponville, 1995). Virtues are moral traits in which the good is manifested. The core of such a trait is that its meaning is optimally expressed. A good knife is a knife that excels in cutting. Similarly, a good human being is a human being who excels in being human. Moral traits are capabilities, worthy of being cultivated.

Psychological individual differences include two general ways of referring to basic and consequential attributes underlying behavior in various situations. Personality (or character and temperament) is one of them; the other is intelligence or ability. Since ancient history, intelligence has been highly valued. Wisdom, good judgment, and intellectual skills have been considered throughout as characteristics through which a civilized society would fare well. Plato suggested that philosophers were intellectually most qualified to govern the state. According to Aquinas, those with weaker intellect have great difficulty in understanding what is explained to them and they fail to acquire perfect knowledge. Both Gardner, Kornhaber, and Wake (1996) and Sternberg (1990) have reviewed the philosophical history and have pointed out how the philosophical history has influenced contemporary issues fundamental to thinking about intelligence. Elements of intelligence, judgment, knowledge, and direction have their origin in views that date back centuries (Sternberg, 1990, p. 32). Gardner (1999, p. 1) writes that, during the last few centuries, the ideal of the *intelligent person* has become pervasive, particularly in Western societies.

Equilibrium and morality in character and temperament

The ancient Greek meaning of *character* was derived from *inscribing* onto a surface. The inscribing would leave a distinctive mark, for example on a coin or a letter. The first psychological use of the term is now reserved for the person who is distinctively marked, the "distinctive mark" comprising the sum of the moral and mental qualities that distinguish an individual (cf. Kupperman, 1991). The best-known antique "psychological" system is that of Theophrastus, who described thirty characters, all with a suggestive, edifying meaning, conveying aspects of the morals of the time. In the writings of Theophrastus, Plato, and many others, a major theme is to point out the societal importance of the scarce psychological resources of high moral and educated nature.

The moral aspect has been attached to *character* throughout history. Aristotle's *Nicomachean ethics* is about vices and virtues of character; Theophrastus' *Characters* is about faults and vices; de la Bruyère's translation of *Characters* and his additional sketches mostly illustrate moral failings. Also, other related works on character were usually imbued with moral and edifying intentions (cf. Kouwer, 1963; Rusten, 1993).

There are no indications that the thirty characters described by Theophrastus were meant to be comprehensive, although the number might suggest that. Recently, De Raad and Ceulemans (2001) analyzed the semantics of the traits represented in the thirty characters in terms of the Big Five system. They concluded that the characters are best described by combinations of the negative poles of the factors agreeableness, conscientiousness, and intellect. The emphasis is on the combination of agreeableness and conscientiousness, which are indeed the typical character dimensions. Thus, the characters cover a relatively narrow area of the trait domain, and the findings support the frequently heard conjecture that Theophrastus' *Characters* conveys a moral message.

Among personality psychologists it is now widely accepted that the gist of personality is *temperamental*. The history of temperamental thinking closely paralleled that of characterology, but had, instead of a moral, a medical emphasis to begin with. Proto-temperamental thinking like that of Empedocles, Hippocrates, and, half a millennium later, Galen, emphasized the medical function of their elementary principles, the meaning of which was colored by mythological and cosmological thinking. Galen put forward the idea that illness was caused by an imbalance of the four humors. He recommended specific diets to help in the "cleansing of the putrefied juices" and often purging and bloodletting would be used. The optimal situation for a person would be one in which the humors are in balance. Although Galen made some reference to character, those references were at best fragmentary; the four humors blood, phlegm, black bile, and yellow bile "were foremost the determinants of illness, constitution, and physiognomy" (Stelmack & Stalikas, 1991). No trait or dispositional meaning was involved. Quite the contrary, temperament, consisting of mixtures of those four humors, could change by the minute. About one-and-a-half millennia later, when the medical function was taken over by a moralistic function, under the influence of Thomism, temperaments came to be conceived of as having a stable form. Behaviors were seen as resonating physical processes and characteristics of the nerve tissue. Interestingly, although "temperament" originally had the meaning of a *mixing in proper proportions* or *bringing into balance*, the term was used later for the non-ideal mixtures in which certain qualities were in excess.

In the time that typological uses of temperament emerged, moral features also came to play a role with respect to temperament. Aquinas (1226–1274), strongly emphasized the importance of harmony among the humors, in order to approach an ideal accommodation for the "perfect soul". The idea of a mixing of humors, and with that the medical function, disappeared and was replaced by fixed sets of physical accommodations, or "imprisonments or dungeons", such as the cholerical, sanguinical, melancholical, and flegmatic dungeons (cf. Kouwer, 1963).

In the large majority of modern handbooks on personality, the term "character" has been replaced by "personality", and the moral aspect has faded into the background (cf. Allport, 1927, 1937; McCullough & Snyder, 2000). With "character" almost disappearing from the stage of personality research, moral aspects of personality substance tended to be ignored or were considered to be of only philosophical or methodological interest. However, with the emergence of interests in "positive psychology" and, more specifically, in *emotional intelligence*, the tide seems to have turned. Emotional intelligence is conceived of as the ability to understand and manage emotional information. Part of this process involves the level of regulating emotion (Mayer & Salovey, 1997; Salovey & Mayer, 1990). In the preface to their book on character strengths and virtues, Peterson and Seligman (2004) expressed "the hope that positive psychology will be able to help people evolve toward their highest potential".

The theatrical personality

Allport (1937, pp. 25–26) discussed the etymology of the concept "personality" by referring to the Latin *per sonare*, meaning "to sound through", that is, to sound through the mouthpiece of a mask as used by actors in Greek theatre. To make it easier for the audience to tell which character was speaking at a particular time, the narrator used different masks to represent the various characters. These plays were performed in natural amphitheatres on the hillside and, to make the narrator's voice travel over the whole area, the masks were given large funnel-shaped mouths like megaphones. This "verbal" meaning is hardly recognized nowadays, and has been replaced by the mask concept of personality through the noun *persona*. The mask concept is about the public personality, the appearance, which is controlled by a variety of expressive means. A partial reading of the common-sense understanding of personality conveys this conception: A person who "has" personality is one who makes a strong, lasting, good impression.

The study of personality is often understood as the approach to "unmask", to uncover the hidden reality concealed by the mask. Of all personality conceptions, the public personality is the least associated with veridicality; it is most under the control of the agent or actor, who aims to manage how he or she gets across to others (cf. De Raad & Kokkonen, 2000). This "treacherous" aspect of personality is expressed in the Greek word for actor, namely "hypocrites". The management of one's own personality indeed refers to the "theatrical" (Goffman, 1959) conception of situations in which the person aims at certain goals through a strategic use of one's dispositional resources (cf. De Raad & Kokkonen, 2000).

Psychologists tend not to listen to the content of what the voice conveys through the mask. Rather, they listen to how the person talks and to characteristics of the voice. Formal and stylistic features are emphasized in studying behavior for its recurrent pattern. That is the way to find out about the person behind the mask. Listening to the content, and therefore listening to the person, would mean communicating with that person as a unique individual. The unique person is someone to talk with, not to try to describe and to study. Uniqueness is thus not an object of scientific investigation, but rather a presupposition.

Content and style

Temperament is usually distinguished from personality, in that the first emphasizes formal (Strelau, 1987) or stylistic aspects (Thomas & Chess, 1977), and the second emphasizes the content of traits and behavior. According to Strelau (1998), such expressions as style, intensity, energetic characteristics, or temporal components of behavior illustrate temperamental features. In contrast, content is reflected in specificity of reactions, of people to themselves, to each other, and to the world (p. 48). Some empirical studies on the relationship between personality and temperament (e.g. Angleitner & Ostendorf, 1994; Strelau & Zawadzki, 1996) suggest more congruence than earlier expected. If one prefers to emphasize the differences, certain dimensions (i.e. extraversion and neuroticism) were particularly supposed to belong to the domain of temperament, and certain other dimensions (i.e. agreeableness, conscientiousness, and intellect) rather refer to the domain of *character* (Strelau & Zawadzki, 1996; see, however, Ten Berge & De Raad, 2002).

Historically, character—less so personality—may have emphasized the description of individualizing features instead of focusing on generalization and abstraction of behavior. Ultimately, however, in all domains of individual differences the emphasis is on recurrent patterns, stable structures, paradigms, or typical tales, and therefore on form and style.

The factors "g" and "p" and their corruptive interaction

Sir Francis Galton (1822–1911) was the first to attempt to measure intelligence, which he referred to as "natural ability" covering "those qualities of intellect and disposition, which urge and qualify a man to perform acts that lead to reputation . . ." (Galton, 1869, p. 37). Galton conceived of intelligence as a single, underlying, pervasive, mental power. The emphasis on single, pervasive constructs was reinforced by the psychometric method of the time, namely Charles Spearman's two-factor method. Spearman (1904) sustained the search for a single, unitary construct of ability, which he envisaged as the general factor "*g*" of mental ability.

In the search for non-intellective factors contributing to success in learning environments, the first candidate of a similarly unitary nature was probably provided in Webb's (1915) conception of character. After Galton (1907) had directed attention to this topic, Webb, who worked under the guidance of Spearman, performed a first "attempt at an exact study of character". Webb's conception of personality was twofold: intelligence, on the one hand, and character, which was defined as "the sum of all personal qualities which are not distinctly intellectual" (1915, p. 2), on the other hand. In his study, Webb, using a prototype of factor analysis, found support for the general factor of intelligence, "*g*", and he found evidence for a second factor of wide generality, representing character, which he named "*w*" (*will*).

Webb's "*w*" has been interpreted later mainly in terms of conscientiousness (or persistence; see De Raad & Schouwenburg, 1996; cf. Deary, 1996). Hofstee (2001) concluded that the large majority of personality traits are scored in a socially desirable direction; they intercorrelate positively, thus forming a positive manifold. Hofstee proposed to call their first principal component the *p*-factor, which he labeled "Competence, in the sense of adequacy of reaction to situations".

Of particular interest with respect to the two general factors "*g*" and "*p*" has been their presumed potency to bring people to strive towards an optimum, to excel, or to use one's capacities to maximal advantage. This was probably characteristic of the reasoning until the middle of the twentieth century. In 1966, Wallace noted that students were led to eschew *efficiency–evaluative* conceptions of personality in favor of a dispositional conception, and he suggested to explore the consequences of conceiving personality as sets of abilities. Together with studies on self-presentation (Baumeister, 1982; Goffman, 1959), personality capability studies involve an individual's ability to control what he or she wants to be. The Self-Monitoring scale of Lennox and Wolfe (1984) expresses this well, witness the following two items: "I have the ability to control the way I come across to people, depending on the impression I wish to give them" and "I have found that I can adjust my behavior to meet the requirements of any situation I find myself in" (p. 1355).

There is a reverse of the abilities metaphor of personality in a temperamental or dispositional understanding of abilities. In exploring the boundaries between personality and intelligence, Goff and Ackerman (1992) and Ackerman and Goff (1994) investigated the distinction between intelligence as typical engagement and intelligence as maximal engagement. Motivational and temperamental factors are supposed to make actual intelligence different from maximal intelligence (Goff & Ackerman, 1992). Intelligence as typical engagement or—more briefly—typical intelligence, is essentially the same as what is supposed to be captured by the fifth factor of the Big Five model (De Raad, 2000), called intellect, intellectual autonomy, and, sometimes, openness to experience (see also Cacioppo & Petty, 1982).

Theories and metaphors

Personality theories are usually classified into psychodynamic, behavioral, and humanistic theories. According to Freud (1857–1939), the core of human personality is formed by the dynamic unconscious. In Freudian theory, humans are staged as voracious, lustful, and aggressive; metaphorically they were depicted as a tank full of bubbling and boiling energy, difficult to control. The picture was elaborated by Freud to explain neurotic symptoms, humor, dreams, and interpersonal conflicts (Monte, 2000). Freud's ideas formed the "prototypical canvas on which other theorists painted, added detail, or against which they reacted by overpainting the original with a radically different portrait" (Monte, 2000, p. 129).

Psychodynamic theory explained personality largely in terms of inner states and processes. Behavioral theorists, in contrast, tried to understand personality in terms of inferences and explanations based on observable behavior. In terms of Skinner's (1904–1990) conceptions, personality came to be understood as the organism's behavioral repertoire in interaction with the environment. "Understand the pattern of rewards and punishments that maintain or suppress behavior and you understand personality" (Monte, 2000, p. 131). To a certain extent, the metaphor of personality underlying behavior theory is that of a well-trained monkey (cf. Skinner, 1948). With their combination of the study of cognitive phenomena and controlled experimentation, Bandura and Walters (1963) set the stage for a multidimensional personality conception based on interactive phenomena, including a person's expectations and interpretations.

The humanistic tradition launched an optimistic view on human personality, in which the status of freedom and self-determination was emphasized. Rogers (1902–1987) theorized all motivation to be subsumed under the so-called *actualizing tendency*, "the directional trend which is evident in all organic and human life—the urge to expand, extend, develop, mature—the tendency to express and activate all the capacities of the organism, or the self" (Rogers, 1961, p. 351). Maslow (1908–1970) attributed predominantly healthy innate tendencies to human beings, including the capacity for constructive growth, kindness, generosity, and love. Maslow (1968) postulated the *hierarchy of needs* with lower needs (e.g. need for food) needing to be at least partially satisfied before higher needs (e.g. needs for security or belongingness) become influential. *Self-actualization*, the highest need in the hierarchy, is satisfied if human potentials are maximally realized.

Grand theories, as described briefly above, do not lend themselves very well to scientific testing, and it is hard to confirm or disconfirm them on the basis of empirical findings (Meehl, 1990). Rather, these theories may function as general orientations that can be of help in interpreting results obtained under a particular perspective. Psychodynamic theory is about personality in conflict with itself (inner conflicts or difficulties). For behavior theory the inner problem is replaced by an outer problem: It is about situations and conditions that control behaviors that form personality. Humanistic theory considered psychodynamic theory to present a limited and demeaning image of human nature, and behavior theory to provide a narrow portrait in which humans are characterized in terms of mechanical reactions. Humanistic theory, as the "third force", emphasized human strengths and aspirations. All three approaches, however, function mainly at the level of human nature; there is a huge gap between this human nature level of analysis and the study of individuality and individual differences (cf. Larsen & Buss, 2005).

The language of individuality and personality

The various ideas and concepts with respect to personality that have passed in revue provide diverse perspectives through which a person may be understood. Pirandello's *To clothe the naked* (1923), is metaphorical in this context. The main character in this play, Ersilia, who tried to commit suicide, is attributed by the surrounding people with different characteristics, each of which should explain her desperate deed. She is clothed with different personalities, so to speak. In a comparable creative attribution process, psychologists may construe concepts of various kinds, motives, cognitions, emotions, the unconscious, self-esteem, adaptations, morality, equilibrium, etc., which concepts are supposed to explain why an individual tends to behave, feel, or think in a certain way. Actually, language is replete with personality-defining concepts or traits, which is expressive of the general belief that such traits define the nature of personality and determine how personality operates. There is no lack of concepts, however, there is a lack of a system in terms of which these concepts can be organized. An additional question, then, is what the basic units are in terms of which personality is best described.

The fourth major approach to personality, the dispositional trait approach, aims at this fundamental question of how to describe people psychologically. This approach starts with everyday language in the search for a compelling taxonomy of personality traits. The basic idea is simple and straightforward, and is expressed in a so-called lexical hypothesis, namely that "all aspects of human personality which are or have been of importance, interest, or utility, have already become encoded in the substance of language" (Cattell, 1943, p. 483). A first listing of virtually all differential characteristics was constructed by Allport and Odbert (1936), who collected 17,953 lingual expressions with differential capacity from the lexicon. They tried to separate the wheat from the chaff by distinguishing temporal and stable characteristics, good and bad, appearance and reality, superficiality and depth. Allport and Odbert selected 4,504 expressions from their full set to represent stable traits, many of which (e.g. alacritous, bibulous, chrematistic, dorty, frampoid) are too unfamiliar to use. Norman (1967) updated the list of stable traits to a set of 2,797 more familiar personality descriptors. Goldberg (1982) reduced that list further to a set of 1,710 even more familiar and typical trait terms considered useful for rating purposes. De Raad and Doddema (1999) constructed a rather exhaustive and familiar set of 4,595 trait descriptive expressions, of which 2,365 were used for ratings of self and other (De Raad & Barelds, 2004).

The mere number of trait descriptors is not only indicative of the objective of the trait approach and of the determination in the endeavor to arrive at a full description of all personality traits, but also of the formidable richness of semantics in terms of which human individuality may be portrayed. Such an extensive listing of familiar trait descriptors can also be of great help in explaining rather technical psychological constructs that otherwise very often need to be explained in glossaries.

With those extensive vocabularies of trait descriptors the field of personality and individuality has constructed a resource of momentous substance. Alphabetical listings of such descriptors may function as specialist dictionaries of particular use to applied psychologists for writing psychological reports. The list could, for example, be exploited to provide full and refined descriptions of the various possible motives attributed to Pirandello's Ersilia. More generally, for any situation where one would want to portray a person's personality in detailed writing, going through this vocabulary quite probably may enrich one's initial conception. However, such uses may be enhanced rather drastically if the vocabulary is systematically ordered. Such an ordering is given in the so-called Big Five model.

Personality and individuality in context

Behavior takes place in a situation, and personality always refers to behaviors in situations. The behavior-in-situation combinations are best conceived of as expressions of traits. Put another way, traits imply behaviors in situations (De Raad, 2005). For example, a person who frequently shows compliance (behavior) upon reasonable requests (situation), can rightly be considered *cooperative* (trait). The trait cooperative stands for *behavior-in-a-situation*. As formulated by Johnson (1999): "Both behavior and context are tacitly built into the socially shared meaning of the trait word". Similarly, the trait *impudent* refers to *unwarranted behavior* towards *superiors*; a role relationship is implicit in the definition of this trait. *Sociable* refers to *behavior with other people*, *aggressive* refers to behavior in *situations of confrontation, friendly* refers to behavior with *positive interaction*, and *shy* refers to behavior in certain *social situations, especially with strangers.* Each trait is thus to be considered as implying situational information. For a full and specified vocabulary of traits, it would thus be necessary to specify each personality trait in terms of behavior in situation.

The outcome of such a specification enterprise is not necessarily a match in terms of scope and dimensionality of behavioral specifications and situational specifications of traits. For some traits it may turn out that many behaviors can be specified in a small range of situations, and for other traits it may be the other way around. The more stylistic traits, for example, may be less defined by particular types of situation (Johnson, 1999). Alston (1975) offers *methodical* and *energetic* as examples of stylistic traits, for "It would seem that one may proceed in a methodical or energetic manner in any situation in which one is doing *anything*" (p. 21). The term "style" is often used to stress the formal aspects of behavior, because the question "how" may be asked for any kind of behavior, whatever its contents or direction (Strelau, 1987).

Ten Berge and De Raad (2001, 2002) performed studies according to the definitions of trait given above, and concluded that there are four types of situation relevant for trait descriptive purposes. This "situational four" comprises: *Situations of adversity*, characterized by, for example, having a setback, losing control, and not sleeping well; *situations of pleasure and prosperity*, characterized by, for example, throwing a party, hearing good news, and passing an exam; *situations of positioning and demand*, with examples such as being in a discussion, organizing an event, and suing someone; and finally *situations of conduct and conflict*, with examples such as making obscene gestures, being teased, and being in doubt.

Ultimately, vocabularies of personality traits should be systematically provided with the proper situational specification. This should lead to an increase of the capacity to convey a sense of uniqueness and contextualization in the description. Moreover, since contextual factors are generally considered more important than traits in collectivistic cultures (cf. Church, 2000), future trait studies with "universal" intentions would gain much firmer footing in diverse cultures if contextual meanings of traits are more systematically sampled.

Basic variables, universals, and cultural variations

Authors with quite different theoretical and methodological orientation towards the study of personality structure agree that the lexicon of personality may be captured in some three to thirteen underlying factors (e.g. Benet & Waller, 1995; Buss & Plomin, 1984; Cattell, 1957; Costa & McCrae, 1985; De Raad & Peabody, 2005; Eysenck, 1970; Goldberg, 1990; Guilford, 1975; Norman, 1963; Zuckerman, 2002). These sets of factors always include extraversion, one of "the big two" (Wiggins, 1968), the other being anxiety or neuroticism. These two constructs have obtained a measurable form since the beginning of the twentieth century and are the two to which by far most of the references have since been made in abstracts of studies over a period of a hundred years (De Raad, 2000, pp. 87–88). Neuroticism appears in a large majority of the studies mentioned above, for which reason it made sense indeed to ask the question "What lies beyond E and N?" (Zuckerman, Kuhlman, & Camac, 1988). Diversions in answering that question should probably be attributed to differences in pools of variables with which one starts (Guilford, 1975). Eysenck started with items representing Guilford factors (Guilford & Guilford, 1934, 1936). However, both Guilford and Cattell were outclassed in terms of input variables by Goldberg's (1990) psycholexical approach. Orientations with a more specific theoretical (temperamental) perspective (e.g. Buss & Plomin, 1984; Zuckerman, 2002) than comprehensive psycholexical perspective, tend to produce fewer factors or more specific factors that deviate from the mainstream findings.

The Big Five model, which summarizes most of the empirical searches for basic factors for the description of personality, now functions as a fruitful working hypothesis with the factors extraversion, agreeableness, conscientiousness, emotional stability, and intellect or intellectual autonomy or creativity. The structure has been supported in independent studies in a large variety of languages (e.g. Ashton et al., 2004; De Raad, Perugini, Hrebíckóvá, & Szarota, 1998).

Since the Big Five model was established as a starting point for further analysis, it has functioned as a general reference framework. This is justified by the extensive, omnibus character of the psycholexical approach that suggests that with the Big Five factors one can find a peg for almost every hole. The semantic coverage is, however, also questioned. Ashton et al. (2004), for example, provide evidence of an additional sixth factor, called honesty–humility, which emphasizes trustworthiness, modesty, lack of greed, and lack of slyness.

If one had available an optimal set of trait variables on which ratings would be obtained from an optimal sample of subjects, it might be possible to find more than six factors. Ashton et al. (2004) suggested this possibility but were not able to find a consistent seven-factor solution in their datasets. De Raad and Barelds (2004) also tried to identify such an optimal set of variables. All lingual expressions, including adjectives, adverbs, nouns, and verbs were used for that purpose. The earlier-mentioned list of 2365 trait descriptive expressions was used in a (tentative) sample of 275 subjects (the final sample will be around 1500 subjects). The early results are promising. The Scree Test suggested five to eight factors. Factor solutions with up to eight factors were investigated. The first four factors of the Big Five were easily identified. In addition, four candidates announced new traits in themselves: maliciousness/sensitivity, criminality/pathology, integrity/honesty, and sensation seeking. Maliciousness is characterized by *destructive, treach-*

erous, malicious, emotionless versus *acts instinctively, is easily touched by things*, and *seeks security.* Criminality is characterized by such items as *steals, does not know his/her limits, violent* versus *unreasonable, ungrateful, likes dispute*, and *often differs in opinion.* Integrity is characterized by such items as *respects others, honest, someone with integrity* versus *flatterer, fools people*, and *does things for profit.* Finally, sensation seeking is characterized by *daredevil, takes risks, leads turbulant life*, versus *home-loving, coward*, and *likes to play safe.* Maliciousness and criminality are of interest because of their immediately obvious clinical relevance. Integrity seems to be identical to the sixth factor identified by Ashton et al. (2004) whereas sensation seeking has been extensively described and investigated by Zuckerman (e.g. Zuckerman, 1984, 1992).

If one focuses on rather strict rules for the identification of universal trait factors, it may be wiser to throttle down a little. Cross-language studies almost without exception disconfirm the cross-cultural replicability of the fifth—intellect—factor (e.g. De Raad et al., 1998; De Raad & Peabody, 2005; cf. De Raad & Van Heck, 1994). Interestingly, the intellect factor was also not replicated in De Raad and Barelds (2004). De Raad and Peabody (2005) and Peabody and De Raad (2002) give evidence of clear cross-cultural identification of only three factors, namely extraversion, agreeableness, and conscientiousness.

In conclusion, one could envisage here a cross-culturally replicable three- or four-factorial structure, supplemented with factors such as honesty–humility, that seems to be replicable in many languages but not all (certain other factors may be identifiable in certain types of culture only, for example, in collectivistic oriented cultures or individualistic oriented cultures; cf. Hofstede, 2001). Allik and McCrae (2004), using data from thirty-six different cultures, provided a view on the geographic distribution of traits. A multidimensional scaling plot showed, for example, that the extraverted and antagonistic traits turned out to be particularly characteristic of European and American cultures, while introverted and compliant traits were more characteristic of Asian and African cultures.

Recently, the Big Five model has undergone a metamorphosis through a newly developed fine-grained representational configuration (Hofstee, De Raad, & Goldberg, 1992) that shows a maximum of ninety distinct facets within the five-dimensional system. The concept makes use of the observation (taken from factor-loading matrices in many large-scale trait investigations) that the majority of trait variables load on two factors instead of one, thus emphasizing the importance of representing blends of factors. Eighty of the ninety facets in this model do indeed represent blends of factors. Due to its explicit and extent unfolding of the five factors, this so-called Abridged Big Five Circumplex (AB5C) model provides an excellent starting point and resource for the development of personality questionnaires, as well as for writing individualized psychological reports.

Trait research methodology

The trait approach to personality is largely based on ratings of self and others on representative and comprehensive listings of trait relevant descriptors. In certain cases, self-report forms the sole source of information, often justified on the basis of specific access to inner conceptions individuals would have. The latter feature seems to be in contrast to reputational information, which is more easily provided from an observer viewpoint. A distinct psychometric advantage of using observers is that there are more of them—as opposed to the single self—which permits more stable and reliable trait assessments.

Main issues in the psychometric–taxonomic enterprise of the descriptive trait approach are still with the choice of relevant variables, numbers of factors to summarize those variables, and, increasingly, cross-cultural replicability of trait factors. In that perspective, one main concern is the veridicality of trait ratings, which may be distorted intentionally (as in faking) or unintentionally (as in response sets). Another main concern is about accurate reflection of culture-related traits. Much effort in trait research should focus on the articulation of an accepted reference system of traits in which trait factors that may be considered universal, and those that may be specific for certain cultures, are specified. Such an accepted reference system has provided important momentum to the development of other assessment systems, such as objective tests (cf. Cattell & Warburton, 1967) and observations in natural settings (cf. Fahrenberg & Myrtek, 2001).

Impact of trait approach

Personality handbooks are usually provided with chapters on the dispositional or trait approach. Some handbooks (e.g. Larsen & Buss, 2005; Mischel, Shoda, & Smith, 2004) have recently moved the dispositional chapter to the beginning of the text, thus emphasizing the central position of the approach to the study of personality. Traits by which behavior in situations can be understood have been vigorously searched from the beginnings of personality psychology. With the establishment of the Big Five they seem to be within reach.

The Big Five model has served as a basis for the development of assessment instruments, including Big Five trait markers, Big Five inventories, and some instruments that have been shaped after the Big Five framework. This variety of instrument development shows the potential of the model. Moreover, the Big Five model is used in many different types of investigations, such as in the judgments of faces (Henss, 1995), the comparison of polar workers with a normative population (Steel, Suedfeld, Peri, & Palinkas, 1997), the construct validation of the concept of "argumentativeness" (Blickle, 1997), and in the categorization of free descriptions of children provided by parents (Kohnstamm, Halverson, Mervielde, &

Havill, 1998). Barrick and Mount (1991) investigated the role of the Big Five factors in relation to job performance. According to Smith and Williams (1992) the application of the five-factor model in the health domain would lead to a more coherent conceptual and empirical foundation in that area. De Raad and Schouwenburg (1996) organized the literature on personality, learning, and education using Big Five factors and facets (AB5C) as an accommodative framework. Many more examples of exploitation of the Big Five framework can be mentioned, such as in *behavior genetics* where the Big Five factors have been taken to classify behavior genetic findings with respect to adult personality (e.g. Bouchard, 1993). In *psychotherapy* the Big Five model can be utilized to facilitate psychotherapy treatment (e.g. Miller, 1991). Van Dam (1996) shows that the Big Five model provides for a useful framework to understand the ways selectors perceive the personalities of job applicants.

For each of the separate factors of the Big Five, specific domains of relevance can be pointed out to demonstrate the impact of the trait approach and the Big Five model in research. Extraversion, for example, has been studied in relation to the number of leadership roles assumed (e.g. Watson & Clark, 1997), the frequency of partying, and to nonverbal decoding skills in social interaction (Lieberman & Rosenthal, 2001). Mak and Tran (2001) related extraversion to intercultural social self-efficacy. Extraversion relates employees' absenteeism (Judge, Martocchio & Thoresen, 1997) to their level of pay and promotions (Seibert & Kraimer, 2001).

Agreeableness is probably the factor most concerned with interpersonal relationships. Agreeableness is related to elevated ratings of peer performance on group exercises (Bernardin, Cooke, & Villanova, 2000), to interpersonal skills in teams (Neuman & Wright, 1999), to tactics that minimize disruption during conflict episodes (Jensen-Campbell & Graziano, 2001), and to optimism with respect to future health risks (Vollrath, Knoch, & Cassano, 1999).

Conscientiousness plays a prominent role in school performance (e.g. Wolfe & Johnson (1995), in job performance (Barrick & Mount, 1991; Salgado, 1997), and in health (e.g. Vollrath et al., 1999).

Neuroticism was found relevant as a factor in school attainment (e.g. Eysenck & Cookson, 1969). In the organizational context, emotional stability was related to job performance and job satisfaction (Judge & Bono, 2001). Neuroticism plays an important role in commitment in a relationship (Kurdek, 1997) and in marital satisfaction (Karney & Bradbury, 1997). Neuroticism is relevant in the assessment of personality disorders (cf. Schroeder, Wormworth, & Livesley, 1992), and it correlates significantly with various measures of illness (e.g. Friedman & Booth-Kewley, 1987).

The fifth factor—intellect, or openness to experience—seems to be related to several disorders (Costa & Widiger, 1994) and to high-risk health behavior (Booth-Kewley & Vickers, 1994). In contexts of learning and education, openness to experience has been related to learning strategies (cf.

Blickle, 1997). In organizational settings, openness to experience has been associated with increased creative behavior (George & Zhou, 2001) and job performance (Salgado, 1997). Clower and Bothwell (2001) found low openness to experience to be related to inmate recidivism.

Concluding comment

Many topics of personality issues of debate with respect to personality have not been discussed in this chapter; the focus in this chapter was rather on consensus. Such a statement may be seen as presumptuous by some readers. Although it is admitted that the psycholexical approach with the Big Five model of personality description as its main result are subjects of continuous criticism, the approach has defined the field of personality throughout the main part of its scientific history. Moreover, through its "provocative" nature, the psycholexical approach has not only stimulated the assessment tradition and the applied fields of research, particularly in the clinical and in the organizational areas, but has also sharpened the knives of those researchers who expressed their opposition to the approach and the Big Five model.

Strong developments are now being made, especially in the biological basis of personality with an emphasis on behavioral genetics. Psychophysiological evidence has been relatively weak. The cognitive developments in most areas of psychology had relatively little impact on personality. Yet, recent strengthened interest in regulation of emotions, emotional intelligence, and in the staging of self, may be considered indicative of the continuing interest of people in who and what they are and what they could become. Developments in personality psychology may be hindered by wishful thinking, school and language barriers, and fashions and hypes. To establish the horizons of understanding of personality, it is important that personality psychologists are forearmed with the right tools. Conceptual analysis, knowledge of history, and articulation of descriptive language are indispensable on the highway to understand and explain personality.

References

Ackerman, P. L., & Goff, M. (1994). Typical intellectual engagement and personality: reply to Rocklin. *Journal of Educational Psychology, 86*, 150–153.

Allik, J., & McCrae, R. R. (2004). Toward a geography of personality traits: Patterns of profiles across 36 cultures. *Journal of Cross-Cultural Psychology, 35*, 13–28.

Allport, G. W. (1927). Concepts of trait and personality. *Psychological Bulletin, 24*, 284–293.

Allport, G. W. (1937). *Personality: A psychological interpretation.* New York: Holt.

Allport, G. W., & Odbert, H. S. (1936). Trait-names: A psycho-lexical study. *Psychological Monographs, 47*, No. 211.

Alston, W. P. (1975). Traits, consistency and conceptual alternatives for personality theory. *Journal for the Theory of Social Behaviour*, 5, 17–48.

Angleitner, A., & Ostendorf, F. (1994). Temperament and the Big Five factors of personality. In C. F. Halverson, Jr., G. A. Kohnstamm, & R. P. Martin (Eds.), *The developing structure of temperament and personality from infancy to adulthood* (pp. 69–90). Hillsdale, NJ: Lawrence Erlbaum Associates Inc.

Aristotle (D. Ross Trans.). (1988). *The nicomachean ethics.* Oxford, UK: Oxford University Press.

Ashton, M. C., Lee, K., Perugini, M., Szarota, P., De Vries, R. E., Di Blas, L., Boies, K., & De Raad, B. (2004). A six-factor structure of personality-descriptive adjectives: Solutions from psycholexical studies in seven languages. *Journal of Personality and Social Psychology*, 86, 356–366.

Bandura, A., & Walters, R. (1963). *Social learning and personality development.* New York: Holt, Rinehart, & Winston.

Barrick, M. R., & Mount, M. K. (1991). The Big Five personality dimensions and job performance: A meta-analysis. *Personnel Psychology*, 44, 1–26.

Baumeister, R. F. (1982). A self-presentational view of social phenomena. *Psychological Bulletin*, 91, 3–26.

Benet, V., & Waller, N. G. (1995). The Big Seven factor model of personality description: Evidence for its cross-cultural generality in a Spanish sample. *Journal of Personality and Social Psychology*, 69, 701–718.

Bernardin, H. J., Cooke, D. K., & Villanova, P. (2000). Conscientiousness and agreeableness as predictors of rating leniency. *Journal of Applied Psychology*, 85, 232–236.

Blickle, G. (1997). Argumentativeness and the facets of the Big Five. *Psychological Reports*, 81, 1379–1385.

Booth-Kewley, S., & Vickers, R. R. (1994). Associations between major domains of personality and health behavior. *Journal of Personality*, 62, 281–298.

Bouchard, T. J., Jr. (1993). Genetic and environmental influences on adult personality: evaluating the evidence. In J. Hettema & I. J. Deary (Eds.), *Foundations of personality* (pp. 15–44). The Netherlands: Kluwer Academic Publishers.

Buss, A. K., & Plomin, R. (1984). *Temperament: Early developing personality traits.* Hillsdale, NJ: Lawrence Erlbaum Associates Inc.

Cacioppo, J. T., & Petty, R. E. (1982). The need for cognition. *Journal of Personality and Social Psychology*, 42, 116–131.

Cattell, R. B. (1943). The description of personality: Basic traits resolved into clusters. *Journal of Abnormal and Social Psychology*, 38, 476–507.

Cattell, R. B. (1957). *Personality and motivation: Structure and measurement.* Yonkers-on-Hudson, NY: World Books.

Cattell, R. B., & Warburton, F. W. (1967). *Objective personality and motivation tests: A theoretical introduction and practical compendium.* Urbana, IL: University of Illinois Press.

Church, A. T. (2000). Culture and personality: Toward an integrated cultural trait psychology. *Journal of Personality*, 68, 651–703.

Church, A. T. (2001). Introduction. *Journal of Personality* (Special Issue), 69, 787–801.

Clower, C. E., & Bothwell, R. K. (2001). An exploratory study of the relationship between the Big Five and inmate recidivism. *Journal of Research in Personality*, 35, 231–237.

Comte-Sponville, A. (1995). *Petit traité des grandes vertus* [Little treatise of great virtues]. Paris: Presses Universitaires de France.

Costa, P. T., Jr., & McCrae, R. R. (1985). *The NEO Personality Inventory*. Odessa, FL: Psychological Assessment Resources.

Costa, P. T., Jr., & Widiger, T. A. (Eds.), (1994). *Personality disorders and the five-factor model of personality*. Washington, DC: American Psychological Association.

Deary, I. (1996). A (latent) big five personality model in 1915: A reanalysis of Webb's data. *Journal of Personality and Social Psychology, 71*, 992–1005.

De Fruyt, F., & Salgado, J. F. (2003). Personality and industrial, work and organizational applications. *European Journal of Personality, 17* (S1).

De Raad, B. (2000). *The Big Five personality factors: The psycholexical approach to personality*. Seattle, WA: Hogrefe & Huber Publishers.

De Raad, B. (2005). Situations that matter to personality. In A. Eliasz, S. E. Hampson, & B. De Raad (Eds.), *Advances in personality psychology* (Vol. 2, pp. 179–204). Hove, UK: Psychology Press.

De Raad, B., & Barelds, D. P. H. (2004). *Structuring the vocabulary of stable characteristics of people: A neo-taxonomy of Dutch personality traits*. Paper presented at the 12th European Conference on Personality, July 18–22, Groningen, The Netherlands.

De Raad, B., & Ceulemans, E. (2001). The trait-dimensional scope of the characters of Theophrastus. In R. Riemann, F. M. Spinath, & F. Ostendorf (Eds.), *Personality and temperament: Genetics, evolution, and structure* (pp. 168–184). Lengerich: Pabst Science Publishers.

De Raad, B., & Doddema, M. (1999). *Book of traits: The language of stable characteristics of people and their behaviors*. Groningen: Unpublished manuscript, University of Groningen.

De Raad, B., & Kokkonen, M. (2000). Traits and emotions: A review of their structure and management. *European Journal of Personality, 14*, 477–496.

De Raad, B., & Peabody, D. (2005). Cross-culturally recurrent personality factors: Analyses of three factors. *European Journal of Personality, 19*, 451–474.

De Raad, B., Perugini, M., Hrebícková, M., & Szarota, P. (1998). Lingua franca of personality: Taxonomies and structures based on the psycholexical approach. *Journal of Cross-Cultural Psychology, 29*, 212–232.

De Raad, B., & Schouwenburg, H. C. (1996). Personality in learning and education: A review. *European Journal of Personality, 10*, 303–336.

De Raad, B., & Van Heck, G. L. (1994). The fifth of the Big Five. *European Journal of Personality, 8(4)*.

Eysenck, H. J. (1970). *The structure of human personality*. London: Methuen.

Eysenck, H. J., & Cookson, D. (1969). Personality in primary school children: ability and achievement. *British Journal of Educational Psychology, 39*, 109–122.

Fahrenberg, J., & Myrtek, M. (2001). *Progress in ambulatory assessment: Computer-assisted psychological and psychophysiological methods in monitoring and field studies*. Goettingen: Hogrefe & Huber.

Fourier, C. (1808). *Théorie des quatre mouvements* [Theory of four movements].

Friedman, H. S., & Booth-Kewley, S. (1987). The "disease-prone personality": A meta-analytic view of the construct. *American Psychologist, 42*, 539–555.

Funder, D. C., Parke, R. D., Tomlinson-Keasey, C., & Widaman, K. (1993).

Studying lives through time: Personality and development. Washington, DC: American Psychological Association.

Galen (ca. AD 170/1938). *Peri kraseon (On temperaments).* (K. Lamera Trans, ancient to modern Greek). Papyros Library: The collected works of ancient Greek writers (Vol. 24), Athens: Papyros (original work written ca. 170 AD).

Gall, F. J. (1819). *Anatomie et physiologie du systeme nerveux, IVme Volume* [Anatomy and physiology of the nervous system, Vol. 4]. Paris: Maze.

Galton, F. (1869). *Heredity genius: An inquiry into its laws and consequences.* London: Macmillan.

Galton, F. (1907). *Inquiries into human faculty and its development.* New York: Duttin.

Gardner, H. (1999). *Intelligence reframed: Multiple intelligences for the 21st century.* New York: Basic Books.

Gardner, H., Kornhaber, M. L., & Wake, W. K. (1996). *Intelligence: Multiple perspectives.* Fort Worth, TX: Harcourt Brace.

George, J. M., & Zhou, J. (2001). When openness to experience and conscientiousness are related to creative behavior: An interactional approach. *Journal of Applied Psychology, 86,* 513–524.

Goff, M., & Ackerman, P. L. (1992). Personality–intelligence relations: Assessment of typical intellectual engagement. *Journal of Educational Psychology, 84,* 532–552.

Goffman, E. (1959). *The presentation of self in everyday life.* Garden City, NY: Doubleday-Anchor.

Goldberg, L. R. (1982). From ace to zombie: Some explorations in the language of personality. In C. D. Spielberger, & J. N. Butcher (Eds.), *Advances in Personality Assessment* (Vol. 1, pp. 203–234). Hillsdale, NJ: Lawrence Erlbaum Associates Inc.

Goldberg, L. R. (1990). An alternative "description of personality": The Big-Five factor structure. *Journal of Personality and Social Psychology, 59,* 1216–1229.

Govers, P. C. M. (2004). *Product personality.* Doctoral dissertation. Technical University of Delft, Delft, The Netherlands.

Guilford, J. P. (1959). *Personality.* New York: McGraw-Hill.

Guilford, J. P. (1975). Factors and factors of personality. *Psychological Bulletin, 82,* 802–814.

Guilford, J. P., & Guilford, R. B. (1934). An analysis of the factors in a typical test of introversion–extroversion. *Journal of Abnormal and Social Psychology, 28,* 377–399.

Guilford, J. P., & Guilford, R. B. (1936). Personality factors S, E, and M, and their measurement. *Journal of Psychology, 2,* 109–127.

Hall, C. S., Lindzey, G., & Campbell, J. B. (1998). *Theories of personality.* New York: John Wiley & Sons.

Hampson, S. E., & De Raad, B. (1997). Personality and chronic disease. *European Journal of Personality, 11(5).*

Henss, R. (1995). Das Fünf-Faktoren-Modell der Persönlichkeit bei der Beurteilung van Gesichtern [The Five-Factor model of personality in judging faces]. *Report Psychologie, 20,* 28–39.

Hoffman, E. (1988). *The right to be human: A biography of Abraham Maslow.* New York: Plenum Press.

Hofstede, G. (2001). *Culture's consequences: Comparing values, behaviors, institutions, and organizations across nations.* Thousand Oaks, CA: Sage.

Hofstee, W. K. B. (1984). What's in a trait: Reflections about the inevitability of traits, their measurement, and taxonomy? In H. Bonarius, G. Van Heck, & N. Smid (Eds.), *Personality psychology in Europe: Theoretical and empirical developments* (pp. 75–81). Lisse: Swets & Zeitlinger.

Hofstee, W. K. B. (2001). Intelligence and personality: Do they mix? In J. M. Collis & S. Messick (Eds.), *Intelligence and personality: Bridging the gap in theory and measurement* (pp. 43–60). Mahwah, NJ: Lawrence Erlbaum Associates Inc.

Hofstee, W. K. B., De Raad, B., & Goldberg, L. R. (1992). Integration of the Big Five and circumplex approaches to trait structure. *Journal of Personality and Social Psychology, 63,* 146–163.

Hsu, F. L. K. (1985). The self in cross-cultural perspective. In A. J. Marsella, G. De Vos, & F. L. K. Hsu (Eds.), *Culture and self* (pp. 24–55). London: Tavistock.

Jensen-Campbell, L. A. & Graziano, W. G. (2001). Agreeableness as a moderator of interpersonal conflict. *Journal of Personality, 69,* 323–362.

Johnson, J.A. (1999). Persons in situations: Distinguishing new wine from old wine in new bottles. *European Journal of Personality Psychology, 13,* 443–453.

Judge, T. A., & Bono, J. E. (2001). Relationship of core self-evaluations traits—self-esteem, generalized self-efficacy, locus of control, and emotional stability—with job satisfaction and job performance: A meta-analysis. *Journal of Applied Psychology, 86,* 80–92.

Judge, T. A., Martocchio, J. T., & Thoresen, C. J. (1997). Five-factor model of personality and employee absence. *Journal of Applied Psychology, 82,* 745–755.

Karney, B. R., & Bradbury, T. N. (1997). Neuroticism, marital interaction, and the trajectory of marital satisfaction. *Journal of Personality & Social Psychology, 72,* 1075–1092.

Kohnstamm, G. A., Halverson, C. F., Jr., Mervielde, I., & Havill, V. L. (1998). Analyzing parental free descriptions of child personality. In G. A. Kohnstamm, C. F. Halverson, Jr., I. Mervielde & V. L. Havill (Eds.), *Parental descriptions of child personality: Developmental antecedents of the Big Five?* (pp. 1–9). Mahwah, NJ: Lawrence Erlbaum Associates Inc.

Kouwer, B. J. (1963). *Het Spel van de Persoonlijkheid: Theorieen en systemen in de psychologie van de menselijke persoon* [The game of personality: Theories and systems in the psychology of persons]. Utrecht: Erven J. Bijleveld.

Krahé, B. (1992). *Personality and social psychology: Towards a synthesis.* London: Sage Publications.

Kupperman, J. (1991). *Character.* New York: Oxford University Press.

Kurdek, L. A. (1997). Relation between neuroticism and dimensions of relationship commitment: Evidence from gay, lesbian, and heterosexual couples. *Journal of Family Psychology, 11,* 109–124.

Larsen, R. J., & Buss, D. M. (2005). *Personality psychology: Domains of knowledge about human nature.* Boston, MA: McGraw-Hill.

Lennox, R. D., & Wolfe, R. N. (1984). Revision of the Self-Monitoring Scale. *Journal of Personality and Social Psychology, 46,* 1349–1364.

Lieberman, M. D., & Rosenthal, R. (2001). Why introverts can't always tell who likes them: Multitasking and nonverbal decoding. *Journal of Personality and Social Psychology, 80,* 294–310.

Mak, A. S., & Tran, C. (2001). Big Five personality and cultural relocation factors in Vietnamese Australian students' intercultural social self-efficacy. *International Journal of Intercultural Relations, 25*, 181–201.

Maslow, A. H. (1968). *Toward a psychology of being.* New York: Van Nostrand.

Mayer, J. D., & Salovey, P. (1997). What is emotional intelligence? In P. Salovey & D. J. Sluyter (Eds.), *Emotional development and emotional intelligence: Educational implications.* New York: Basic Books.

McCullough, M. E., & Snyder, C. R. (2000). Classical sources of human strength: Revisiting an old home and building a new one. *Journal of Social and Clinical Psychology, 19*, 1–10.

Meehl, P. E. (1990). Why summaries of research on psychological theories are often uninterpretable. *Psychological Reports, 66*, 195–244.

Miller, T. R. (1991). The psychotherapeutic utility of the Five-Factor Model of personality: A clinician's experience. *Journal of Personality Assessment, 57*, 415–433.

Mischel, W., Shoda, Y., & Smith, R. E. (2004). *Introduction to personality: Toward an integration.* Hoboken, NJ: John Wiley & Sons Inc.

Monte, C. F. (2000). Theories. In A. E. Kazdin (Ed.), *Encyclopedia of psychology* (pp. 128–133). Oxford, UK: Oxford University Press.

Neuman, G. A., & Wright, J. (1999). Team effectiveness: Beyond skills and cognitive ability. *Journal of Applied Psychology, 84*, 376–389.

Norman, W. T. (1963). Toward an adequate taxonomy of personality attributes: Replicated factor structure in peer nomination personality ratings. *Journal of Abnormal and Social Psychology, 66*, 574–583.

Norman, W. T. (1967). *2,800 personality trait descriptors: Normative operating characteristics for a university population.* Ann Arbor, MI: Department of Psychology, University of Michigan.

Peabody, D., & De Raad, B. (2002). The substantive nature of psycholexical personality factors: A comparison across languages. *Journal of Personality and Social Psychology, 83*, 983–997.

Peterson, C., & Seligman, M. E. P. (2004). *Character strengths and virtues: A handbook and classification.* Oxford, UK: Oxford University Press.

Pirandello, L. (1923). *Vestire gli ignudi: commedia in tre atti* [To clothe the naked]. Firenze: Bemporad.

Revelle, W. (1995). Personality processes. *Annual Review of Psychology, 46*, 295–328.

Revelle, W. (2000). Individual differences. In A. E. Kazdin (Ed.), *Encyclopedia of psychology* (pp. 249–252). Oxford, UK: Oxford University Press.

Roback, A. A. (1952). *The psychology of character, with a survey of personality in general.* London: Routledge and Kegan Paul.

Rogers, C. R. (1961). *On becoming a person: A therapist's view of psychotherapy.* Boston, MA: Houghton Mifflin.

Rusten, J. (Ed. and Trans., 1993). *Theophrastus: Characters.* Cambridge, MA: Loeb Classical Library, Harvard University Press.

Salgado, J. F. (1997). The five factor model of personality and job performance in the European Community. *Journal of Applied Psychology, 82*, 30–43.

Salovey, P., & Mayer, J. D. (1990). Emotional intelligence. *Imagination, Cognition, and Personality, 9*, 185–211

Schroeder, M. L., Wormworth, J. A., & Livesley, W. J. (1992). Dimensions of personality disorder and their relationships to the Big Five dimensions of personality. *Psychological Assessment*, *4*, 47–53.

Schultz, D. P., & Schultz, S. E. (2005). *Theories of personality*. Belmont: Thomson Wadsworth.

Sechrest, L. (1976). Personality. *Annual Review of Psychology*, *27*, 1–27.

Seibert, S. E., & Kraimer, M. L. (2001). The Five-Factor Model of personality and career success. *Journal of Vocational Behavior*, *58*, 1–21.

Skinner, B. F. (1948). *Walden two*. New York: Macmillan.

Smith, T. W., & Williams, P. G. (1992). Personality and health: Advantages and limitations of the Five-Factor model. *Journal of Personality*, *60*, 395–423.

Spearman, C. (1904). General intelligence objectively determined and measured. *American Journal of Psychology*, *15*, 201–293.

Steel, G. D., Suedfeld, P., Peri, A., & Palinkas, L. A. (1997). People in high latitudes: The "Big Five" personality characteristics of the circumpolar sojourner. *Environment and Behavior*, *29*, 324–347.

Stelmack, R. M., & Stalikas, A. (1991). Galen and the humour theory of temperament. *Personality and Individual Differences*, *12*, 255–263.

Sternberg, R. J. (1990). *Metaphors of mind: Conceptions of the nature of intelligence*. Cambridge, MA: Cambridge University Press.

Strelau, J. (1987). The concept of temperament in personality research. *European Journal of Personality*, *1*, 107–117.

Strelau, J. (1998). *Temperament: A psychological perspective*. New York: Plenum Press.

Strelau, J., & Zawadzki, B. (1996). Temperament dimensions as related to the Giant Three and the Big Five factors: A psychometric approach. In A. V. Brushlinsky & T. N. Ushakova (Eds.), *V. D. Nebylitsyn: Life and scientific creativity* (pp. 260–281). Moscow, Russia: Ladomir.

Ten Berge, M. A., & De Raad, B. (2001). The construction of a joint taxonomy of traits and situations. *European Journal of Personality*, *15*, 253–276.

Ten Berge, M. A., & De Raad, B. (2002). The structure of situations from a personality perspective. *European Journal of Personality*, *16*, 81–102.

Thomas, A., & Chess, S. (1977). *Temperament and development*. New York: Brunner/Mazel.

Triandis, H. C. (1995). Collectivism and individualism as cultural syndromes. *CrossCultural Research*, *27*, 155–180.

Van Dam, K. (1996). Persoonlijkheidswaarneming in het selectie-interview [Personality perception in the selection-interview]. *Gedrag en Organisatie*, *9*, 1–14.

Vollrath, M., Knoch, D., & Cassano, L. (1999). Personality, risky health behaviour, and perceived susceptibility to health risks. *European Journal of Personality*, *13*, 39–50.

Wallace, J. (1966). An abilities conception of personality: Some implications for personality measurement. *American Psychologist*, *21*, 132–138.

Watson, D., & Clark, L. A. (1997). Extraversion and its positive emotional core. In R. Hogan, J. Johnson & S. Briggs (Eds.), *Handbook of personality psychology* (pp. 767–793). San Diego, CA: Academic Press.

Webb, E. (1915). *Character and intelligence: An attempt at an exact study of character*. Cambridge, MA: Cambridge University Press.

Wiggins, J. S. (1968). Personality structure. *Annual Review of Psychology*, *19*, 293–350.

Wiggins, J. S. (1973). *Personality and prediction: Principles of personality assessment.* Reading, MA: Addison-Wesley.

Wolfe, R. N., & Johnson, S. D. (1995). Personality as a predictor of college performance. *Educational and Psychological Measurement, 55,* 177–185.

Zuckerman, M. (1984). Sensation seeking: A comparative approach to a human trait. *Behavior and Brain Sciences, 7,* 413–471.

Zuckerman, M. (1992). What is a basic factor and which factors are basic? Turtles all the way down. *Personality and Individual Differences, 13,* 675–681.

Zuckerman, M. (2002). Zuckerman–Kuhlman Personality Questionnaire (ZKPQ): An alternative five-factorial model. In B. De Raad & M. Perugini (Eds.), *Big Five assessment* (pp. 377–396). Seattle, WA: Hogrefe & Huber Publishers.

Zuckerman, M., Kuhlman, D. M., & Camac, C. (1988). What lies beyond E and N? A factor analysis of scales believed to measure basic dimensions of personality. *Journal of Personality and Social Psychology, 54,* 96–107.

15 The self

Qi Wang and Nandita Chaudhary

All the things in the world are already complete in us.
(Mencius)

The self is a microcosm playing out in the macrocosm of family, community, society, and culture. This humanitarian view of the self, which derives from Confucian scholars, points to the nature of the self as both an autonomous entity taking charge of its own actions and a relational being inextricably connected with people, things, and the entire universe (Elvin, 1985). In this chapter, we discuss the individuality and collectivity of the human self that develop through different developmental pathways across cultures.

Contemporary intellectual interests in the self can be traced back to William James (1890/1983), who devoted an extensive discussion of "the self" in his seminal treatise on the *Principles of psychology*. James viewed the self as consisting of two fundamental aspects: the "I", the self as subject, and the "Me", the self as object. For James, the I-self is the active knower and experiencer responsible for constructing the Me-self, who, in turn, represents the aggregated knowledge of one's own personal characteristics. A century after James, the self remains a fascinating and vibrant topic of study. In spite of the failure to agree on the precise definition of the self, researchers generally concur about several central characteristics that reflect the basic meaning of the self. As summarized by Baumeister (1998), "Self begins with the human body and involves the construction of a definition that entails unity and temporal continuity. Self is an entity marked by reflexive consciousness, interpersonal roles and reputation, and executive function" (p. 683). In particular, one crucial feature of the self reflected in many theoretical models is that the self is a multi-faceted, complex, dynamic construct encompassing many interacting aspects or components (Baumeister, 1998; Harter, 1998; Jopling, 1997; Neisser, 1988).

One of the ways of looking at the complexity of self-development is by examining two interrelated aspects of the self—autobiographical memory and self-concept. Autobiographical memory, construed by Neisser (1988) as the "extended self" or the "remembered self", refers to distinct, long-lasting memories of significant personal experiences from an individual's life. Self-concept, or the "conceptual self" (Neisser, 1988), refers to an individual's conceptual representations of himself or herself. Many theorists have posited that these two reflective aspects of the self exhibit a dynamic interplay in which the conceptual self operates on the encoding, organization, and retrieval of personally meaningful events, and autobiographical memory, in turn, sustains the development, expression, and maintenance of a dynamic self-concept (Conway & Pleydell-Pearce, 2000; Fivush, 1994; Neisser, 1997; Nelson, 1996; Pillemer, 1998; Ross & Wilson, 2000; Wang, Leichtman, & White, 1998). In addition, the onset of autobiographical memory and the emergence of the conceptual self appear to be ontogenetically interconnected (Harley & Reese, 1999; Howe & Courage, 1993; Povinelli, 1995; Welch-Ross, 2000). Because the two aspects of the self are both believed to be sensitive to social influences, they have been underscored in contemporary self theories (Fivush, 1994; Harter, 1998; Nelson, 1993; Wang, 2004).

Many theorists maintain that the ultimate goal of human development in any society is to establish social connections and to achieve individuation (Costanzo, 1992; Damon, 1983; Harter, 1999; Kagitcibasi, in press; Kihlstrom, 1993; Spiro, 1993). Individuals thus develop both personal (self-perceived distinctiveness) and social (self-perceived connectedness) identities through their cultural experiences. During the early years of life, children develop a sense of individual agency and in the meantime learn about the rules and conventions of their society. The youth period is the time for education and employment training, followed by the establishment of early career. An essential goal of this period is for an individual to develop an identity that comprises both unique personal attributes (e.g. being imaginative, efficient, and perfectionist) and important social roles and categories (e.g. being a son, a democrat, and a young scientist). When individuals reach early midlife, many have both career and family in place. They are expected to be responsible not only for themselves but also for others in the family, community, workplace, and so on. During peak midlife, individuals are reaping the rewards of career and family, and their personal and social identities become further stabilized. Note that although individuals in different cultures may differ in their ages corresponding to various life periods, the stages of lifespan development are generally consistent across cultures (Alexander & Langer, 1990; Clausen, 1993; Erickson, 1963; Levinson, 1986; Wethington, 2000). Thus, through ontogenetic development individuals incorporate increasing autonomy (as opposed to heteronomy) and relatedness (as opposed to separateness) in the construction of their self and identity (Kagitcibasi, 1996a, in press; Wang & Conway, 2004).

Although autonomy and relatedness emerge in response to basic human needs and universal societal expectations, the crystallized belief system in any cultural or subcultural group tends to prioritize the development and expression of one over the other (Kagitcibasi, 1996b; Markus & Kitayama, 1991; Shweder & Bourne, 1984; Triandis, 1989; Wang & Brockmeier, 2002). As shown in empirical work in anthropology and psychology, many Western cultures, especially that in the USA, place important emphasis on individuality, agency, and self-assertiveness. Individuals are encouraged to develop and maintain their autonomous sense of self by attending to their private beliefs, attributes, and personality traits, which are conceivably impervious to other people, social groups, or interpersonal contexts. In contrast, in cultures such as those in East Asia, Africa, Latin America, and Southern Europe, the priority is often given to interpersonal harmony, group solidarity, and the maintenance of social hierarchy. Individuals are therefore encouraged to develop a strong sense of a relational self by attending to their significant social roles, duties, and responsibilities.

We here use the framework of developmental pathways to characterize these cultural differences in self-conceptions (Greenfield, Keller, Fuligni, & Maynard, 2003). We refer to the greater cultural emphasis on autonomy in the human self and its development as the "independent pathway", and the greater cultural emphasis on relatedness in the human self and its development as the "interdependent pathway". Drawing on the empirical findings of self-development in various cultural contexts, we analyze the content and manifestation of cultural constructions of the self in practical everyday activities through each developmental pathway. We view the development of the self through the two different pathways as reflecting varied degrees of emphases on the two important dimensions of the human self rather than two dichotomous categories that function in multiple combinations within and among individuals (Barth, 1997; Hollos & Leis, 2002; Voronov & Singer, 2002; Wang & Li, 2003). Moreover, it is possible and sometimes even necessary for the coexistence of multiple-self ideologies, both at personal and collective levels of manifestation, as well as different approaches to self–other orientations in intra-personal dynamics depending on the domain of activity. Importantly, "despite the variability . . . all forms of the self are responses to the basic human predicament; they necessarily have a lot in common" (Neisser, 1997, p. 12). It is the commonality of the human self that we first turn to.

The universal aspects of self-development

Biological maturation, cognitive growth, and social experience together interact to facilitate the development of the self. This holds true in all cultural settings. Infants demonstrate an early awareness of the self as an active agent in space, a sense of volition over self-generated acts (Harter, 1998; Stern, 1985). For example, visual self-recognition is present at least as early as 9 months when infants are able to recognize the images of themselves based on the principle of contingency (Amsterdam, 1972; Lewis & Brooks-Gunn, 1979). There is a greater chance of response from the infant to concurrent movements of the self, whether these are in the mirror or through video recordings, thereby implying a higher responsivity to these images in comparison with visually noncontingent self-images (e.g. in pre-recorded videos) or images of other infants. Infants at this age often display exuberance when they show control over certain environment events such as making a mobile move (Case, 1991). These responses imply a clear sense of personal agency, a rudimentary form of James's I-self.

The Me-self, a sense of the self as an object of one's knowledge, emerges during the second half of the second year (Harter, 1998). Infants now show "full" or conscious self-recognition where they can recognize the self based on their physical features independent from contingency clues. When infants of this age are placed in front of mirrors with their noses surreptitiously dabbed with rouge, they display self-directed behavior like wiping their own nose (Amsterdam, 1972; Lewis & Brooks-Gunn, 1979), suggesting the presence of an internal representation of their stable facial features and the ability to compare it with their mirror image. This form of self-cognition is regarded as a milestone for the emergence of a cognitive sense of self, a rudimentary form of self-concept (Harter, 1998; Howe & Courage, 1993). By the end of the second year of life, infants have also achieved other accomplishments that signal their cognitive self-awareness (Case, 1991; Damon & Hart, 1988; Harter, 1998; Kagan, 1989). Of particular importance, the advent of language enables the verbal expression and representation of the Me-self. Infants show increasing use of self-descriptive statements ("I sit", "Mary eat", "I do it myself") that reflect an awareness of their active constituents and capacities, in addition to knowledge of the physical constituents of the self. The early cognitive sense of self constitutes a foundation for constructing more sophisticated representations of the self as well as the self in relation to others.

The self-concept develops with further cognitive growth and social experience, and shows increasing complexity, integration, and differentiation (Damon & Hart, 1988; Harter, 1988, 1998; Selman, 1980). By the age of two, many children have come to understand some of their most basic characteristics, knowing, for example, whether they are girls or boys and that they are children rather than adults. In the preschool years, children's self-concepts often concern their physical features, possessions, and preferences and typically focus on concrete, here-and-now attributes and observable behaviors. These self-representations tend to be isolated and lacking in coherence. During middle childhood, children begin to understand their less tangible characteristics such as traits and emotions, and show interest in the continuity of the self over time and that people have enduring dispositions (Ferguson, Van Roozendaal, & Rule, 1986). They use social comparisons more often to understand themselves and to evaluate their skills or talents relative to those of friends or classmates (Ruble & Frey, 1991). In addition, children of this age show some abilities to coordinate previously compartmentalized self-representations. Adolescents' cognitive abilities lead to more abstract and hypothetical understanding of their inner attributes, personality traits, and personal beliefs. They also show awareness of conflicting attributes within the self, such that a person can be shy in class but outgoing with friends, and are able to integrate different representations into a coherent self-portrait. Thus, as children grow older, their characterizations of themselves become more coordinated, more abstract, more comparative (with peers), and more differentiated based on specific social roles and relational contexts. Their self-evaluations also become more realistic for both their positive and negative attributes.

In addition to the conceptual self, researchers have examined the development of the extended or remembered self (Neisser, 1988) that relates to episodic memories of personal experiences, i.e. autobiographical memory (Foulkes, 1999; Povinelli, 1995; Wang, 2004; Welch-Ross, 2000). This form of self-knowledge is crucial because it highlights the temporal dimension of the self and constitutes an enduring self-concept and individual identity. The development of autobiographical memory takes place across preschool years and extends beyond adolescence and adulthood. Toddlers, equipped with their general memory skills and newly emerging language abilities, are able to provide some fragmentary information about their past experiences with adult scaffolding. With further neurological maturation, language and cognitive growth, and particularly through participation in memory conversations with adults (e.g. Fivush, 1994; Nelson, 1993; Peterson & McCabe, 1994), preschoolers come to construct more temporally coherent and elaborate accounts of the past, and these skills continue to develop in complexity and organization across middle childhood. The further sophistication of cognitive skills and social experiences enable adolescents to construct more comprehensive life stories that integrate thematically and causally related episodes, which contributes to the identity formation and stabilization (for reviews, see Fivush & Hudson, 1990; Habermas & Bluck, 2000).

The pattern of self-development with cognitive progress and social participation from infancy through adolescence has been observed in children from different cultures (Hart, Lucca-Irizarry, & Damon, 1986; Kagan, 1989; Miller, Mintz, Hoogstra, Fung, & Potts, 1992; Wang, 2004). For detailed discussions of the universal aspects of self-development, see Harter (1998, 1999). We now turn to the discussion of cultural specificity in the development of the self.

Cultural processes of self-construction

The study of the self within the traditions of psychosexual and psychosocial writing, object-relations theories, identity studies, attachment theory and cultural studies, are mostly constructed around an initial social unit of the self and other, undifferentiated at birth, while gradually moving toward a mature independent sense of self (Bosma & Gerlsma, 2003). When researchers from diverse disciplines of linguistics, anthropology, and psychology start to explore cultural differences in self-formulation, it becomes clear that the notion of a bounded, unitary entity, the self as a developmental outcome, as it is understood in the Western tradition, is indeed a culturally specific one, and is in reality, fraught with "complexity about the elusive phenomenon that the self is" (Hermans, 1996, p. 31). This developed into the cultural study of selfhood, now a dynamic field of investigation (Obeyesekere, 1990; Pratkanis & Greenwald, 1985; Smith, 1985; Valsiner, 2001).

The influence of culture on self-construction takes place through multiple processes that are inextricably linked on the one hand and functionally distinctive on the other. In the following pages, we will be focusing on four cultural processes that are constitutive in the construction of self-processes: cultural conceptions of selfhood, language of the self and others, organization of social activities, and cultural homogeneity and diversity.

Cultural conceptions of selfhood

Many economic–ecological factors impinge on the notion of selfhood in a given culture. The meaning of the self and its relative positioning within the social network is guided by social, religious, and philosophical traditions. The reality of individual existence is thus stamped with cultural meaning in every social setting, and indeed, in every social interaction. This may be explicit, as in a legal discussion of responsibility, or implied, as in the pragmatics of an intimate relationship. More specifically, any cultural setting, be it domestic, economic, ecological, educational, legal, or social, and no matter whether it concerns the experience of adolescence (Kagitcibasi, 2002; Saraswathi, 1999), childrearing practices (Keller, 2001), or patterns of marital arrangement, places constraints on the experience of being a person. Using family size and household space as an example, the following extract from the Indian Census illustrates that sharing of space in India is more the norm than otherwise; and that space may have a profound meaning for Indian selfhood:

> Collected by an army of two million drafted by the Census of India, the first of its kind household survey—which preceded the once in a decade population census—has unfolded a numerical fabric of the country . . . the census man knocked at the doors of every single Indian household across 593 districts in 35 states and Union territories of India . . . The outcome is both instructive and amusing. There are 179 million residential houses in India—that is about six people to each house. About 40 per cent of Indian families live in one-room houses. Thirty-nine per cent of all married couples in India (about 86 million) do not have an independent room to themselves. There are more places of worship in the country (2.4 million) than schools, colleges and hospitals combined.
> (Saran, 2003, p. 34)

Epistemology, reality, and individual experience are deeply intertwined (Marsella, 1985) and one's "believing" and "knowing" are often intimately linked with one's "being". Individuals in each cultural setting direct "attentional focus" towards certain dimensions of lived experiences (Kitayama, 2003), thereby creating specific "domains of heightened activity" (Chaudhary, 2004) that are the substance of cultural content and therefore also of cultural differences. These socially manifested domains are the ambient cultural material from which ways of being are appropriated by functional groups and individuals (Wang, Ceci, Williams, & Kopko, 2004), what Kojima (1998) refers to as the "pool of ideas" in any society. One version of the interdependent views of the self is exemplified in African social thought, which recognizes three basic components of being—the social, the ancestral, and the spiritual. Within this paradigm, those dimensions that are limited by birth and death are separated from those that transcend biological limits, being part of the spiritual, ancestral reality (Nsamenang, 1999). The social practices surrounding the individual are constructed around these self-construals and it is believed that the individual exists "in and for the community" (Atado, 1988, p. 7).

This understanding of the person–community interface is directly in contrast with the Western independent notion of the self, which views the individual as an essentially detached entity with "dispositional attributes" (Markus & Kitayama, 1991). In Western ideology, a newborn baby is close to nature, innocent, and therefore vulnerable and dependent on the adult (Hockey & James, 1993). The subsequent social practices are designated to instill autonomy and self-sufficiency in the child so as to bring up an independent, "mature" individual who thinks, feels, and acts according to his or her own inner beliefs, attitudes, and wishes (Shweder, Goodnow, Hatano, LeVine, Markus, & Miller, 1998). There is thus a great cultural emphasis on the inherent separateness of distinct persons who are encouraged to seek and maintain their independence from others by attending to the self and by discovering and expressing their unique inner attributes, especially positive ones (Kagitcibasi, 1996b; Markus & Kitayama, 1991, 1998; Shweder & Miller, 1991; Triandis, 1989; Wang, 2001a). The formation of an independent self with higher-order abstractions and internal consistency is regarded as an essential component of intellectual maturation.

Such a nagging focus on individuality and autonomy in the Western self-conception is not easily communicated in the native vocabulary in other cultural settings, and may even invoke laughter or amazement (Chaudhary & Sriram, 2001). Indeed, an independent "self" or separate identity often has much less significance in communities where roles and relationships are marked very clearly and where overzealous ascription to the group can even lead to the phenomenon of "hyper-identity" (Valsiner, 2000b, p. 498). For instance, Mwamwenda (1999) discussed the debate behind accepting the existence of an African identity or personality, arguing that the *interdependence* of a person with the context and others in the environment was introduced as an important point of departure from the Western sense of self. Given the political significance of race in African contexts, Mwamwenda (1999) further integrated a racial perspective into the African selfhood. Similarly, in the many East Asian cultures that are influenced by Confucian philosophy, the self is viewed as formulated with supremacy of relations, especially kinship, and a great emphasis is placed upon an individual's appropriate place and behavior among his fellowmen, a characteristic Hsu (1953) termed "situation-centered". Such an interdependent, relational self is regulated and monitored by social rules embedded in specific interpersonal contexts and is often characterized by an individual's overt behaviors as opposed to his or her inner world (Bond, 1991; Chao, 1995; Shweder et al., 1998; Wang & Hsueh, 2000).

Selfhood in Hindu thought illustrates yet another version of self-conception in the interdependent pathway. The self was the central topic of inquiry of the ancient Hindu scriptures, the *Upanishads*, dating back to the period between 1500 and 600 BC. There is a fundamental affirmation of the existence of a self in the *vedanta* tradition (Paranjpe, 1998), one of the main streams of ancient Hindu philosophy. According to the treatise, the ultimate unified reality is the *brahman*, within which individual selves are constituted. The living being, or the sentient, empirical self, is the *jiva* (literally meaning that which breathes) that consists of *prana* (breath) and *manas* (consciousness). The experiences of the self (and therefore all worldly experiences) are seen as illusionary and inconsequential for true happiness and a meaningful life. A focus on *jiva* may further lead to *ahankara* or undesirable pride (*aham* is the Sanskrit word for I or me), which is a strong tendency in every human being and has to be overcome in order to gain a comprehensive grasp of reality. In addition, within the physical limits of this life-world, the sense of self among Hindus is believed to be constantly changing, evolving "partly because the context is given primacy". Bodies are considered to be relatively "porous", "permeable", and predicated upon the different life-circumstances and relationships (Menon, 2003). The possible transformations are determined by one's social and biological states, of being woman or man, pregnant or young and so on. Furthermore, a fundamental connectedness is assumed among all living beings (collective selves or *advaita*). The existence of human beings is seen as essentially linked to society, and social processes are believed to have the same organicity as bodies (Menon, 2003; Trawick, 2003).

Conceptions of selfhood in predominantly independent and interdependent pathways are further reflected in the differential self-defining functions of autobiographical memory across cultures (Chaudhary & Keller, 2003; Wang, 2004; Wang & Conway, 2004). It is a predominant view in Western philosophy and psychology that the self is developed, expressed, and reconstructed from one's accumulated life history (Bruner, 1990; Hume, 1739/1882; Nelson, 1996; Pillemer, 1998). As Hume (1739/1882, p. 542) stated, "Had we no memory, we never shou'd have any notion . . . of that chain of causes and effects, which constitute our self or person". In this view, a coherent, elaborate, well-integrated life history with the individual cast as the central character is indispensable for psychological integrity and well being. In other words, "the sureness of 'I was' is a necessary component of the sureness of 'I am'" (Wyatt, 1963, p. 319). In many East Asian cultures, by contrast, the self is defined less by one's unique autobiographical history but more by an individual's place within a web of relationships (Markus & Kitayama, 1991; Triandis, 1989; Wang, 2001a). Social status and roles, be it as a member of a family, a profession, a group, or a nation, are regarded as crucial elements constituting one's self and identity. Autobiographical memories therefore tend to be judged as less important for personhood in this context (Wang & Conway, 2004). On the other hand, the moral and intellectual values placed on the past in these cultures entail a different usage of autobiographical memory. According to Confucian ethics, a person should examine himself every day on three things: "Have I done my best in doing things for others? Have I been trustworthy in my dealings with friends? And have I failed to revise what the Master had taught me?" This practice of self-reflection (*zi-xing*, 自省) is regarded as an essential means for an individual to achieve *ren* (仁), the supreme virtue of benevolence, moral vitality, and a sensitive concern for others, which is, by Confucian ethics, the highest purpose of life. Thus, autobiographical memory serves an important directive function where in their pursuit of *ren* individuals are urged to routinely examine their own past mistakes for the purpose of perfecting a moral and social self.

That the self has social origins in itself is not a recent notion (Paranjpe, 1998). It is the acceptance of a socially oriented self, quite different from the Western notion of an individual, that has become fascinating to encounter. Indeed, cultural conceptions of selfhood, just like other symbols and terms, constitute an intricate part of the cultural meaning system. They give rise to culture-unique developmental pathways—independent and/or interdependent and the many versions and variations of each—in which individuals come to construct their self and identity, a process that is mediated by or formulated through language.

Language of the self and others

The world of human beings is not just lived, it is created and constructed, and language plays a central role in the reconstitution of reality. The linguistic semiotic system provides "relative stability" to personal encounters (Valsiner, 2001, p. 87) without which it would be difficult to maintain experiential constancy while at the same time being both temporary (in a given instance) and permanent (in the stable meaning-system) (Nelson, 2001). As Polkinghorne (1988, p. 152) claims, "the self is that temporal order of human existence whose story begins with birth, has as its middle the episodes of a lifespan, and ends with death". In this manner, the self can be argued as being a social creation to provide a "sense" of stability to individual life-worlds, while at the same time being dynamically constructed within the time–space manifestations of reality. Both of these processes occur in the realm of linguistic formulation. Narratives of commonplace episodes thus become an important source of self-development, such as childhood memories (Bruner, 1987; Gullestad, 1996; Miller, 1981; Nelson, 1989; Wang, 2001a), emotion talk (Fivush, 1994; Ochs, 1996; Wang, 2001b), person indexing (Budwig, 1990; Rabain-Jamin & Sabeau-Jouannet, 1989), and even narratives surrounding death (Abu-Lughod, 1988).

The available vocabulary within any given language is an important dimension of the canalizing forces within culture. Relationships, both with the self and with others, are dependent on experience, notwithstanding the universal cultural task of constructing an adult person from a biological offspring; this remains a common task in all societies. Each language makes distinct the degree to which relationship details are required; these enumerations then serve the purpose of constructing the social and personal worlds of the interlocutors. At this point, even the relation between language and cognition has to be unfurled as it is not free from confusions. To believe that the two processes are completely overlapping, that language is a transparent view of intrapersonal reality, is misplaced (Kim, 2002). The degree to which speaking one's mind is valued is in itself dependent on the time and place of the episode. Chinese traditional thinking, for instance, does not accept the complete correspondence between language and thought (Kim, 2002). The degree to which speaking is valued, appropriate, or even necessary, can also vary. For instance, silence can be of considerable semantic value, and can be understood as fluctuating between having nothing to say and positive silence, or not needing to say anything in a situation of full intersubjectivity (Markova, 2001; Valsiner, 2001).

The governing power of language is further reflected in its more subtle or implicit operation during interpersonal exchanges. Very often, the social distance between one person and another is largely determined by the context within which the relationship is manifested. For instance, the relationship between two colleagues in a multinational company may be quite unlike the dynamics between a *guru* (teacher) and a *shishya* (student) in the process of learning classical Indian music. The social rules that guide the two situations are embedded in the conventional codes of conduct, constrained by the rules, allowing only a certain degree of acceptable variation. To transact these relationships adequately, languages within culture develop various features of grammar, vocabulary, and usage over the years. For instance, Elgin (2000) compared the sentence "I was riding a horse" in English and its closest translation in Navajo: "The horse and I were moving about". Whereas the English version illustrates a subject–object relation between the rider and the ridee, the Navajo version expresses an equal relationship between two parties engaging in a joint endeavor. Thus relationships can indeed be said to be packaged in and by language, without necessarily arguing which takes precedence.

Thus, language not only serves as a means of reflecting and expressing underlying thought (i.e. communicative function) but is also instrumental in the construction of the self (i.e. representational function) (Budwig, 2000). As proposed within the language socialization approach, language plays an essential role in the communication of cultural content while, at the same time, contributing to meaning construction through language forms (Ochs, 1996). Language learning thus enables children in both linguistic and sociocultural competence. Indeed, language is so deeply embedded in cultural practices that the acquisition of a new language, either for a young child or for an adult immigrant, often entails the establishment of a novel self-system that is conditioned by the newly acquired linguistic representational codes and the accompanying new ways of constructing the sociocultural world (Schrauf, 2000).

Furthermore, the term "self" as a pronoun and pronominal adjective, is a declaration, an indexical act, that the reference is to the specific person or thing mentioned and not to another. In a sense, that which is truly and essentially she or he in a person, versus what is accidental, and therefore not part of that person or thing. The self has also been used to refer to the characteristics constituting conflicting personalities within a human being, the different selves. Speaking about the self has been a central source of information about self-systems. However, talking in general and talking about the self in particular may not be considered a positive action in all situations or in all cultures, and is often linked to the ethos of individualism (Bellah, Madsen, Sullivan, Swidler, & Tipton, 1996; Kim, 2002). Self-presentation and speaking one's mind are taken for granted as a positive personal qualities in cultures that value independence and autonomy. Notably, talking about oneself with others is not equally valued in many other cultures, where people often show clumsiness and even reluctance to discuss their own life experiences and do not encourage others to do so. As Röttger-Rössler (1993) observed in a rural Indonesian community, the villagers "obviously felt very uncomfortable and embarrassed when requested to talk about themselves, and always tried to avoid it" (p. 366). On the other hand, the same villagers were often apt and able to talk about other persons in extensive gossiping and other forms of storytelling in daily life. Thus it is vital to acknowledge the prevailing sociocultural dynamics around speaking about the self and others, whether in everyday or research situations, during self-analysis in any locale.

The evidence of varied degrees of self-focus is readily available in the yarns that we weave as storytellers in the narratives of the everyday. "It is part of the *othering* nature of language that it forces upon its subjects an endless series of value-laden representational choices. . . Thus ordinary language and casual conversation have by now gained huge ontological respectability" (Nair, 2002, p. 4, emphasis added). Human beings are thus "centers of narrative gravity" (Dennett as cited in Nair, 2002, p. 5) as, in making conversational choices, they keep themselves in perpetual focus, even when they speak about other people and places. Narratives may not be a display of the self to the same extent in different cultures, however. In the narratives of European American children during a storytelling task, it was found that the narratives centered on children's own roles and actions. By contrast, Chinese children tended to focus much more on social and interactional details (Wang & Leichtman, 2000). In the telling of their own stories, therefore, children displayed different degrees of self-focus and of attention to social details. Interestingly, even at American preschools, it is a common practice that, every Monday morning, the youngsters sit in a circle each telling a story about the fun things he or she did over the past weekend. Cultural practice thus organizes the ways in which people talk about themselves and others, and here we can see the intersection of culture and language. This principle is effective even in talking about collective identities. Among Bedouin Arabs for instance, one cannot really talk about "women" *per se*. "Every woman is a sister, daughter, wife, mother or aunt and it is the role and relationship that usually determines how she will be perceived and treated" and therefore also how she will see herself (Abu-Lughod, 1988, p. 152).

The person-talk in Hindi—one of the official languages of India, spoken by a large proportion of the population, particularly in north-central India—provides another illustration for the influence of language on self-construction. Based on the ways in which person-talk is expressed in conversation in Indian families, Mohanty (1999) identified four socialization goals of communicative competence: orientation towards social status and role-appropriate language use; instruction, practice and exposure to culturally appropriate communication; transmission of values and affect; and communicating in different languages, appropriate to the domain and person. The communication patterns within the family are located in the contextual, highly empathic relationships typical of the Indian family system. If these empathic overtures are missed, there is a tremendous scope for misunderstanding intended communications, as has been found in some of the research on Indian families. In a study of the patterns of person talk in Indian families, Chaudhary (1999) found that there was a predominant reference to other people in mothers' conversations with children. These people were mostly addressed by kin terms appropriate from the child's perspective, even when there was no relationship with the person. Children were socialized for and began to express a rich repertoire of kin terms by the time they were 3 years of age, and they seemed to use these terms accurately, even in new encounters. Age and gender markings were particularly emphasized in the conversations. Similarly, Das (1989) observed in north-Indian homes that "(M)others not only teach infants the use of language and other social skills but also in their very manner of communicating make a gift of self and the world to the child. I may say that often the mother not only talks *to* the child but she *'talks'* the child into being—gives it, as it were, an embodiment in language" (Das, 1989, p. 265).

In the indexing of selfhood in Hindi, we encounter a very elaborate kin terminology, with several minor variations within the lexicon to allow delicate maneuverings in the expression of perspective, regard and respect that support the expression of social positioning and interpersonal dynamics. Such form of person-talk is in direct contrast with the self-focused narrative genre populated in many Western societies, and they are aimed at different communicative and representational goals. Linguistic discourse, through the structure and lexicon of the particular language spoken and the social arrangement of the communicative context, makes salient some qualities or representations in conceptions of the self and others. In other words, talk as a form of action directs individuals' attention to particular cultural models of self and others in their efforts to create inner meaning for themselves and to understand social meaning shared with significant others and the community, thus having powerful psychosocial consequences (Holland & Quinn, 1987). However, it is not only the sociohistorical features of the community, the particular folk-beliefs about the self, and the linguistic features of the language used that contribute to the interactive creation of the particular cultural realities in independent or interdependent pathways; it is also through adults' deliberate or implicit socialization intention and children's own participation and agency that conceptions of the self and others become fashioned. We turn to this next.

Organization of social practices

The emergence of the self in the ontogenetic span of a human being is closely linked with the knowledge of and experience with other fellow human beings. Everyday activities and rituals, and the social relationships they entail, supply an important resource for the construction of the self that is culturally adaptive and interpersonally functional. For instance, the Indian conception of "*samskara*", the rituals of refinement, includes the transformative experiences that are believed to guide a person's life-course and prescribe certain activities that are central to a spiritually appropriate life-course. Participating in these rituals is also believed to influence the peace and well-being of ancestors as well as future generations and is therefore regarded as an essential function of a household and its members (Menon, 2003). *Samskara* hence provides individuals with social affordance through which the self and self-in-relation (to significant others and to gods) are constructed and shaped. Thus, the self is a cultural creation formed within social interactions and negotiations that are embedded in particular cultural organization of social practices.

There is no denying that different cultures value and socialize children in different pathways relevant within particular world views that carry specific ideas about ontogenesis. These ethnotheories steer the community towards structuring of childhood environments, socialization practices, and educational endeavors in culturally appropriate ways (Bruner, 1996; Nsamenang, 2000). For instance, in a Western home, the face-to-face, verbal interaction of a caregiver and her infant with the inclusion of interaction with play material is a common event (Keller & Greenfield, 2000), whereas in others, physical activity and body contact may be considered far more essential for young babies (Keller, Yovsi, & Voelker, 2002). These different practices are intended by socialization agents to facilitate the development of characters and behaviors in children that are culturally adaptive. As Kagan, Kearsley, and Zelazo (1980) reported, when asked to rank traits on a scale from most to least characteristic of their children, Chinese mothers tended to believe that physically staying close to the mother was the trait most characteristic of their children, whereas European American mothers often gave top ranks to laughing easily, being active, and being talkative.

Different childcare arrangements across cultures also reflect and reinforce self-development in independent and interdependent pathways. In many Western societies, although the cultural ideal for early childhood is still centered around care by the mother, many children start daycare at around 2 years of age, or even younger, because both their parents have to work. Whereas many other societies share this ideology for maternal childcare, they appear to offer more options than leaving young infants in strangers' hands. One important and common practice has to do with the involvement of grandparents, who have become frequent caregivers of young children whose parents are both employed. Indeed, such a childcare arrangement appears to be preferred by the parents over daycare. For instance, in a study of daycare choices of young Indian urban employed parents, Kapoor (2005) found that there was an order of preference for the family. The best alternative was believed to be the grandmother (maternal or paternal), followed by another family member, domestic helpers in the home, and lastly daycare. Institutional care was opted for as a last resort as it was considered basically inappropriate for the young child. In the words of a grandfather, ". . . It is torture for a child to be in a centre at such an early age . . . as and when she starts speaking . . . then, I suppose she can happily go" (Kapoor, 2005). Even after moving to other countries, many Asian couples maintain this value for home-based care. They often request the assistance of their own parents, who willingly travel to participate in the "appropriate" care of the young baby in an alien society. Evidently, the interdependence among kinship members in Asian cultures makes possibly home-based care for young children, which, in turn, is likely to facilitate self-development towards interdependence.

Family narrative practices, especially family conversations about shared experiences, play a crucial role in children's acquisition and development of autobiographical and conceptual self (e.g. Fivush, 1994; Fivush & Hudson, 1990; Nelson, 1993, 1996; Pillemer & White, 1989; Tessler & Nelson, 1994).

As Middleton and Edwards (1990) claimed, family memory-sharing serves as a rich learning environment "in which the parent takes pains to elicit perceptions, memories and judgments from the children, to examine and elaborate upon them, to contextualize and assign significance to them, in terms of a shared past in which personal identity, family relationships and the landmarks of development can be reconstructed" (p. 41). Thus, from parents' modeling of conversational styles and ways of thinking and talking about the past, children learn to create narratives about their own experiences and to further construct an enduing self-concept. More importantly, family narrative practices are interwoven into the larger fabric of the culture, where culture-specific values, beliefs, and ideologies are institutionalized in various material and symbolic ways that create and reconsolidate different views of selfhood in children (Wang & Brockmeier, 2002).

Family memory-sharing often takes different forms and contents across cultures, reflecting the prevailing cultural orientations toward autonomy versus relatedness. Mullen and Yi (1995) conducted a 1-day observation of conversational interactions between Euro-American and Korean mothers and their 3-year-old children. Mother and child each wore a vest containing a small tape-recorder during the day that recorded their naturally occurring conversations. European American mothers engaged their 3-year-old children in talking about past events three times as often as Korean mothers. Studies by Wang and colleagues (Wang, 2001b; Wang, Leichtman, & Davies, 2000) showed that when European American and Chinese mothers talked with their 3-year-old children at home about shared past events, American mothers often used an elaborative conversational style where they dwelled on specific episodes, supplemented children's responses with rich and embellished information, and provided immediate feedback to scaffold children's participation. Such conversations created an opportunity for children to learn to construct elaborate stories about themselves. In contrast, Chinese mothers often employed a pragmatic conversational style where they directed the conversations by frequently posing and repeating factual questions, provided little detail or embellishment to assist the child's participation, and often tried to elicit correct answers in a way that emulated a memory test. Such conversations seem not to focus on personal storytelling but more on reinforcing the position of the mother as an authority figure.

Furthermore, memory talk between European American parents and their preschool-aged children often takes a child-centered approach, where the child remains the focal point of the conversation and the mother frequently refers to the child's interests, preferences, opinions, and personal attributes. By contrast, memory talk in Korean (Mullen & Yi, 1995) and Chinese (Wang, 2001b; Wang et al., 2000) families often takes a mother-centered, hierarchically organized approach in which mothers set the direction of the conversation, emphasize interpersonal relations, and frequently refer to moral rules and behavioral expectations with their children. For instance, Miller and colleagues (Miller, Fung, & Mintz, 1996; Miller, Wiley, Fung, & Liang, 1997) observed that during memory-sharing with their two-and-a-half-year-olds, Taiwanese Chinese parents often narrated the child's past transgressions in front of a nonfamily member, repeatedly invoking moral and social norms, and structuring their stories so as to establish the child's rule violation as the point of the story. By contrast, European American parents, in the rare instances when they acknowledged the child's past transgressions, tended to downplay the child's wrongdoing and to tell the story in a humorous, nonserious manner. The researchers argued that, by operating with an explicitly evaluative, overtly self-critical framework, Chinese parents encouraged children's obedience to authority, appropriate conduct, and a sense of shame. By contrast, American parents used an implicitly evaluative, overtly self-affirming framework intended to protect or enhance the child's self-esteem. Evidently, the didactic attitude of Asian parents accords with the Confucian ethics shared in these cultures, which emphasize discipline, moral rectitude, and filial piety (Ho, 1986; Wu, 1996), whereas the narrative interactions between American parents and their children reflect the cultural emphasis on autonomy and self-affirmation.

In a similar vein, Chaudhary (1999) observed that during everyday conversations in Indian families, adults—mothers, grandmothers, and aunts—frequently referred to other people and rarely mentioned themselves when conversing with children. Such conversations created a complex and vibrant group of people with whom the child was affiliated, no matter whether these people were present in the immediate setting. The omission of oneself in a conversation implies a need to highlight others and to avoid attention to the speaker (Buhler, 1990), thus in consonance with the cultural importance placed on other people within the Indian family. Through such conversations, Indian adults model to their children the mode of highlighting the social–cultural dimensions of reality when constructing stories of oneself. In addition, due to the multiplicity of caregivers in Hindu India, mothers often encourage their children to actively interact with others instead of remaining in exclusive closeness with the mother (Chaudhary, 1999; Kakar, 1978; Kurtz, 1992; Minturn & Hitchcock, 1966). Narrative is often evoked to help "incorporate" the child into the social group and to instill a sense of belonging.

Social practices, especially those within the family, structure the everyday activities children engage in and determine whom children interact with. They are organized in varied cultural contexts that comprise culturally prescribed role negotiation between parents and children (e.g. hierarchical and/or equal), parent's implicit and explicit child-rearing goals (e.g. to establish autonomy and/or relatedness), and the culture's prevailing views of selfhood (e.g., independent and/or interdependent). Social practices thus constitute an important cultural dimension that directs self-development in culturally favored fashions. Ultimately, culturally organized social practices assume an important forum of intergenerational transmission of independent or interdependent pathways.

Cultural heterogeneity

Although the development of the self in a particular society may observe a predominant developmental pathway, independent or interdependent, within-culture variations are more than common between subcultural groups and among individuals. There are further variations within an individual such that one's self-views may change across domains and contexts. In addition, cultures in favor of a particular developmental pathway may often have internal differences rather than being homogeneous as implied in the general terms of independence and interdependence (e.g. Nakamura, 1964). All these variations reflect the complexity of the human self and indeed highlight the cultural specificity of its constructive process. They reveal culture as "a mode of configuration" (Wang & Brockmeier, 2002) that manifests itself in not only social institutions but also in the actions, thoughts, emotions, beliefs, and moral values of individuals and thereby regulates both intrapersonal and interpersonal psychological functions (Bruner, 1990; D'Andrade, 1992; Valsiner, 2000a; Vygotsky, 1978). We here discuss various forms of variations as they unfold with the heterogeneity of a culture and its social settings.

Differences within cultures could be brought about by various factors associated with different demographic patterns, economic progress, educational facilities, and a host of other factors. Findings on gender, for instance, illustrate that the discourse of women and girls is essentially different from that of men, reflecting inherent differences in the relational profile of women and men. Women tend to tell their personal stories with detailed interpersonal episodes and vivid emotions, whereas men tend to provide skeletal descriptions of personal events focusing on autonomy and often remember for the purpose of savoring a triumph or evaluating their progress in life (e.g. Buckner & Fivush, 1998; Davis, 1999; Gilligan, 1992; Merriam & Cross, 1982; Ross & Holmberg, 1990; Thorne, 1995). Theorists argue that becoming a person through the course of sexual maturity (Behar, 1996) and the accompanying multiple societal influences (Cross & Madson, 1997; Gilligan, 1992) lead women to focus on social connectedness and men to focus on individual agency. Another example comes from varied self-construction processes between different social–economic groups. For instance, Wiley, Rose, Burger, and Miller (1998) did extensive observations of adult–child personal storytelling in families from two European American urban communities (the working and middle classes). In both communities, family members engaged young children in conversations in ways that encouraged autonomy where children were given ample opportunities to navigate the talk of their past experiences. However, while to express one's view was a natural right for middle-class children, it had to be earned and defended for working-class children. Thus, parents in these communities differed in the versions of autonomy they tried to promote, each of which is conceivably adaptive to the specific social features of the respective communities.

In addition to considering subcultural factors, the development and expression of the self must be understood within specific domains and contexts. Some researchers have argued that the self is not a unitary entity but is expressed through multiple identities in different contexts, that is, a "simultaneous and situational" multiplicity, not time-less and context-free (Gullestad, 1996, p. 6). The establishment of identities encompasses various levels or domains such as personal, ethnic, religious, legal, minority and national identities (Hermans, 1996; Nelson, 1989; Neisser, 1988; Roland, 1988). Based on their analysis of data on children's self-concepts, Wang and Li (2003) proposed that attending to specific domains of psychological functioning helps to locate culture-specific conceptions of the self and their effects on child development in meaningful contexts. Individuals in real life move in and out of different domains and contexts that constitute different aspects of their lives (e.g. children live in the family and also go to school regularly), which sometimes leads to a mismatch or what Hymes (1972) called "sociolinguistic interference" (p. 287). Although some personality traits may remain relatively stable, the components of one's self can be subject to changes to adapt to the requirements put forth by various domains. Thus, the same Chinese child who is very yielding to her siblings at home can be quite competitive and independent in academic work at school. Indeed, helping children adjust their behavior and cognition to meet different expectations of the settings is seen as an important goal of family socialization in many Asian cultures (Bosma & Gerlsma, 2003; Kaura & Chaudhary, 2003).

Furthermore, Wang and Li (2003) emphasized that the self within any single domain is complex and multi-layered. The self may be predominantly social in some aspects of a domain, more autonomous in others, and mixed in yet others, as exemplified in the domain of social relations for Chinese individuals. In Chinese family life—an important component subsumed under the larger domain of social relations, the social orientation is often so strong that individual boundaries are least delineated (although there are very clear boundaries for certain aspects, such as sexual privacy). This phenomenon was termed "expressive tie" (Hwang, 1987), whereby a Chinese individual can comfortably and willingly merge with other family members (Hsu, 1953; Yang, 1996). Thus, because of the enduring Confucian value placed on the family, family life constitutes a particular context in the social domain in which Chinese individuals exhibit probably the most interdependence. However, Chinese individuals sometimes draw a clearer boundary between themselves and others in social circles, such as acquaintances, classmates, and co-workers (Hwang, 1987). For instance, in friends' circles, there is a more mixed mode where individuals may display in some contexts a great sense of relatedness (e.g. giving and requesting help without reservation) but remain cautious in other contexts with the same people (e.g. not criticizing each other's children). The social boundary between the self and others thus tends to be more restrictive under such circumstances than in one's own family. These domain-specific views pertain to the self both within and across cultures (Wang & Li, 2003).

Individual differences within a culture constitute another important dimension of cultural heterogeneity. Cultural ideologies, beliefs, and practices may not be accepted by every individual in that culture to the same extent or in the same fashion. Given the immense individual variations in biological predisposition, physical–social environment, psychological constituents (e.g. personality), there is bound to be a gap between the collective and personal manifestations of the self. After all, it is through specific individual minds and within specific social contexts that a particular developmental pathway comes to unfold. Individuals do not act mechanically according to cultural expectations. Instead, they actively participate in social–cultural activities and thus create their own experiences in the developmental niche (D'Andrade, 1992; Shweder et al., 1998; Valsiner, 2000a; Wang et al., 2004). During this process, they select, modify, and dispute ideas from the "public pool" they share with other members of their culture, which results in individual variations in the internalization and application of cultural views of the self. Some variations may be deviant from the predominant developmental pathway in a given culture, nevertheless their existence may be functional for the individual in adapting to specific situational or contextual demands. The individualized enculturation processes give rise to both commonality and diversity among individuals within a single culture.

Cultural heterogeneity is further reflected in the encouragement of individual agency in societies that favor interdependent pathways. For instance, in many East Asian cultures a long tradition, originating from Confucian teachings, emphasizes a life-long pursuit of self-perfection. As reflected in the Confucian concept of self-cultivation, individuals are encouraged to strive to achieve intellectual and moral integrity, that is, to acquire *ren*, through continuous active learning, practice, and self-examination (Li, 2001). Those who commit themselves to this process are regarded as "Jun-zi" (君子), i.e. moral persons (Tu, 1979). These humanitarian views entail a sensitive concern for the agentic side of the individual self, in addition to its social side that is also well defined and equally emphasized in Confucian ethics. The acknowledgement of individual agency can also be found in Hindu belief system. Instead of imposing a uniform moral code of conduct, the notion of right and wrong that is prescribed, the very foundation of morality (*dharma*), is linked to the situation in the time–space–person dynamics. Furthermore, the ultimate subject, according to the *Vedantic* traditions, is the *atman* (literally meaning breath of life) or the real self—a component and manifestation of divinity in every individual. All other forms, the *jiva*, the ego, the mind, the body, and the outside world, are the known elements, or objects, associated with worldly experiences. The fundamental purpose of an individual is to gain gradual but effective separation from all worldly experiences, whether they are material, personal, or social. This process requires *"karma"*—the act of doing, creating or making something, through which individuals eventually achieve a true understanding of the *atman* and thus a state of self-realization (Menon, 2003; Paranjpe, 1998; Radhakrishnan, 1997). Such a notion of the essential but indiscernible selfhood in Hindu thought is, teleologically speaking, highly "individualistic" in nature.

Notably, the individual agency elaborated in Asian philosophies is dissimilar in fundamental ways to the "free will" or "self-rule" sense of agency in Western thinking. Whereas the former entails actively seeking one's intellectual, moral, or spiritual potential with a possible outcome for the larger good, the latter emphasizes motivated action of an individual to act willingly, with a sense of efficacy and volition, toward a desired outcome of the self (Kagitcibasi, in press). Thus, individual agency appears to show varied manifestations in different developmental pathways consistent with the culture's emphasis on autonomy or relatedness. Equally importantly, a cultural preference for individuality does not imply that individuals in these cultures do not care about social relations. On the contrary, altruism, empathy, and sensitive concerns for others' well being are no less common in these cultures than in those with an interdependent focus. Nevertheless, unlike in interdependent cultures where significant others and social contexts are constant defining features of the self, social relations in independent cultures tend to be voluntary and individuals generally perceive themselves as separate from other people, including significant others such as family members (Hsu, 1953). Again, relatedness seems to take different forms in constituting the self in independent and interdependent pathways.

The development of the self is in response to not only the predominant cultural views and practices pertaining to selfhood, but also to the ideologies of particular social groups individuals belong to (e.g. gender, race, class), to the psychosocial demands of various domains constituting individuals' lives (e.g. social relations, achievement, morality), to the enculturational processes individuals actively contribute to, and to the ethnotheories of what constitutes individual agency and relatedness. Such cultural heterogeneity in self-development does not imply chaos or lack of order. Instead, it underscores the cultural and contextual sensitivity of the constructive process of the self and demonstrates that it is through the dynamic interplay between culture and the individual that the human self eventually comes into shape. The various forms of variations in self-construction further reveal the quantitative nature of cultural differences both between and within independent and interdependent developmental pathways, where autonomy and relatedness as two integrated processes are complementary and co-constructive.

Self-development in different cultural contexts

We have discussed how the four cultural processes operate to produce cultural specificity in the development of the self in independent and inter-dependent pathways. We now turn to the cognitive consequences of their manifestation, presenting empirical data on self-concept and autobiographical memory in children and adults in different cultures. Research investigations take place within the cycle of theory–method–phenomena dynamics (Valsiner, 2000b) and the unpackaging of research process can provide important insights into the cultural (academic and everyday culture) construction of selfhood and identity.

Although self-theorists have long recognized the importance of culture in the development of the self, empirical research has been more recent. In one of the few pioneer studies, Stigler, Smith, and Mao (1985) administered the Perceived Competence Scale for Children (Harter, 1982) to 714 fifth-graders in Taiwan. They then compared the results with those in equivalent US samples. It was found that Chinese children rated their own competence significantly lower than their American counterparts, downgrading themselves in relation to other children. As Stigler et al. suggested, this finding reflects the endorsement of humbleness and self-effacement in Chinese culture as a means of facilitating social harmony, compared with the cultural emphasis on self-enhancement and affirmation in the USA. It thus provides evidence for the self-development of Chinese and US children along different developmental pathways. Many early studies like this one, however, often suffered from methodological limitations, where measures developed for Western populations were administered to non-Western samples (see Greenfield, 1997; Harter, 1999 for critiques of this strategy).

Recent work has used more culture-sensitive methodologies. In particular, many researchers favor open-ended, interpretive methods, where children "generate their own self-descriptions, using their own vocabularies and guided by their unique perspectives on themselves" (Hart & Edelstein, 1992, p. 304). Compared with psychometric measures with pre-existing norms often favoring Western children, open-ended techniques are more neutral and appear more natural to children in different cultures (e.g. Harter, 1999; Shweder et al., 1998; Wang & Leichtman, 2000; Zahn-Waxler, Friedman, Cole, Mizuta, & Hiruma, 1996). For example, Hart et al. (1986) used an open-ended format to elicit self-descriptions of children and adolescents (6- to 16-year-olds) from the USA and from a small, communally oriented fishing village in Puerto Rico. They found that in response to questions such as "What kind of person are you?" Puerto Rican children frequently described themselves in terms of their social qualities (e.g. "I have a brother" and "I try not to hurt my friends' feelings"), whereas US children tended to focus on their psychological qualities (e.g. "I am a happy person" and "I believe in world peace"). Using a storytelling paradigm, Zahn-Waxler and her colleagues (1996) examined Japanese and European American preschool children's verbal and behavioral responses to hypothetical interpersonal dilemmas. They found that US children expressed more anger and aggression than Japanese children, who more often reported positive emotions even in response to potentially distressing situations. These differences in children's emotional reactions were associated with the greater encouragement of children's emotional expressivity among US mothers and the greater emphasis on psychological discipline and control of emotions and impulses among Japanese mothers. They further suggest that, by preschool age, US children had acquired the cultural script of autonomy and defending one's position during interpersonal conflict, whereas Japanese children have developed a sense of sameness of self and other.

Studies have further examined the narrative construction of autobiographical experiences in children of different cultures. As Bruner (1990, p. 8) maintained, narrative is an instrument for making meaning that dominates much of life in one's culture, and the child's improvement in narrative skill is "not simply a mental achievement, but an achievement of social practice that lends stability to the child's social life". One of the first studies in this approach was done by Han, Leichtman, and Wang (1998). Euro-American and native Korean and Chinese 4- and 6-year-olds recounted their past experiences (e.g. their last birthday) with a familiar adult interviewer in respective cultures. Compared with their Asian peers, US children provided more elaborate and detailed memory narratives in which they produced lengthier propositions (subject–verb constructions) and used more descriptives (words that provide descriptive texture to the narrative, such as adjectives, adverbs, and modifiers) when talking about their experiences. US children also made more references to specific past events than did Asian children, who talked more frequently about daily routines or script events. In addition, US children made greater usage of internal state language, including talks about inner emotional and cognitive processes and personal preferences and evaluations. In particular, they mentioned more than twice as many personal preferences and evaluations as Asian children did, which furthers the notion that Asian children are less practiced than US children in formulating and focusing on their own subjective judgments. By contrast, both Korean and Chinese children spoke more of other people relative to themselves than did US children, which reflects the emphasis on social relations, knowledge of other people, and attention to obligations to others during Asian family narrative practices (Chaudhary, 1999; Miller et al., 1996; Mullen & Yi, 1995; Wang et al., 2000).

To further capture the social characteristics of children's personal narratives, Wang and Leichtman (2000) asked Chinese and European American kindergartners to recount instances in which they felt a particular emotion such as happiness, fear, sad, or anger. Content analyses revealed that, compared with US children, Chinese children showed a greater tendency to introduce social interactions and positive interpersonal relations, a greater concern with moral correctness and authority, and less of a tendency to express individual judgments, opinions, or self-determination in their memory narratives. In a more recent study, Wang (2004) examined the emergence of cultural self-construct as reflected in children's remembered and conceptual aspects of the self. Euro-American and Chinese children in preschool and through to second grade participated. During individual interviews, children were invited to play a "question-and-answer game" in which they recounted four autobiographical events and described themselves in response to open-ended questions. US children tended to provide lengthy, detailed, and emotionally elaborate memories and to cast themselves as the central character of the story; they also frequently described themselves in terms of personal attributes, abstract dispositions, and inner traits in a positive light. By comparison, Chinese children provided relatively skeletal accounts of past experiences, which tended to center on social interactions and daily routines; and they often described themselves in terms of social roles, context-specific characteristics, and overt behaviors in a neutral or modest tone. These findings support the notion that the self is a constructed meaning system of culture that emerges early in life.

The stylistic and content differences in personal narratives of children in different cultures become even more prominent among adults, including adults' recollections of childhood experiences. Mullen (1994) found that earliest childhood memories of Koreans frequently involved scolding or discipline and, most strikingly, "the majority of the memories of Koreans (78%) involved other people, while 50% of the memories of Caucasians involved only the self" (p. 74). MacDonald, Uesiliana, and Hayne (2000) compared earliest childhood memories of New Zealanders. They found that growing up in an environment where funerals are an important part of community life and often involve active participation of young children, many Maori adults recalled in their earliest memories funerals that occurred when they were as young as age three, while none of the participants of European or Asian descent did. In a study of adults' earliest childhood memory and self-concept in the USA and China, Wang (2001a) found that European Americans often provided memories that were voluminous, specific, self-focused, and emotionally elaborate. By contrast, memories of native Chinese tended to be brief and centered on collective activities, general routines, and emotionally neutral events. In addition, Americans placed a greater emphasis on individual attributes in describing themselves (e.g. "I am honest, happy, intelligent") than did Chinese, who included a greater number of social roles and group memberships in their self-descriptions (e.g. "I am a Buddhist, a son, a student"). The same pattern of cultural differences in memory style and content has also been found in autobiographical memories from later life periods (Wang & Conway, 2004). Furthermore, when contrasting responses of self-remembering between German and Indian young adults, Chaudhary and Keller (2003) found that the German youth tended to describe past events, objects and people from their own point of view, without mentioning that of others. In comparison, the Indians had particular ways of not only including but also taking the perspective of others fairly constitutive in their remembering (e.g. "My mother used to tell that I used to love singing as a child" and "Everyone in my family used to say that I was a fussy child"). Although in both cases memories of the self were constructed around one's own understanding, the remembering seemed personal for the German youth while fundamentally social for the Indians, for whom the voices of others having an important place in the act of remembering and recounting of the self.

Intriguingly, different ways of self-understanding are not only reflected in how people remember and convey autobiographical information but also in the accessibility of such information over time (see Wang, 2003, for a review). For instance, Mullen (1994) found that Caucasian Americans had earliest childhood memories approximately 6 months earlier than Asian Americans, and 17 months earlier than native Koreans. Similarly, Wang (2001a) found that Caucasian American adults remembered events they experienced at about age 3.5, almost 6 months earlier than native Chinese. MacDonald et al. (2000) also showed that European New Zealanders recalled earlier childhood experiences than did Asians. Furthermore, consonant with their oral tradition and their cultural emphasis on the importance of the past, Maori adults (32.6 months) reported earliest memories from 10 months earlier than Europeans (42.9 months) and more than 2 years earlier than Asians (57.8 months). Wang, Conway, and Hou (2004) asked Chinese, British, and Caucasian American adults to recall as many childhood memories (of events occurring below the age of 5 years), including their earliest memory, as they could in a 5-minute period. Caucasian Americans (12.24) recalled the greatest number of childhood memories, followed by British (9.83), and then Chinese (5.68); and Chinese adults again had earliest memory 6 months later than either of the Western groups.

Taken together, the existing cross-cultural data indicate that people, both children and adults, show systematic differences in the ways they perceive themselves and remember their personal experiences, which reflect the manifestation of independent and interdependent developmental pathways. A focus on autonomy versus relatedness in the cultural conception of selfhood may affect whether and to what extent cognitive processes and resources are channeled into the early development of an articulate, detailed, and self-focused personal history. Relevant language usage and social practices in a culture further shape self-development in ways that support the predominant self-views. In particular, elaborative, child-centered memory talk acts to promote the encoding and retention of personally unique autobiographical information in independent cultures where the development of autobiographical memory is prioritized. Memory in these cultures serves to differentiate the self from others and so provides an important means of constructing a unique individual identity, even at early ages.

Conclusion: "One mind, many mentalities"

Summing research in diverse disciplines, we have shown that the development of the self comprises an active constructive process within which culture, community, and psyche coordinate and facilitate the transformation of one mind into many mentalities (Shweder et al., 1998). First of all, the universally evolved biological heritage of ontogeny and the corresponding societal expectations make common threads in the pattern of self-development among children from different parts of the world possible. For example, at the "age of reason" (5 to 7 years of age), children of all cultures or communities are expected to begin their formal schooling or to help out in the household or field, a societal demand corresponding with children's physical and intellectual maturation (Sameroff & Haith, 1996). Children then develop skills of self-understanding and remembering that reflect their cognitive progress and social participation.

Such commonality in individual self-development further interacts with and is shaped by cultural processes that are themselves manifestations of norms, beliefs, linguistic symbols, and social practices of a particular culture, community, or family. These cultural processes can be characterized, among many possible ways, as functioning in independent and inter-dependent pathways through development. Depending on the predominant views of self and relevant social–linguistic practices in their culture, children develop their conceptual and remembered aspects of the self in respective pathways, which are thus both the cause and the consequence of the dynamic constructive process of self-development. In addition to the varied patterns in the ways children and people understand themselves and others in different cultural settings, it is equally true that cultural groups can have internal divergences in the form and manner in which the self is manifested in systematic and spontaneous ways. Such within-culture heterogeneity reflects the multi-faceted nature of the self and creates patterns of self-development with coexisting contradictions and different levels and domains of cultural specificity, which perhaps can be called alternative pathways or sub-pathways.

Importantly, the cultural processes of self-construction are themselves dynamic and transformative under the influences of migration, urbanization, industrialization, intercultural exchange, and so on. Such changes may create new ways in which individuals creatively construct their selves in response to requirements and challenges of the historical era they live in. For instance, Asian American parents are found to emphasize independence and personal sufficiency to their children to a greater extent than do Caucasian American parents, and this is not done at the expense of family interdependence that is equally valued in their socialization practices (e.g. Lin & Fu, 1990; Wang & Hsueh, 2000). Such emphases on both autonomy and relatedness may result in the development of what Kagitcibasi (1996a) termed "autonomous relational self", a construct adaptive to the conditions of life and social structures of the contemporary US society. Indeed, children growing up in this modern age are constantly encountering new ideologies, new technologies, and new ways of thinking, which makes the construction of the self an ever-complex process during which the individual and the collective interact, negotiate, and accommodate for the development of an adaptive and well-functioning psyche.

References

Abu-Lughod, L. (1988). Fieldwork of a dutiful daughter. In S. Altorki and C. F. El-Solh (Eds.), *Arab women in the field: Studying your own society* (pp. 139–161). New York: Syracuse University Press.

Alexander, C. N. & Langer, E. J. (1990) (Eds.). *Higher stages of human development: Perspectives on adult growth*. London: Oxford University Press.

Amsterdam, B. K. (1972). Mirror self-image reactions before age two. *Developmental Psychology*, 5, 297–305.

Atado, J. C. (1988). *African marriage customs and church law*. Kano, Nigeria: Heinemann.

Barth, F. (1997). How is the self conceptualized? Variations among cultures. In U. Neisser & D. A. Jopling (Eds.), *The conceptual self in context* (pp. 75–91). New York: Cambridge University Press.

Baumeister, R. F. (1998). The self. In D. T. Gilbert, S. T. Fiske, & G. Lindzey (Eds.), *The handbook of social psychology* (Vol. 1, 4th edn, pp. 680–683). Boston, MA: Mcgraw-Hill.

Behar, R. (1996). The girl in the cast. In M. Gullestad (Ed.). *Imagined childhoods: Self and society in autobiographical accounts* (pp. 217–240). Oslo, Norway: Scandinavian University Press.

Bellah, R. N., Madsen, R., Sullivan, W. M., Swidler, A., & Tipton, S. M. (1996). *Habits of the heart: Individualism and commitment in American life*. Berkeley, CA: University of California Press.

Bond, M. H. (1991). *Beyond the Chinese face*. Hong Kong: Oxford University Press.

Bosma, H., & Gerlsma, C. (2003). From early attachment relations to the adolescent and adult organisation of the self. In J. Valsiner, & K. J. Connolly (Eds.), *Handbook of developmental psychology* (pp. 450–488). London: Sage.

Bruner, J. (1987). Life as narrative. *Social Research*, *54*, *1*, p. 15.

Bruner, J. (1990). *Acts of meaning*. Cambridge, MA: Harvard University Press.

Bruner, J. (1996). *The culture of education*. Cambridge, MA: Harvard University Press.

Buckner, J. P., & Fivush, R. (1998). Gender and self in children's autobiographical narratives. *Applied Cognitive Psychology*, *12*(4), 407–429.

Budwig, N. (1990). A functional approach to the acquisition of personal pronouns. In G. Conti-Ramden & C. E. Snow (Eds.), Children's language (Vol. 7, pp. 121–146). Hillsdale, NJ: Lawrence Erlbaum Associates Inc.

Budwig, N. (2000). Language and the construction of self. In N. Budwig, I. Uzgiris, & J. V. Wertsch (Eds.), *Communication: An arena of development* (pp. 195–214). Stamford, CT: Ablex Publishing Company.

Buhler, K. (1990). *Theory of language: The representational function of language*. Philadelphia, PA: John Benjamin Publishing Company.

Case, R. (1991). Stages in the development of the young child's first sense of self. *Developmental Review, 11*, 210–230.

Chao, R. K. (1995). Chinese and European American cultural models of the self reflected in mothers' childrearing beliefs. *Ethos, 23*(3), 328–354.

Chaudhary, N. (1999). Language socialisation: Patterns of caregiver speech to young children. In T. S. Saraswathi (Ed.), *Culture, socialisation and human development* (pp. 145–166). New Delhi: Sage.

Chaudhary, N. (2004). *Listening to culture.* New Delhi: Sage.

Chaudhary, N., & Keller, H. (July, 2003). *Memories of me: Autobiographical memories of youth from Germany and India.* Presented at the conference of the International Association for Cross Cultural Psychology, Budapest, Hungary, July, 2003.

Chaudhary, N., & Sriram, S. (2001). Dialogues of the self. *Culture and Psychology, 7*(3), 379–393.

Clausen, J. A. (1993). *American lives: Looking back at the children of the Great Depression.* New York: Free Press.

Conway, M., & Pleydell-Pearce, C. W. (2000). The construction of autobiographical memories in the self-memory system. *Psychological Review, 107*(2), 261–288.

Costanzo, P. R. (1992). External socialization and the development of adaptive individuation and social connection. In D. N. Ruble, P. E. Costanzo, & M. E. Oliveri (Eds.), *Social psychology and mental health* (pp. 55–80). New York: Guilford.

Cross, S. E., & Madson, L. (1997). Models of the self: Self-construals and gender. *Psychological Bulletin, 122*, 5–37.

Damon, W. (1983). *Social and personality development.* New York: Norton.

Damon, W., & Hart, D. (1988). *Self-understanding in childhood and adolescence.* New York: Cambridge University Press.

D'Andrade, R. G. (1992). Schemas and motivation. In R. G. D'Andrade & C. Strauss (Eds.), *Human motives and cultural models* (pp. 23–44). New York: Cambridge University Press.

Das, V. (1989). Voices of children. *Daedalus, 116*(4), 236–293.

Davis, P. J. (1999). Gender differences in autobiographical memory for childhood emotional experiences. *Journal of Personality and Social Psychology, 76*, 498–510.

Elgin, S. H. (2000). *The language imperative.* Cambridge, MA: Perseus Books.

Elvin, M. (1985). Between the earth and heaven: Conceptions of the self in China. In M. Carrithers, S. Collins, & S. Lukes (Eds.), *The category of the person* (pp. 156–189). Cambridge, UK: Cambridge University Press.

Erickson, E. H. (1963). *Childhood and society.* New York: Norton.

Ferguson, T. J., Van Roozendaal, J., & Rule, B. G. (1986). Information basis for children's impressions of others. *Developmental Psychology, 22*, 335–341.

Fivush, R., & Hudson, J. (1990) (Eds.). *Knowing and remembering in young children.* New York: Cambridge University Press.

Fivush, R. (1994). Constructing narrative, emotions, and self in parent–child conversations about the past. In U. Neisser & R. Fivush (Eds), *The remembering self: Construction and accuracy in the self-narrative* (pp. 136–157). New York: Cambridge University Press.

Foulkes, D. (1999). *Children's dreaming and the development of consciousness.* Cambridge, MA: Harvard University Press.

Gilligan, C. (1992). *In a different voice: Psychological theory and women's development*. Cambridge, MA: Harvard University Press.

Greenfield, P. (1997). Culture as process: Empirical methodology for cultural psychology. In J. W. Berry, Y. H. Poortinga, & J. Pandey (Eds.), *Handbook of cross-cultural psychology. Vol. 1: Theory and method* (pp. 301–346). Boston, MA: Allyn & Bacon.

Greenfield, P., Keller, H., Fuligni, A., & Maynard, A. (2003). Cultural pathways through universal development. *Annual Review of Psychology, 54*, 461–490.

Gullestad, M. (1996). Modernity, self and childhood in the analysis of life-stories. In M. Gullestad (Ed.), *Imagined childhoods: Self and society in autobiographical accounts* (pp. 1–40). Oslo, Norway: Scandinavian University Press.

Habermas, T., & Bluck, S. (2000). Getting a life: The emergence of the life story in adolescence. *Psychological Bulletin, 126*, 748–769.

Han, J. J., Leichtman, M. D., & Wang, Q. (1998). Autobiographical memory in Korean, Chinese, and American children. *Developmental Psychology, 34*, 701–713.

Harley, K., & Reese, E. (1999). Origins of autobiographical memory. *Developmental Psychology, 35*(5), 1338–1348.

Hart, D., & Edelstein, W. (1992). Self-understanding development in cross-cultural perspective. In T. M. Brinthaupt & R. P. Lipka (Eds.), *The self: Definitional and methodological issues* (pp. 291–322). New York: State University of New York Press.

Hart, D., Lucca-Irizarry, N., & Damon, W. (1986). The development of self-understanding in Puerto Rico and the United States. *Journal of Early Adolescence, 6*, 293–304.

Harter, S. (1982). The perceived competence scale for children. *Child Development, 53*, 87–97.

Harter, S. (1988). Developmental processes in the construction of the self. In T. D. Yawkey & J. E. Johnson (Eds.), *Integrative processes and socialization: Early to middle childhood* (pp. 45–79). Hillsdale, NJ: Lawrence Erlbaum Associates Inc.

Harter, S. (1998). The development of self-representations. In W. Damon (Ed.), *Handbook of child psychology* (pp. 553–617). New York: Wiley.

Harter, S. (1999). *The construction of the self: A developmental perspective*. New York: Guilford Press.

Hermans, H. J. M. (1996). Voicing the self: From information processing to dialogical interchange. *Psychological Bulletin, 119*, 31–50.

Ho, D. Y. F. (1986). Chinese patterns of socialization: A critical review. In M. H. Bond (Ed.), *The psychology of the Chinese people* (pp. 1–37). Hong Kong: Oxford University Press.

Hockey, J., & James, A. (1993). *Growing up and growing old: Ageing and dependency in the life-course*. London: Sage.

Holland, D., & Quinn, N. (1987). *Cultural models in language and thought*. New York: Cambridge University Press.

Hollos, M., & Leis, P. E. (2002). Remodeling concepts of the self: An Ijo example. *Ethos, 29*, 2.

Howe, M. L., & Courage, M. L. (1993). On resolving the enigma of infantile amnesia. *Psychological Bulletin, 113*, 305–326.

Hsu, F. L. K. (1953). *Americans and Chinese: Two ways of life*. New York: Henry Schuman.

Hume, D. (1739/1882). *A treatise of human nature* (Vol. 1). London: Longmans Green.

Hwang, K. K. (1987). Face and favor: The Chinese power game. *American Journal of Sociology, 92*, 944–974.

Hymes, D. H. (1972). On communicative competence. In J. B. Pride & J. Holmes (Eds.), *Sociolinguistics: Selected readings* (pp. 269–292). Harmondsworth, UK: Penguin.

James, W. (1890/1983). *Principles of psychology*. Chicago: Encyclopedia Britannica.

Jopling, D. A. (1997). A "Self of selves"? In U. Neisser & D. A. Jopling (Eds.), *The conceptual self in context: Culture, experience, self-understanding. The Emory symposia in cognition* (pp. 249–267). New York: Cambridge University Press.

Kagan, J. (1989). *Unstable ideas: Temperament, cognition, and self*. Cambridge, MA: Harvard University Press.

Kagan, J., Kearsley, R. B., & Zelazo, P. R. (1980). *Infancy: Its place in human development*. Cambridge, MA: Harvard University Press.

Kagitcibasi, C. (1996a). The autonomous-relational self. *European Psychologist, 1*, 180–186.

Kagitcibasi, C. (1996b). *Family and human development across cultures: A view from the other side*. Hillsdale, NJ: Lawrence Erlbaum Associates Inc.

Kagitcibasi, C. (2002). Rites of passage to adulthood: Adolescence in the Western world. *Human Development, 45*, 136–140.

Kagitcibasi, C. (in press). Autonomy and relatedness in cultural context: Implications for self and family. *Journal of Cross-Cultural Psychology*.

Kakar, S. (1978). *The inner world: A psychoanalytic study of childhood and society in India*. New Delhi: Oxford University Press.

Kapoor, S. (2005). Alternate care for infants of employed mothers: Experiences in different childcare arrangements. Unpublished doctoral dissertation. Department of Child Development, University of Delhi.

Kaura, I., & Chaudhary, N. (July, 2003). *Continuity and change: Narratives of conflict from the lives of Indian adolescents*. Presented at the conference of the International Association for Cross-cultural Psychology, Budapest, Hungary, July, 2003.

Keller, H. (2001). Report on the advanced research and training seminar on pathways across development: cross-cultural perspectives. *International Journal of Psychology, 36*, 200–201.

Keller, H., & Greenfield, P. (2000). History and future of development in cross-cultural psychology. *Journal of Cross Cultural Psychology, 31*, 52–75.

Keller, H., Yovsi, R. D., & Voelker, S. (2002). The role of motor stimulation in parental ethnotheories. The case of Cameroonian Nso and German women. *Journal of Cross-Cultural Psychology, 33*, 398–414.

Kihlstrom, J. F. (1993). What does the self look like? In T. K. Srull & R. S. Wyer, Jr. (Eds.), *The mental representation of trait and autobiographical knowledge about the self. Advances in social cognitive* (Vol. 5, pp. 79–90). Hillsdale, NJ: Lawrence Erlbaum Associates Inc.

Kim, H. S. (2002). We talk therefore we think? A cultural analysis of the effect of talking on thinking. *Journal of Personality and Social Psychology, 4*, 828–842.

Kitayama, S. (2003). *Culture, self and social relationships*. Keynote address, "Cultures in Interaction" Regional conference of the International Association for Cross-cultural Psychology, July 15, 2003, Budapest, Hungary.

Kojima, H. (1998). The construction of child rearing theories in early modern to modern Japan. In M. Lyra & J. Valsiner (Eds.), *Child development within culturally structured environments. Volume 4: Construction of psychological processes in interpersonal communication* (pp. 13–34). Stamford, CT: Ablex Publishing Corporation.

Kurtz, S. N. (1992). *All the mothers are one: Hindu India and the cultural reshaping of psychoanalysis*. New York: Columbia University Press.

Levinson, D. J. (1986). A conception of adult development. *American Psychologist*, *41*(1), 3–13.

Lewis, M., & Brooks-Gunn, J. (1979). *Social cognition and the acquisition of self*. New York: Plenum Press.

Li, J. (2001). Chinese conceptualization of learning. *Ethos*, *29*, 111–137.

Lin, C-Y. C., & Fu, V. R. (1990). A comparison of child-rearing practices among Chinese, immigrant Chinese, and Caucasian–American parents. *Child Development*, *61*, 429–433.

MacDonald, S., Uesiliana, K., & Hayne, H. (2000). Cross-cultural and gender differences in childhood amnesia. *Memory*, *8*, 365–376.

Markova, I. (2001). Social representations and communicative genres. Papers in honour of Serge Moscovici. *Penser la vie, le social, la nature*. Paris: Editions de la Maison des sciences de l'homme.

Markus, H. R., & Kitayama, S. (1991). Culture and the self: Implications for cognition, emotion and motivation. *Psychological Review*, *98*, 224–253.

Markus, H. R., & Kitayama, S. (1998). The cultural psychology of personality. *Journal of Cross-Cultural Psychology*, *29*(1), 63–87.

Marsella, A. J. (1985). Culture, self and mental disorder. In A. J. Marsela, G. DeVos & H. L. K. Hsu (Eds.), *Culture and self: Asian and western perspectives* (pp. 282–308). New York: Tavistock.

Menon, U. (2003). Morality and context: A study of Hindu understandings. In J. Valsiner & K. J. Connolly (Eds.), *Handbook of developmental psychology* (pp. 431–449). London: Sage.

Merriam, S. B., & Cross, L. H. (1982). Adulthood and reminiscence: A descriptive study. *Educational Gerontology*, *8*, 275–290.

Middleton, D., & Edwards, D. (1990). Conversational remembering: A social psychological approach. In D. Middleton & D. Edwards (Eds.), *Collective remembering* (pp. 23–45). London: Sage.

Miller, A. (1981). *The drama of the gifted child*. New York: Basic Books.

Miller, P. J., Fung, H., & Mintz, J. (1996). Self-construction through narrative practices: A Chinese and American comparison of early socialization. *Ethos*, *24*(2), 237–280.

Miller, P. J., Mintz, J., Hoogstra, L., Fung, H. & Potts, R. (1992). The narrated self: Young children's construction of self in relation to others in conversational stories of personal experience. *Merrill-Palmer Quarterly*, *38*(1), 45–67.

Miller, P. J., Wiley, A. R., Fung, H., & Liang, C. H. (1997). Personal storytelling as a medium of socialization in Chinese and American families. *Child Development*, *68*, 557–568.

Minturn, L., & Hitchcock, J. T. (1966). *The Rajputs of Khalapur, India*. New York: John Wiley.

Mohanty, A. K. (1999). Language socialisation in a multilingual society. In T. S.

Saraswathi (Ed.), *Culture, human development and socialisation* (pp. 125–144). New Delhi: Sage Publications.

Mullen, M. K. (1994). Earliest recollections of childhood: A demographic analysis. *Cognition, 52*, 55–79.

Mullen, M. K., & Yi, S. (1995). The cultural context of talk about the past: Implications for the development of autobiographical memory. *Cognitive Development, 10*, 407–419.

Mwamwenda, T. (1999). Culture and the self: An African perspective. In M. M. Mboya (Ed.), *Culture and self: Theory and research from an African perspective* (pp. 1–18). Pretoria, South Africa: Ilitha.

Nair, R. B. (2002). *Narrative gravity*. New Delhi: Oxford University Press.

Nakamura, H. (1964). *Ways of thinking of Eastern peoples: India–China–Tibet–Japan*. Honolulu: East-West Center Press.

Neisser, U. (1988). Five kinds of self-knowledge. *Philosophical Psychology, 1*, 35–59.

Neisser, U. (1997). Concepts and self-concepts. In U. Neisser & D. A. Jopling (Eds.), *The conceptual self in context: Culture, experience, self-understanding* (pp. 3–12). New York: Cambridge University Press.

Nelson, K. (1989). Monologue as the linguistic construction of self in time. In K. Nelson (Ed.), *Narratives from the crib* (pp. 284–308). Cambridge, MA: Harvard University Press.

Nelson, K. (1993). The psychological and social origins of autobiographical memory. *Psychological Science, 4*, 7–14.

Nelson, K. (1996). *Language in cognitive development: The emergence of the mediated mind*. New York: Cambridge University Press.

Nelson, K. (2001). Language and the self: From the "Experiencing I" to the "Continuing Me". In C. Moore & K. Lemmon (Eds.), *The self in time: Developmental perspectives* (pp. 15–34). Mahwah, NJ: Lawrence Erlbaum Associates Inc.

Nsamenang, A. B. (1999). The image of the self in African social thought. In M. M. Mboya (Ed.), *Culture and self: Theory and research from an African perspective* (pp. 19–42). Pretoria, South Africa: Ilitha.

Nsamenang, A. B. (2000). Issues in indigenous approaches to developmental research in Sub-Saharan Africa. *International Society for the Study of Behavioural Development Newsletter, 1*, 1–4.

Obeyesekere, G. (1990). *The work of culture*. Chicago, IL: University of Chicago Press.

Ochs, E. (1996). Linguistic resources for socialising humanity. In J. Gumperz & S. Levinson (Eds.), *Rethinking linguistic reality* (pp. 407–437). Cambridge, UK: Cambridge University Press.

Paranjpe, A. C. (1998). *Self and identity in modern psychology and Indian thought*. New York: Plenum Press.

Peterson, C., & McCabe, A. (1994). A social interactionist account of developing decontextualized narrative skill. *Developmental Psychology, 30*, 937–948.

Pillemer, D. B. (1998). *Momentous events, vivid memories*. Cambridge, MA: Harvard University Press.

Pillemer, D. B., & White, S. H. (1989). Childhood events recalled by children and adults. In H. W. Reese (Ed.), *Advances in child development and behavior* (Vol. 21, pp. 297–340). New York: Academic Press.

Polkinghorne, D. E. (1988). *Narrative knowing and the human sciences*. Albany, NY: State University of New York Press.

Povinelli, D. J. (1995). The unduplicated self. In P. Rochat (Ed), *The self in infancy: Theory and research. Advances in psychology* (Vol. 112, pp. 161–192). Amsterdam, Netherlands: North-Holland/Elsevier Science Publishers.

Pratkanis, A. R., & Greenwald, A. G. (1985). How shall the self be conceived? *Journal for the Theory of Social Behaviour, 15,* 311–329.

Rabain-Jamin, J., & Sabeau-Jouannet, E. (1989). Playing with pronouns in French maternal speech to pre-lingual infants. *Journal of Child Language, 16,* 217–238.

Radhakrishnan, S. (1997). *The principal Upanishads.* New Delhi: HarperCollins.

Roland, A. (1988). *In search of self in India and Japan: Towards a cross-cultural psychology.* Princeton, NJ: Princeton University Press.

Ross, M., & Holmberg, D. (1990). Recounting the past: Gender differences in the recall of events in the history of a close relationship. In M. P. Zanna & J. M. Olson (Eds.), *Self-inference processes* (pp. 135–152). Hillsdale, NJ: Lawrence Erlbaum Associates Inc.

Ross, M., & Wilson, A. E. (2000). Constructing and appraising past selves. In D. L. Schacter & E. Scarry (Eds.), *Memory, brain, and belief* (pp. 231–259). Cambridge, MA: Harvard University Press.

Röttger-Rössler, B. (1993). Autobiography in question: On self presentation and life description in an Indonesian society. *Anthropos, 88,* 365–373.

Ruble, D. N., & Frey, K. S. (1991). Changing patterns of comparative behavior as skills are acquired: A functional model of self-evaluation. In J. Suls & T. H. Wells (Eds.), *Social comparison: Contemporary theory and research* (pp. 79–113). Hillsdale, NJ: Lawrence Erlbaum Associates Inc.

Sameroff, A. J., & Haith, M. M. (1996) (Eds). *The five to seven year shift: The age of reason and responsibility.* Chicago, IL: University of Chicago Press.

Saran, R. (2003). How we live: Census India household survey. *India Today, July 28,* 2003.

Saraswathi, T. S. (1999). Adult–child continuity in India: Is adolescence a myth or an emerging reality? In T. S. Saraswathi (Ed.), *Culture, socialisation and human development* (pp. 213–232). New Delhi: Sage.

Schrauf, R. W. (2000). Bilingual autobiographical memory: Experimental studies and clinical cases. *Culture and Psychology, 6*(4), 387–417.

Selman, R. L. (1980). *The growth of interpersonal understanding: Developmental and clinical analysis.* New York: Academic Press.

Shweder, R. A., & Bourne, E. J. (1984). Does the concept of the person vary cross-culturally? In R. A. Shweder & R. A. LeVine (Eds.), *Culture theory: Essays on mind, self, and emotion* (pp. 158–199). New York: Cambridge University Press.

Shweder, R. A., & Miller, G. (1991). The social construction of the person. In R. A. Shweder (Ed.), *Thinking through cultures* (pp. 156–185). Cambridge, MA: Harvard University Press.

Shweder, R. A., Goodnow, J., Hatano, G., LeVine, R. A., Markus, H., & Miller, P. (1998). The cultural psychology of development: One mind, many mentalities. In W. Damon (Series Ed.), & R. M. Lerner (Vol. Ed.), *Handbook of child psychology. Volume 1: Theoretical models of human development* (pp. 865–937). New York: Wiley & Sons.

Smith, M. B. (1985). The metaphorical basis of the selfhood. In A. J. Marsella, G. de Vos & F. L. K. Hsu (Eds.), *Culture and self: Asian and Western perspectives* (pp. 56–88). New York: Tavistock.

Spiro, M. E. (1993). Is the Western conception of the self "peculiar" within the context of the world cultures? *Ethos*, *21*(2), 107–153.

Stern, D. (1985). *The interpersonal world of the infant*. New York: Basic Books.

Stigler, J. W., Smith, S., & Mao, L. W. (1985). The self-perception of competence by Chinese children. *Child Development*, *56*, 1259–1270.

Tessler, M., & Nelson, K. (1994). Making memories: The influence of joint encoding on later recall by young children. *Consciousness and Cognition*, *3*, 307–326.

Thorne, A. (1995). Developmental truths in memories of childhood and adolescence. *Journal of Personality*, *63*, 139–163.

Trawick, M. (2003). The person behind the family. In V. Das (Ed.), *The Oxford companion to sociology and social anthropology* (Vol. 2, pp. 1158–1178). New Delhi: Oxford University Press.

Triandis, H. C. (1989). The self and social behavior in differing cultural contexts. *Psychological Review*, *96*, 506–520.

Tu, W. M. (1979). *Humanity and self-cultivation: Essays in Confucian thought*. Berkeley, CA: Asian Humanities Press.

Valsiner, J. (2000a). *Culture and human development*. London: Sage.

Valsiner, J. (2000b). Data as representations: Contextualising qualitative and quantitative research strategies. *Social Science Information*, *39*(1), 99–113.

Valsiner, J. (2001). Process structure of semiotic mediation in human development. *Human Development*, *44*, 84–97.

Voronov, M., & Singer, J. A. (2002). The myth of individualism-collectivism: A critical review. *Journal of Social Psychology*, *142*(4), 461–480.

Vygotsky, L. (1978). *Mind in society*. Cambridge, MA: Harvard University Press.

Wang, Q. (2001a). Cultural effects on adults' earliest childhood recollection and self-description: Implications for the relation between memory and the self. *Journal of Personality and Social Psychology*, *81*, 220–233.

Wang, Q. (2001b). "Did you have fun?": American and Chinese mother–child conversations about shared emotional experiences. *Cognitive Development*, *16*, 693–715.

Wang, Q. (2003). Infantile amnesia reconsidered: A cross-cultural analysis. *Memory*, *11*, 65–80.

Wang, Q. (2004). The emergence of cultural self-constructs: Autobiographical memory and self-description in European American and Chinese children. *Developmental Psychology*, *40*(1), 3–15.

Wang, Q., & Brockmeier, J. (2002). Autobiographical remembering as cultural practice: Understanding the interplay between memory, self and culture. *Culture & Psychology*, *8*, 45–64.

Wang, Q., Ceci, S. J., Williams, W. M., & Kopko, K. A. (2004). Culturally situated cognitive competence: A functional framework. In R. J. Sternberg & E. L. Grigorenko (Eds.), *Culture and competence: Contexts of life success* (pp. 225–249). Washington, DC: American Psychological Association.

Wang, Q., & Conway, M. A. (2004). The stories we keep: Autobiographical memory in American and Chinese middle-aged adults. *Journal of Personality*, *72*(5), 911–938.

Wang, Q., Conway, M. A., & Hou, Y. (2004). Infantile amnesia: A cross-cultural investigation. *Cognitive Sciences*, *1*(1), 123–135.

Wang, Q., & Hsueh, Y. (2000). Parent–child interdependence in Chinese families:

Change and continuity. In C. Violato, E. Oddone-Paolucci, & M. Genuis (Eds.), *The changing family and child development* (pp. 60–69). Aldershot, UK: Ashgate.

Wang, Q., & Leichtman, M. D. (2000). Same beginnings, different stories: A comparison of American and Chinese children's narratives. *Child Development, 71*, 1329–1346.

Wang, Q., Leichtman, M. D., & Davies, K. (2000). Sharing memories and telling stories: American and Chinese mothers and their 3-year-olds. *Memory, 8*, 159–177.

Wang, Q., Leichtman, M. D., & White, S. H. (1998). Childhood memory and self-description in young Chinese adults: The impact of growing up an only child. *Cognition, 69*, 75–105.

Wang, Q., & Li, J. (2003). Chinese children's self-concept in the domains of learning and social relations. *Psychology in the Schools, 40*(1), 85–101.

Welch-Ross, M. (2000). Personalizing the temporally extended self: Evaluative self-awareness and the development of autobiographical memory. In C. Moore & K. Lemmon (Eds.), *The self in time: Developmental perspective* (pp. 97–120). Mahwah, NJ: Lawrence Erlbaum Associates Inc.

Wethington, E. (2000). Expecting Stress: Americans and the Midlife Crisis. *Motivation and Emotion, 24*, 85–103.

Wiley, A. R., Rose, A. J., Burger, L. K., & Miller, P. J. (1998). Constructing autonomous selves through narrative practices: A comparative study of working-class and middle-class families. *Child Development, 69*, 833–847.

Wu, D. Y. H. (1996). Chinese childhood socialization. In M. H. Bond (Ed.), *The handbook of Chinese psychology* (pp. 143–154). Hong Kong: Oxford University Press.

Wyatt, F. (1963). The reconstruction of the individual and of the collective past. In R. H. White (Ed.), *The study of lives* (pp. 304–320). New York: Atherton Press.

Yang, X. Y. (1996). Examination of the self in a culture of affinity. *Journal of Social Psychology, 1*, 26–32 (in Chinese).

Zahn-Waxler, C., Friedman, R. J., Cole, P. M., Mizuta, I., & Hiruma, N. (1996). Japanese and United States preschool children's responses to conflict and distress. *Child Development, 67*, 2462–2477.

Author index

Subject index

Abridged Big Five Circumplex (AB5C), 313, 315
Absolutism, 56
Accommodation, 74, 176
Acculturation, 51, 52–53
Achievement goal-orientation, 255, 260–62, 264
Achievement motivation, 254–55, 260, 262, 263
Active organism models *see* Organismic models of development
Actualizing tendency, 308
Adaptation, 176
Adaptive capacity, 86
Adolescence, 67, 70, 75, 76, 328–29
Advaita Vedanta, 39
Affect, 102, 114
Affections, 106, 109
Africa
  child development, 186
  click languages, 215
  culture, 51, 52
  human migration from, 206, 208, 216
  intelligence concept, 167–68
  interdependent view of the self, 327, 331–32
  personality traits, 313
African-Americans, 54
Agreeableness, 304, 306, 312, 313, 315
Algorithm level, 16–17, 288
Altered states of consciousness, 30–31, 36–37
Amae, 55, 130
American Psychological Association, 1, 3
Amnesia, 227, 228
Analogical representations, 19, 20, 144
Analytical thinking, 35

Anger, 104, 107, 115, 119, 129
Animal communication, 197, 198, 199–200, 201–2, 216
Annual Review of Psychology, 8
Anxiety, 312
Aphasia, 184
Appraisal theory, 115, 131
Arousal, 35
Art, 200, 271, 293
Articulatory phonology, 210, 211
Artificial intelligence, 15–16
Asia
  childcare, 338
  children's narratives, 346
  culture, 51
  family socialization, 342
  intellectual traditions, 133
  intelligence concept, 167
  interdependent view of the self, 327, 332, 333
  personality traits, 313
  psychodynamic approaches, 130
  self-perfection, 343
Asian Americans, 348, 349
Assimilation, 74, 176
Associationism, 278, 279
Atman, 39, 343–44
Attachment, 112
Attention
  brain areas, 35
  cognition, 12
  consciousness, 30, 32
  'filter theory', 31
  mental imagery, 156
  PASS theory, 184
Attribution theory, 255
Australia, 166, 215
Autobiographical memory, 325–26, 329, 332–33, 347, 348